# PALESTINE
*and*
# JEWISH HISTORY

# PALESTINE *and* JEWISH HISTORY

Criticism at the Borders of Ethnography

JONATHAN BOYARIN

University of Minnesota Press
Minneapolis
London

Copyright 1996 by the Regents of the University of Minnesota

Chapter 2 first appeared in *New Literary History* 23 (1992), reprinted by permission.
Chapter 6 first appeared in *Found Object* (Journal of the CUNY Center for Cultural Studies) 3 (spring 1994), reprinted by permission.

All rights reserved. No part of this publication may be reproduced, stored in a retrieval system, or transmitted, in any form or by any means, electronic, mechanical, photocopying, recording, or otherwise, without the prior written permission of the publisher.

Published by the University of Minnesota Press
111 Third Avenue South, Suite 290, Minneapolis, MN 55401-2520
Printed in the United States of America on acid-free paper

**Library of Congress Cataloging-in-Publication Data**
Boyarin, Jonathan.
    Palestine and Jewish history : criticism at the borders of ethnography / Jonathan Boyarin.
    p.   cm.
    Includes bibliographical references.
    ISBN 0-8166-2764-9 (hc). — ISBN 0-8166-2765-7 (pb)
    1. Israel—Description and travel.  2. Boyarin, Jonathan—Journeys—Israel.  3. Israel—Ethnic relations.  4. Zionism—Philosophy.  I. Title.
DS107.5.B69   1996
915.69404'54—dc20                                  95-39566

The University of Minnesota is an
equal-opportunity educator and employer.

# Contents

Introduction: Old Things    1

1
My Trip to Israel: Beginning    26

2
Reading Exodus into History    40

3
My Trip to Israel, Continued    68

4
In Search of "Israeli Identity":
Anecdotes and Afterthoughts    194

5
Enough Already with My Trip to Israel    207

6
Ruins, Mounting toward Jerusalem    238

Bibliography    253

# Introduction
# Old Things

> These chronicles' lapses and incoherencies, their redundancies and paradoxes, represent the limits of discourse, the moments in which discourse does not know what to say.... If an account of the past includes its indeterminacies, parts of the account are very likely to remain terminally "nonproven" and others incoherent.
>
> MYRA JEHLEN (1993: 692)

> The best way of all to approach the book is to read it as a challenge: to pry open the vacant spaces that would enable you to build your life and those of the people around you into a plateau of intensity that would leave afterimages of its dynamism that could be reinjected into still other lives, creating a fabric of heightened states between which any number, the greatest number, of connecting lines would exist.
>
> BRIAN MASSUMI (1987: xv)

> Like everyone else I have at my disposal only three means of evaluating human existence: the study of self, which is the most difficult and most dangerous method, but also the most fruitful; the observation of our fellowmen, who usually arrange to hide their secrets from us, or to make us believe that they have secrets where none exist; and books, with the particular errors of perspective to which they inevitably give rise.
>
> MARGUERITE YOURCENAR (1954: 21)

> No, not history.
> His is a stranger dream.
>
> SALMAN RUSHDIE (1989: 209)

From my Jerusalem fieldwork diary, September 7, 1991: "Charles [my friend from college, now living in Jerusalem] told me about a story Chana Hacohen told about herself at a party in the neighborhood. She had asked somebody what the verb *lezaken* means, because she kept hearing men in the street shouting, *"Al tezaken."* What they were actually saying, of course, was *"Alte zakhen,"* "old things," which they buy and resell. This is a classic nostalgia figure of immigrant Jewish life, both here and in America — the *alte zakhen* man, but only in Israel do people of my generation still remember him, generally as an old Ashkenazi Jew. The day after Charles told me this story I heard a young man in the street with the same cry I'd heard the day before, only now I understood it for the first time: *"Zakhe-e-e-n! Al-te zakhe-e-e-n!"* And another man the next day... And I don't think they were Yiddish speakers either; the phrase removed from its original language has taken on its own character in Hebrew. This marginal profession, then, has been maintained and been passed on, along with its characteristic announcement, to a different immigrant ethnic group.

My reference to a "different immigrant ethnic group" at the end of this passage suggests that I assumed, because I was then living and heard this call in a poor neighborhood of Jerusalem occupied largely by Moroccan Jews, that the men who walked the streets in search of old things were themselves Moroccans. Eventually I realized, somewhat to my embarrassment, that these "immigrants" weren't Jews at all, but poor Palestinians. The phrase *alte zakhen* had survived the cataclysmic history of Palestine in this century, its phonics and intonation transformed as it "migrated" from the lumpen class among East European Jews in Palestine as well as in Western Europe and North America to the lumpen class among Palestinians dispossessed and suffering under military occupation, but with its meaning still recognizable to a Yiddish speaker. Perhaps indeed the *alte zakhen* collectors for an intermediate time had been Moroccan Jews, shortly after their arrival in the first years after the State of Israel was established. The trajectory the phrase has followed — always coming through the window to haunt immigrant dwellings; always insisting on the memory of the old, the worn out, the rejected, the obsolete — from Yiddish to Arabic, perhaps by way of Hebrew, in the process throwing all of these petrified names for "languages" into question, is the trajectory of this study. In this book I — a speaker of Yiddish as my adopted *mame-loshn*, my "mother tongue" — have tried to open myself to different meanings of "Palestine" than seem to be available to those Jews of European origin who have forgotten or rejected Yiddish in favor of modern Israeli Hebrew. Indeed, the joke the radical political activist Chana Hacohen tells about herself bears an ironic witness to that very rejection, and not only because she failed to understand the phrase as Yiddish: *al tezaken*, as she reports originally hearing the phrase, does not mean anything in modern Hebrew, but since *zaken* means "an old man," *al* can indicate a negative imperative, and the prefix *te-* can also indicate an imperative, if *al tezaken* did mean anything it would very likely be "Do not grow old."[1]

---

1. Another kind of "old thing" that continues to echo in Zionist culture is the Yiddish names that often lie hidden underneath Israeli Hebrew ones, often as direct glosses (for

In contrast to this emphasis in European secular Zionism on innovation and on rejection of the *alte zakhen* of the diasporic Yiddish past, Palestinian culture and collective identity are sometimes portrayed as unalienated, authentically rooted in the land and in the past. Yet formulations of both Zionism and Palestinian nationalism are marked by a curious combination, on the one hand, of claims of priority, of being the nation that "really" belongs to the land, and, on the other hand, of claims to representing the side of progress in this national struggle. The Israeli-Palestinian conflict is thus a struggle for both land and history, space and time. History is as basic to the two peoples' identity and security as is land. A great deal has been written about this history with the intent of clarifying the origins of the conflict, but it has rarely been addressed as one of the major stakes over which Israelis and Palestinians still contend.

The very notion of abstract time — in which discrete events can be marked as discontinuous, sequential, or simultaneous — is closely linked to the progressive concept of history that is questioned throughout this book. Yet even on the most straightforward, everyday level the practical relevance of time becomes clear when we consider that the most likely territorial resolution of the conflict — partition into two separate states — was accepted formally and in principle by the Zionist leadership in the 1940s, and is accepted by mainstream Palestinian leaders today, but has never been accepted simultaneously by the contending parties. Even after the signing of a vague agreement between the Israeli government and the Palestine Liberation Organization in September 1993, the question of whether the Israelis would ever agree to the establishment of a separate Palestinian state, and whether the Palestinians would ever agree to anything less, cast the realization of even the minimal initial terms of the agreement in doubt. This research is intended to clarify both why such a compromise is so difficult to achieve and in what ways it is inadequate as a solution to the problem of conflicting histories.

Research into these questions can benefit from the insights of contemporary cultural theory — a body of work that draws on all the humanities and social sciences. Cultural theory addresses global social dynamics without ignoring particular cultural frameworks of perception. Thus my approach neither shuts out the larger framework of world history in which the Israeli-Palestinian conflict is set nor treats the Israelis and Palestinians as mute

---

example, Sela for Stein). Unlike similar name changes by Jewish immigrants to countries with non-Jewish majorities these cannot be said to conceal the Jewishness of their bearers, but they do precisely conceal their Yiddishkayt, their Yiddishness. The revelation of this covert history should help to nuance the notion of the absolute, "phallic" Ashkenazi ruler of Israeli society (Shohat 1988; Lavie 1992) precisely by bringing back a reminder of the Yiddish subaltern uneasily contained within that exalted Ashkenazi.

pawns in a global chess game. It is not intended to imply any symmetry in the experiences on which Israeli and Palestinian identities are based. It provides a starting point for an effective critique of various theories of conflict genesis and resolution: European models of conflict resolution through mediation by "neutral" powers; the progressive idea that "religion" or "nationalism" is the essential problem; and well-intentioned "dialogism" without sufficient grounding in the cultures, histories, and differential powers of the parties to the conflict.

This approach also questions the employment of value-laden political goals based on Euro-American models, such as the desire for independence and the doctrine of democratic pluralism, as well as security concerns deemed "natural" or "commonsense," such as the mutual fear of irredentism. Employing it, I sometimes find myself struggling to repress a naive or liberal belief that "People are basically good at heart" and to remember that the worst nightmare scenarios of those who mistrust all treaties sometimes come to pass. Yet it is important to remember that such projective scenarios remain grounded not in the holy spirit of prophecy but in a complex mix of information, anxieties, emphases, and desires.

•

My subtitle, "Criticism at the Borders of Ethnography," represents not only the format of this book but also the record of two years of library and office work in New York, followed by roughly six months of fieldwork in Israel/Palestine, with the writing of "Ruins, Mounting toward Jerusalem" coming as a fortuitous summation. It is of course unconventional for an ethnographer to conclude a research project with the fieldwork: usually the writing comes after. I kept my time in the field for last, first of all because of an illness in my immediate family that would have made it impossible to go earlier, and then — as a somewhat post hoc yet fruitful rationalization — in a deliberate attempt to question the territorializing epistemological claims of both anthropology and nationalism, by questioning the rhetorical authority of information "from the ground." My intent in assembling the book in this way is to avoid, on one hand, the simple empiricism of an unrelieved travelogue; on the other, the arid theorism of much cultural studies; and on the *third* hand (Shehadeh 1982), the post hoc fashioning of a synthetic ethnography that would just happen to be neatly consistent with my theoretical framework.

Hence *Palestine and Jewish History* offers a juxtaposition between critical articulations (two of which actually interrupt the field narrative at appropriate points) and an edited version of a deliberately eclectic, anecdotal, and unprofessional field diary. Those who are irritated by a highly personal tone in ethnography are therefore excused from reading the bulk of this book; and if they do read it, they will be forgiven if they need to vent their spleen.

Aside from my own predilections, there are two simple and compelling reasons for presenting the journal itself — shortened by about two-thirds and lightly annotated and glossed. The first reason is precisely as a counter to the abstract and categorical formulations contained in my synthetic essays. I did not want to leave the entire book suggesting that the situation, beliefs, or associations of any individual or group were adequately described or explained by those provocative critical constructs. Indeed, to some extent — but it is still not clear even to me to *what* extent — in my fieldwork I deliberately sought to counter some of the implicit or explicit judgments made in the essays. Certainly the damning attitude toward right-wing Israelis expressed in the original "Palestine and Jewish History" essay would not suggest a sympathetic attitude toward West Bank settlers, which I tried to adopt on the two occasions I visited them. But I invite readers to realize this juxtaposition I have suggested, to use the material presented in "My Trip to Israel" in their own complications, confirmations, and challenges to the critical pieces.

The second, and closely related, reason for presenting the ethnography in this "raw" form is my conviction that much scholarship on Israel and Palestine is hampered by the solipsistic confirmation of preconceived religious, ethnic, and political categories, starting with the dichotomy between Israelis and Palestinians but encompassing internal categorizations as well. I have occasionally made the cynical observation that scholarly collections bearing titles along the lines of *Religion and Politics in Israeli Society* have as their primary function the reinforcement of the idea that there is something identifiable and objectively isolated that can be called "Israeli society" — a notion I explicitly contest in this book. Nor do I wish to reproduce the notion of the people living in Israel/Palestine as a mosaic of discrete and neatly differentiated groups. Had I attempted to interview and profile a cross section, for example, of "Israeli Arabs," "West Bank intellectuals," "Palestinian radicals," "secularist liberal Israelis," "Orthodox nationalists," and "Oriental Jews," that is precisely what I would have accomplished — at the same time failing to register much of the worthwhile incidental information that forms the bulk of this report.

•

*Palestine and Jewish History* explores in depth points first articulated in a programmatic essay by the same name, which appears as the last chapter of my earlier book *Storm from Paradise: The Politics of Jewish Memory* (J. Boyarin 1992). One of the key themes raised there was the differential career of the term "Palestine" in modern Palestinian and Jewish identity. For Palestinians, the name as a designation of *their* country, the lost or occupied homeland that marks them as a people, has grown ever more salient throughout the twentieth century. For many Jews prior to the establishment of the State of Israel, the term represented a project and a goal — either of personal immigration or as the geographic base for a project of the territorial regeneration of the Jewish people. After the State of Israel came into being, the term "Palestine" fell into disuse among Jews, and with its increasingly insistent embrace by Palestinians, it even acquired a generally suspect connotation in public Jewish discourse.

Another theme in the earlier essay was the transformation of the attitude toward "ancestors" in modern Jewish experience. One of my operating assumptions when I try to discover particular moments where the relations among history, identity, and politics are revealed is that what seem to be political blind spots, failures to adjust received ideologies to changing situations, are closely related to an ideal of fidelity to political forerunners. General credos that such "ancestors" formulated may be taken as eternally valid rather than specific to the situation in which they were first uttered (see the quote from Rabbi Kook on p. 69, below). More poignantly perhaps — certainly so in the case of Zionism — it seems that fidelity to forerunners could more readily be maintained, along with a critical distance from the actions they took or slogans they formulated in other situations, if it is acknowledged that they attempted solutions to "impossible" situations: those where no program for political action can be simultaneously pragmatic and just. Jacques Derrida, writing about the identity of Europe generally but quite possibly alluding to the way that the disastrous events surrounding World War II have thrown that identity into more general question, actually places this *"experience and experiment of the possibility of the impossible"* (Derrida 1992: 41) at the heart of the question of historical responsibility.

The essay "Palestine and Jewish History" began by making a differentiation between two meanings of the term "Palestine" itself:

> The first designates that region between Lebanon, the Sinai, the Mediterranean, and the Jordan, particularly as it became a focus of activist Jewish collective aspirations in the modern period. The second is the name of a new state, declared at the meeting of the Palestine National Council in Algiers in November 1988, intended to be the national home of the Palestinian Arab people. (J. Boyarin 1992: 116)

This book does describe numerous meetings with Palestinian Arabs, both citizens of Israel and noncitizens under Israeli occupation, but for the most part it is probably not so much about the Palestinians as about the Jews who are understood as being *in Palestine* (to say that, after 1948, itself bears a very sharp political valence).

My initial and to some extent still primary identification with the Israeli Jewish "side" of this conflict is clearly reflected in the unfolding of the project documented here. My training in graduate school, and my prior research and fieldwork, concentrated on East European Jews and the communities of their descendants in Paris and New York City. My studies of the multifarious pre–World War II political involvements of East European Jews have taught me that Zionism has been identifiable as the sole mass ideology of European Jewry only since, and largely as a result of, the Nazi genocide. My original political involvement in the fate of Israel and Palestine was sparked at some level by an ambivalent sympathy for the goals of Jewish independence espoused by classical socialist Zionism and by the ironic progress of the Israeli state further and further away from the ideal of national liberation as independence from outside military powers.

Beginning in 1983 and continuing through to the period during which this book was written, I was active in the International Jewish Peace Union, which argues for recognition of the PLO, the establishment of a Palestinian state alongside Israel, and support of the Israeli peace camp. This work involves convincing Americans that rapprochement between the two peoples is possible, understanding the difficulties Palestinians have in accepting a two-state compromise, and considering how the history and situation of the Jews lead the majority of them — both in Israel and elsewhere — to reject the idea of partition today. This experience has largely generated the questions informing this project.

My most general thesis in planning research on this issue was that particular group identities at the end of the twentieth century neither persist in an unreflective way nor are about to disappear. The present situation of the world's various peoples represents a choice of either ahistorical, rigid, exclusive identity or a transcultural reintegration of our own history and the history of the Other. In our cultural system, where identity is justified by history — it is legitimate and proper to be shaped by what has happened to you and to make claims based on those experiences — the challenge "to see the other as historically constituted rather than ontologically given" (Said 1989: 225, quoted in D. Boyarin and J. Boyarin 1989: 626) necessarily impinges on the normative and "given" accounts of our own history. This is a difficult enough challenge in itself, but insofar as it is based on a rhetoric of "history" that is broadly shared but still specifically grounded in modern European culture, we may have to learn to embrace it more self-consciously than we are accustomed to doing. To stress historicity, as Edward Said does, reinforces this particular (even if potentially inclusive) notion of history as the most general, bottom-line framework of legitimation we can imagine ourselves accepting. But in a recent essay assessing the currently fashionable critical emphasis on the dynamics of diasporic identity, James Clifford writes a sentence that brings into sharp focus the link between historicity and group identity:

> In conditions of permanent historical exile — or what amounts to the same thing in an exile that can *only* end with the Messiah — ethnocentrism is just one tactic, never an absolute end in itself. (Clifford 1993: 20)

Clifford simultaneously offers a sensitive paraphrase of the diasporic sensibility affording groups such as Jews an identity that is ethnocentric without being actively triumphalist and suggests the vision of a messianic advent as the limiting horizon of the very notion of history. This is a "traditional" understanding that posttraditional people like myself and most readers of this book can understand more readily thanks to the piercing insights of Walter Benjamin's *Theses on the Philosophy of History.*

One of the most important lessons that Benjamin has left us is that the messianic vision is not simply oriented toward the future but entails the redemption of our ancestors' lives as well. Benjamin claims in fact that *no* moment in "history" has ontological precedence for a redeemed humanity. If this notion is seriously entertained, that means there is no privileged present, let alone (and this is more broadly understood) a privileged future. That clamoring of each moment at the eastern end of the Mediterranean, if taken to its conclusion, may lead to a radical indeterminacy regarding the precedence of collective claims to a land title grounded in suffering ancestry — reminding us once again that revolutions, whether "violent" or no, can never be carried out only in thought. It is true that our notion of "action" suggests both an ultimate moral demand, because it is efficacious in a way that, for example, reconceiving history is not, and that such "action" is conceivable only in the present. But once again, the ethnographic exploration of notions of temporality among people whose identities are not grounded in a progressive worldview shows the limitations of our constructed "present" as the current example of a series of moments. As Judith Butler suggests, "The notion of the 'moment' may well be nothing other than a retrospective fantasy of mathematical mastery imposed upon the interrupted durations of the past" (Butler 1993: 245). Hence an activist morality no longer enjoys an unquestioned pride of place. I hope the reader will bear this point in mind below, especially in those sections of "My Trip to Israel" that document my episodic participation in my leftist friends' various actions on behalf of Palestinians in Israel and the Occupied Territories. More generally, this confusion of temporal sequence properly *should* throw into prolonged question the presumed priority of field presence and the sequentiality of ethnographic recollection.

•

At a time in this century when most cultural anthropologists were still working with an ideal type of isolated cultural wholes whose systemic integrity needed to be documented before the cultures were irrevocably "contaminated" and destroyed, the anthropologist Gregory Bateson was profoundly interested in the question of antagonistic and symbiotic relations between cultures. In one of his conclusions, as further articulated by Gabriele Schwab, Bateson claimed that

> general interaction patterns show that all forms of culture contact that tend to rigidify boundaries in order to maintain an unchanged internal coherence lead to an increase of external conflict and hostility ultimately destructive for all agents involved. (Schwab 1986: 134, referring to Bateson 1972: 61–72, quoted in Sarris 1993: 60)

In one critical respect, this formulation is consistent with the common assumption that cultures "normally" exist prior to contact and that such pre-contact cultures display "unchanged internal coherence": rigidity is thereby yoked to cultural conservatism. Yet in the case of Zionism, I would argue that the colonists' general, though not universal, "rigidity" when confronted with the presence in Palestine of Palestinian Arabs and their culture could not be described as an effort to maintain an unchanged internal coherence. On the contrary, in Amnon Raz-Krakotzkin's recent formulation, the Zionist "'negation of exile' demanded cultural uniformity and the abandonment of the different cultural traditions through which Jewish identity had previously been determined" (Raz-Krakotzkin 1993: 184). If, as the saying has it, *"A yid iz in goles"* (A Jew is in exile), this means not only that Jews live "in conditions of permanent historical exile" but that exile constitutes the Jew. By contrast, the settlers' defensive reaction to the troubling presence of Arab residents in Palestine simultaneously activated a mystified association with the ancient Israelite kingdoms documented in the Bible and drew on a stock of colonialist justifications broadly shared in West European culture. This defensiveness was thus closely linked to the symbolic impoverishment of Zionist culture and the patently invented nature of those symbols that did evolve, all of which was in turn a result of the Zionist *rejection* of the "internally coherent" culture of the European Jewish Diaspora, Yiddishkayt. Zionist demonization of Palestinian Arabs, I am claiming, was profoundly though by no means uniquely traceable to an internal lack consequent on a rejection of the Zionist pioneers' *alte zakhen*.

After all of the debates in contemporary critical theory about the nature of "agency," the unproblematized reference in the quote from Schwab to "all agents involved" also calls for scrutiny. It seems almost inevitable that we take at least one of the terms in such a contact model as given, in order to see how it constructs the Other, how the Other's impingement changes that original term away from a baseline description in given ways, and so forth. The difficulty of writing about a given situation without assuming the objective reality of such collective agents is indicated by my own repeated recourse to the phrase "Israeli-Palestinian conflict" — a phrase whose congealed connotations this project is largely intended to overcome. Attempts to dislodge such rhetorical reiterations of given identities tend at best to regress toward a reliance on alternative agents; hence my move away from writing about "Israel and Palestine" toward Palestine and "Jewish" history and my intent (articulated in the earlier essay "Palestine and Jewish History") to examine the effects of the persistence and evolution of Palestinian identity on "Jewish" agency.

Another instructive illustration of this rhetorical problem appears in the course of François Hartog's *The Mirror of Herodotus*, where Hartog wonders

> How must the Athenians, who so insistently claimed to be of autochthonous birth, have represented this alien figure whose whole being consisted in having no attachment to any place? It is not hard to foresee that the discourse of autochthony was bound to reflect on the representation of nomadism and that the Athenian, that imaginary autochthonous being, had need of an equally imaginary nomad. The Scythian conveniently fitted the bill. (Hartog 1988: 11)

Hartog's focus on the relations among autochthony, nomadism, Self, and Other is also, I claim, very germane to what we must try to think of from now on when we come upon the phrase "the Israeli-Palestinian conflict." But the analogy to the situation analyzed in this book risks becoming dangerous if it is not qualified by the observation that, although Hartog notes the need of an imaginary Other (lacking the landedness of the Athenians) for the Athenians to be themselves, the logical structure of this passage still takes the Athenians as agents who then make the Scythians in their own image. What the passage suggests, against Hartog's explicit syntax, is that a group of people *became the Athenians* at least substantially through an articulation of the Scythians as Other — which is generally what happened as a group of forced and voluntary Jewish migrants to Palestine became Israelis.

A further passage in Schwab's reworking of Bateson's ideas takes fully into account that cultural change and contact are a normal rather than suddenly intruding dynamic and that the question is how groups of people with varying cultural affiliations respond to the imaginative challenges posed by such contact:

> A dynamic balance [between two or more cultures] requires a reorganization of boundaries and a new creation of inner coherence based on chance. Defensive attempts at self-preservation tend to become, in the long run, self-destructive, whereas the open and transformative strategies might, up to a certain limit, be the self-preserving ones. In non-destructive culture contact, self-preservation presupposes self-transformation, or, more generally the recognition of otherness/ Other induces a self-transforming interaction. (Schwab 1986: 134, quoted in Sarris 1993: 60)

Particularly striking here is the insistence on a necessary relation between inner coherence — a symbolic system that makes adequate sense out of the world for a group of people to continue living with mortal uncertainty — and the chance nature of human existence thanks to which, rather than despite, such coherence actually obtains. As Raz-Krakotzkin observes, the way in which awareness of exile has been constitutive of Jewish culture is a vital example of this integration of chance with cultural structure, and the *reintegration* of such an exilic consciousness is, I would argue along with Raz-Krakotzkin, "a necessary step towards the development of bi-national ethics" (Raz-Krakotzkin 1993: 184).

Yet here again an important caveat must be added to the Schwab-Bateson formula. Its sketch of a dynamic balance, and of an apparent choice between defensive and open-ended responses to the challenge of the cultural Other, seems to assume a situation of equal access to power. In such a situation, the question would simply be one of getting groups of people to structure their identities through a more copacetic kind of othering. Other formulations of subjectivity (individual and group) and abjection tend to assume one hegemonic identity against which all others are abjected, hence defined as nonsubjects (Butler 1993). In such a view, there is a tendency on the part of the scholarly analyst to read every aspect of the subaltern identity as a reaction formation within the terms set by the dominant discourse, which is presumed to be the only discourse "really" available to anyone (Genovese 1976; cf. Gutman 1977).

My identification of certain theories or case studies with one or another of these twin traps vis-à-vis the relationship between power and identity — on the one hand, an emphasis on the contact of "cultures" that elides power differentials; on the other, a total fusion of power and knowledge that evacuates the place of a coherent, sustained, "minor" cultural difference — does not diminish my respect for the authors of these theories and studies. If I insist on preserving in this book the provisional nature of my field diary, it is not because I think I have already steered a consistently clear course between Scylla and Charybdis. I doubtless bounce against them time and again in ways that will be differently perceived by differently situated readers. Rather, by keeping the two poles in tension, I hoped to avoid being overly limited by the presumptions of either general formulation of the problem of identity and difference.

Part of the reason "My Trip to Israel" might still seem to overemphasize examples of the relatively benign contamination and subversion of unitary Israeli and Palestinian identities is that the creative and symbiotic possibilities of culture contact as articulated by Schwab express well the somewhat covert vision underlying all my investigations and musings about Israel and Palestine.

Thus when in and around Jerusalem, I was almost always implicitly looking for particular openings for this kind of process. Occasionally I found and recorded what seemed to be flashes of such creativity.

More broadly, once in Jerusalem I quickly began trying out on academic friends a new formulation that seems to move beyond the vision of cultures essentially retaining their integrity but in mutually fructifying ways. I propose that in the case of Israel and Palestine, there exists, usually suppressed and sometimes (usually casually or anecdotally) acknowledged, an everyday, evolving *interculture*. This proposal encompasses the question of cultures in contact reinventing themselves creatively or destructively rejecting the challenge of communication, and it can also take fully into account the dominance of Israeli Jews (and Ashkenazi Israelis in particular) and the subordination of Palestinian Arabs — nevertheless. Such an interculture in another nearby situation of murderous struggle over land and identity has been observed by Michael Herzfeld: "In the case of Greek-Turkish relations in Cyprus... the denial of common cultural grounds obscured the fact that each side understood the other's symbolism with devastating clarity" (Herzfeld 1993a: 2).

Ironically, the increasing "moderation" of the Palestinian leadership in the course of the intifada and subsequently may be seen as the adoption of critical aspects of the Zionist understanding of the link between land and identity. Whatever their actual desires may have been, significant portions of the Palestinian nationalist movement maintained for decades the political demand for a "democratic secular Palestine" — a polity that would be defined not by ethnicity but solely by citizenship within a common territory. The official, majoritarian, and publicly announced agreement finally to accept partition into two states meant an acknowledgment of the principle that certain territories were to be uniquely identified with given ethnic identities. As a Palestinian speaker put it in a conference in New York City in 1990, "For many years we were like the mother in the story about King Solomon — the one who refused to let the baby be cut in two because we loved the baby so much. Now we have realized that a country is not like a baby, and we must accept its being cut in two." For Palestinians this shift (to the unequal extent that it is a shift for different tendencies within Palestinian politics) is either a sound tactical move or a fundamental compromise. For an Israeli liberal such as Amos Oz, the reluctant magnanimity expressed in the notion that Israelis and Palestinians can avoid killing each other only by being separated from each other serves primarily as a reminder of who's got the upper hand.[2]

---

2. Oz describes the conflict as a tragedy, reinforcing the impression that its fundamental terms are fatally and eternally set: "I think the Israeli-Palestinian conflict... is a tragedy in

In both cases, *along with* the different situations out of which the expressions come, the only possible "peaceful" outcome is a diminution of the identities and reach of both sides, rather than a *revision* of the nature of the related identities.

These notions of the interculture, this perception that designations of a situation in binary terms and in zero-sum terms are constitutive of the situation rather than merely descriptions of it, and an awareness of the inevitable slippage in any account of the relation between cultural categories and differential access to power are correlates of the impossibility of ever achieving a stable balance between assuming that the *entire* context is determined "in the last instance" by the hegemonic culture and assuming that "cultures" per se are comparable units, therefore enjoying equal power. Since the very origins of ethnography are bound up in determinate ways with the broad colonial background of the relation between Palestine and Jewish history (Said 1989), ethnography is a *necessarily* inadequate intervention in an unjust situation.

The implicit notion of an ultimate reconciliation — a messianic moment, precisely impossible *in history* as I have suggested above, wherein Jews and Palestinians would experience an empathic understanding of each other's historical constitution so profound that the two identities would henceforth be seen as *fundamentally* costructuring rather than in conflict — does underlie the initial premise of my project. And it is still something to own up to, without shame or renunciation, but at the same time not to take as an absolute. It is intended rather as a kind of *wager* in which ethnography is not redemptive in the totalizing, messianic sense, but rather intended to help keep the game open and going; to nudge "history" ever so slightly in the direction of the Schwab-Batesonian symbiotic vision;[3] neither to owe too much allegiance to a universalist dream of "reconciliation" that *always* presumes some ultimate, objective human yardstick (a Kantian or Augustinian imperative, perhaps [see W. E. Connolly 1993a]) beyond the play of culture nor to accept that political antagonisms inevitably attend cultural difference.

---

the exact sense of the word. It is a clash between one very powerful claim and another no less powerful.... A Chekhovian tragedy... ends with everybody disillusioned, embittered, heartbroken, disappointed — indeed, absolutely shattered, but still alive. I want a Chekhovian, not a Shakespearean, resolution for the Israeli-Palestinian tragedy" (Oz 1993: 17). Contained here is the idea that collective identities are fundamentally inflexible, so the *best* one can hope for is that they survive being "shattered."

3. Bateson did not expect much more: "It is possible that those responsible for the policy of classes and nations might become conscious of the processes with which they are playing and cooperate in an attempt to solve the difficulties. This, however, is not very likely to occur since anthropology and social psychology lack the prestige necessary to advise; and, without such advice, governments will continue to react to each other's reactions rather than pay attention to circumstances" (Bateson 1972: 72).

This notion of the wager[4] also helps make possible the kind of self-exposure entailed by such a provisional account. Freedom from scholarly terror of occasionally being "wrong" — factually or politically — in some instances allows me a more direct presentation in this book of the *alte zakhen* that, by the time this final manuscript is prepared, my fieldnotes have become. As is common with the production of ethnographic monographs, several years have intervened and worked their sea changes upon my own reading of the notes. Some passages have lost their pungent resonance with time, like a package of *zattar* brought home and doled out slowly over the years to be savored with olive oil and pita bread. Others, representing moments of annoyed discomfort in the field, may take on a nostalgic piquancy, like the cassette of the Mizrachi pop group Ha'etnix that irritated me when it was blasted from neighbors' cars and apartments in Jerusalem but moves me almost to tears coming from my own stereo in New York. If one response to the gap in classic ethnography between the risk taking of fieldwork and the closure of the published account is to make "home" the field, by actively entering into the politics of culture back at home (Hale 1992), another is to present the record of fieldwork "there" in a different way, one that attempts to keep the moment of questioning open. The space on each page of "My Trip to Israel" between the journal entries and the commentary is the space of that opening.

Here again, despite a bifurcation between "conscious" and "sensuous" aspects of experience that we might question today, Bateson appears as a profound forerunner of central ideas in current critical theory, as Don Handelman and Lea Shamgar-Handelman have written:

> Gregory Bateson (1972: 128–52, 440–47)...attacks the modern insistence on making all knowledge accessible to the conscious mind, in search of the most powerful and efficient social levers. The positivist, shortest distance between two points produces only the loss of vital information. The (perhaps sensuous) processing and reconfiguration of such information depends upon the absence of conscious intentionality. The fully rational, intentional activation of the knowledge/power conjuncture is shortsighted in the extreme. (Handelman and Shamgar-Handelman 1993: 459)

The Handelmans invoke Bateson in their retort to a synthetic and theorized ethnographic argument that they find overly systematized and dependent on a strict correlation between official discourse and the symbolisms which that discourse frames (Domínguez 1993). But the same argument about the need for rational, logical control over any written account and the importance of permitting expression of contingent, counterintuitive, or even patently "prejudiced" impressions applies as well to the initial scene of writing in

---

4. Partly inspired by Bourdieu 1977.

ethnography, that is, to the field journal. Both the journal entries in this book and my subsequent commentaries to them buzz around this dilemma, on the one hand, often succumbing to the temptation to foreshorten a situation's complexities and do a quick, formulaic analysis, on the other hand, deliberately and overtly resisting that tendency and hence at points perhaps even making the analysis more opaque than need be.

Classically, fieldwork is marked off as a separate time of "data gathering."[5] This is the case here as well. Only the journal entries themselves are marked as particular, as historical, by the dates that separate them: the essays and the commentary are not dated. Indeed, the terms of my research fellowship mandated the period that I spent "in the field." I rhetorically signal my going off by starting the journal with getting on the airplane. In other ways the journal and my general situation in Jerusalem were hardly those of the classic outsider who comes to share an alien world for a time as a participant observer. The everyday life I was trying to live was not so much that of a "typical" Israeli or a Palestinian (there is no such person), nor of a professional field-worker, but more like that of a young American sent to Israel by his parents—hence the journal sections titled "My Trip to Israel."

A classic trope in ethnography is the presentation of the book's crucial point as a discovery that was made, unexpectedly and often suddenly, in the course of fieldwork.[6] Against this temptation, I must say that I did not suddenly *discover* that there was more than one kind of Palestinian and more than one kind of Israeli as a result of my fieldwork. Rather I structured my time in and around Jerusalem partly as an antidote to a series of critical essays I had written[7] that tended to employ these two dichotomous terms as if they did in fact refer to stable, unitary, and symmetrically opposite collective identities. I overcame one barrier to this kind of scattershot or shuttlecock ethnography in my living room in New York, months before arriving in Jerusalem. An Israeli anthropologist doing a stint as a guest scholar at New York University came over for a talk. I told him I was planning to consider the rhetorical construction of both Palestinian and Israeli national identity. He offered some friendly advice: "Don't try to do both of them. There's no way you'll have comparable information from both sides. You'll have a lot of difficulty making Palestinian contacts, and it may be dangerous getting around

---

5. To which some ethnographers now respond with the provocative injunction: "Homework, not fieldwork" (Viswesaran 1994).

6. See, for example, Margaret Mead's description of the realization by the working group that produced *Life Is with People*; the realization involved "discovering the existence of a whole at which we had not guessed" (Mead 1962: 16).

7. In addition to the original "Palestine and Jewish History" essay, cited above, these included "Reading Exodus into History" (see chap. 2, below) and "Hegel's Zionism?" (J. Boyarin 1994a).

the West Bank." But I was already aware that such sensible advice serves precisely to reinforce a range of other boundary-maintenance effects, ranging from patrolling soldiers to different-colored license plates to identity cards, that effectively naturalize the critical dichotomy between Israeli Jews and Palestinian Arabs. I had in fact no illusions or demands on myself to "obtain equal access" to Israelis and Palestinians; rather I intended to pursue and did pursue, in the limited time available, as many different directions as the range of contacts I had — academic, political, and family — afforded me.

Fellow scholars, both Israeli Jews and Palestinian Arabs, not only served as sympathetic sounding boards for my various ideas and helped me to find persons and situations among whom to test those ideas — the usual functions acknowledged by visiting ethnographers — but also appear in "My Trip to Israel" *as* Israelis and Palestinians. All of them, even those wary of my lack of expertise and open-ended approach to fieldwork, were generous in their reception of my ideas, and several of them shared insights that I regard as critical to any value this account may have.

My years of political activism on the Israeli-Palestinian issue afforded me a rich base of contacts on "both sides" of the divide. Obviously these contacts are almost exclusively on the left of both the Palestinian and Israeli political spectra, and once again, my account must not be taken as any kind of representative sample. Yet these contacts were still wide-ranging in their own way, and they made possible certain key ventures during my stay in Jerusalem, such as my stay at the Bedouin village of Ramye and the strange and disturbing night I spent in the refugee camp of Deheisheh. They also made it possible for me to explore further the congruences and divergences between an avowedly progressive political program and a critical account of intercultural politics.

Kinship has, of course, been a central organizing concept in modern social anthropology. Usually this term is related to the subject matter of ethnographic research, rather than to its method. Yet here my own kin — my brother Daniel's family has lived in Israel for almost twenty years — were among the most important "native contacts" I brought with me to Jerusalem, and they are very much present in this book.

I tried to meet and to portray as many different people as I could, but there are certain huge gaps in the impressionistic "cultural map" of my trip to Israel that should at least be signaled here. I regret that I have never traveled to Gaza. I knew all along that I should make greater efforts to meet with what might be called, with some hesitation, "mainstream" Zionist Israelis. Most embarrassing in retrospect, although I lived in a neighborhood of poor, mostly Moroccan Jews for about two months, my evident blindness toward them is reflected by their almost total absence from the journal.

When I began this project I expected that in the course of the research I would become, and be able to market my skills as, a Middle East area specialist. But my knowledge of the history and culture of Mediterranean Jewry, of classical Arab culture, and of Middle Eastern polities was inadequate. Furthermore, while I had a reading knowledge of Hebrew and had begun to study Arabic, in neither case was my knowledge adequate to the standard expected of professional ethnographers. In my office in New York and then later "in the field," I learned a great deal about Palestinian history, something of Arab culture, and my conversational Hebrew improved considerably, but I still am not a Middle East expert.

This disavowal should not be read as a claim that the criterion of expertise is bankrupt. When combined with an awareness both of the encrusted disciplinary taboos that tend to limit creative scholarship and of the everyday experiences that constitute what later gets codified as a "culture," real expertise results in vital writing such as Ammiel Alcalay's new book, *After Jews and Arabs* (Alcalay 1993). Alcalay, in some ways on much surer ground than I, takes what I would call the thesis of a Levantine "interculture" as his starting point and demonstrates its mutual fructifications, in the process putting into question a broad range of cultural and geographical boundaries that have hitherto been taken for granted. Rather than dismissing this kind of expertise, I am very much dependent on it. What I must and do resist in my account is the *rhetoric* of expertise that, for example, dictates that questions of fact are not supposed to remain in the final account: either the question must be settled or the topic must be deleted. Acceding to this kind of rhetorical closure would make me withdraw my wager before the contest begins.

I am not the first ethnographer to note how hard it is to write about a place where identities and ideologies seem to exist in an infinite variety of constantly shifting permutations. Virginia Domínguez has devoted an entire monograph to the reflexive discourse on Israel identity (Domínguez 1990). Earlier on Kevin Avruch titled one of the chapters of his ethnography *American Immigrants in Israel* (1981), "On Fieldwork in an Overly Complex Society." Avruch's title is rueful and mostly, but not solely, ironic. It leaves a hint that one of Israel's problems, and not only for the ethnographer, might be precisely an overabundance of differences and desiderata interfering with solidarity. Primarily, of course, since the chapter's explicit topic is fieldwork, it reflects the dilemma of attempting to apply the synthesizing and reductive model of ethnography in a context where the natives not only speak back to you (as they do everywhere) but speak in your own theoretical language — sometimes also insisting that the ethnographer express solidarity with them, a claim that may be based on your own ethnic identity.

The general approach I take in this book has a number of precedents. The only recent example I know in which a "diary in the strict sense of the word" has been published as an ethnography by the ethnographers themselves is Richard Price and Sally Price's *Equatoria* (Price and Price 1992), an account of an expedition "upriver" into Surinam collecting artifacts for the proposed national museum there. The book contains extended discussions of the politics and ethics of collecting and is disarmingly frank about the situation of the ethnographer: "Now, whoever tried to deny that anthropology is the handmaiden of colonialism?.... There's something about the definition of our role, and the way the town is set up, that leaves little choice" (Price and Price 1992: 141). Nevertheless, their published "diary" still seems much more controlled and coherent than my trip to Israel. Perhaps this is because they really were on a mission, carrying out a mandate; but it may also be that the material was to some extent retrospectively rewritten, something that I have (quite literally) resisted. Not only does their self-exposure (see J. Boyarin and D. Boyarin 1994) actually seem highly controlled; it also pertains to a part of the world that may be in tremendous political, economic, and epistemological conflict, but where those conflicts are not as locally enmeshed in U.S. politics as is the case in Israel/Palestine.

In any case, works like the Prices' help prepare the ground for a book like this one in ways that would have been much more difficult to imagine ten years ago. In fact, "An impressionistic approach to culture that emphasizes subjective experience and evocation is hardly alien to contemporary anthropology" (T. Turner 1993: 419). While the author of that quote might not agree, I take this as welcome news, for impressionism certainly has a place. Turner's observation is intended to be damning, perhaps because some scholars may still argue that the ethnographer is not a fit subject of ethnography. What's lost in the reiterated demand for an accurate representation of the world outside our heads is that most reflexive ethnographies have also found more space than traditional ethnographies for the reflexive articulations of our fieldwork "subjects," those persons whom we engage, who tell us about the world outside our heads that is *their* world. Presenting the ethnographer as a narrative construction, that is, may well help us find room for a fuller presentation of our interlocutors. Certainly here my own central presence in the text is intended as a way of allowing my peers and interlocutors who now live in Israel and Palestine to be more fully in the book. For everyone except my brother Daniel and my wife, Elissa Sampson, that textual presence is nevertheless inescapably marred by my use of pseudonyms — a form of respect that is also a diminution and a distortion.[8]

---

8. A few exceptions to this rule: Virginia Domínguez, with whom I discussed the awkward situation of citing the work of colleagues who are elsewhere referred to by pseudonyms, and who responded by giving me carte blanche to use her name; and, in the "In Search of 'Israeli Identity'" chapter, the colleagues who organized or responded to the panels discussed therein.

There is no master logic to the sequence of meetings and local journeys documented in the journal (it is more like the Israelites' wandering in the desert than like the Lewis and Clark expedition), and the only signposts are the dates that begin the various entries. Thus it may be helpful to point out that these dates are those on which the given text was actually written, so that on occasion a brief point that I noted that day might interrupt an account from one or several days previously that is resumed later. Embedded within certain journal entries as well are bracketed comments, marked as "footnotes" with dates several days later than the entry itself. I have resisted the editorial temptation simply to incorporate these within the postfieldwork commentary. This "fidelity," which might well strike some readers as merely obtuse, is in fact intended as a further disruption of the tendency for readers to suspend disbelief, in ethnography as in fiction. Without entirely surrendering verisimilitude (as you will judge for yourself), I want you to remember at every point that the journal, no less than the critical essays, is something I *made*.

But not arbitrarily, and not without any constraints at all. The experience of travel and the writing of ethnography display the same remarkable tension between experience as a reconfirmation and reinforcement of identity, on one hand, and as an opening and challenge, on the other. Louis Marin, following on earlier writings of Michel de Certeau, aptly expresses this tension:

> As de Certeau has superbly shown the travel narrative authorizes frontiers to be established *and* displaced, founded *and* trespassed over.... Any travel is, first of all, a moment and a space of vacancy, an unencumbered space that suspends continuous time and the ordering of loci. (Marin 1993: 414–15)

Yet at the same time, the democracy and generosity of travel implied in the second sentence quoted here are curtailed sharply by Marin's next sentence: "The traveller enriches this place with a large booty of knowledge and experiences by means of which he states, in this coming back to the 'sameness,' his own consistency, his identity as a subject" (415).

An apt illustration of this that many readers may have experienced is the phenomenon of walking down the street in a city we have come to visit for a time and "recognizing" a passerby as a neighbor or friend from our home community, only to realize that we have never seen this person before. In travel we are constantly filling in gaps with material from our stock of expectations, at the same time as, through a series of revelations, we enlarge our store of recognizable phenomena. Nor is this back-and-forth movement of fabulation and revision limited to concrete phenomena such as persons and landscapes. Faced with a situation that doesn't fit our social or political categories, we may try nevertheless to squeeze it in. Since a great deal of what I am about in

"My Trip to Israel" is the documentation of the making of this ethnographic world, my commentary isn't intended to correct, explain, or "cover" every tendentious comment in the journal. Some readers might find tendentious, for example, the passage in my journal entry for June 23, 1991, where I list the organizations that provided the money for the "reclamation" of the land of a kibbutz in the southern Arava desert near Eilat, and then add, "It's not clear who they thought they were paying to have it reclaimed from." In fact, "reclamation" need not imply that the land was taken or stolen from anybody. Did the Dutch steal the polders from the sea? My baldly ironic comment seems to reveal my own obsession with the theme of Zionism as theft masking itself as redemption. Yet rather than trying to purify my own account, I find it much more productive to insist once again that the ethnography as well is fit material for the critical questions Michael Herzfeld asks about rhetorics of essential identity in relation to the ethnography of the state:

> Instead of spending so much time on *attacking* essentialism and thereby ourselves indulging in a moralistic game, we should devote much more attention to such pragmatic questions as who essentializes what and under what specific circumstances: that is the role of an ethnography that can encompass local actors, state agencies, and scholars. (Herzfeld 1993a: 16)

Inevitably there is a tendency here to "essentialize" the Palestinians as a *foil* for my Jewish ethnography: to take them as a more or less solidary mass of more or less indigenous inhabitants with more or less perfect claims to lands they still possess or lands they lost to the Zionists in the course of this century.

This tendency is most sharply employed, but also interrogated, in my closing chapter, "Ruins, Mounting toward Jerusalem." In so doing, I attempt a kind of "remembrance based on the Palestinian point of view" (Raz-Krakotzkin 1993: 184) and thereby make my own imagination a kind of laboratory for the Batesonian corrective, the promise and risks of which have already been suggested. Inasmuch as this is an attempt at empathy, a momentary becoming-Palestinian, it might seem just another "old thing," relying on the humanism that insists we could all somehow be each other in imagination if we believed hard enough. The difference is perhaps that the older ethic of humanist empathy relied on the possibility and need to empty our own identities of any specific content other than "humanity" in order then to take on for a moment the identity of the Other, whereas my imaginative effort is always contingently grounded in the Jewish identity I have been given and have made for myself.

That identity — even in its securely "traditional" formulations — is not simply inward-looking, resting on internal justifications for its moral and behavioral strictures. *Maasey Alfas*, the introduction to various editions of the traditional Jewish prayer book, explains why Jews must behave in an upright way with all people:

> The Holy Temple was the Jewish formative school [*shule fun bildung*], for the purpose of shining light outward into the world, so that through the Jew's good behavior toward all people, both Jews and the nations of the world, everyone would recognize our great Teacher, the Creator of the World, whose teaching is so important because it purifies the mind, it teaches great knowledge in every aspect of learning, it has a powerful influence on the heart and on the character [*kharakter*]. (*Maasey Alfas* n.d: 3; my translation from Yiddish)

Thus there is a call for just behavior toward Jews and non-Jews alike, the express purpose of the latter especially being the greater glory of God. This is an ethic of generalized or universal decency with a "particularist" purpose behind it. In a perhaps startling way, this is quite analogous to imperialist universalism, which also represents an intimate linkage between generously humanist behavior and the special nature of the imperial power. But this Yiddish prayer book introduction actually reverses the terms of imperialist humanism in at least two major ways. First, it does not directly demand that all the "nations of the world" begin acting like the Jews, but merely asserts that if Jews act the way they are supposed to then the Others will see the virtue in our ways. Second, it does not set out a putatively universally valid framework for behavior and then identify a given, exalted group as the bearer of that ideal (think of Macauley in India), but rather insists that internal standards for just dealing are valid and mandated in dealings with Others as well.

In addition to the argument of the *Maasey Alfas* for generally valid standards of just and civil behavior based on the general need to spread God's glory, the ancient Jewish tradition contains powerful injunctions both of exclusion and of openness toward other specified nations based on the particulars of Israelite history. Remarkably, when it comes to the Egyptians, it is the sojourn rather than the oppression that seems to count: "Thou shalt not abhor an Egyptian, because thou wast a stranger in his land" (Deuteronomy 23:8). In two instances — the command that gleanings be left behind in the field and that unfallen olives be left after the trees are beaten, both for "the stranger, for the fatherless, and for the widows" — the justification and perhaps the purpose as well are "And thou shalt remember that thou wast a bondman in the land of Egypt, and the Lord thy God redeemed thee thence" (Deuteronomy 24:18, 22). These texts are relevant both as an ancient, textually authoritative, and "native" discourse of empathy and also because they bear powerful analogies, which need not be spelled out here, with the relations of different imagined communities in Israel/Palestine today.

Deuteronomy and the *Maasey Alfas* are old things. My own resources for an attempt to understand the dynamics of identity, responsibility, and difference are of course not limited to Jewish texts, ancient or modern. I also find powerful encouragement in critical writings by various writers, all of whom seek to identify important limitations in the liberal conception of the autonomous individual. One of these writers is the political theorist William Connolly, whose avowedly and self-critically secularist account seeks the sources of what we might call "empathy" (although he does not use the word) in an evolving awareness of the contingency of one's own identity. In contrast to this sense of contingency Connolly and others would like us all to cultivate,

> liberalism remains a philosophy of tolerance among culturally established identities more than one of attentiveness to how these identities are established and the ways in which new possibilities of identity are propelled into being. (Connolly 1993b: 178)

Connolly's statement may be taken as a corollary of the Schwab-Batesonian call for a symbiotic formation of the identity of Self and Other. If the liberal ethos of modernity is taken as a baseline, Connolly's insight here and the broader world of thought that makes his formulation possible strike me as a genuinely "new thing."

Ideas about the particular and the universal, about identity and ethics, and about the mutual invention of Self and Other — ideas that are engaged in writings as diverse as *Maasey Alfas*'s chauvinistic ethic of universal decency, Bateson's theory of schismogenesis, and Connolly's disruption of liberal identity — continue to shape my own balancing of identity and difference, both as a practicing Jew and as a practicing anthropologist, and are brought to bear in the accounts of my stay in and around Jerusalem. Recognizing that Bateson's original, provocative investigation of Self and Other was articulated decades ago in the context of American cultural anthropology might lead to some salutary rethinking of the place of anthropology in academic cultural studies, whose practitioners often seem to think that the Other with a capital "O" was invented in France. Nevertheless, for the time being it is within this broad field of cultural studies — more often than not with an institutional home in departments of literature — that the kind of questions about identity, history, language, and genealogy that nurture this account are most sharply articulated and debated.

I received my first concentrated "dose" of cultural theory in the summer of 1988 at the School of Criticism and Theory at Dartmouth College. My primary course there was Edward Said's "Methodologies of Empire." His lectures demonstrated how literature is at the heart of the mechanics of empire building and maintenance and also serves anti-imperialist struggles. His books *Orientalism* (Said 1978) and *The Question of Palestine* (Said 1980), two earlier monographs in this vein, are important models for the present project. However, I contend that in Said's account all of Jewish history that did not result in the establishment of Israel and violence to the Palestinians is invisible. Jewish identity is thereby generally reduced to a monolithic Zionism. Given my claim that history and land are of comparable weight as dimensions of the conflict, this elision of Jewish history and culture in Diaspora has ideological implications analogous to those of early Zionist rhetoric referring to "a land without a people." Nevertheless on the practical level it is absurd to compare the effect of Zionist settlement on the mass of Palestinians to the effect imperfect Palestinian sensitivity may have on Jewish or Israeli intellectuals. Ideology and experience cannot be equated; neither are they separate.

The juxtaposition of ethnography and criticism in this book is likewise intended to mirror and disrupt the received dichotomy between experience and ideology. The placement of criticism at the borders of ethnography here — this extended introduction, "Ruins, Mounting toward Jerusalem" as a sort of coda, the commentary in the footnotes to the journal, and the two essays that break up the travelogue — is thus intended to have an "arhythmic" effect, rather than to constitute a neatly symmetric architecture.

"Reading Exodus into History," the first of the interjected essays, pops out of my account of a discussion with a German scholar living in East Jerusalem like Marshall McLuhan stepping out from behind a movie poster to explain his own theories in Woody Allen's *Annie Hall*. The disjuncture brought on by this sudden and extended exercise in literary history, the *pulling away* from a presentist account of a dialogic encounter, is extreme. Yet the essay is relevant precisely to the immense issue that comes up, albeit in passing, in my conversation with the German historian. That issue is the long history of struggles over interpretation that underlies any question about the relation between a given "authoritative" text and a given political situation. Attempting to understand the persistence of an ideology of Jewish nationhood across generations and despite vast social change has led me to consider the link and slippage between identity and history, "nation" and personal experience. Equally important, work in Jewish ethnography has forced me to focus on text as a bearer and shaper of culture (J. Boyarin, ed., 1993). "Reading Exodus into History" was also influenced by my having read, argued, and studied with Said. It is placed here — even though it leads us "far away in time and space" from the immediate concerns of this book — as an illustration of the "myth models" (Obeyesekere 1992) that we continue to reproduce even in the "West." One of the main points of "Reading Exodus into History" is to disrupt, once and for all, the question whether Zionism is a movement of colonialism *or* of national liberation; these categories are anachronistic vis-à-vis the Bible narrative, and they are not mutually exclusive in the present. Nor is "national liberation" the panacea it was once imagined to be. Yet rather than use my fieldwork as more fodder for my critical mill, I prefer to let the essay stand as more material that readers might draw on in producing their own analyses of the various situations described in "My Trip to Israel."

Initial reactions to the second essay interposed here within the journal — "In Search of 'Israeli Identity'" — were mixed in the two different contexts where I read it as a conference paper. Some of these reactions suggested vaguely but ominously that there I had indeed fallen into one of the culturological traps described above, writing of the construction of both Palestinian and Israeli identity in a way that suggests that they are structurally equal. Why that particular essay, written under specific circumstances, might have turned in that direction is now explored in an extended self-critique appended to the original conference paper. Here let me just mention my guess that it had something to do with the paper's being written "in the field" — that is, in Jerusalem — but more precisely, in an office at the Shalom Hartman Institute, an institution with a generally liberal-Zionist bent and a mission to foster pluralism in Israeli society. This affinity between the tone of an essay and the particular situation in which it was written suggests once again the importance of articulating in this book the leakages among ethnography and criticism, theory and situation, and, indeed, between discovery and ignorance.

"Ruins, Mounting toward Jerusalem" was initially written in response to a fortuitous invitation, received just a few weeks before I was due to leave Jerusalem, to participate in an upcoming conference entitled "The Culture of Ruins" at the University of California at Santa Cruz. It is structured by my intense curiosity about one of the sites that I finally had the chance to explore with my colleague Naomi Seidman when I prepared for the paper and by the stories told me by my wife, Elissa Sampson, and my sister-in-law, Chava Boyarin, about the dispossessed Palestinian Israelis from Ikrit and Biram, the other site explored in the paper. "Ruins, Mounting toward Jerusalem" seems now to incorporate many of the questions about the material, physical, and geographical "presence of the past" that underlie my entire investigation of the links between memory and territory in shaping the Israeli-Palestinian interculture. It completes this book both because it was written immediately after the fieldwork was completed and based on some of the very last bits of fieldwork and because it is a relatively concrete exercise in the articulation of what I implicitly call for in "Palestine and Jewish History" — the evocation and cultivation of contingent memories rather than those that fill a mutually exclusive mental map.

•

Although it was not planned as such, this book might be taken as an attempted realization of the call for a "Jewish ethnography" in my earlier essay "Jewish Ethnography and the Question of the Book" (J. Boyarin 1992).

There I called for an ethnography that would be fragmentary, communicating the partial and tentative nature of ethnographic learning, resisting the still-powerful impulse to portray "whole" cultures. I suggested that, as with the expressed Jewishness of the French poet Edmond Jabès, the ethnicity and other constitutive elements of the ethnographer's identity should be situated in the text, but not grounded or stabilized in an illusory way.

What this suggests to me now is a further call for a diasporic ethnography. In the debate about the relation between Jewish history and Jewish memory, "privileging Diaspora" is not about valorizing those Jews who happen to live outside the Jewish state. Rather it indicates the effort to reclaim the resources of creating and sustaining identity in the presence of different and sometimes dominant Others and in the absence of any possible myth of a unique, perfect, and "organic" connection between a given people and "their" land on which they live. Diasporic ethnography of this kind would not be detached from questions of place and identity (all diasporas are desperately linked to questions of place!) but clear about its own origins in an epistemic regime that worked to *fix* identity in a given and unitary place and that diasporic identity must therefore resist. This move — both the tendency and the resistance — was expressed in one of the stunning and humbling insights shared with me by so many of the people I talked to during my fieldwork, when for the first time I met the activist and scholar known in this text as Judy Levi, and she referred to herself as my "native informant — or rather, migrant informant." We still have some work to do overcoming that aspect of our anthropological inheritance that sees "natives" as more authentic than "migrants." But a diasporic ethnography would not only be *about* Diaspora, much as a Jewish ethnography is not only or not necessarily *about* Jews. Rather it would be diasporic in its content and in its effects: a kind of ethnography where even the final text would not represent a substitute homeland or resting place, but where the reader would be sent out always once again to wander and to wonder about the places where identities and memories meet to struggle and negotiate.

# 1
# My Trip to Israel: Beginning

• 6/10/91 •

Getting on the plane, to Paris and then Tel Aviv. Writing with a small, yellow, lined tablet picked up at the airport, self-consciously, feeling very amateurish, feeling like a high school kid who wants to be a writer. Well, I've been saying to myself for days that this project is deliberately unprofessional.

• 6/11/91 A.M. •

Charles de Gaulle Airport, waiting for my transfer flight to Israel. At the airport café here, I ask the counterman if I can pay for a *café crème* and a croissant with a five-dollar bill. He says yes, but he can't give me change. I say, in that case make it *un grand crème,* and am rewarded with an amused smile from a middle-aged Frenchwoman standing next to me.[1]

I really feel incredibly down to earth, with no particular feeling either of anxiety or of anticipation at the moment. I was just calculating, in a businesslike way, how much time I'll have to spend in Israel (as opposed to here in France) in December in order to earn my stipend. It will depend on how my writing goes, of course. I've brought along (in my carry-on) Roger San-

---

1. This bit also sends me, and the reader, back to the year my wife, Elissa Sampson, and I lived in Paris, while I was doing fieldwork for my dissertation and eventual book on Polish Jewish immigrants (J. Boyarin 1991a). The French coffee I ordered — and the modest *bon mot* that evidently worked — reassured me that even years later, passing through the airport, my hold on Paris was still effective. The Frenchwoman who granted me a smile seems to be blessing my new project by acknowledging my ability to function in other cultures. In earlier ethnographies an extended introductory account of the entry to the field site was a common literary technique (Pratt 1986). This becomes more difficult when the journey to the field, even half a planet away, takes about half a day. On the other hand, "frequent flyers" know that the no-place of airplanes and airports is a place where millions of people spend time, and as such is an appropriate site for ethnography as well. When my father, Sidney Boyarin, is asked where his sons live, he replies, "On an airplane."

jek's book on fieldnotes, but I'm having enough trouble concentrating on the feminist fantasy novel I've brought along to pass time on the plane.

A field situation idea: Biram, compared to Oradour — possibility of getting Father Chacour to go with me?[2]

It's relaxing to be able to just *write* like this, after the painful assemblage of library-based research and closely argued clever sentences I've been producing in my windowless office at the Center for Studies of Social Change for the last two years.

On the flight to Tel Aviv: very sleepy, a twinge of my old FEAR OF IS-RAELIS, which I can only explain as a conviction that they know the real Jewish language and I don't.[3]

Why do they ask for your father's first name on the "registration of entry" form?

Flying in — so quickly you're circling over the hills, over the "territories." How does a Palestinian ("Israeli" or not) feel looking at it from the air?

Ruins of terraced fields along the way to Jerusalem.[4]

Another theme: *Traces in the Landscape* (where does that title come from?). [Fn.: when retyping, 6/27: I think from Monika Krajewska's exhibition of photographs of Jewish cemeteries in Poland at YIVO.][5]

• 6/12/91 •

Sign walking up Yehuda Street: *"Baka shkhuna betukha badrakhim — misrad hatakhbura."*[6] The prevalence of *security* as an obsession of the whole "internal" social system — for example, traffic safety.

---

2. Father Elias Chacour, who has lived and worked for decades in the Galilee town of Ibillin, is a native of Ikrit, further north near the Lebanese border (Chacour and Hazard 1984). For discussions of Ikrit and its sister village, Biram, see the conclusion to this book.

3. The Jewish language I know best is Yiddish. This journal entry now appears to me as the first attempt to formulate what became a key element of my analysis of my continuing uneasiness in Israel: the sense of being an outsider in a place where the prevailing ideology dictates that I belong. Against my presumption that this is essentially an ideological phenomenon, I must say that as I became more comfortable with Hebrew, this sense eased considerably.

4. This entry, part of a series of briefly noted observations about possible themes for further research, actually signals a concern that will become more and more prominent as it is articulated toward the end of this book. As suggested in the introduction, this hint — this foreshadowing or pregnancy — indicates the strange mixture of preconception and the desire for discovery that characterizes ethnographic fieldwork.

5. This was indeed the name of the exhibition. Monika Krajewska is the author of two volumes of such photographs, the more recent containing erudite commentary on the iconography of Polish Jewish cemetery art (Krajewska 1981, 1993). The YIVO Institute for Jewish Research in New York City is one of the major archives on East European Jewish history and culture.

6. "Baka is a neighborhood of safe ('secure') streets — Department of Transportation."

Another poster, in Arabic on top; can't quite make out text, which is something like *"Dhariba el-arnona fi el wake min ajdad"* — showing various nice parts of the city and nice things happening in it (gardening, sweeping, walking on the walks of the Old City) — all marked in Hebrew. What's this about?[7]

I went in to the Shalom Hartman Institute[8] to see about using the office which has Dan's[9] computer in it. One of the people currently using it is Menashe Levin, a philosopher.[10] Later he explains to me that he wasn't using the office much; he'll be working at home. Without my asking, he says that he lives "in the Occupied Territories — in Elon Shvut." His use of the phrase, and the diffident way he says it, make me say, "You don't have to apologize." He insists that he wasn't apologizing, but I had the clear impression that he expected me to disapprove actively.

On the steps of Yemin Moshe,[11] a flash of insight: Charles had shown me

---

7. I got parts of it right, but this transcription is not coherent enough to be translated back into Arabic. However, the *arnona* is a residence tax levied on everyone living in Jerusalem, and toward the end of my stay I saw signs in Hebrew saying, *"Arnona — ze be'etsem beshvilcha"* (Arnona is really for your sake). Evidently the poster was intended to encourage Arabic-reading residents to pay the *arnona* by showing how it improves the quality of life throughout the city.

8. Directed by Rabbi David Hartman, the institute is a place where pressing contemporary issues — such as inter-Jewish tolerance, relations between Arabs and Jews, the place of Jewish law in a Jewish state, and the situation of women in Judaism — are examined in their interaction with rabbinic Jewish teachings and the longer course of Jewish history.

9. My brother, Daniel Boyarin, maintains a home in Jerusalem; at the time of my stay, his wife, Ruth, lived there, and his two sons, Efraim and Avner, were serving in the Israel Defense Forces.

10. In fact he is a Talmud scholar; evidently I confused him here with the Israeli philosopher Yehuda Elkana.

11. Named after the Jewish philanthropist Moses Montefiore, Yemin Moshe is one of the oldest Jewish neighborhoods outside the walls of the Old City. It is built on the slope of the Valley of Hinnom, across from the Tower of David. Because of its age and its proximity to No-Man's-Land between 1948 and 1967, it was considered an extremely poor neighborhood; at that time, "Most of the residents (80 percent) came from Turkey, and the rest from Persia, Iraq, and Kurdistan, and those of Ashkenazi origin were in the minority" (Jaffe 1988: 66). However, "after the Six Day War, with the liberation of the Old City, the idea of evacuating the neighborhood came up again. When the walls separating the east and west sectors of the city came down, the 'other' Yemin Moshe was discovered, now in a central geographical position...with a spectacular view, from olden times, full of magic and splendor" (84). The post-1948 residents were "evacuated," and the neighborhood underwent a decade of renovation. The plan called for Yemin Moshe to become an artists' colony, but it didn't quite work that way: "Initially, a number of artists took advantage of the terms offered to them, but apparently the large financial investment required for the restoration and repair of the buildings was beyond the means of many other artists. Therefore, it was decided to sell the apartments to (almost) anyone who could take on the expenses connected with the purchase and restoration of an apartment in the area. The result was the establishment of an exclusive neighborhood with a high standard of living" (141–42). Now, in fact, Yemin Moshe is an extremely wealthy neighborhood populated largely by Jews from English-speaking countries. Through the kindness of a mutual friend, I was able to stay for several weeks at the beginning

a paper, by physicists he works with, commenting on a quote from Einstein which suggests he believed in a series of momentary, discontinuous selves.[12] The beginning of fieldwork may be a moment when that is most true. I am poised on a step toward the next several months, but I don't know who I'll be when I'm done. Not being with Elissa heightens that, of course. In some ways being alone — without Elissa, who of course has her own strong opinions — furthers that sense of openness and indeed dependency. [Fn. 6/27: Blanche Dubois — "I have always depended on the kindness of strangers."][13] This notion seems to be based on the disruption the removal from familiar surroundings to strange ones causes to the sense of a continuous self. But on what basis do we assume that the very *place* remains consistent? I know that's not the case here, since, for example, I can't go to the Old City as freely, even, as I did in 1983, or certainly as Elissa and her friends did in the mid-1970s — all to see her friend Riah, which is why I'd like to go to the Old City right now. I expect to commiserate with him about bad business here and there, but we'll see.

Two bumper stickers on a car on Emek Refaim last night: one says, *"Ani lo skud v'al tehiye li lepatriot — shamor merekhok!"*[14] Other nice evidence of the internal-external security issue. Charles told me that the traffic accident rate in Israel is twice that of the United States, and since the Arab police in the territories quit when the intifada started, the rate in the territories has been five times that of Israel — so the government is proposing to impose Israeli traffic law on the territories, in violation (Charles says) of the Geneva Convention.

The second bumper sticker (seen also on other cars, on signs, and so on) says, *"Khatima lekhayim — hitkhayavut ishit limniyat haketa bedrakhim."*[15] The "signature for life," of course, is taken from the imagery of Yom Kippur judgment, and thus the civic slogan is another reminder that this country is *Jewish*.

I call Sandy and Beth Brisker — Sandy is a friend from my Tifereth Yerusha-

---

and end of my stay in what may be the last unrenovated apartment in Yemin Moshe. It should be declared a national historic site.

12. The physicist Charles Waters, my closest friend at Reed College in the mid-1970s, has been living in Jerusalem since 1982. The paper referred to is Horowitz, Arshansky, Elitzur 1988.

13. This embedded footnote falls into the category of high camp: one of the standard ways for narrative ethnography to recruit the sympathies of its readers is to stress the personal vulnerability inherent in fieldwork.

14. "I'm not a Scud, so don't be a patriot — keep your distance!"

15. "Signature for life — personal responsibility for the avoidance of slaughter on the roads." *Keta badrakhim* is a common journalistic phrase for fatalities in traffic accidents in Israel, the high rate of which is universally regarded as an urgent problem.

layim[16] days. I speak to Beth first — she says to him that it's me, and his first reaction is, "That Jew-hater?"[17] (God he's fast; how do you convey to a notebook that he was kidding?) Later she says to him that I'm here for six months, and he says, "He probably owes somebody in New York money." Later when I talk to him directly, I tell him one of my main goals is to keep myself "healthy and cheerful," a simple formula I adopted today. He promises to help with the latter.

Last night I told Ruth that one of my goals is to convey the sense that the lives of Israelis don't consist entirely of oppressing Palestinians. She tells me the only way she can stand the everyday expressions of racism is by wearing a Walkman to shut them out, and she illustrates this with a couple of examples she heard on Shavuot, when she couldn't wear the Walkman.[18]

A question raised I think in my "Palestine and Jewish History" piece can be extended now: Is the problem with Zionism for me just the dispossession of the Palestinians, or the very project of centralization and state power? What if I decided that (as it seems at the moment, after warm contact with relatives, old friends, and prospective friends, and in a beautiful place) the project for "people like us" at least was "working"? And, given that it isn't the same as Yiddishkeit, but it's nice once in a while to be in a big place full of Jews — Is that an OK substitute for Yiddishkeit? Why was my brother a committed Zionist now anti-Zionist, while I'm a "committed" non-Zionist, and it never (apparently) mattered that much to my sister? I'll walk some more — and now think that it's interesting and troubling that I could even imagine that it's possible to hypothetically separate out the Palestinians from my problems with the Israeli formulation of Jewishness — as if, on one hand, I could be content to remain with a conception of "us" that is all Jews (as "part of me" could) and, on the other, things would be intellectually/morally/politically more convenient and simpler if there had never been and weren't now any Palestinians — a suspicion that, I suspect, haunts many Zionists (left)[19] as well. But — but what? Shall I say that my life would be poorer? How egotistical can you get? Shall I say this does not take the rights and lives of the Palestinians into account? But there are no hypothetical rights and lives. The answer is rather: this is the world, and these are the people in it.[20]

---

16. A yeshiva on the Lower East Side of New York (see J. Boyarin 1989).

17. A teasing reference to my views — certainly radical for someone who is an even fitful participant in the Orthodox Jewish community — on Israel and Zionism.

18. Orthodox Jewish law forbids contact with electrical devices on the Sabbath and festivals.

19. I mean here leftist Zionists, not those who are still Zionists.

20. An embarrassingly puerile answer to a badly formulated question. Perhaps entertaining the hypothetical nonexistence of the Palestinians — taking as plausible the convenient Zionist rhetoric of "a land without people for a people without land" — is valuable if it helps me or

Two reviews in the window of a restaurant called Marhaba[21] on Shlomzion Hamalka 14 — the one from the *Jerusalem Post* and the one in Hebrew (no source listed, my guess is *Kol Ha'Ir*)[22] — both refer to the fact that you just can't really go to Bethlehem for good Arab food anymore. The one in Hebrew is more sardonic about this — its headline is *"Avoda aravit."*[23] [Fn. when writing this up, 7/4: the other day Ruth showed me an article about Arabs with Ph.D.'s who can't get jobs in Israeli universities; apparently there are no Arabs with tenure at — Hebrew University? any Israeli university? — and the headline was *"Aravim lekembridg,"*[24] an obvious play on the right-wing slogans calling for the expulsion of the Arabs.]

The symbol for Israeli tourism — the spies coming back with two huge bunches of grapes[25] — what were they *thinking* about when they adopted it? "You, too, can conquer this land"? A mixed message at best: the giant grapes, like the giant people, must have been a source of fear.[26]

• 6/13/91 •

Part of an incredibly involved dream just before waking up: I'm at some institution where, I think, I'm a professor (or maybe a researcher like I was

---

anyone else to understand the overwhelming desire that drives Zionism, not only to ensure the physical safety of Jews, but to relieve Jews of that terrible and fruitful *contingency* that defines the situation of Yiddishkeit. Once this is stated, it becomes obvious that Palestinian existence in our times is one of the central defining conditions of Jewish existence. After the establishment of the State of Israel, Jewishness is impossible without the Palestinians.

21. "Hello" in Arabic.
22. The local alternative newspaper in Jerusalem, which contains a remarkable amount of critical journalism aimed at a mass audience.
23. "Arab work," a slang term for slipshod workmanship. The term may also have ironic echoes of the early twentieth-century Zionist slogan of *"Avoda ivrit,"* or Hebrew labor, which promoted the development of a Jewish working class in Palestine, rather than the hiring of cheaper Arab labor.
24. "Arabs to Cambridge!"
25. More precisely, the symbol for the Israeli ministry of tourism shows the spies who have been sent into Canaan returning to the Israelite camp in the desert.
26. In fact the majority report from ten of the spies sent out to scout the land at the end of the Israelites' journey through the desert in the biblical narrative leaves a mixed impression. On one hand, they cut down "a branch with one cluster of grapes, and they bore it upon a pole between two" (Numbers 13:23), the precise source of the modern symbol. And indeed, they told Moses that the land "flows with milk and honey; and this is the fruit of it" (Numbers 13:27). They were also convinced of the impossibility of Israelite conquest, because "it is a land that eateth up the inhabitants thereof" (Numbers 13:32), who were in any case giants; "we were in our own sight as grasshoppers, and so we were in their sight" (Numbers 13:33). One might comment that this is a mixed message to be impressing upon twentieth-century tourists. More to the point, in terms of the relation between Zionism and Jewish culture, most of the spies (except for Joshua and Caleb) are explicitly despised in the biblical account because of their negative propaganda.

at the New School), but which is also Jonah's[27] nursery school. A worker asks me, like all the other people there, to sign a nonexistent gift book he's holding in his hands. I refuse, and ask who it's for. "The Arab mugger," he laughs. I ask the person I'm walking with what that's about, and he says there was a mugging at the institution, but it was actually committed by a Greek Jew.[28]

Many languages go by my window here in Yemin Moshe — French, Italian, English, Hebrew, Arabic, others I don't recognize. One could stay in Jerusalem indefinitely without learning Hebrew.

On the phone, Ruth tells me she's thinking of going to an organ concert at the Lutheran church in the Old City tonight — but only if she can find someone to accompany her from the Jaffa Gate.

Ruth also tells me that I'll have plenty of anthropology to do in the family — not only Avner's induction ceremony, but also sending him off on the bus with the other boys' families, and so on.[29] She seems amused by the idea of being an expert informant.

Postnap: another scary dream, violent as well, as I often have when I sleep with a headache, which is frequent [Fn. 7/5: frequent in New York, anyhow]: I'm buying vegetables from a couple of young Palestinian guys, chatting easily with them, and they're intrigued by the fact that I "know five languages." I get into my car, start pulling away, realize that I forgot the lettuce, and a Jewish man offers to hand it to me. Suddenly he turns abusive, and we start to exchange ridiculous, sexist sexual epithets. The woman (?) sitting with me in the car tries to calm me down, saying, "It's the doubleness that drives him crazy."

---

27. Our older son, who was five years old at this time.

28. This reporting of dreams in the field may be the ultimate in ethnographic subjectivism; it is precisely the kind of material that should not automatically be expunged. The association in this dream between an Arab and a "Greek Jew" illustrates the unstable boundaries between my own ethnic categorizations and judgments and the categorizations and judgments I'm analyzing. As in a distorting mirror, the conflation mimics the theme of Ammiel Alcalay's book *After Jews and Arabs: Remaking Levantine Culture* (A. Alcalay 1993). Alcalay seeks to document the fruition of a regional interculture that exceeds its "parts" without making them disappear (in much the same way that New York City functions whenever it prospers). My dream, by contrast, might be said actually to hinge on a catechresis. On one hand, there is a vicious reinstatement of the dichotomy between Jews and Arabs, since the dream contains the "moral lesson" that a crime was committed by one of "our own" — or rather, by a Jew but the wrong kind of Jew. On the other, there is the reiteration of a single category in which generic "Arabs" and Greek Jews can be confused. This is not the Hellenic Greek as European precursor, but the despised Oriental Greek (Herzfeld 1987; Lambropoulos 1992). Does finding what you're looking for in the field extend to planting Orientalist dreams in your own head?

29. Different moments in the entry of eighteen-year-old non-Arab Israeli citizens into their period of mandatory army service.

An ad in the Jerusalem Yellow Pages: "The greatness of a people is judged by its attitude toward animals — Mahatma Gandhi."

Another traffic-safety bumper sticker: *"Venahagta lere'ekha kamocha,"*[30] with the little Sonol[31] symbol in the corner. This, it seems, is the kind of stuff Virginia could have picked up on much more easily than counting uses of *tarbut* in newspapers. Maybe she wouldn't have recognized the quote, but I suspect I owe her a debt for guiding me to pick up on this phenomenon.[32]

The names of two of the gates of the city — Damascus[33] and Jaffa — and another street named Derech 'Aza, reflect broken connections. The Aza Road is no longer the road to Gaza; the Damascus Gate and the Jaffa Gate are no longer the beginning of journeys to those places. And whatever else happens, they will never again be that: only reminders of possible journeys past.[34]

OK wise guy — but Derekh Bet-Lechem, "thanks" to the occupation, *is* once again the road to Bet Lechem. Two questions pose themselves: Will it remain so? And if so, for whom?

---

30. "And you shall drive (behave) toward your neighbor as toward yourself."

31. One of the oil companies operating in Israel.

32. Virginia Domínguez is a U.S. anthropologist and the author of a painstaking and innovative study of rhetorics of national identity among middle-class Israelis, especially academics and other intellectuals (1990). Doubtless I sell her knowledge of Judaism short; my somewhat catty remark perhaps betrays my anxiety that she had already done a great deal of the research I was assigning myself. I'm not sure why I refer to her by her first name; although we have subsequently become acquainted, at this time we only knew each other's writing. One chapter in her book analyzes uses of the word *tarbut* (culture) in the Israeli press.

33. The Hebrew name of this gate is Shaar Shekhem, which links it to the city Crusaders named after Naples, and which Palestinians call Nablus. I almost got away here with simply referring to "the names of two of the gates of the city" as if these names in English, the ones given by the colonizers, simply "were" their names; as if colonizers had the same power of absolute naming the Bible grants to Adam. States too would like to have this power of absolute naming, but at various points in this book I give examples where the State of Israel does not enjoy such power.

34. In fact, there is no reason why a journey to Jaffa — which, engulfed by Tel Aviv, still has a remnant Palestinian Arab population — could not still begin at the Jaffa Gate, or why a journey to Nablus (see previous note) would not begin at the Damascus Gate. What I'm trying to evoke in this journal entry is the sense of a lost *unity* of the area under the Ottomans. Ammiel Alcalay evokes this loss by citing a passage from Hachette's *Blue Guide to the Eastern Mediterranean and Egypt* for 1938 describing a recommended four-day trip from "Beirut to Jerusalem via Damascus." Alcalay comments that "the subsequent events — the actual partition of Palestine, the establishment of the State of Israel in 1948, and the mass population movements of 'exile' and 'return' — made following the itinerary of the *Blue Guide* difficult for many, impossible for some. Old and familiar routes with their enduring lines of communication had unnaturally and abruptly been cut off" (A. Alcalay 1993: 61). Alcalay adds, though, that "a new Levant — more discrete and fragmented but still aware of the possibilities of its space — is in the making" (61). For an illustration of the way the "old and familiar routes" once worked, see my conversation with Elissa's friend Riah in the journal entry for the evening of July 18.

## • 6/16 •

At the suggestion of Gila Nadav, of the A.I.C.,[35] I buy *Hadashot* to practice my Hebrew instead of *Yediot*,[36] because, she says, there's more politics in it. Two stabbing incidents are featured — one, by a fifteen–year-old Arab girl, against a thirty-two-year-old Italian tourist at the Damascus Gate. (This had been reported at the Yedidya Synagogue yesterday as the stabbing of two female tourists — but maybe I heard that rumor wrong.) The other is the stabbing of three Thai workers at a moshav[37] near Jericho. The sad irony of Thai immigrant workers being stabbed by Palestinians while working for Jews in the Occupied Territories is too obvious to require more detail.

On the #9 bus toward Scopus now — my first time "north"? of Yaffo Street, through Geula and along French Hill. Yesterday with Ruth, looking out across Nadian to Scopus and the Mount of Olives, I realized for the first time how this bus route curves around, not just avoiding the deep valley but Arab neighborhoods as well. Actually it does go down, past poorer *shikunim*[38] in the neighborhood called — I don't know, even after looking at the map.[39] The new Hyatt is finished up here now, between French Hill and Scopus — it's ugly, and what's it doing here?[40]

These last notes taken going to and from a meeting on Scopus[41] with Greta Grünfeld, a German sociologist/historian who specializes in the history of the

---

35. The Alternative Information Center, an anti-Zionist press and documentation service.
36. *Hadashot* (The news) and *Yediot Aharonot* (The latest news) are two of Israel's daily newspapers, the former of which is both newer and considered more to the left on the political spectrum.
37. An agricultural settlement consisting of private holdings with some cooperative aspects.
38. Public housing, generally substandard.
39. Shmuel Hanavi.
40. A representative of the public relations department at the Hyatt chain headquarters whom I contacted in December 1993 contented herself with telling me, "We have no information on that. It's not something we would keep in our files." I did not press. However, the staff of the Alternative Information Center in Jerusalem tracked down an item published in the Jerusalem weekly *Kol Ha'Ir* under the title, "A Brief History of the Hyatt." The first paragraph explains: "The chronicles of the hotel, the first to depart from the principle of building in stone in Jerusalem, begin shortly after the Six Day War when Pinchas Sapir, then the minister of the treasury, invited a group of wealthy Jews to Jerusalem for what he called a 'council of millionaires.' In the days after the conquest the government sought to establish solid building projects in the eastern part of the city, and Sapir, in conjunction with Minister of Tourism Moshe Kol, dealt with the head of the international Hyatt chain. No room for doubt was left concerning the preferred location. The Hyatt people understood that if they agreed to place the hotel on French Hill, across the Green Line, their company would enjoy the full cooperation of the government."
41. The Hebrew University faculties in the humanities and social sciences are located on Mount Scopus in East Jerusalem. This was the original site of the Hebrew University, inaccessible to Israelis from 1948 until 1967.

Palestinian national movement, and who is married to a Palestinian musician named Massoud Kamel, whom she met in Germany. I met Greta at the New School a couple of years ago, when she was passing through New York and wanted to meet Chuck Tilly and speak at the center. She is a good friend of Rachel and Alex's,[42] and knows the activists I know here.

Greta had passed on my "Palestine and Jewish History" article to Ahmed Abu Saleh, a physician who isn't interested in being a doctor. He now organizes the medical work of In'ash el-Usra,[43] but the project he's starting to work on is the establishment of a Palestinian center for Israel and Jewish studies.[44] Greta is trying to get him funding from the German Protestant Friedrich Ebert Stiftung,[45] but so far the connections have been difficult. His idea is mainly to get materials by Israelis and other Jewish scholars translated and published in the Arabic press, and then maybe to set up a journal. He has already translated my "Palestine and Jewish History" piece, which is profoundly gratifying to me, and Greta says he wants to translate "Hegel's Zionism?" as well. Greta will try to arrange to introduce me to him this week before she, Massoud, and her son go to Germany for eight weeks.

Their son (Mahmoud) says he wants to go to Germany — it's his idea of a really free, civilized place. As Greta points out, he doesn't know German history yet. Mahmoud told her recently that he wanted to go to a place where there weren't any Palestinians, so she took him to the Tayelet near Talpiot[46] — only she doesn't call it that; I'm pretty sure Greta doesn't even read Hebrew. The problem was that security guards followed them around wherever they went, so it wasn't much of a break.[47]

Greta confirms "from the other side" that things in general are worse than they've ever been. She takes me to the faculty lounge, and out the terrace there's an incredible view of the Old City and East Jerusalem. To the left, past Scopus (nearer the Mount of Olives, I think) is the "village" where she

---

42. Rachel Peleg is one of the foremost human rights lawyers in Israel. Alex Kracauer is the director of the Alternative Information Center.
43. "Aid for the Family," one of the best-known and oldest Palestinian social welfare agencies.
44. As of 1994, the project continues, and Dr. Abu Saleh is currently studying toward a Ph.D. in Jewish history at the Hebrew University.
45. A major philanthropic foundation.
46. An elaborate promenade and landscaped garden, on lands just over the Green Line (the armistice line that separated Israel from Jordan from 1948 until 1967) in East Jerusalem, boasting a dramatic view of the Old City. Talpiot is the neighborhood of West Jerusalem just east of Baka, where I lived for part of this period.
47. This claim is hard for me to judge. On various visits to the Tayelet, I certainly saw individual Arabs and family groups, who did not seem to be attracting any official attention — which should not gainsay the potency of Greta's sense that she and her son were being watched, and the consequent feeling of being inescapably trapped, both among Palestinians and among Israeli Jews.

lives, Suwan. She tells me there's a house above Suwan which was sold by a Palestinian in America to an American Jew in 1987. Then it was sold to Mafdal,[48] who were thinking of using it as their headquarters, and then changed their minds. Now it belongs to a group of settlers, who had a great big noisy party when they moved in with Shamir and other big shots present. On Yom Yerushalayim,[49] they had a big party, with several buses pulling up. It started at 10:00 P.M., and they had loudspeakers playing music. At midnight she called the police and pointed out that it was illegal to play music that loud. He said, "But it's Yom Yerushalayim." She pointed out that all the other parties had quieted down. He said the police were already there. She asked him to have the police there do something about the noise. Shortly after the loudspeakers were turned up, and the party continued until 1:30. The buses left empty, and the revelers marched through the streets of Suwan and Wadi Joz, back to the Old City. Now every Friday there's a little parade of about a dozen Jews, wearing dark pants or skirts and white shirts, some carrying guns.[50]

I'm going back to Friday night now — last night, *motsaei shabat*,[51] I was too tired to write. Friday night I was invited to dinner with Sandy and Beth Brisker. They've moved from an area called North Talpiot — partly because it became uncomfortable as a result of the intifada — to old Katamon,[52] having bought a place they can't quite afford. Sandy, a jazz guitarist, is now teaching at the Reuben Academy of Music at Hebrew University, and at Tel Aviv, and privately. Beth teaches theater. Beth prepared a lovely vegetarian meal — I can't really convey the warmth I feel at their home. As it grew dark the new moon was visible through the window, and after dinner we sat on the balcony talking until 11:30.

Middle-aged, middle-class, Ashkenazi-looking guys patrolling the garden above Yemin Moshe with rifles; a Yemenite (or Kurdi?) guy wearing "traditional" clothes and a submachine gun slung over his shoulder; sixteen-year-old kids in the Civil Guard wearing rifles (unloaded); a tall soldier with a pistol in his belt, playing with his two small children.[53]

---

48. The National Religious Party.
49. The annual commemoration of the "reunification" of Jerusalem under Israeli control in 1967.
50. Especially since Greta notes that this "little parade" takes place on Friday, the small crowd she describes is presumably going to the Western Wall for Sabbath evening services.
51. Saturday evening after the Sabbath ends.
52. North Talpiot is a small Jewish neighborhood of relatively recently built apartment buildings just west of the highway called Derekh Hebron. It is thus technically across the Green Line in East Jerusalem and actually quite close to Arab parts of the city and to a forest/park that is frequented by both Arabs and Jews. On "old Katamon" and the significance of its name, see below, n. 59.
53. This is Jonathan attempting the "collage" technique of writing. Except for the first

• 6/17/91 •

Before my first appointment this morning, I went over to the Jerusalem Municipal Cultural Department office, off Strauss near Mea Shearim.[54] I had decided to sign up for a trip their Torah Branch[55] is sponsoring, to *ikvot* (the dictionary doesn't tell me what this means in this context)[56] in the south on Monday. I'm not sure exactly what I'm getting myself into — a visit to the power plant at Ashkelon seems to be part of it — but it definitely includes some antiquities and lunch. The man whom I paid for my registration didn't know what an anthropologist was, but he seemed pleased that I was going, and in a burst of promotion, told me I should bring some friends along. "Maybe," I said; I don't suppose he can imagine why anybody would want to do this alone.

Walking then through Katamon to my appointment with Enoch Isaacson,[57] I remembered that it's called "Gonen" on the map. Furthermore, the *katamonim* — the neighborhoods of *shikunim* extending farther out[58] — are also called Gonen Bet, and so on, on the map. Except that everyone still calls Katamon Katamon — there's even a housing complex opening up called

---

item, note that without specific locations or situations, the images come across as ubiquitous Jerusalem scenes. My shock at seeing Jewish civilians carrying guns in Jerusalem might be compared to an English tourist's possible reaction to seeing every policeman in New York with a pistol in his belt.

54. That is, in one of the oldest neighborhoods of West Jerusalem, whose residents are considered "ultra-Orthodox" and officially if sometimes ambivalently anti-Zionist.

55. More precisely, the Branch for Torah Culture. My impression, based on the attendance at a subsequent trip (not the one referred to in this paragraph) and on the appearances of the staff at the Branch office, is that it is generally oriented toward, if not controlled by, the National Religious Party, rather than the non-Zionist or anti-Zionist Orthodox communities who might have been expected given the office's location.

The very phrase "Torah culture" (*tarbut torani*) is striking here since the modern Hebrew term *tarbut* has its social origins in the Haskalah, the Jewish Enlightenment, where it conveyed something very much like the German Enlightenment term *Bildung*. As such, it connotes a "cultivation" of the individual away from and above the traditional practices and beliefs broadly signaled by the word "Torah." The neologism *tarbut torani* thus indicates quite precisely the complex relation to modernity of a population that is willing to be associated with, to benefit from, and even to form part of a government dominated by the secular parties.

56. This word puzzled me for quite a while. Here it apparently must have meant something like "the footsteps of...," as in "the footsteps of the ancestors," although I am still almost certain that the poster read simply *"Be'ikvot badarom,"* "To *ikvot* in the south."

57. An Israeli anthropologist and psychotherapist.

58. "Gonen" is derived from the Hebrew root meaning "defense," suggestive of the location of these new slum neighborhoods right by the 1948–67 border between Israel and Jordan. That location actually contributed to their relative undesirability, but naming the area "Gonen" may have been intended either to commemorate the defense of Jerusalem in the 1948 war, to enhance the patriotic value of this area as a residential "line of defense" (thus ironically reflecting back on the associations between "security" and "defense" in Israeli public discourse), or both.

Ganei Katamon.[59] This seems to be a case of a failed name change away from the old Arab name to a freshly invented Israeli Hebrew one.

[During my meeting with Enoch Isaacson, he relates that] a Palestinian said to Enoch recently, "The settlers must not like their children — they put them behind barbed wire."

Then on to Scopus for my meeting with Tsvi Ben-Zev.[60] Yesterday I had mentioned my interest in the traffic-safety campaign, and he told me that his wife was the administrative assistant of the person in charge of it, a nice man from Gush Emunim. Tsvi offered me his phone number, but I was in too much of a hurry to take it, and today I failed to. I should follow this up.[61]

Tsvi is a bit concerned when I say that I'm going to East Jerusalem, and, careful not to offend me, he wants to make sure I'll take off my yarmulke first.[62] He and the department secretary Ronit both say that Israelis don't go to East Jerusalem anymore. Tsvi suggests that I try to look as much like a tourist as I can — wear shorts, carry a camera (I don't have one), that sort of thing. [I'm willing to take off my yarmulke, but wearing shorts really seems too tacky — I suppose what I'm trying to look like is an American who has business in East Jerusalem, which might be too subtle for my own good. But why should Palestinians in East Jerusalem like naive tourists any more than Jews at this point?][63]

---

59. The name means "Katamon Gardens." In this case the use of the older name for the neighborhood clearly adds to its appeal and may even subtly suggest the appeal of the elegant pre-1948 "Arab houses" that are so prized in this part of Jerusalem (see "In Search of 'Israeli Identity,'" below).

60. An anthropologist at Hebrew University.

61. I was already beginning to analyze the traffic-safety campaign as part of an effort to secularize traditional Jewish religious motifs into a secular Israeli culture that would still be marked as "Jewish." The information that the campaign was in fact organized by a religious nationalist seemed to confirm the hypothesis — so neatly, perhaps, that I never did get around to interviewing the man from Gush Emunim.

62. Thus, on a preliminary field trip while I was beginning to plan dissertation research in Paris, I noted several responses to my wearing of the yarmulke there and commented that "it works effectively, almost dangerously, as a two-way sensor, inducing Jews to present themselves to me and forcing me to try to understand how I am reflected in their eyes" (J. Boyarin 1988: 62). On one occasion, when visiting Ramallah, my brother tried putting on his yarmulke *inside* a Palestinian house, with distressing results (J. Boyarin and D. Boyarin 1994).

63. Generally, tourists may have been associated with the Israeli occupation, since the only usable airport is inside Israel, and the Israelis had formal control over all persons moving into and out of the Occupied Territories, including East Jerusalem. Yet I think my bracketed comment here actually reflects too much conflation on my part between settlers, as literal colonizers, and tourists, as metaphorical ones. It seems quite likely in retrospect that even at this low point in Palestinian self-confidence, Palestinians in East Jerusalem would have been more friendly to tourists, who may be goodwill ambassadors for them and in any case are likely to bring them business, than to Jews, whom they perceive as potential if not actual usurpers of their land.

I walked over to the American Colony[64] the same way as last time — along Shivtei Yisrael and St. George, more confidently than last time. Ahmed was waiting when I got there. By his looks — average height, an unremarkable face, glasses — he could as well be Israeli as Palestinian. He's translated about a dozen scholarly articles on Israel into Arabic — the first being Mordechai Bar-On's article about the effect of the intifada on Israel — and had them published in magazines here and abroad. My "Palestine and Jewish History" was also published in this fashion. He wants to know what I think he should be translating, and also what Israeli scholars he might talk to. I promise to reflect on it.

We had a long and (for me) dissatisfying discussion about my plans to spend time in the territories. Ahmed spoke of spending two hours in Jalazoun with two American Jews, who had called him five times to make sure their plans to meet him in Ramallah were safe. I tried out my formula on Greta and Ahmed: I'm not an adventurer, but I don't want to just stay away — because the more people stay away, the more they grow apart, and the more dangerous it becomes to go. . . . They didn't dispute this, in any case. Ahmed also offered to introduce me to Um Sabri, the head of In'ash el-Usra. I said I'd heard she "doesn't like Jews," which he rephrased as she "doesn't like Israelis." He also said she sometimes gets very emotional. Today a woman had come in complaining about the fact that some Italians who were supporting her family had suddenly stopped doing so, and demanding their address. Um Sabri wept and shouted: "I've been in prison five times. I haven't seen my son for seventeen years, and you want me to break our rules?" (Ahmed explained that families aren't allowed to contact their benefactors directly, since that would seem like begging.) Ahmed offered to introduce me to Um Sabri, as long as I don't mention his research project, of which she apparently disapproves.

I said to Greta that I realized East Jerusalem was now mostly surrounded by Jewish development on the heights. She said yes, she has begun to feel physically hemmed in. She also complained that the new Israeli roads — "settler's roads," for example, from Ramallah to the airport — don't respect the landscape, but are bulldozed right through the hills. She cited a recent article by Johann Galtung in the *Canadian Journal of ? and Development,* about the culture of imperialism — the idea that Puritans in America and Boers in South Africa have of themselves as chosen people. She speculates that the Israelis share this same "Judeo-Christian" culture (shades of Edward Said); and that this helps explain that "special relationship."[65] I didn't tell her I thought it was more complicated — but someday I'll show her my Exodus paper.

---

64. One of the major hotels in East Jerusalem.
65. That is, between the United States and Israel.

# 2

# Reading Exodus into History

In an earlier essay in my book *Storm from Paradise* (J. Boyarin 1992: 116–29) on the shifting significance of Palestine as the ground of Jewish historical identity, I broached several critical questions, one of which was phrased as follows: "What are the grander links among the ancient Jewish state, the Western cultural complex of 'Zion' through the Bible, traditional Jewish culture in the modern period, Zionism, and what I will call here a post-modern ideal of diaspora?" Here I will be considering the link between only two of those elements: the use of the Exodus–Promised Land narrative in writings from various points of Christian European, and particularly English, history; and the ways that same narrative has been drawn on for the legitimation of Zionism. Perhaps most of all, I hope to show that real insight into the narrative construction of history cannot do without close attention to the precise language of ancient source texts, to the translation of such texts as a practice that helps define collective identity, and to the multiplicity of readings they have afforded in widely differing historical circumstances.[1]

The politics of Exodus constitute an exemplary case of the link between history and interpretive reading. The case is first of all "exemplary" in the loose sense that there are so many cases, over such a wide area and long period, in which that narrative has been used to make events cohere into meaningful constellations. It is also more precisely exemplary because the narrative cannot be understood solely as pertaining to the time in which it purports to be set,[2] nor yet solely in the series of new presents in which it is

---

[1]. Talal Asad, Hannah Davis, Uri Ram, Elissa Sampson, and Shalom Goldman all read and commented on the first draft of this chapter. It was first presented to a seminar at the Shelby Collum Davis Center for Historical Studies at Princeton University. My thanks to the director, Natalie Zemon Davis, and to the participants in that discussion. Further thanks to the participants in the Proseminar on Knowledge, Power and Culture at the Center for Studies of Social Change, New School for Social Research.

[2]. One reason why I will not even pretend to deal here with what "really happened" during the Biblical period, except to quote a recent assertion in the *New York Times* of "a growing consensus among Egyptologists, Biblical scholars and archaeologists that most of the

taken up as a model. Rather it "is suspended between its own age and a later one" (Lloyd 1989: 36). Far from exhausting itself, it reacquires its force (and it will be central to my argument that its force is multivalent) in its repeated invocations. I intend, therefore, to trace out a trajectory of readings linking source texts, the ways they have been used and interpreted in the meantime, and the ways they are or can be used and interpreted now. This differs from the established notion of a "hermeneutic circle" linking only a given reader and a given text as sources and interpreters of each other, because it acknowledges the shaping force of a history of readings on the latest in their sequence. At no present moment are the potential readings of a text fully determined by its previous readings; but the range of plausible readings, of new directions of meaning, is constrained by the work the text has been used for in the past. This is what I mean by a trajectory.

The ancient tale of Israelites, Egyptians, and Canaanites resonates with a long series of historical narratives of conquest and of liberation. As I will attempt to show in the next section, the multiplicity of readings the text affords surpasses any attempt to contain that tale within the modern world-system model of imperial, adventurist conquest versus autochthonous liberation. By the end of the essay, in fact, I hope to convince the reader that Exodus is not as anomalous against that model as we might think at first. Instead I will suggest that European culture contains a discontinuous "tradition" of narratives of oppression, flight, and subsequent conquest. Some of these will include all three terms — liberation, migration, and the establishment of a new (and "pure") homeland. Others will focus on migration and conquest.[3] In these latter cases, lacking the prior history of covenant and oppression, it would be worthwhile to contrast whatever moral justification might appear for that di-

---

early Israelites were Canaanites" (Wilford 1990). According to Sari Nusseibeh, on the other hand, "Present-day Palestinian Arabs regard Canaanites, Hittites, Jebusites, etc. [along with more recent waves of migrants], as their ancestors" (1990). One conclusion that might be drawn, to paraphrase Michael Walzer, is that whoever you are, you're probably a Canaanite. Regarding the relation between the history of Exodus and the current Palestinian-Israeli conflict, Nusseibeh justly writes that "while one can certainly respect the Jewish people for its astute self-consciousness and continuity, such respect cannot in fairness be used as grounds for disinheriting the wave after wave of political manifestations of the non-Jewish Arab communities of Palestine, whether through denying them their rightful historical role, or their rightful contemporary claims" (ibid.).

3. The folklorist Yael Zerubavel, whose work analyzes the careers of Israeli national myths (Masada, Bar Kokhba, Tel Hai), emphasizes the importance of understanding how the older legend is "spliced" for understanding the politics of its subsequent applications (1994). This will be a critical point in my discussion below of the contemporary Exodus debate. Zerubavel gains much of her insight from spending time in Israeli history classrooms. It is worth emphasizing that scholars interested in the relation between literature and collective ideology need to pay close attention to the mechanisms by which narratives and their determined readings circulate and gain social authority.

vine one-sidedness with the sequence of divine promise-servitude-covenant in the Bible.[4]

In order fully to see the hermeneutic trajectory of Old Testament reading, we would, of course, need a much more sophisticated comparative ethnography of biblical literacy and interpretation. Good work on the typological uses of the Bible in early British America has been done (see references in Reventlow 1985: 141 n. 437). Two very recent studies — one concerning the rabbinic midrash literature, the other dealing with the Anglo-Saxons — will ground two of the sections of this chapter. However, as far as I know we still lack, for example, a comparative study of the workings of the Exodus model in British America and South Africa or of the biblical sources employed in the rationalizations of Catholic and Protestant imperialisms.[5]

Such a lack lends itself to wild claims, on one hand, and apologetics, on the other. Perhaps because the uses of the Old Testament narrative are so prevalent in European cultural history and so often enlisted in the justification of colonizing missions, Exodus and the biblical narrative in general have sometimes been used to identify the Jewish origins of Western "dominationism." Thus in his book *Beyond Geography: The Western Spirit against the Wilderness,* Frederick W. Turner locates the origins of intolerance in Israelite monotheism:

> It was the Israelites who established monotheism in the spiritual geography of humankind. And with it came the terrible concomitants of intolerance and commandments to destroy the sacred items of others (Exodus 23:23-24; 34:13-16) and to "utterly destroy" polytheistic peoples wherever encountered.... The conception of genocide is foreign to polytheistic cultures. But the distinctions

---

4. Not that God's promise and a history of suffering justified Joshua's expulsion of the prior inhabitants of Canaan to the satisfaction of quite all the voices canonized in the Old Testament; W. D. Davies (1982: 15-16) has listed the traces of biblical "bad conscience" concerning the former-day Palestine question. Robert Cohn (1990) has detailed various qualifications of God's promise of the Land to the people of Israel: in Genesis, the reminder that "the Canaanites were then in the land" (12:6); in Leviticus 18 and 22, explanations that the Canaanites were expelled because of sexual perversions and warnings that Israel will suffer a similar fate if it does not obey God's law; in Deuteronomy, the reminder that not only for Israel has God driven out prior inhabitants to make room for newcomers (2:10-12, 20-23). Cohn sees "a steady transformation in the narrative of the Torah from God's unqualified promise of a homeland to God's conditional offer of a holy land" (1990: 14). He ties this to the situation in Babylonian exile of the Torah's final redactors, "painfully aware that, like the Canaanites before them, they too had been dispossessed" and anticipating "their own return to a homeland where one could never be quite at home" (14).

5. Robert Thornton assures me that the Exodus narrative has been very richly employed in South African history, both by colonialists and Africans. Currently it is used by African liberationist churches; Chief Buthelezi employs the book of Joshua to frame his claim to re-create Chaka Zulu's state. The theme of crossing rivers is also important in South African historical geography. Thornton concludes that the Bible is in fact the South African master narrative: "The question is who gets to be the Israelites" (personal communication, Shelby Collum Davis Center, October 1990).

raised in the covenant between religion and idolatry are like some visitation of the *khamsin* to wilderness peoples as yet unsuspected, dark clouds over Africa, the Americas, the Far East, until finally even the remotest islands and jungle enclaves are struck by fire and sword and by the subtler weapon of conversion-by-ridicule (Deuteronomy 2:34; 7:2; 20:16–18, Joshua 6:17–21). (F. W. Turner 1980: 45)

Now this statement is astonishing, if hardly unprecedented. In its sweepingly simplistic equation of polytheism and pluralism, on one hand, and monotheism and chauvinism, on the other, it suggests that the Jews (like some irresistible oriental force of nature, an evil wind) are ultimately responsible for all the evils of colonialism. Even more (though Turner does not write this, and perhaps if it had crossed his mind he would have been more cautious), it implies that the Jews, as inventors of genocide, are ultimately responsible for getting themselves killed by the Nazis! The monotheist-polytheist dichotomy is matched, in Turner's account, by a dichotomy between primitive mythological, cyclical conceptions and closeness to nature, on one hand, and Israelite historical linearism and hostility to nature, on the other (43).[6] A recent Jewish celebrant of the Exodus narrative discussed in the next section unwittingly walks into Turner's trap, insisting on the "linear" as opposed to "cyclical" character of Exodus and on Exodus as a universal Western model.

A key term in the quote from Turner is the claim that the Israelites are commanded to annihilate polytheistic peoples "wherever encountered." In fact, ruthless as the divine warrants are, they are aimed precisely at those peoples that might impede the Israelites' progress toward the land or whose continued presence *there* (not "wherever") might lead them astray and is in any case not legitimized by divine covenant. Turner's need to find an ancient original of the "warrant for genocide" leads him to overlook this critical difference between a strictly local, highly particular account of intolerance and the modern West European "universalist" propensity to dominate weaker peoples everywhere encountered, in the name of Christ or progress. If I may be allowed a brief totalization of my own, the Jewish biblical text in sum constitutes a redemption narrative of partially global pretensions but with precise ethnic and territorially based referents. "Mature" Christianity — that is, Christianity once it has become an imperial religion and is clearly no longer a

---

6. This distinction has a substantial prehistory, which it would be helpful to have documented. The classical discussion of "cyclical" conceptions of time is, of course, Eliade 1959. A rather more dialectical account, emphasizing the role of astronomy in the shaping of early civilizations' conceptions of time, is contained in de Santillana and von Dechend 1977. Specifically regarding the ancient Israelites, for a corrective account emphasizing homologies between the human body and the "natural" world in the Jewish Bible, see now Eilberg-Schwartz 1990.

Jewish sect — constitutes rather a deterritorialized, universalized, allegorized narrative of spiritual redemption. This difference is not an ontological one between the respective "essences" of Judaism and Christianity but a historical one grounded in the ideological paradoxes of ancient nationhood and ancient imperialism. Thus our focus turns for a moment toward the earliest Jewish-Christian period and toward a less deterministic articulation than Turner's of the changes in relations among land, ethnicity, and tolerance from the Old Testament to the modern period. I will content myself here with citing W. D. Davies's telling point that "one of the startling aspects of early Christianity is that, at a very early date, Gentiles, for whom the question of the land could not possess the interest that it had for Jewish Christians, soon became the majority" (1974: 371). Because gentile converts to Christianity did not share the deep attachment to the Land of Israel that Jewish Christians had been born with, Christianity largely dropped those elements of Judaism that were inconsistent with its increasingly catholic character. Davies suggests, in effect, that aspects of the early social history of Christianity caught it ideologically off its guard. For the first few centuries, when Christianity was spreading among an ethnically varied multitude throughout the late Roman Empire, the links between covenantal destiny and promised lands were hardly relevant.

I will discuss some examples of how, starting a few centuries later and at various points thereafter, the model of a covenantal relation between a given people and a given land was integrated into Christian self-understandings. When this happened, it did not represent the workings of an autonomous logic contained in a text (as Turner would have it) but the employment and reshaping of an authoritative textual model.

Without denying that ancient Judaism is a major source of Christian European self-understandings, we would do well not to make a beeline to the Pentateuch for the premodern origins of Western European colonial discourse. Thus Robert A. Williams grounds his synoptic account of European conquistador legalism in the universalist discourse of the medieval church. First of all, Williams claims that law, and not, as one might suppose, Old Testament legends of conquest, was "the West's most vital and effective instrument of empire" (1990: 6). For Williams, the crucial innovation in Christian legal thought that paved the way for the rationalization of Renaissance-era conquests occurred during the Crusades, in a mid–thirteenth-century commentary written by Pope Innocent IV. True, the fact that the Crusades, as a model for European colonization, focused on the land once promised and now holy reminds us that the culture of colonialism has biblical grounds as well. Yet, according to Williams, Innocent IV's argument rested on nonbiblical sources, consisting of an adroit synthesis of the doctrine of natural law and the doctrine of papal responsibility for the "spiritual well-being of all the souls of Christ's human flock, including infidels and heathens" (14). From these Innocent IV derived the principle that infidel and heathen peoples behaving in gross violation of natural law were subject to Christian intervention in their affairs.

Natural law and papal infallibility are not "Jewish" doctrines. Whatever ideas about humanity in general may be sprinkled throughout ancient, rabbinic, and modern Jewish thought, they are not cast in terms of natural law; and whatever notions about a special place for the Jews in the divine plan for humanity there may be, no one has imagined the Jews in a universal pastoral role.[7] The basic ways of dealing with the natives in both the biblical conquest narrative and, *mutatis mutandis*, Zionist ideology[8] — either avoiding contact with the natives or getting rid of them — are a far cry from such early European colonial techniques as the Spanish *encomienda* (the wholesale consignment of groups of Indian slaves to loyal Spaniards) or the *requerimiento* (a "charter of conquest" that "informed the Indians in the simplest terms that they could either accept Christian missionaries and Spanish imperial hegemony or be annihilated") (Williams 1990: 91).

Given the different views of the broader sources of colonialism in general indicated by this cursory look at Turner and Williams, it is hardly surprising that there is a confusion about the "discourses of conquest" concerning Palestine and Israel. The links among knowledge, culture, and power pertinent to this region, compared to places such as the Indian subcontinent or Latin America, seem relatively underdeveloped in contemporary cultural studies. Thus in his introduction to a recent collection entitled *Nation and Narration* (1990), Homi Bhabha appropriately apologizes for the failure to include considerations of Palestinian national culture. Yet he seems unaware of the ways in which modern Hebrew and Yiddish fiction were critical to the formulation of Jewish nationalism, including Zionism (cf. Eisenzweig 1981); and as vital

---

7. Intriguingly, Williams derives "the basic idea of the Church as a universal body" (1990: 15) in part from the Pauline notion of the mystical body of Christ, "'whether we are Jews or Greeks, whether we are slaves or freemen'" (15) (see also D. Boyarin 1994). In other words, the sources of this universalist, organicist, hierarchical metaphor are to be found, as Davies noted in the above-cited passage, in the doctrinal pressures caused by the quick spread of "Christianity" among non-Jews.

8. I must stress that I am talking about Zionist *ideology* here, and I should specify that I am thinking primarily of Labor Zionism. "Zionist" capitalist-colonial planters gladly hired inexpensive Palestinian laborers, and the integration of the Occupied Territories into the Israeli economy has added a major source of disadvantaged "underclass" labor to the preexisting pools of Israeli Arabs and Oriental Jews. Nevertheless, the hiring of Palestinians in the early settlements was combatted by Labor Zionists on both pragmatic and ideological grounds (Shafir 1989), and the presence of the new Palestinian underclass since 1967 significantly contributed to the undermining of Labor Zionist hegemony in the Israeli state.

as the image of the Jewish Other was to the culture of nineteenth-century European nationalism, there is only one passing reference to anti-Semitism in the entire collection (Thom 1990: 40).[9]

I attribute this underdevelopment (of which Bhabha's collection is only a recent and convenient example) at least in part to a failure to articulate the critique of anti-Semitism with the critique of imperialism. Even the most careful and thoughtful criticism tends to slide in one of two directions. Either overwhelming horror at centuries of anti-Semitism and the culminating genocide leads to the celebration of Israel as a redemptive movement of national liberation; or anger at the denial of independence to Palestinians results in a slighting of the crucial struggle for Jewish freedom in modern Europe. To put it another way, since (with the rare and recent exception of a study like Williams's) the critique of dominant Christianity lags behind the critique of empire, those most concerned with Jewish well-being are hard put to integrate the Palestinians into their account, and the reverse holds as well.[10] Furthermore, versions professing equal concern for both seem unable to go beyond the simplistic mold of a tragic, mirrored conflict between two national rights. The Israeli-Palestinian conflict is *not* a Greek tragedy, nor is it fated. An inquiry equally concerned at understanding European anti-Semitism and European imperialism would, I submit, lead to a perception that the construction of Israelis and Palestinians as being on two opposite "sides" is not at all inevitable. A more nuanced understanding of the workings of Exodus in history might contribute toward that perception. On the other hand, to continue debating whether the biblical text feeds directly into either secular liberation or religious chauvinism is to reinforce many of the assumptions underlying the reification of the Jewish and Arab, Israeli and Palestinian collectives. And thus on to the more immediate occasion of this chapter.

---

9. Edward Said is perhaps the exception that proves the rule here. A great deal of his critical energy stems from his position as a Palestinian exile and attempts to illuminate the wider sources of that situation. Yet with a few exceptions (for example, Shohat 1988), those who draw on his model analysis of Orientalism do not discuss the case of Palestine/Israel.

10. Gershon Shafir, citing his colleague Baruch Kimmerling, puts it this way: "Whereas Israelis tend to focus on the non-colonialist reasons and motivations for their immigration to Palestine, Arabs directed their attention to its results.... At the outset, Zionism was a variety of Eastern European nationalism, that is, an ethnic movement in search of a state. But at the other end of the journey it may be seen more fruitfully as a late instance of European overseas expansion, which had been taking place from the sixteenth through the twentieth centuries" (1989: xiv, 8). I'm not sure I would fully endorse this formula; it still smacks of apologetics, especially since Shafir himself cites explicitly colonialist proposals for Jewish development in Palestine (10–11). But it does represent an attempt at just nuance that is rare in writing on Palestine/Israel.

## The Said-Walzer Debate

Michael Walzer's *Exodus and Revolution* is both a cultural intervention into this modern history of Palestine and a valuable attempt to trace the career of a central narrative in Jewish and Christian history. Walzer's primary concern in that book is not with bondage, nor with conquest, but with the struggle to form a responsible political community in the context of newly achieved freedom. Accordingly, he explicitly announces his intention to read Exodus not as a divine act of liberation but as a secular and basically rational political effort that will echo through Western history. Among the historical examples available as reinvocations of Exodus, Walzer focuses on Latin American liberation theology and the English Puritans. Perhaps the main virtue of his account is the simple fact of broaching the topic of the collective, political uses of Exodus, thus transcending the purely individualist, spiritual, and typological analysis of the use of Exodus in early modern Europe (cf. Galdon 1975). Evidently Walzer's account, which sees a radical thrust in the biblical text itself, represents some revision in his own thinking, for earlier he had described Puritanism as "the earliest form of political radicalism" (1965: vii).

Edward Said responded to Walzer's book with his own "Canaanite reading" (1986).[11] These texts embody, in a particularly dramatic and bitter way, the political stakes of the conflict of interpretations. Both have more to teach us than their tone suggests. Throughout this chapter I will be using the issues raised by the Walzer-Said debate to identify critical questions about the use of the Exodus narrative in the past. At the same time, I will use these historical examples to point out the shared limitations of Walzer's and Said's ideologically secularist hermeneutics.[12]

The title of Said's review makes an extremely telling point against the way Walzer "edits" Exodus, as I will discuss shortly; the review also contains what strike me as at least three particularly blind spots of its own, with which I want to deal first.

First, on reviewing the biblical text, it seems to me that Said is correct to note that, unlike Africans brought to America as slaves, Jacob's family is described as having gone to Egypt voluntarily. Yet the narrative seems equally clear in its description of them as having become a coerced labor force there.

---

11. Said's reply was reprinted in Said and Hitchins 1988. I cite the original publication.

12. Two caveats are called for here. First, nowhere do I mean to suggest that the meanings of Exodus, whether ancient or contemporary, are only those discussed in this essay. Second, Gayatri Spivak points out that in the Walzer-Said debate, and despite Said's protests, Exodus remains the hegemonic narrative of oppression and liberation, the narrative that must first be responded to. She suggests, in effect, that remaining within this framework and debating it back and forth, as Walzer, Said, and I do, perpetuates and reinforces the colonial crowding out of nonmonotheistic or even nonnarrative discourses about politics and the cosmos (personal communication, Shelby Collum Davis Center, October 1990).

Thus it seems strange for Said to argue that "when Egypt fell on hard times, so too did the Jews, and because they were foreign they were the targets of local rage and frustration" (1986: 91). This assertion by Said goes against Pharaoh's reported statement that his fear is precisely that the Children of Israel will leave, that he will lose his work force. Most readers, I submit, whether secular or religious, Jewish or not, would agree that the narrative describes them as being more exploited than scapegoated. Yet Said's explanation sounds more like Simmel than like Marx; he makes the Old Testament out to be a proto-Zionist text, explaining oppression through the brute fact of cultural minority difference. It seems that, by his irresistible choice of a title, Said himself has fallen too readily into the typological association of Israelites and Zionists and has offered readings as willful and tendentious as those he accuses Walzer of providing. Said is driven to assert flatly that the Israelite story is "hardly comparable with that of American Blacks" (91), but African-American history is replete with examples of how richly the slaves drew on precisely that comparison: "Where whites sang 'Lord, I believe a rest remains / To all thy people known,' blacks used the same tune to sing of Moses leading his people out of Egypt" (Levine 1977: 23). Had he acknowledged this, Said might be less puzzled at the sympathy for Zionism of someone like Martin Luther King, whom Said identifies as an anti-imperialist (1986: 98). Equally important, his denial of this connection makes it harder to understand the reciprocal reinforcements between liberal American Jewish sympathy for Zionism and for black civil rights. These are both expressions of an implicit "Exodus" liberalism, drawing both on the biblical command not to oppress the "stranger" and on the empathic memories of having been liberated en masse from "bondage" in Russia to "freedom" in America,[13] which has until recently been a very comfortable ideology for American Jews, both politically and morally.

Second, because Said's polemical approach entails his rhetorical acceptance of the direct link between Exodus and Zionism posited by Walzer, he is compelled to assert the continuity in Judaism of the biblical warrants for slaughter. Against Walzer's claim that the violent exclusiveness of the commands regarding prior inhabitants was never really carried out and was in any case vitiated through later Jewish commentaries "arguing over its future applications" (Walzer 1985: 143), Said retorts that these commentaries are irrelevant because "*after* the destruction of the Temple,...Jews were in no position at all collectively to implement the commandment" (1985: 93). This is a misreading of Walzer because the commentaries he refers to speculate about a time when Jews will again be both collectively able and collectively

---

13. "Immigration to the United States was compared to the Exodus from Egypt because it was a mass exodus, unlike the tiny settlements [in Palestine] of the *Hovevei Zion*" (Shavit 1990: 68).

responsible for carrying out all the biblical commandments — the time of the Messiah, though Walzer does not spell this out. For Walzer, this is evidence that Jewish doctrine has grown "progressively" less exclusive and more universalist. Said, on the other hand, sees a continuum of religious prejudice. Neither Said nor Walzer acknowledges the possibility of a complex and ambivalent interaction between the loss of political power and a greater rabbinic emphasis on the demands of human empathy, with sources both in Greek philosophy and in the biblical commands forbidding mistreatment of strangers. Neither, for their own reasons, acknowledges the profound difference between the Zionist ethos and that which was understood for centuries as Jewish — a difference readily acknowledged by both the early Zionists and their Jewish opponents, along with the theme of Jewish fulfillment through return to Zion (see Selzer 1970: 11–18; D. Boyarin and J. Boyarin 1993).

This leads to my third criticism of Said: his contention that early Zionism "was primarily religious and imperialist," that "the concepts of Chosen People, Covenant, Redemption, Promised Land and God were central to it" (1986: 98). No one can deny, of course, that traditional "religious" associations with Israelite history and the Land of Israel were crucial to whatever level of popular Jewish support Zionism had. They coexisted alongside much more mundane arguments, however, and one would be hard pressed to find them as "central" themes in the writings of Leo Pinsker, Theodor Herzl, or Max Nordau. These men were not religious and imperialist but rather secularist and imperialist. As I understand their ideas, the concepts of "Chosen People" and "Promised Land" were subservient to the desire for *any* land (to be sure, one available from a friendly imperial power) on which Jews could raise themselves to the level of a worthy European people.[14] Nor were the concepts Said lists necessary for giving "identity to a people scattered in exile" (98), who already had a powerful shared identity. Such concepts may to some extent have been "useful in getting crucial European support," but this was mainly because they were grounds for preexisting support among European "non-Jewish Zionists" (see Sharif 1983).

None of this vitiates Said's most telling charge: that Walzer's account barely mentions the Canaanites and that, consistent with Walzer's emphasis on the continued relevance of the Exodus model, ignoring the Canaanites serves to

---

14. In 1896, Herzl asked, "Shall we choose [the] Argentine [Republic] or Palestine? We will take what is given us and what is selected by Jewish public opinion" (1980: 425). The first Zionist Congress, of course, settled decisively on Palestine in 1897. But insofar as Said is talking about the "origins" of Zionism, I believe the point stands that the ideology does not arrive full-blown out of Jewish tradition. Below I will have more to say about how traditional associations with the geography of Palestine affected the "spatial history" of Jewish colonization.

reinforce the invisibility of the Palestinians. Where Said is concerned with the geographic, spatial movements of colonialism, Walzer is concerned to link Exodus to modern examples of the establishment of a just society against tyranny. Contrasting Exodus politics to messianic apocalypticism, Walzer repeatedly emphasizes the partial and this-worldly redemption that Exodus aims for, and the somewhat ambivalent hostility toward enemies in Exodus movements as against the demonization of enemies in Messianism. Consistent with his claim that Labor Zionism represents Exodus politics against a messianic right-wing fundamentalism, Walzer notes that the attention of the narrative "is focused on internal rather than external wars, on the purges of the recalcitrant Israelites rather than on the destruction of the Canaanite nations" (1985: 142). If Said denies Israelite slavery in Egypt, Walzer reads with the grain of the text: his interpretation complicitly declines to confront the Exodus model with the destruction of the nascent Palestinian nation.[15]

In this exchange, both Said and Walzer seem to need to cast the question of Palestine in typological terms, as a reenactment or fulfillment of an archetypal narrative. Otherwise why would they need to read the Old Testament narrative in ways that so closely match their respective visions of Israel, Palestine, and "Western" politics?

For Walzer, the invocations of Exodus are carried out primarily in time. There is an analogy between his approval of the Exodus model of historical-political understanding, in which "events occur only once, and they take on their significance from a system of backward- and forward-looking interconnections, not from the hierarchical correspondences of myth" (1985: 13), and his stress on all subsequent "Exodus histories" as being basically rational, this-worldly, gradualist, progressive. On the other hand, Walzer not only shows us latter-day politicians invoking the Exodus narrative as a model but feels perfectly free himself to discuss Exodus "anachronistically" (59), as if it were in fact a founding legend that still charters his politics. There is a major problem here: Walzer does not confront the critical question whether the Exodus narrative autonomously "works" in history or whether it is merely available for effective rhetoric in a wide variety of situations.[16] If it is merely available,

---

15. The debate between Walzer and Said has received critical attention from Mark Krupnick in *Tikkun* (1989). My responses to Krupnick, some of which are elaborated here, can be found in a letter to the same journal (J. Boyarin 1990). Elissa Sampson's essay (1990) on the debate focuses more directly than this chapter on critical issues of contemporary Zionist tendencies and their understanding of Palestinians.

16. In an essay on the general switch from the biblicism of the "saints" to the Romanism of the Royalists in the second half of the seventeenth century, Steven Zwicker offers some very acute insights on this dialectic: "Royalist vindication reclaimed materials that Puritans had once used to celebrate their triumphs; but Royalists also looked harshly and derisively at Puritan scripturalism.... The combination of Puritan demise and Royalist vindication

how important is it in shaping action? If in fact it "works," how can we accept Walzer's strategy of giving us only his preferred "secular" reading, since that would give us a very distorted picture of its effects in history? Outside the limited range of Walzer's polemic against right-wing "messianic" Zionists (who in any case are not likely to be swayed by his secular reading of Exodus!), why should we think that anyone's emancipatory interests are best served by that reading?

Said calls implicitly for a history of the Exodus narrative that would raise these issues in a more substantial way. But in their polemic, neither approaches the necessary synthesis of historical grounding of the text with sensitivity to its narrative power.[17] In particular, close attention to the text — concern for responsible reading of its *words* — seems to fly out the window. This is evident on the grossest level, as I just suggested, in Walzer's choice to present us with an anachronistic "secular" reading divorced from a "sacred" reading, which he disowns. On a more detailed level, it reappears in a bizarre dispute over the "original" meaning of the word "redemption" (Said 1986: 253; Walzer 1986: 248). Walzer claims the word originally means "redemption from slavery"; if he has in mind the Hebrew word *ge'ula,* he is correct. Said in turn questions the possible meaning "of a secular politics heavily dependent on the notion of redemption (whose first meaning is delivery from *sin*)" (253). But surely the meaning of the Hebrew Bible is not to be determined by checking the dictionary for its definition of a word in English!

There is an odd logic linking the shared, avowed secularism of Walzer and Said to their claims for the power of Exodus as Genesis, that is, as a myth of origin. The ancient or "religious" Jewish Other is effectively treated by both as inert, raw, original material, available for molding. Said's intention is to combat what he calls Walzer's overly assimilating, overly comfortable approach in the name of those who suffer today. Yet Walzer's insistence on the secularist reading of the ancient text is ultimately more complemented than deconstructed by Said's attitude, which is now ironic, now horrified, but always distanced.

Walzer is "inclined to prefer an argument that depends on the vividness of the present rather than the past" (1985: 87).[18] This refreshing assertion, how-

---

complicated the potential for Scripture as a social and political language, but eventually such complication also undermined its authority, its capacity to sustain praise and the burden of a national life imagined in its terms" (1988: 41).

17. For an essay that does, in my opinion, approach that synthesis, although focusing on the question of state power versus moral community in the Israelite kingdoms, see Berger 1989.

18. David Harlan cites Walzer's book approvingly as an example of historiography free from the illusions of contextualism. Harlan describes *Exodus and Revolution* as "a history of meaning rather than a history of the production and transmission of meaning" (1989: 606).

ever, is based on a dichotomy that robs Exodus of the power it has contained among such people as Jews, English Puritans, and African Americans, none of whom saw reading as a choice between the secular and the sacred or experience as a choice between living in the past and living in the present. For Walzer convincingly to sustain both his own gradualism and his overtly selective interpretation of Exodus as origin, one would expect either an account of how Exodus has been subsequently purged of its "sacred" or chauvinist side or a modification of gradualism to include the possibility of periodic recourse to "mythical" archetypes. The former would be difficult if not, as I suspect, impossible; chauvinist and liberationist readings of the text continue to appear, and as I discuss below, they are often inseparable. Walzer can have no recourse to the latter since, like Turner, he has already declared Exodus as "the crucial alternative to all mythic notions of eternal recurrence" (12). The reader who sees Exodus as the origin of domination and the reader who sees it as the origin of liberation are in agreement on its "linear" rather than "cyclical" character. The ways in which poets and politicians have *interacted* with the Old Testament narrative of the Israelites throw light on notions of primitive myth versus civilized progress that should henceforth bar such simplistic dichotomies and make us wary of commentators who flash their credentials either as secularists or as participants in the tradition.

## Creating the Anglo-Saxon Exodus

Walzer gives us no indication of the intervening tradition that enabled the "Exodus politics" of the Protestant saints. Perhaps he regards these invocations as isolated flashes of inspiration; more likely he is relying on the general notion of a Protestant rediscovery of the Old Testament, which had been buried by centuries of Catholic ritualism and restricted literacy. But the rhetoric of affinity with the Israelites has roots in Eusebius's early Christian historiography (Hanning 1966: 23ff.) and long predates the Reformation. That affinity was explored in the most sustained way by the English (Stinson n.d.).[19] Reviewing pre-Reformation English uses of Exodus should thus serve

---

Since Harlan is hardly arguing for a return to a rarefied history of ideas and strongly questions the possibility of determining past meanings, it is hard to see what this can mean but an arbitrary selection out of the repertoire of putative past meanings for the purpose of present rhetoric.

19. Although for the medieval period as well, a comparative account of Exodus readings is wanted. Beryl Smalley pointed out decades ago, for instance, that "the Frisians, comparing themselves to the chosen people, inverted the order of events in their history, so as to get a closer correspondence with the Old Testament. This group of Frisian chronicles supplies an extreme example of the tendency to pour one's material into a traditional mould. In the middle ages tradition began with the story of Creation as it is told in the book of Genesis" (1964: xi–xii). It should be said that I am focusing on England here not only because the Exodus seems to have played an extraordinary role in its self-imagining over the course of

as a useful way to check Walzer's claim that Exodus has been primarily used for "secularist" and progressive narratives of collective identity and destiny.

A book by Nicholas Howe shows, in fact, how the Old Testament narrative served as a versatile template for the articulated self-understandings of the origins of people in Britain. Howe's general thesis is that "the Anglo-Saxons...envisioned their migration from continent to island as a reenactment of the biblical exodus" (1989: 2). Howe thus anchors the identification of the English with the Chosen People, and of the Emerald Isle with the Promised Land, much further back than the sole emphasis on the Protestant intimacy with the Old Testament would suggest.

Howe's book is significant not only for what it tells us about the workings of the Exodus story in early English literature and in the process of shaping an English *folc* out of the various Angles, Saxons, and Jutes who invaded the island, but also for what it tells us about how to investigate interactions among history, ideology, and narrative.

One important lesson is contained in Howe's discussions of intertextual history. He does not confine himself to the general point that the Anglo-Saxons read and used the Old Testament but looks for further connections within the early history of writing in Britain. Thus he sees models within models, types within types: when Wulfstan wrote in 1014 "to inspire [the English] to resistance against Viking attacks" (8), he cited Gildas, a Celtic poet who had written before the Anglo-Saxon invasion. Through this reference back to a representative of the British who had been conquered during the *adventus Saxonum,* Wulfstan was able to warn the English that sinful and irresponsible behavior could cost them their promised land. Similarly, in discussing Bede's use of Virgil's myth of Roman origin (of course, Exodus was not the only model used), Howe makes the point that it is not necessary to demonstrate that Bede read the *Aeneid* because "a cultural myth of this type becomes canonical when it achieves general currency in the literary as well as the popular imagination" (62). In this particular case Howe was able to trace an indirect literary source; but the point is that, while careful detective work is indispensable, narrative models may work most powerfully where their presence is most diffuse.

Second, Howe is able to show that the crucial link enabling repeated modelings of Anglo-Saxon history on the Old Testament narrative is the parallel suggested by the crossing of water. Thus, for the author of the Old English epic called *Exodus,* "The crossing is the exodus" (Howe 1989: 102; see also

---

centuries but also because of the particular importance of the English heritage both for the history of Zionism and the history of the United States, and because England's was the preeminent modern world empire.

46, 179); episodes such as the Canaanite wars are barely mentioned.[20] But the point is not only Howe's careful attention to the splicing of the model narrative. Howe also recognizes the importance of what Paul Carter (1989) calls "spatial history"—the geographical contingencies with which historians contend when they reshape narrative models as memorials to new adventures. The Exodus story continued to be so productive in England not only because of its parallels with a series of events in English history, and not only because of institutional reinforcements of textual authority, but largely because, drawing partly on Exodus, the Anglo-Saxon migration myth "translated chronology into a spatial pattern" (Howe 1989: 34) and thus helped to fix memory.

Third, Howe understands that our conventional divisions of ancient textual material should not blind us to earlier readers' inclusion of material other than that we ourselves focus on. The early insular writers he discusses—the British Gildas, the Anglo-Saxons Alcuin and then Wulfstan—not only read *Exodus* and used the Old Testament as a model for triumphal self-justification but also employed the material for cautionary exhortation. In the cases of Alcuin and Wulfstan, he points to their references to the Jews' being taken into Babylonian captivity, the model of "'a disobedient people being punished by God by wars and defeat at the hands of foreign invaders'" (22, citing Bethurum). Those who used Old Testament templates to warn of impending invasion and expulsion, therefore, were not presenting "Canaanite" readings but rather referring to a more potently relevant crisis period in Israelite history when the "covenantal" inhabitants were endangered.

Finally, with reference to the Old English *Exodus*, which he analyzes most closely, Howe utilizes a uniquely appropriate method. Relying on the importance of compounds in Old English, he looks carefully at a series of compounds contained in that text and possibly nowhere else, regarding them as a site of fusion between the Old Testament model and the Anglo-Saxon material. A particularly revealing example in Howe's analysis is the compounds including the element *flod*, here used not just as a synonym for a body of water but imbued with religious meaning. God is the *flodweard* (guardian of the flood). The Israelites journey on the *flodwege* (floodway). The Egyptians, on the other hand, are *flodblac* (floodpale) and *flodegsa* (in terror of the flood) (85). Thus the same element is used in compounds that point toward the heightened moral powers of the model (the doom of the Egyptians) and to the adaptation of the model to the new material (these Israelites do not walk through on dry land; they are sailors). The technique of compounding,

---

20. Shades of *Exodus and Revolution*! On the other hand, unlike Walzer's fearful Israelites, "the Israelites of the Old English poem seem unmarked by enslavement in Egypt" (Howe 1989: 79).

particularly rich in Old English, serves as the means by which multiple semantic valences are bound in the same text, or as Howe puts it: "Far from being a translation or paraphrase, the Old English *Exodus* represents the rarer achievement by which a foreign story is absorbed into the native imagination and idiom" (73).

## Puritan Analogues

What happened after Wulfstan? I do not find in the secondary literature any strong claims for the Exodus model in the period between William the Conqueror's triumph and Henry VIII's revolt against Rome. The Norman period seems to represent a break in the chain of historiographic readings of the Old Testament. Robert Hanning notes several changes in the approach to history during the twelfth-century "Renaissance" in Anglo-Norman culture: human causation was given more weight; the concept of fortune was brought in; cyclical notions of history appeared; and the analogy between individual and national careers was loosened (1966: 126). While, on one hand, the Normans were treated as yet another "new Israel," their significance was also cast in a classical mold: they were "imperial repressors of English liberty" (128). These new themes of secular narrative, human greatness, the cyclical rise and fall of individuals and nations, and the Greco-Roman theme of the struggle for liberty reached their culmination in the influential writings of Geoffrey of Monmouth (128; see also Leckie 1981). The evidence of this shift in the rhetorical grounds of historiography should warn us against any tendency to suppose that national identity ultimately *depends* on a single narrative model. Nor, of course, did the Normans need to see themselves as Israelites in order to conquer Britain (cf. Searle 1988).

The Exodus typology was not permanently suppressed, however, and Walzer is right to insist on its role in the debates of English Protestantism. Its prominence in Protestant rhetoric was signalled as early as the reign of Henry VIII. In 1534, William Turner wrote that Henry's Declaration of Supremacy "intended suche a thynge as all myghty god dyd when he delyuered the chylder of Israel from the bondage of Pharao / and drove the chanaanites of theyr lande that the true Israelites myght haue that land and succede them" (quoted in Reventlow 1985: 111). Whether or not such rhetoric played any significant role at all in Henry's rebellion, that rebellion was extremely consequential for the initiation of English settlement in the New World and hence for the further career of the Exodus narrative. The confiscation of church lands made the state rich, brought power to an ambitious class of "new men," enabled Henry to build a powerful navy, and encouraged the displacement of former peasants to the cities, thus meeting "the vital material conditions for English expansion and colonization" (Williams 1990: 126).

Finally, Protestant anti-Catholic ideology provided a rationale for challenging the Spanish monopoly in the New World.

In *Exodus and Revolution*, Walzer cites a fair sampling of Puritan associations between their own revolution and the Exodus narrative. But it is not clear how sharply those associations can be distinguished from the broader link between Protestant millennialism and Christian encouragement of the ingathering and conversion of the Jews. Among at least certain segments of English society, this link was indeed articulated with the imperial project. The millennium would entail "the conversion of the Jews and the spreading of Christianity to all nations ... [along with] the destruction of the Turkish Empire, which controlled Palestine and under whose rule most Jews lived" (Hill 1986a: 271). Eventually some radicals came to give highest priority to "the reign of the saints on earth which was to proceed the Second Coming" or even to equate the English with the Jews (277).[21] The ingathering of the Jews was reworked into "the gathering of the Gentiles," thus serving as another justification for conquest in America (278).[22]

Yet the importance of the Anglo-Saxons' memory of an actual sea crossing in enabling their identification with the Old Testament Israelites suggests that explicit evocations of the Exodus narrative would be even more prevalent among English Protestants who had themselves crossed the ocean to America. There was first the ethnic-moral analogy, in which Israelites were to Egyptians and to Canaanites as Puritans were to Papists and to Indians. There was also the geographical analogy, in which Egypt was to England as Canaan was to America. In the Puritan project of justifying conquest, these associations complemented the claims that the lands held by Indians were in fact vacant and that they had to be settled and civilized in order to fulfill the biblical command that man "occupy the earth, increase, and multiply" (Eisinger 1948: 131).[23]

---

21. Nabil Mattar (1989) provides important documentation of anti-Restorationist strands in British Protestant theology, but his rhetoric is confusing. His contention — directed especially against Barbara Tuchman's *The Bible and the Sword* (1956) — is that previous scholarship has ignored this anti-Restorationist tradition because of Zionist bias. The claim is somewhat undercut by his own citation of Sharif 1983, a clearly anti-Zionist reading that focuses on British Restorationism as a motivation of Zionism quite separate from concern for the Jews' well-being. Mattar's sweeping claim that *all* British support for the "return" of the Jews to Palestine is linked to the vision of Jewish conversion to Christianity seems unwarranted; at least this claim is disputed by one scholar (Mayr Vereté, summarized in Popkin 1988). Mattar further betrays his own partisanship by assuming that *all* non-Jewish Zionism is motivated by anti-Judaism or anti-Semitism.

22. Considerably later the epochs marked by Moses, the advent of Christianity, and the reign of Alfred were invoked in a work called *Christian Policy the Salvation of the Empire*. The work called for the restoration of what its author conceived to be the republican, communist, agrarian societies of those three periods (Hill 1986a: 110–11).

23. When Perry Miller, earlier in this century, began to take a fresh critical look at the

This Puritan heritage contributed in turn to the range of myths of origin that inspired the generation of the American Revolution. In addition to the classical model of democracy (Arendt 1965), they, like the generations before them, looked back to the Exodus story. Like English radicals of their time, they also employed the idealized image of the free Anglo-Saxon yeomanry before the Norman Conquest, living justly together by natural law and recognizing each other's property rights (Williams 1990: 252ff.).[24] Of course, they also drew on images of Native American tribal organization, which sometimes at least was explicitly analogized to the Saxon model (Hill 1986a: 62).

The conjunction of the Israelite and Anglo-Saxon inspirations is dramatically displayed in Thomas Jefferson's idea for the seal of the United States: one side was to bear a representation of the Israelites crossing the Red Sea, while the other was to show the Saxon chiefs Hengist and Horsa, from whom, Jefferson claimed, "we have the honor of being descended" (cited in Howe 1989: 1). The two associations complemented each other: lest the Saxon image cause second thoughts about rebelling against the motherland, the seal would remind its viewers that they had, after all, left Egypt; lest they become fearful thinking of themselves in the wilderness, they were reminded that they were, after all, bred of a pure and warlike Teutonic race.

This scattered discussion of the links between colonialism and mythmaking in seventeenth- and eighteenth-century England and America should be enough to suggest that the Exodus narrative was used; that it was not necessarily distinct from a Christian kind of messianism; and that it was linked both to the colonial project and to visions of a radically egalitarian reorga-

---

ideology of the American Puritans, he too seemed really to perceive the land they came to as a "wilderness." The preface to one of his books evokes yet another case of empire imagining its genealogy: "To bring into conjunction a minute event in the history of historiography with a great one: it was given to Edward Gibbon to sit disconsolate amid the ruins of the Capitol at Rome, and to have thrust upon him the 'laborious work' of *The Decline and Fall* while listening to barefooted friars chanting responses in the former temple of Jupiter. It was given to me, equally disconsolate on the edge of a jungle of central Africa, to have thrust upon me the mission of expounding what I took to be the innermost propulsion of the United States, while supervising, in that barbaric tropic, the unloading of drums of case oil flowing out of the inexhaustible wilderness of Americao" (Miller 1956: viii). The passage shows clearly how the continued invocation of foundational tropes — a sense of being "in the tradition" — enables Miller's powerfully influential historiography. Myra Jehlen, in the course of an insightful discussion of Miller's work, points out that Miller continued to see America as having been a "vacant wilderness," which of course it was not (Jehlen 1986: 28). The continued blanking of the Native American presence, in this sense analogous to the continued blanking of the Palestinians, shows how difficult it is to make a clean separation between history and historiography. On American intervention in Vietnam as a latter-day "errand in the wilderness," see Spanos 1990: 241–43.

24. Williams (1990: 266ff.) analyzes Jefferson's "radical mythology" partly in terms of his and other colonial businessmen's argument against the Crown for the right to speculate freely in land purchased from the Indians.

nization of society in England.²⁵ With the substitution of "nineteenth- and twentieth-" for "seventeenth- and eighteenth-," of "Europe and Palestine" for "England and America," and of "Jewish" for "Christian," that sentence could also describe the modern Zionist movement, to which I now turn.

## Zionism

Is it possible to determine to what extent the Exodus narrative plays a direct role in Zionist ideology, both informing the articulated Zionist vision and helping that vision gain resonance among Jews at the turn of this century? Two linked premises shared by both Walzer and Said are that effective analogies can be drawn between the biblical narrative and the history of Zionist settlement and that this analogy was actively drawn on in shaping Zionist ideology. It seems to me the connection is neither as uniquely determinant nor as immediate as the Walzer-Said debate would suggest.

The Exodus, as commemorated in daily Jewish prayer and in the Passover ritual, is taken to be a founding event in several senses. First, it is "the birth of a nation." In one sense, while the liturgy praises God for delivering to the Jews the lands of several nations, the high point at which we truly become a people is the giving of the law on Mount Sinai. On the other hand, the conquest and the assignment of lands to individual families reinforce the connection between the people and the land in a way that the covenant Abraham makes with God as an individual does not (Davies 1982: 62, 71). The full narrative, including at one end bondage and at the other the responsibilities toward "strangers" assumed by the people newly established in their conquered land, authorizes the separate existence of the nation on two mutually reinforcing bases: first, the memory of bondage, redemption, and promise; and second, the empathic, superior morality demanded on the basis of this history. This sense of a special providence and a special responsibility is at the core of Jewish existence in vastly changing fortunes.

All this — the social compact at Sinai, the detailed ancient title to Palestine, and the combination of national distinction with a model of empathy — would seem to suggest Exodus as the blueprint for Zionism that both Walzer and Said would make of it. Yet to the extent that this narrative does work as a template for the Zionist project, there are good indications that its applica-

---

25. Walzer asserts that "among the English Puritans, for example, it is possible to make out two groups of ministers, the one committed to what I want to call Exodus politics, expounding the Sinai covenant, the other committed to (or at least experimenting with) apocalyptic and millennialist politics, expounding the Abrahamic covenant" (1985: 78–79). Walzer obviously knows infinitely more about the subject than I do, but without documentation, I cannot take him on faith.

tion in Zionism does not come directly from "traditional" Jewish culture but from other, more diffuse sources.

On the basis of Walzer's account, this question would be difficult to judge. Walzer fails to cite a single *actual* evocation of Exodus by one of the pre-state founding fathers of Labor Zionism, contenting himself with the general observation that gradualist, liberal, realist Labor Zionists practiced Exodus politics.[26] Said, as I have noted, makes the contentious but complementary claim that "religious" notions of divine promise and right to the land were central to early Zionist discourse, but he does not cite examples either. On the other hand, a representative selection of Theodor Herzl's occasional writings reveals a concentration on the position of Jews in fin de siècle Europe, not a vision of the past glories on which a shining future can be modeled (1973). On one occasion when Herzl did cite the Exodus from Egypt, it was only by way of contrasting it to the movement he envisioned: "We cannot journey out of Mizraim [Egypt] to-day, in the primitive fashion of ancient times" (1980: 424).

This is not to deny that the Exodus narrative, precisely as enshrined in daily prayer and in the Passover ritual, was a significant resource for recruiting Jews from "traditional" backgrounds to the Zionist vision. It was doubtless used rhetorically for this purpose, as it was used rhetorically by pre-Zionist Reform Jews and later by anti-Zionist Jews, who claimed that their native lands (Germany, America, England) were "the Promised Land" and who denied that they were waiting for a Messiah to come take them anywhere else.[27]

Against this I submit the hypothesis that the intimate association of Exodus with the Jewish settlement in Palestine and establishment of Israel is largely a product of the 1940s and after. I remember, for example, that as a child I first learned of the Nazi genocide while watching a documentary entitled *Let My People Go*; significantly, that film was broadcast on the night of Passover. The memories and images of the concentration camps lent themselves readily to an association with enslavement in Egypt, while the British restrictions on Jewish immigration to Palestine cast the British as latter-day Pharaohs, refusing to let the Jews out of "Egypt"-Europe. The association was popularized immensely through Leon Uris's novel *Exodus*, named after one of the ships taking Jewish refugees to Palestine, and through the film made

---

26. Walzer does note that "a few socialists, like David Ben-Gurion, still entertained messianic hopes" (1985: 138). Ben-Gurion remains such a towering figure in Zionist history that this acknowledgment might at least have given Walzer pause.

27. As the Reform Rabbinical Conference, meeting in Frankfurt in 1845, resolved: "The messianic idea should receive prominent mention in our prayers, but all petitions for our return to the land of our fathers and for the restoration of the Jewish state should be eliminated from the liturgy" (in Mendes-Flohr and Reinharz 1980: 165; see also Meyer 1988: 122).

from that novel. It is significant that (perhaps like Moses the Egyptianized liberator) the hero of the film *Exodus,* the "new Jew," the product of liberation from Zionism, is blond and blue-eyed Paul Newman. Furthermore, as suggested above, for liberal American Jews the "Exodus connection" helped to cement the connection between their sympathy for the new Israeli nation and their sympathy for the civil rights struggle of American blacks.

This is not to say that ancient associations played no significant part in the formation of Zionism, nor that the Exodus narrative is simply an extraneous, ex post facto import. The Exodus narrative, for all that Walzer emphasizes its "linear" character, is itself mixed with the memory of other exiles and returns. Thus the Passover Haggadah, the retelling of the Exodus, culminates in the hopeful shout of "next year in Jerusalem." This is clearly a reference to the return from exile in Babylonia, since Jerusalem does not figure in the biblical narrative until generations after Joshua's conquest.[28] Though this is by all means an expression of Messianic hope, the tradition hardly finds it incongruous as the climax to the retelling of the Exodus narrative.

This latter theme — the loss of a commonwealth and the hopes for its return — seems more salient in Rabbinic Judaism. In prayer Jews *remember* and express their *gratitude* for delivery from Egypt, but they beseech God for the *restoration* of David's kingdom and of the Temple in Jerusalem. The possibility needs to be considered that the model of Babylonian exile and return was more salient than Egyptian exile and Exodus in the interplay between Zionist goals and the popular (mostly East European) Jewish imagination. As Yaakov Shavit suggests, for a brief period — from the advent of the Hovevei Zion (Lovers of Zion) in 1882, through roughly the 1920s, when the Balfour Declaration was explicitly analogized to that made by the Persian king Cyrus — the role of Cyrus in permitting the return to Zion was prominent in Jewish "historical memory," that is, in a collective "memory" stimulated by both historiography and a set of circumstances analogous to those at a point in the distant past. Shavit makes several points relevant to the respective prominence of the return model and the Exodus model, noting that in the prestate period there was

> recognition that the Return to Zion was an indisputable historical event (unlike the Exodus from Egypt) and an outstanding messianic event.... [The East

---

28. In modern, non-Jewish usages of the biblical narrative, the two exiles are if anything less distinct. For example, there is the Rastafarian Bob Marley's chant that proclaims, "Exodus,... we're leaving Babylon." The Exodus model of liberation and mass movement is certainly more dramatic a model than the gradual and partial return from Babylon. Yet the Rastafarians' focus on Babylon as a model of captivity, partly because of its reputation for corruption and partly because it is more explicitly depicted as a place of exile, such as in Psalm 137 ("By the rivers of Babylon").

European Hovevei Zion] explained [Cyrus's] Declaration and the subsequent Return to Zion as an outstanding example of redemption by natural means, as opposed to the redemption from Egypt by miraculous means.... Cyrus simply served as a good case — in fact the only one in historical experience — which symbolized what should be expected from diplomacy and legitimized the latter as a historical political method. (1990: 68–72)

During the 1930s, when Zionists became disappointed with the policies of the British "Cyrus" and the project of creating an independent state became increasingly favored, the figure of the original Cyrus "revert[ed] to the status of a passive memory" (Shavit 1990: 62). If indeed the model of the return from Babylon was more prominent than the Exodus from Egypt in early Zionism, this would have considerable bearing on the debate over Zionist conceptions of history and self. At least three consequences can be identified.

First, the ancient images of the Land of Israel (or more particularly Jerusalem) as desolate (Lamentations 1:1) would promote a justification of colonial settlement in Palestine on the basis that the land there was desolate now as well. This would be consistent with tropes of fertilizing the wilderness employed in other colonial contexts; for Methodist missionaries Africa was "a 'wilderness' to be turned into a 'fruitful field'" (Comaroff 1985: 138).

A corollary of the desolation of the land is that it is implicitly understood as not being genuinely populated. Much as the Puritans had justified their taking of Indian land by the claim that it was *vacuum domicilium,* perhaps in the imagination of the early European Zionists, the Palestinians were not so much "Canaanites" as simply *not there.*[29] This blanking out of the Arab presence may have been accomplished more through the shaping of an acceptable range of Zionist discourse that set the terms of polemic and therefore enabled a range of exclusions (Aronoff 1990), most notably that of the Palestinians,

---

29. Herzl described Zionism as "a modest demand which does not jeopardize or injure anyone's rights" (1973: 145). Not the rights of any Europeans, at least; there's the rub. Compare Edward Said's analysis of Algerian Arabs as an inert, mute, ahistorical presence in the novels of Camus (Said 1990). Clearly the place of Palestinian Arabs in the imagination of Zionists shifts according to both spatial and temporal coordinates. Its possible formulations differed, for a first approximation, according to whether the land was being imagined from Europe, being settled by colonists (in which case, as noted above, Zionist workers and Zionist planters often saw Palestinians quite differently), or constituted as the possession of a sovereign "Jewish state." Against my argument that the Babylonian model fits with the notion of an "empty land," Shavit claims as one of the situational analogies between the ancient return and modern Zionism the "struggle with the 'people of the land' (the Arabs) who opposed the national revival" (1990: 56). Unfortunately, Shavit does not cite any such rhetorical analogies made by modern Zionists. The "people of the land" at the time of the return from Babylon were "the Arabians, and the Ammonites, and the Ashdodites, [who, when they] hear that the repairing of the walls of Jerusalem went forward, then they were very wroth; and they conspired all of them together to come and fight against Jerusalem, and to cause confusion therein [but to no avail]" (Nehemiah 4:1).

than through explicit arguments against their legitimate presence. Such considerations may well be moot to displaced Palestinians, nor are they intended as a claim that the early Zionists were naive. Yet they are extremely pertinent to understanding how certain categories of persons are signified and others are not, in differing nationalist and colonialist conflicts.[30]

Note also that this vision of the land as desolate, barren, and abused is directly contradictory to the picture of Canaan brought back by the Israelite spies. In the scene memorialized by the symbol of the Israeli National Tourist Board, they return bearing immense clusters of cultivated grapes (Numbers 13:23). The land is already rich and cultivated, already flowing with all good things. In order to make this rhetoric work in support of the modern Zionist project, the sequence had to be reversed: in 1944 Senator Clark of Missouri described the Jewish immigrants as having "converted a barren land into a literal Biblical land of 'milk and honey'" (quoted in Sharif 1983: 110). While the quote shows how easily the two narrative models could be mixed, the emphasis is certainly on the right to possess barren land through working it rather than on a divinely mandated conquest.

Second, the Zionist settling effort really was a "return," at least in imagination. This is attested to by the fact that names were already there in the lexicon: some of these names were still in use; some echoed through Arabic variants; some were contained in Jewish texts and could be plausibly reattached to new particular locales. The whole phenomenon represented a close overlay of the legendary and the referential: it is impossible simply to say that people came in and assigned biblical names as if they were Israelites, and it is also impossible simply to say that they started using biblical names again (see Benvenisti 1986). Unlike, for example, Australia, where European explorers and settlers had to transform space that to them was initially "raw" into space that was marked by and within their culture, Palestine was already an "occupied territory of the Jewish imagination" (Eisenzweig 1981).

Third, the Exodus narrative and the Babylonian exile and return narrative differ significantly in terms of the relationships between Israelites and empire obtaining at the end of the respective stories. The Exodus, of course, represents a complete divorce from the oppressor, whereas later there is a complex and in many ways benevolent continuing relationship with the Babylonians. An emphasis on the latter, then, would foster the simultaneous idea of Zion-

---

30. It is no revelation to note that the topic of racism in Zionist and Israeli ideology is a tortured one. Anything like an adequate account of this issue would have to start by making certain discriminations within the history of Zionism — such as that between "Western" and "Eastern" Zionism, which differ significantly in terms of notions of identity and progress. It would also, I think, gain strength and coherence from the perception of Zionism as an attempt to negate Jewish religion while preserving the Jewish people (see Luz 1988: xiii–xix).

ism as a colonizing mission and as a redemptive mission. The entire popular Zionist effort of mass fund-raising, gradually rebuilding the land, and sending settlers with the broad support of the majority of non-settler Jews also fits this model better.[31]

While Walzer tries, inter alia, to associate liberal Zionism with a democratic "Western" tradition via the Exodus narrative, the Babylonian analogy thus seems closer to the ambivalent attitude Israelis bear toward the West. On one hand, Israel is a frontier, an outpost along a "narrow coastal strip," the "only democracy in the Middle East." On the other hand, this very association with "Western" values allows liberal Zionists to be retrospectively (and fairly effectively) tarred as "Hellenizers" by the right-wing territorial maximalists whom Walzer opposes. These demagogues are thereby able to elaborate a sort of antiliberal, "anticolonial" Zionist counterdiscourse, which is increasingly attractive to many Israelis as the hollowness of Labor Zionism sets in.[32]

Is it possible to construct a relation between Israeli Jewish identity and the Jewish textual tradition that transcends the weakness of Labor Zionism and the irresponsible chauvinism of Gush Emunim? Reading secularism or chauvinism back through the tradition will hardly serve as a basis for accomplishing that task. Rather we should learn both to see more richly the range of associations and exclusions that make up Israeli identity and to think beyond the "Western" polarizations of secularism and fundamentalism. By way of conclusion, I will suggest a few tentative steps toward grounding the second of these two tasks.

## Decolonizing Hermeneutics

What are we to make of my breathless overview of the history of Exodus reading? If I have indeed identified weaknesses in Walzer's and Said's political hermeneutics, what alternatives are or could be available?

---

31. Baruch Kimmerling has an insightful discussion of the symbolic significance of the seven hundred thousand Jewish National Fund collection boxes circulating in 1937: "Thus a linkage was formed between land redemption, which was a central component in the Jewish-Arab conflict, and participation in the Zionist community, both in Palestine and in the Diaspora. This linkage was not highly visible, and it is difficult to estimate its significance, but it was part of a three-part process: a) taking the conflictual sting out of as many aspects of the Jewish-Arab conflict as possible and defining them in 'positive' terms unconnected with Jewish-Arab relations; b) raising those aspects to the symbolic level; c) making use of the mechanisms of socialization and social control to implant these symbols" (1983: 76). On the other hand, when Kimmerling discusses the various ways in which the settlers related to the local Arab population (184ff.), a failure really to acknowledge them does not figure on the list.

32. Shavit, citing the veteran right-wing Zionist Israel Eldad, notes that "in Israel today the image of Cyrus and the erection of the Temple under the aegis of a foreign king are placed in opposition to the purity of the Temple and the conquest of the land in ancient times or in the period of the Hasmoneans" (1990: 83 n. 46).

I hope it is clear that the Exodus narrative is susceptible to both colonizing and liberationist readings, that the two variations are not often identified as such, and that they are frequently mingled in the minds of readers. All of these uses represent one aspect of the heritage of modern politics, in a complex sense. Exodus was inherited by the shapers of modern imperialism and liberationism, used by many in their own projects, and thereby passed on as their heritage to us. There is a useful distinction to be made, therefore, between our ability to account for the role of Exodus (or any other preexisting narrative complex) in the ideological construction of modern politics and our own interaction with that text as we have received it.

The continuing power of this imperial heritage — its potential for continued or innovative ideological effectiveness — is an open question, especially in view of the claims made recently for the "death of master narratives" (Lyotard 1984), such as the biblical stories of oppression, liberation, and conquest, or of exile and restoration. Since we are simultaneously critics and producers of ideology, the question is both descriptive and prescriptive. Will the grand narratives continue to sway large numbers of people? Should we be engaging them as authoritative? The problem may in fact be with the trope of narratives shared by large numbers of people, encompassing much history and an inexhaustible store of potential readings, as "master" narratives, since the qualifier itself implies imperial domination.

There is a different approach to the political history of reading: the recuperation of earlier "anti-imperialist," or at least anamnestic, reading strategies. Thus, for example, Daniel Boyarin's book entitled *Intertextuality and the Reading of Midrash* examines the rabbinic readings of the Exodus narrative in the centuries following the final Roman destruction of the Jewish commonwealth. In such a situation, textual tradition and language in general are made to bear perhaps an even greater weight than when a collective enjoys temporal power. Boyarin's reading of the rabbis on Exodus is free of dichotomies between "secular" and "sacred" or between Exodus-as-conquest and Exodus-as-liberation. By treating language as part of the material world and part of history, Boyarin escapes the Hobson's choice of deciding whether narrative is autonomously effective or merely available to political rhetoric, much as critical theory seems finally to have moved beyond the compulsion to declare certain aspects of our world as merely reflective of others that are "determinant in the last instance."

Furthermore, Boyarin understands the rabbis themselves as having treated language as that part of the world given by God to humanity in order to make sense of our world. For that reason, as a "religious" obligation the rabbis were bound to stretch language to its utmost, to make it reveal as many of its potential meanings as possible. The midrash does not aim to discover the "true" meaning of the text; on the contrary, "The cumulative effect of the midrash as compiled is to focus on the ambiguity and the possibilities of making meaning out of it" (D. Boyarin 1990: 58).

A striking example of this approach pertains to the references in the Bible to the Israelites "murmuring" in the desert. According to Walzer, who pays relatively close attention to these references:

> The conflict...is between the materialism of the people and the idealism of their leaders, or it is between the demands of the present moment and the promise of the future. These are common political formulations, and one can find them developed in a great variety of ways in the rabbinic literature, usually, but not always, in ways unsympathetic to the people and the present moment. (1985: 51)

Boyarin closely traces the rabbis' evaluation of one such murmuring and of subsequent verses, as recorded in a midrashic compilation called the Mekilta. The first verse in point is Exodus 16:2, "And the whole congregation of Israel murmured." This certainly seems like a pejorative description of cranky ingrates. It is subjected to contrasting interpretations by two rabbis, whom the Mekilta represents as consistently evaluating the text in opposite ways. Rabbi Yehoshua, who tends throughout to a more positive account of the generation in the wilderness, does his best to remove its sting. Rabbi Elazar, who consistently denigrates the Israelites, "enthusiastically activates the pejorative connotations of the word 'murmured,' and even enhances them dramatically" (D. Boyarin 1990: 71). Slightly later, another verse reads, "And the Lord said to Moses: I hereby rain bread from Heaven for you." Rabbi Yehoshua gives this verse what we would probably agree is its commonsense reading, as a sign of divine goodwill. Rabbi Elazar, however, stretches the interpretation to contend that "He says 'hereby' only to mean by the merit of your ancestors" (cited on 72).

What is going on here? Have Rabbi Yehoshua and Rabbi Elazar, for reasons extrinsic to the text, already made up their minds about the generation in the wilderness and proceeded to force each verse into their preconceived molds? On the contrary, Boyarin suggests that it is fallacious to assume that the Mekilta represents an accurate "transcript" of exactly what two historical figures said. Rather, he suggests, the Mekilta itself has molded them into representatives of two possible, antithetical readings contained in the biblical text itself, one depicting the Israelites as faithless and servile, the other as faithful and bold:

> The midrash seems to present a view of an ancient reader who perceives ambiguity encoded in the text itself with various dialectical possibilities for reducing that ambiguity, each contributing to but not exhausting its meaning(s).

...Moreover, the Mekilta does not speak discursively and abstractly in metalanguage *about* the ambiguity of the Torah. It represents the tension and inner dialogue of the biblical narrative by tension and inner dialogue of its own. (79)

This approach to the politics of reading, which Boyarin implicitly claims to share with the rabbis, bears several lessons. It takes seriously the idea of language in and as history and examines closely particular cases of readers interacting with "foundational narratives" as they shape techniques for narrativizing memory against oblivion. It has ample room for contentious voices within a shared tradition, rather than either claiming that one trend must be dominant or opting to speak of only one trend as more congenial to our own views. It renews the potential of creative (and even subversive) interaction with the tradition beyond the poles of affirmation and denunciation. Most important, because it integrates powerful currents of both textual authority and interpretive heterogeneity, it suggests a positive answer to Said's question whether one can "both 'belong' and concern yourself with Canaanites who do not belong" (Said 1985: 106). The more one is equipped to read, the greater the number of plausible interpretations one is able to entertain, the less one is compelled to view "belonging" as a monodimensional loyalty, and the better able one is to work through such seeming contradictions in creative practice.

A legitimate objection can still be raised. Even though this intense and detailed interaction with the stuff of textual traditions helps avoid reification of the "ethnic community" that maintains them, it still entails a common set of competences and a shared reference to an authoritative tradition. Furthermore, no matter how difficult philologic and interpretive work on midrashic or Anglo-Saxon texts may be, and no matter how indispensable such work may be for discussions of text as ideology, it does not present the same challenges as the attempt to articulate ancient models with current political situations. Is a form of "midrashic dialogism" possible beyond the boundaries of a tightly knit hermeneutic/political tradition? Could it possibly be an intercultural model? Though I might be tempted to cast Said as "Reb Edward" and Walzer as "Reb Michael," to do so now would both neutralize the complex power relations implicated in their debate and fictionalize the suffering of Palestinians for whom Said wishes to speak. The image of relatively comradely interpretive dialogues preserved in the midrash may be one ideal, but it cannot serve as a *standard* for judging debates in the present.[33]

---

33. Nor should we assume that all the rabbis' debates were as calmly recollective of their own past as the record might sometimes lead us to believe. We should bear in mind that they worked under conditions of Roman rule or Babylonian exile that were considerably analogous to the situation of the Palestinians today. There were doubtless bitter schisms and crises of communication in their ranks, motivated by political pressures and also by the range of ego anxieties that "Western" *men*, then as now, beyond their differences, are prey to.

I believe that, beyond and encompassing both Walzer's "belonging to the tradition" and Said's "embattled intellectual" stance, we are necessarily engaged in a search for models of interpretation that are translatable across cultural boundaries. What this search demands I would not call enlightenment, not least because viewing our ancestors as having been in darkness constitutes much of the problem. We do need to struggle for social conditions that will permit us to realize, much more than we have until now, the innate ability of human beings to operate within a great variety of cultural idioms, and that will "authorize" a much larger and more diverse human group effectively to create culture and intervene in politics. The goal of expanding our peoples' capacity for reading, writing, speaking, and understanding is inherently political, inseparable from the humane goals that give the term "humanities" whatever value it has. Stated at this level of generality, of course, there is a danger of falling back into a liberal universalism that erases not only cultural differences but the world system of collective discriminations and deprivations that is still very much in force. In the search for models of intercultural and contentious dialogue, the only possible procedure is one that maintains simultaneously the equal importance of each human life and the almost inexhaustible reiterative power of our particular narrative associations through time.

# 3

# My Trip to Israel, Continued

• 6/20/91 •

Let's face it — the Israeli "right wing" and "center" are probably going to be about as well represented in this diary as are the Occupied Territories, if that, the one distortion being a matter of personal bias, the other a matter of situational restraint.

This afternoon: I'm off for a long walk. Now I'm on — I think — Ramban Street in Rechavia (not a neighborhood of people who especially appreciate the Ramban,[1] but then I imagine most people here don't give as much thought to street names as I do). The neighborhood is astonishingly lush, with a dozen shades of green — pine trees and a variety of plants I can't begin to guess. I remember walking here one evening years ago at dusk, and looking at a scene that made me feel I was in a Magritte painting — the light was so pure and its shades so subtle that it was surreal. A middle-aged "Arab" (I don't know sometimes whether to write "Arab" or "Palestinian," and I make a note to note who uses which word when) is sweeping the street, wearing blue workers' clothes and a green knit cap.

Someone could write an article about the geography of hotels in Jerusalem.[2]

---

1. The Rechavia neighborhood was built and settled by generally secular German Jews in the 1930s; its architecture reflects the modernism of that period. The implication here that the neighborhood is made up of secularists is apparently misleading, with reference both to the time Rechavia was built and to the present. Israeli readers of this manuscript assure me that, in fact, this part of Rechavia has always been at least half-Orthodox, and in particular, religious intellectuals such as Professor Saul Lieberman lived there. Consider this parenthetic remark as part of my reflection on the disjuncture of coexisting times and associations in urban landscapes.

2. There are two main clusters in West Jerusalem, one at the "center" of town along King George Street, the second, which I describe here, nearer the Knesset. Then there are the Palestinian hotels in East Jerusalem — the Jerusalem, the American Colony, the National Plaza — each associated as meeting places of different international journalistic, diplomatic, and relief cliques and different Palestinian political factions. Then, as mentioned, there's the newish Hyatt near the Mount Scopus Campus.

Here's one cluster, at the corner of Ruppin and Shderot Herzl, near the Government Center, the Givat Ram university campus, and Mount Herzl — the Sonesta (which I always think of as the Canasta),[3] the Ramada Renaissance, the Migdal Knesset,[4] maybe one other. A tennis court is screened with green plastic emblazoned with the Head sports products emblem. A large kidney-shaped pool glimmers blue, and I catch a whiff of chlorine. A boy tumbles his nubile, bikinied, solid-thighed sister out of a lounge chair. They move off, speaking Hebrew. I count the pages in my diary (not bad) and move on as well.

Here's the poster for the Gush lecture series again — I take down the dates and times, and resolve to make at least one. The exact quote from Rav Kook is: *"Dorenu dor nifla.... Kashe meod limtso lo ledugma bechol divrey yameynu,"* translated on the poster as "Our generation is wonderful.... It would be hard to find another one like it throughout history."[5]

Two yellow, new buses go by, with the name Hakhevra Lepituach Mate Benjamin.[6] It would be helpful if I knew what part of the "West Bank" that referred to. Of course I blanch at the terms Yehuda and Shomron, because of the current process of dispossession they imply, but it strikes me for the first time that the term "West Bank" is awfully neutral, doesn't have a bit of emotional power.[7] Most of it anyway is hill country which has little to do with

---

3. Shimon Schneebalg notes, "I always think of it as the Siesta."
4. Parliament Tower.
5. This refers to a series of lectures sponsored by Gush Emunim. Rav Kook, the first chief rabbi of Israel, is regarded as the spiritual inspiration of the Gush Emunim movement because of his synthesis of Orthodoxy and the Zionist pioneering ethos. Rav Kook died decades ago, and his son, the spiritual leader of Gush Emunim, also died several years ago (Lustick 1988). Hence the generation Rav Kook had in mind was the generation of prestate "pioneers," not the generation of post-1967 settlers. The invocation of this enthusiastic description of the earlier generation in the present perfectly illustrates the thesis, discussed in detail by Ian Lustick and widely noted by Israeli journalists and intellectuals, that West Bank settlers in particular inherited the pioneer aura of the earlier *halutzim*. The sense of being a *unique* generation contained in this quote might seem to undercut the association between the earlier and later "pioneers," but it seems more to have the effect of bringing them together within a general conception of the Zionist twentieth century as a premessianic epoch.
6. Benjamin Region Development Corporation.
7. Yet it is not clear that we could therefore assign the term "West Bank" to the workings of *place*, "those operations that make their object ultimately reducible to a fixed location," and "Yehuda and Shomron" (Judea and Samaria) to *space*, "created by the actions of historical *subjects*" (Patraka 1992, citing de Certeau 1984). "West Bank" is produced by historical subjects as well — modern politicians and diplomats — even if the intended *effect* of the term is reductive. Nor is it clear that the "actions" that produce Yehuda and Shomron "multiply spaces and what can be positioned between them" (ibid.). Yet certainly, for those who might be interested in the reconciliation of competing histories and claims, it is bootless to simply banish terms that have particular resonance for certain of the contending parties and potentially useful to think of ways that many memories could be "positioned" within the same territory.

the Jordan River. Now I'm right at Mount Herzl by Herzl's grave, but I'm not going to go in and describe it. It's too complicated for today. I'm heading for the woods.

Walking way out on Har Hazikaron,[8] through a forest with no one present, I reach a place called "Garden of the Righteous."[9] On a simple stone wall are plaques bearing the names of a few hundred Gentiles — mostly in Poland — who saved Jews during World War II. Scrambling toward the top of the hill, I realize better what the forest is intended to be. Each tree in this section has its own, numbered plaque with the name and country of one of the Righteous Gentiles next to it. From here I can see, I believe, a strip of the highway to Tel Aviv, and a stunning half-ring of hills, mostly still undeveloped. And here too is the unfinished "Valley of the Destroyed Communities."[10] It doesn't look like a map of Europe from here; I'll go down. There's a tablet with the names of "Founders" and "Patrons" engraved; on it are a few names I recognize, such as Benjamin Meed and Jack Eisner.[11] No, it's too unfinished to see what they have in mind, except that it will involve walking through an irregular maze of ten-foot-high walls — perhaps with plaques affixed to them? Engraving must be a major trade here. And then I think of the water that irrigates this forest, and I think of the six shallow Palestinian wells on — yes — the West Bank that were recently destroyed by the occupation authorities, and it makes me sad.[12]

I can see the moon clearly here, even in the late afternoon. Its waxing comforts me, reminds me that as I'm here day after day watching it change, so too my time to come home will arrive (but how can time arrive?).

---

8. Literally, "The Mountain of Memory."

9. Mount Herzl, with its military cemetery, and Har Hazikaron, which contains the Yad Vashem memorial to the Nazi genocide, are central parts of the "geography of commemoration" in Israel (Handelman and Shamgar-Handelman 1991).

10. The newest part of the memorial complex, this is an excavated hillside through which the visitor walks, passing names and representations of a vast number of destroyed Jewish communities in the Diaspora. As such, it evidences among other things the new respect for the particulars of diasporic memory, which is one of the hopeful developments in Israeli culture over the past two decades.

11. Benjamin Meed is the most important leader of organized Jewish victims of Nazi genocide in the United States. Jack Eisner is the author of a best-selling memoir entitled *The Survivor* (Eisner 1980).

12. There's bad writing in this journal too, such as this blatant pitch for the reader to identify with my baldly stated emotions: but there it is. The "and then" beginning this sentence is also jarring: What did this thinking of water follow, exactly, and why wasn't I sad before at this Holocaust memorial forest? I am perhaps inured to rhetorics of Holocaust commemoration, having done so much documentation myself (Kugelmass and Boyarin 1983, 1988; J. Boyarin 1991a). What saddened me, it seems, was the sense that even the purity of mourning is here poisoned by the immorality of occupation.

• 6/21/91 •

Kibbutz Qetura, in the Arava Valley, fifty-two kilometers north of Eilat. My sister-in-law (Elissa's sister) Randi's kibbutz for many years — I visited here with Elissa for the first time when we came for Pesach from Paris in 1983, while I was doing my doctoral fieldwork. I still describe this place to people as a wonder: an oasis of date palms, after a frighteningly bare desert landscape, coming down from Tel Aviv (as I did this morning) or from Jerusalem. The Arava — the northernmost extension of the Great African Rift, ending in the Dead Sea — is a few miles wide here, with steep sloping hills on the Jordanian side and rough red cliffs perhaps five hundred feet high on this side. Most of the people who live here are under forty and American. For the first time now, Randi tells me, there are a couple of fifteen-year-old kids (children of members) here. Some of the Americans make a point of speaking Hebrew, there are a few Israeli members or people from other countries, and there's often a *nachal* group — kids doing their army service who spend a certain amount of their service working on (usually fairly new) kibbutzim,[13] so there's a good mix of Hebrew and English around.

Randi rarely leaves the place. Once in a while she'll go north to visit friends — such as my brother's family — or on kibbutz business, such as the time she did a stint as culture organizer for the kibbutz and took a course run by the central kibbutz movement. She's allowed a trip abroad to see her family, paid for by the kibbutz, once every four years or in case of emergency — such as when Elissa was undergoing chemotherapy a year and a half ago.

This isn't really my kind of place — a harsh and beautiful landscape, where physical labor is the basic activity — and yet I am drawn here each time I visit Israel. Thinking before I came that I'd be spending a fair amount of time here (although now I don't know if that's the case), I decided on a "hook" to relate it to my concerns with ideology — I needed the hook precisely because Qetura seems so far removed from "the conflict" — and the hook was that this place, where hardly a shrub was living before this kibbutz was established, let alone people, seems more than anywhere else to be a place where the original pioneering dream — including the fruition of a empty land — seems plausible.[14] Ironically enough, this is only very questionably part of

---

13. Originally *nachal* units were intended as the nuclei of new kibbutz communities, and the new settlements at which they were stationed eventually became full-fledged kibbutzim. In recent years some *nachal* units in the Occupied Territories have functioned primarily to anchor an Israeli presence. Although they carry out some agriculture and other modest economic enterprises, it is understood that their stations will not become kibbutzim. At the same time, *nachal* units are commonly sent to already established yet younger kibbutzim.

14. Even if no one lived in this part of the Arava before the kibbutzim were established, the Israeli settlement of the northern Negev has entailed massive disruption of the Bedouin

"biblical" Israel — although according to my official Carta guide to Israel, Solomon's kingdom extended down to the Red Sea. (King Solomon's Mines are close by.)[15]

• 6/23/91 •

An hour and a half before the bus back to Jerusalem, I'm sitting in the dining room at Qetura, where two members of the kibbutz have the TV on — they're showing Bob Saget, the director of "America's Funniest Home Videos,"[16] who's inviting people here to send their best to him. Then the Israeli version, which is quite distinctive to Israel — including one having to do with people trying to run past a sprinkler at a kibbutz, one about a kid trying not to laugh as he reads his bar mitzvah speech, and one involving a *brit milah*[17] and water sounds (?). The one about the bar mitzvah goes on, with the kid completely unable to get through his speech, cracking up despite the best efforts of teacher and parents to calm him down. And so on.

Back to Friday night. A relatively elaborate Friday night service; Randi told me later that they only have a morning *minyan*[18] here about once a month. What impressed me most about the *bet knesset* — it seems weird to use the word "synagogue" at all here — was the inscription above the ark: "*Shuva hashem et shiviteynu k'afikim banegev*," "Return us Lord, like the wellsprings in the Negev."[19] It's especially effective here precisely because water is such

---

way of life, and in the broadest sense, it cannot be neatly separated from the Zionist displacement of Palestinians. Still, one cannot point to a row of cactus bushes here in the Arava as living witness to such displacement. Yet another factor giving the impression of health here is the youth of the kibbutz: the membership overwhelmingly consists of young families, and the kibbutz itself was established only in 1973. Youth per se seems to be an essential part of the kibbutz mystique, and the average age in many of the more established, Socialist-Zionist kibbutzim has been skewed toward the elderly in recent years.

15. Randi assured me later with a broad smile that "King Solomon never had mines down here." According to the *Encyclopedia Judaica* entry on Solomon, "The interruption in the renewed archaeological survey of the metal mines in Edom has precluded the possibility of ascertaining whether in the days of Solomon these mines were indeed worked intensively, in particular those in the Punan bloc, southeast of the Dead Sea" (*Encyclopedia Judaica* 1971: 104) — that is, in the Arava.

16. I am informed that he is actually the producer.

17. Circumcision ceremony.

18. Communal prayer services.

19. My translation here is consistent with that used in the popular ArtScroll prayer book, which has "return our captivity like springs in the desert" (Scherman 1985: 201). Professor Chana Kronfeld notes, "Not a good translation. *Afikim banegev* are the creek/wadi beds, dry in summer but apt to be filled instantaneously with rushing water, even to overflow with sudden flash floods." The general image is the same, however, linking the cyclical return of water and thus of vegetation to the hoped-for epochal return of the Jews to life in their own land. Yet the specific reading of *afikim* as desert flood-beds rather than simply springs makes clearer

an important theme of life here. Randi warns visitors to drink frequently, not to become dehydrated. The few horses left on the kibbutz from the time they had a tourist riding enterprise have a hose strung over their paddock with holes, so they can stand underneath, get wet, and get some relief from the sun. The swimming pool seems an incredible luxury — such a mass of water in one place. The spout for drinking water here in the dining room has a sticker which says, "Don't waste water — every drop's a loss!" It makes me think of *Dune*. The water here in fact comes from underground aquifers. Anyway the observation about the inscription over the ark — it's a phrase included in the introduction to the grace after meals, which a million Jews around the world recite regularly. But almost everywhere the second part of the metaphor is dead — it's the return of the Jews that's on people's minds (if they think about the words at all), not the springs of the Negev.[20] Being here, where life is so closely dependent on water, makes the first part more poignant as well.

As Randi explained to me once before, agriculture here is even more totally dependent on water than elsewhere. The sand is full of noxious chemicals, and has none of the nutrients the various crops — dates, mangos, melons, peppers, and so on — need. So a mix of necessary nutrients is included in the water that drips out of irrigation pipes to the plants. In addition to helping the plants grow, the water makes the sand more of a neutral base, leaching out the noxious chemicals.

Several kilometers south of here is Yotvata, the oldest, largest, and richest kibbutz in the Arava. The water table is relatively high there. This means that the "wild" plant life — most noticeably acacia trees — is considerably more widespread. It also means that the aquifer is more vulnerable to contamination. The residents of Yotvata are becoming convinced that the nutrients they feed to their crops — nitrogens, potassium, and one other, Randi doesn't remember which — are poisoning their water supply. Randi says she doesn't know what they'll do about it — they seem to think that they have to convince people outside the kibbutz that this is indeed happening before they can decide what to do about it.

Near the laundry here there's a big plaque listing various bodies — the Keren Kayemet,[21] the JNF of Australia and New Zealand, and so on — that

---

how the use of this verse as a motto for Judaism at Qetura makes Qetura, with its classically Zionist inhospitable terrain, into a *model* of Zionist return.

20. The control of water resources — particularly in the West Bank, where a vastly disproportionate portion of the available water is now allotted to Israeli settlements or to Israel proper — is also a key aspect of the struggle for territorial control that is similarly disregarded in outside representations of the conflict.

21. Jewish National Fund.

provided the money for the "reclamation" of Ketura's lands. It's not clear who they thought they were paying to have it reclaimed from. In the north, of course, the classic image is draining the swamps in the Hula Valley, and there it's pretty clear that the reclamation they had in mind was from centuries of absentee ownership and Turkish neglect. Here, aside from personalized Nature, the only candidate seems to be the ancient Nabateans, the previous civilization in this region, gone for millennia. This morning Randi took me to see a Nabatean archaeological site. It's a village along the route of a tunnel, tens of miles long, that they built to bring water down from a place where the water table was higher. Portions of it have been excavated, along with the pits dug to construct it originally. It's an impressive underground construction, not large but with solid stone sides and an arch-shaped roof to keep it from caving in. Evidently, Randi says, the climate here was somewhat wetter when the Nabateans lived here — but equally clearly, they too had to worry about irrigation.[22]

Two things I was wrong about in my notes on Friday. First, there is (at least in public) more Hebrew spoken here than English, often by people with a strong American accent. At least that's my impression this time around. Second, my comparison of the heights on either side of the Arava here did not do justice to the Jordanian mountain range, which is indeed a true mountain range. Its erstwhile "facing ridge" is in the Sinai, a hundred-odd kilometers south of here. That's why they call this the Great Rift Valley. It moves about a millimeter a year. One of Randi's friends says he can hardly feel it.

Friday night *Singin' in the Rain,* one of Randi's all-time favorite movies, is on, and we go looking for a TV we can watch it on. Several people have their own TVs now, something new on the kibbutz. They're either veterans with first priority, or they had their own money, or someone else bought it for them. This is a kind of progress people like Randi (who doesn't have her own TV) aren't thrilled about. Anyway, we needed to find a TV that wasn't private — since we had several people — and wasn't in a "public" place (the dining room or the "clubhouse"), because those TVs can't be turned on on Sabbaths or holidays, as a gesture to the semireligious nature of this kibbutz. Eventually we found one in a cool bomb shelter, and enjoyed the movie immensely.

---

22. When Randi visited New York in October 1993 for her sister's wedding, she heard me read "Ruins, Mounting toward Jerusalem" at the New York Academy of Sciences. Afterward, in response to my implicit claim in the paper that ruins *always* entail loss and destruction, she asked me how I would respond to the Nabatean ruins. She herself, as she told me, does not respond to them as a site of loss; rather she admires the people who knew how to live in that environment thousands of years ago.

• 6/24/91 •

A detail from my brief stay in Tel Aviv last week: at Gil's[23] office there's a big poster (which he probably put up) which reads, *"Sovlanut ba'ad artseynu,"* "Tolerance for the sake of our country," which is a parody of Trumpeldor's supposed famous last words, *"Tov lamut ba'ad artseynu,"* "It is good to die for our country."[24] I think this is part of a campaign mounted several years ago, with bumper stickers, an office apparatus, and so on. A good bit of wit, certainly, but troubling as well: the word *sovlanut*, like "tolerance," implies putting up with something unpleasant — suggesting that quietly accepting the proximity of people who are different is a sacrifice you have to make for the good of the country. And if it's for "the country," then how far do the limits of tolerance extend? Anyway, the idea seems an imposed "Western" one to begin with. Who would it really speak to except "European" or "Anglo-Saxon" Jews (with the further, perhaps unintended, implication that they're the ones who have to be tolerant of everybody else)? It seems clear that some other model of coexistence needs to be put into play.

Incidentally, Gil says that the man from the Ministry of Transportation who developed the *chatima lechayim*[25] campaign — whom Tsvi Ben-Zev, whose wife is his administrative assistant, described as a very nice guy — is a "fascist."[26] Gil tells me he is also (assuming we're talking about the same person here) the boss of Gingy Stein, another Yesh Gvulnik who came on a speaking tour to the United States this year, and whom I hope to see soon.

Back at Qetura, a lackluster pool party — warm beer, few swimmers, music coming out of only one speaker. I told one of Randi's friends I was doing fieldwork in "Israel and Palestine." She asked me, a bit sharply, to define my terms, and I told her I meant pre-1967 Israel, on one hand, and the Occupied Territories, on the other. She calmed down, saying, "Those words can mean

---

23. Gil Cohen, one of the founders of the Yesh Gvul organization. Yesh Gvul, originally established as a support group for Israeli soldiers who refused service during the Lebanon invasion in 1982, now supports Israeli soldiers who refuse to serve in the Occupied Territories. Gil became a friend of ours when he was studying at the Graduate Faculty of the New School for Social Research in New York.

24. Joseph Trumpeldor is one of the legendary heroes of the Zionist pioneering era. In an exemplary analysis of the way the legend of Trumpeldor's death in defense of the Tel Hai settlement has focused Israeli political discourse, Yael Zerubavel points out that it had regained currency as a reference in the debate over the return of the Sinai to Egypt (Zerubavel 1991).

25. The "signature for life," discussed earlier.

26. The syntax is awkward here, of course: Gil described this official as a fascist; Tsvi Ben-Zev described him as a very nice guy. I placed Gil's opinion in quotes without thinking about it, but presumably to distance myself from it. Possibly Tsvi's more positive judgment had to do not only with the fact that he knows the man personally but also with his being an anthropologist, hence more likely to "correct" his personal judgments of various persons by filtering out beforehand his own religious, cultural, or political tendencies.

a lot of things, you know," but I can't imagine what else they could mean in combination.

Randi was free until 3:00 on Sunday, and after ascertaining that one of the vehicles belonging to the kibbutz was free, she took me on a little tour, including the Nabatean site mentioned above. From that site — more or less equidistant from the heights on both sides — I could see through the binoculars the set of fences marking the Jordanian border, close to the mountains on the other side — not running down the middle of the Arava, that is. The border is loosely patrolled from this side, and the fences aren't even that well maintained, and the renegade Jordanian soldiers who sometimes infiltrate [generally] do so further north. Halfway up one of the mountains not far from Qetura there's a prison — presumably the authorities figured prisoners would think twice before trying to escape, either over the mountain or across the fence into Israel.

Nor does anyone from the Israeli side particularly want to be caught on the wrong side of the border, but sometimes it happens. Every year there are flash floods in the Arava, some more severe than others. The dips in the Arava highway have poles with red markers next to them, to show drivers trying to get through how deep the water is at a particular spot. The rain may last for two hours, the flood for six — sometimes starting as a trickle, sometimes rolling down the valley in a single wave. Two years ago Randi's friend Shel and another fellow from Qetura rode kayaks down to Grofit.[27] This year they tried windsurfing. Their boards almost immediately got away from them, and haven't been seen since. Shel was eventually able to stand on the Jordan side of the flood. Friends drove back and forth, keeping even with him, looking for a place where he could get across, but every time he entered the water the current was too strong. Eventually he made it back to the Israeli side without being shot. [Fn. 11/7: I really like that paragraph; it sounds like something John McPhee would write, with the combination of anecdote, geology, and politics.]

Randi went to work at 3:30, I worked on the journal entry dated yesterday, and then I walked over to the dairy area to say goodbye to her. She was driving a huge tractor, and she had me climb up in the cab with her while she fetched a bale of oats, then drove me down to the road to catch my bus back to Jerusalem. One red Egged bus drove by while we approached, but she assured me it couldn't be mine. Three minutes later we reached the bus stop, and my bus almost immediately pulled up.

The bus — like all Egged buses, a Mercedes — roars up the Arava and

---

27. The next kibbutz down the valley. The residential and other buildings of Grofit are spectacularly located on a small mesa above the valley floor.

along the Dead Sea toward Jerusalem. Just before En-Gedi, I noticed the driver bouncing up and down in his seat, and reflected that he was zipping along nicely. He slowed down a bit just then — I thought because another bus was approaching from the other side. Then I noticed in a flash a car just in front of us, trying to pass the other bus; as soon as I noticed it the driver of the car had pulled around to the right of our bus — fortunately at this point there was a shoulder rather than an embankment. I couldn't see in back, but apparently the car was undamaged, and the bus continued without stopping. A split second separated this paragraph from a fatal accident.[?]

(5:30 P.M. — finally cool enough to walk on the hottest and stickiest day since I've been in Jerusalem. The whole park around Yemin Moshe is still filled with Arab families. Kids are climbing on Max Bill's sculpture, "Four cubes cut into halves which make eight elements, 1973–1985." They seem very unself-conscious, hardly asserting their rights to "Jewish territory." Across a small parking lot, half a dozen soldiers in off-white uniforms — what unit?[28] — consulting maps outside the French consulate, looking like they're on a treasure hunt.

(Wandering around French Hill, trying to find Stan and Debbie Greenberg's[29] house — they're going to the States and I have a little mail for them to bring. Next to the supermarket, an incredible view of the hills leading, I think, down toward the Dead Sea — perhaps the road I came back in on last night. The Arab houses in the villages — one might be Isawiya — on the hills just a bit lower than this one look similar to the "villas" on the side of this hill — being the same size and covered with the same stone — and yet entirely different, being spread out in no symmetric pattern while these are close together, and without green while these have trees. French Hill, I remind myself, is over the Green Line.

(The Greenbergs live in Mavo Hama'avak, which Debbie translates for me as Struggle Alley. On the street sign there's an explanation, in Hebrew, saying that it's named after the struggle of the Jewish population against British mandatory rule. The sign in English just says, "HaMa'avak Ally" [sic].)

• 6/25/91 •

(My descriptions of Jerusalem so far make New Jerusalem [that seems a quaint term by now as well] seem almost entirely well-off and "Anglo-Saxon" — that's, incredibly enough, the term they use here for Jews from English-speaking countries. By that logic, they should call Jews from German-speaking

---

28. Probably they weren't Israeli soldiers at all.
29. Stan is a senior member of the Department of Sociology and Anthropology at Hebrew University.

countries "Aryan Jews." Anyway, there are of course substantial portions of the city which are either Ashkenazi-religious, "Sephardi," or both mixed together. I walked through one of the latter yesterday — the area along Shmuel Hanavi, down from Ramat Eshkol toward Geulah and Sheikh Jara. Nothing especially interesting to report, unfortunately.)

To finish my Qetura notes: the last half-hour or so of the trip is the climb toward Jerusalem from the northern end of the Dead Sea. It was near dark by this time, so all I could see was the lights from the settlements around Maalei Adumim, which certainly seem to have grown a lot since the last time I rode past them, three years ago. I hadn't realized how close they are to "Jerusalem" — or I should say to French Hill, the edge of the Jewish city of Jerusalem. Yesterday I saw the bus ads for Maalei Adumim again, and realized that the word *mitsape* — "looking out" — also meant that the settlement is a *mitspe*, a "lookout."[30] So the campaign is combining the cachet of Zionist pioneering and defense with the secular welcome of a new community. They're having an open house from Sunday, July 7, through Tuesday — I probably should try to figure out a way to get there. [Fn. 11/7: should have, but didn't after all.]

On Saturday at Qetura, I spent a few minutes reading the very end and beginning of *Fieldnotes* — partly unwilling to read more because I couldn't take notes on it then, partly afraid that it will already know things I think I'm discovering all by myself. It's dedicated "to the next generation of ethnographers." I don't know whether that includes me — I'm not in the same "generation" as Roger,[31] who's been teaching since before I started college, but I've already done some ethnography of my own. Makes me feel a bit stuck in between. And the end of the book — reaffirming fieldnotes as the material *from which* ethnographies are made, invoking several classics from "the classic age" (Kearney 1991) as models, and reaffirming that the people ethnographers write about are more "interesting" than ethnographers — confirms my suspicion that my plan to publish *this* is still somewhat radical.

Finally, as to my space-time dynamics vis-à-vis Qetura — I'd say that space is overwhelmingly important to what in fact works as a strong collective identity for the people there, and that it is not, however, "sacred space." To Randi it is an ecology with which she is identified, that she has made herself part of — and her fascination with the Nabateans is not because she sees in them "ancestors," but because she sees them as a model of a people who know how to live in this landscape. To the people at Qetura, the fact of living together seems most important — after that I couldn't say whether living in Israel or

---

30. A bus ad campaign for a three-day "residence fair" in this large West Bank suburb had featured the slogan, *"Maalei Adumim metsape lekha,"* "Maalei Adumim is looking (or looking out) for you."

31. Sanjek, the editor of the volume.

living in the desert is more important. But if Randi had to leave Qetura and live in Jerusalem instead, she would certainly grieve.

My brother Dan called at 6:00 this morning from Berkeley, and we commiserated about being away from our families. I told him about how it comforts me to watch the progress of the moon, and he told me about the midrash which speaks of Adam's anxiety as he watched the sun go down the first day of his life, thinking that the world was about to end.[32] Now *that's* anthropology!

• 6/26/91 •

The Shalom Hartman Institute, in Emek Refaim. Shoshana Even, my brother's former student who lives in a settlement called Tekoa and has invited me there, is in the next room, the library, sorting out over a thousand of my brother's books, which she has rescued from a wet cellar and is now cataloguing so that they won't disappear here. He doesn't even know she has done this, and she is well aware that she's doing him a big favor. "Students better than children," she says, paraphrasing a rabbinic saying. "You see what a student will do for you? Get yourself some students." I assure her that I'd like to, if only someone would make me a teacher first.

Back to yesterday. Yesterday was a good time for my new glasses to have arrived, because I got a chance to try them out on some amazing landscapes I had never seen.[33] I followed up Efraim's invitation to go with Avner to visit him at his *he'achzut*[34] just south of Bet Shean.

Avner at seventeen has plenty of interesting things to tell me, and wanted to understand better what sort of things I'm interested in. I gave him the example of the Arab families at the bathing fountain.[35] He told me that Arab kids often come to the Liberty Bell Garden, and that the night before when he played basketball there, two Arab kids had been part of the game. "They were a bit nervous, but they weren't really afraid to be playing with us, and nobody said anything or called them any names." I said that basketball is a

---

32. "When Adam the First Person saw the day diminishing and departing, he said 'Woe is me, perhaps because of my sin the world has darkened on my account and is returning to the void, and this is my death, a punishment upon me from Heaven!'" (Babylonian Talmud, Avoda Zara 8A).

33. It was also a good time for my glasses to have arrived so that I could employ the trope of ethnographic perspective or vision here: "progress" in fieldwork is well captured in the image of a scene coming into focus, details taking on their own identity and forming more and more coherent patterns among themselves. See "Ruins, Mounting toward Jerusalem."

34. An army settlement, historically regarded as the forerunner to a new kibbutz.

35. Yemin Moshe and the park above it are extremely close to several Arab neighborhoods. The park, and during the summer in particular the fountain (which is not, in fact, properly a bathing fountain), were very much used by Arab families during the summer I was there.

democratic game — even at the park near my parents' house in a basically segregated suburb of New Jersey, there are mixed black and white basketball games. Avner wasn't so sure: he remembers that when he was younger, visiting during summers, and used to play there, he was called "Jewboy" because of his yarmulke. The place where he really feels comfortable with the mix of people is the schoolyard next to our apartment building in New York, where "white," Latino, black, Bangladeshi, Chinese, Guatemalan kids all play.[36]

•

We got on the bus from the Central Bus Station, and it headed out back the same way I'd returned from Qetura, due east from Jerusalem to the top of the Dead Sea rather than south as I'd imagined. Avner told me that recently there'd been a plan to put the main cemetery for all of Jerusalem outside Maalei Adumim, but it had been quashed because the government won't allow cemeteries inside areas that aren't officially Israel. An interesting technicality: because cemeteries are permanent,[37] in a way that Shamir's declarations (in a headline here yesterday) that "Judah, Samaria and Gaza are an inseparable part of the Land of Israel" aren't, there remains at least this area of life (that is, death) in which the territories haven't been integrated into the Jewish state.

For the first of the many times I've come down the hills this way, the bus turns left toward Jericho rather than right toward the Dead Sea, and in a few minutes we're actually driving through the Palestinian town of Jericho — which is a lovely place, large, spread out, with substantial-looking and fairly new houses, with date palms scattered around and various orchards, including bananas, interspersed among the bananas right up to the main road. Just outside of town there's a cluster of poor small houses with no green among them at all; on the way back I caught the sign that said, "En Sultan refugee camp." Just outside of town the desert begins again. Then there's another, smaller, but still reasonably prosperous-looking Palestinian town with its fields laid out in modern symmetrical style. Then there are several kilometers of evidently Jewish agriculture, until the road climbs into the hills above the Jordan Valley. Avner pointed out the border[38] to me, but I didn't see it at first because I

---

36. The value of coexistence underlying my account is rooted not only in a vague American liberalism but in personal experiences. The sickness I feel at being associated with a bullying dominant ethnic group in Israel is rooted in the sickness I felt when I was bullied as a preadolescent recently arrived at that segregated suburb.

37. By Jewish law, that is, gravesites are not to be disturbed. This has been the proximate cause of many famous conflicts between traditionalist Jews and archaeologists in Israel — as between Native Americans and archaeologists or physical anthropologists in North America.

38. Not the actual border between Jordan and the occupied West Bank, which is the Jordan River. This fence, however, marks a "border" in the sense of a limit beyond which civilians without particular business are forbidden to pass, although some of the settlements

was looking too far away; starting north of Jericho, it hugs the road just a few meters to the east, and the entire Jordan Valley in this area belongs to Jordan. The Jordan side looks well farmed, green, and fairly densely populated.

We get off the bus at a place called Mechola, which turns out to be a religious moshav, with considerable fields including dates, grapes, and I don't know what else. We talk for a few minutes with the three middle-aged reservists guarding the entrance to the residential part of the moshav. One of them asks me a question I don't catch even the third time he asks me — "So how are the Israelis, good or bad?" Before I walked up, Avner had told them I was doing research on the Israelis. They're thrilled to see us, bored out of their minds, ask us if we want cold drinks or hot. Before we say goodbye to them, one of them says, "Yonatan, you should stay here. Call your wife and tell her to come."[39]

Then we spend an hour at the *pundak*, the roadside refreshment stand, waiting for a car from the *he'achzut* to pick us up. A few buses pull in at the *pundak* for a rest stop — a tour bus of older women (Avner says they're Moroccan), another one full of young yeshiva guys all in navy pants and white or light-blue shirts. Palestinians go by with a small herd of cows, a larger herd of mixed sheep and goats; it seems there's a Palestinian village right next to the lands of the moshav. A couple of young Palestinian men sit at another picnic table outside the *pundak*, without buying anything.

I remark to Avner that after seeing all this new Jewish agriculture, it's hard to imagine Israel giving up the territories. He agrees, and we review the options: giving up the territories and the establishment of a Palestinian state; absorption of the territories and the redefinition of the state, so that it's no longer a Jewish state; apartheid; another war.[40]

Eventually the folks from the *he'achzut* come down to get us — five of them as it turns out, apparently coming down just for the chance to pick something up (felafel, cigarettes) at the *pundak* and see who else might be there. We drive back into the hills and turn off onto the small road that leads up the hill to the *he'achzut*. There's a large herd of goats with two young goatherds on the hill — my reaction, unarticulated even to myself, is "how picturesque."

---

in the region as well as Efraim's *he'achzut* had planted date palms on the other side. Certain areas east of the fence are mined, and a pathway runs along it that is patrolled once an hour and checked for footprints in the sand.

39. It would be worthwhile comparing the experiences of various ethnographers who have done fieldwork in a place where the "natives" insistently want you to become one of them. The sense of instant camaraderie and acceptance here was particularly dramatic to me because it contrasted so sharply with my awkward awareness of my lack of fluency in Hebrew.

40. Several months after the Israel-PLO agreement of September 1993, these still seem to be the options. It remains unclear what the outcome will be. It might well be misleading to think in terms of some eventual stable "outcome" altogether.

The driver stops, calls the goatherd over, and speaks to him in Arabic: "You have to get the flock out of here. You can't graze them here. Where are you from?" The goatherd, scared, gestures vaguely behind himself. "Where?" "En Hilwa," the kid says, reluctant. "Take them back down the hill!" And that's the end of the incident, everyone in the car — me included — impressed with the driver's Arabic, and I and, I presume, the goatherd as well, relieved that it had been that innocuous. "Did you see how scared that guy was?" Avner asks me later. "He knows he's not supposed to bring the goats there — it's too close to the *he'achzut*." But I wasn't thinking about that — I was thinking how resentful I would be, unarmed, watching my goats eat grass that nobody else wants, facing a carload of armed soldiers who are maybe two years older than me and a hell of a lot bigger. Maybe he isn't resentful; maybe it's just normal for him; maybe it would be for me too.

At the hilltop we quickly find Efraim, and he and Avner greet each other with the "*Ahlan!*"[41] that seems to be hip Israeli slang here. Efraim leads us to his room, turns on the stereo, and the comforting sounds of Lou Reed's *Transformer* come on. It's a quick tour around the place; what's remarkable about it is the site itself, at the top of a bare hillside with a valley before it and even bigger hills behind it, and with a strong wind constantly blowing. The atmosphere of the place is a strange (to me) mix of military discipline and frontier-communal freedom; in fact there are currently twenty-four young women serving there and twenty young men. Outside one of the living quarters someone has posted a sign saying in Hebrew, "Soon to be established here — a nude beach, under the supervision of Rabbi Shach."[42] Definitely this is not a religious settlement.

At the bottom of the hill there are a few fields in the stony soil; they have no crops right now, and if Efraim hadn't pointed them out I wouldn't have quite noticed them. There is a chicken coop, which Efraim is in charge of. I guess there are 300 chickens, but Efraim corrects me: 870. So much for my powers of estimation. Efraim tells "a bit of a sad story: the day before yesterday an Arab came up with a truck and a couple of helpers to buy 300 chickens for their holiday, their *khag ha-kurban*."[43] (I'll ask Riad more about it — I remain utterly ignorant about Islam.) "They wanted the chickens even though they're still immature. So we were loading them five by five, counting as we went. Then I saw that the Arabs were loading them seven by seven. I told our commander, and he said, 'Don't worry, I'm telling them to load them

---

41. The standard short-form informal Arabic greeting.
42. Rabbi Eliezer Shach, in his nineties at the time of this writing, is the head of the Lithuanian-style Orthodox Ponevezh Yeshiva and the titular leader of one of the non-Zionist Orthodox political factions in Israel.
43. *Id ul-daha*; see entry for July 24.

eight by eight, and I'm counting them ten by ten.' " Why did Efraim think this was a sad story? After all, it's the kind of story anthropologists love. The implications of Efraim's thinking it's sad (I could have asked him why, and I should have) are (*a*) that Arabs persist in sharp dealing, and therefore increase the derogatory feelings of Jews toward them; or (*b*) that Jews and Arabs here don't trust each other enough to do business straightforwardly.[44] Is he being naive in assuming that "Western" businesslike relations are the way things should be, or am I romanticizing "traditional" ways of dealing? What would Clifford Geertz say?[45]

On the bus coming back to Jerusalem the same way we came, I get nervous as the driver turns off to the right, further into "Samaria," on a road marked "to Shechem." But he only goes in a couple of kilometers, past another poor village and farmlands that look more prosperous than the village does, up to the gates of a well-fenced Jewish settlement called something like Nachlat Arye. So this is where the Jews who have agricultural lands down in the valley live, I think — back here toward the hills, but very close to Palestinians. And I wonder who does all the work in the Jewish farmlands — some is done by Jews themselves, of course, but isn't this the region where, as I read last week, three Thai laborers had been stabbed by a Palestinian? The driver is in a hurry — he complained to Avner that I hadn't run fast enough to get on, and he complains to a soldier who gets on at a stop in the middle of nowhere, "Climb up already — what are you, sleeping?" So when he raced through Jericho coming back, was it for fear of another Molotov cocktail or just his usual impatience?

•

Back in Yemin Moshe, I reach Ahmed Abu Saleh at In'ash el-Usra, and we make tentative plans for me to come to Ramallah and meet some people from Bir Zeit next week. I had mentioned to him that I'd like to meet Um Sabri, the director of In'ash el-Usra and the aunt of a Palestinian activist friend of ours from New York, Samiha Abdel-Kadir. He suggests that I call her directly, and mention the family connection: he could introduce me to Um Sabri and mention Samiha, "but then she might wonder why you didn't mention it yourself." So when our plans for next week are firm, I'll call her. Meanwhile Ahmed tells me that I can take the taxi from Jerusalem to Ramallah for two shekels, and for a shekel or two more,[46] the driver will let me off

---

44. Asked in February 1994 why he thought it was sad, and without prompting on my part, Efraim gave me reason (*b*) only.

45. Never mind what Clifford Geertz would say. The answer to this question lies below, in the journal entry for August 13.

46. In the summer of 1991 the exchange rate was roughly two and a half shekels to the dollar.

right in front of In'ash el-Usra: "Everybody knows where it is, and people are used to seeing visitors here."

•

On the grounds here[47] I meet Elias, the Palestinian caretaker. (So I will have to be careful to write Palestinian rather than Arab: as soon as I'm considering someone whom I acknowledge by name, as here, it becomes unthinkable for me to call him an "Arab."[48] I must then make the effort to extend the name to those I don't know personally.) I try out my Arabic: *"Masa elheer,"* "Good morning." Wrong: he corrects me, *"Saba elheer."* I should know better. My brother has sent him regards. Earlier in the intifada, Elias saw my brother on Jordanian television: during the tax strike at Bet Sahur, my brother had been part of a convoy of Israeli peaceniks who set off on a solidarity visit to the town. Everyone was turned away except for the one carload of religious Jews, presumably because the army thought they were settlers and had "legitimate business" there. People from Bet Sahur managed to come out of the blockaded town and pass a message from the people of the town to the "peace-loving people in Israel." It is an utterly eloquent statement.[49] Jordanian television was there, and my brother stood up on a large rock and read the statement out loud, and that same evening it was broadcast. For weeks Palestinians were stopping my brother in the street and saying, "Hey, I saw you on TV!"

---

47. At the Hartman Institute, where for most of my stay I used the office that my brother uses when he's in Israel. Toward the end of my stay the new internal phone list at the institute was printed, with two entries saying "Boyarin, Daniel," and "Boyarin's brother."

48. This, because "Arab" as used by Israelis and by Westerners often implies a refusal to accept the distinctive Palestinian identity, dissolving it into an undifferentiated mass of interchangeable "Arabs." Palestinians may well refer to themselves at times as Arabs without such ambivalence.

49. The statement, in part, reads: "To the peace forces of Israel, greetings from the people of Beit Sahour: All the town knows of your visit today, though we cannot host you there as we have in the past. But many of you know Beit Sahour as a safe and welcoming place, where any Israeli who comes as a visitor and not an occupier can sleep and pray and break bread. Now in Beit Sahour checkpoints and rooftop patrols and curfews prevail. No new food supplies reach us; we are under economic siege. The confiscation, which has reached 120 shops, factories and houses, is accompanied by beatings, humiliation, looting and damage to the goods. We challenge the laws that permit brutality and collective punishment for the purpose of collecting taxes; that permit seizure of 10 times the claimed amount. But nothing that is done to us will stop us from talking peace.... Peace and coexistence is our message. We have repeated it often: peace in Palestine and Israel, each free and secure. Our tax resistance campaign is part of our protest against occupation and our commitment to a national Palestinian identity.... The way to peace is to recognize the existence of the Palestinian nation on this land and its legitimate rights to self-determination and its own choice of representatives. We want no more than what you have: freedom and our own representatives to pay taxes to. The Palestinians throughout more than 40 years of homelessness and suffering have proved that they are strong enough not to be removed from this land. The Palestinians also, like all peoples, long for peace. It is up to you to ask your fellow Israelis to decide when they will realize these incontrovertible facts."

So the first thing Elias asked me was whether I shared by brother's views on politics. I told him I did, except that my brother calls himself an anti-Zionist and I don't. But I did say that I think it's simply unacceptable to have a state with a privileged class of citizens and an underprivileged class, and we agreed that the Israelis are trying to get the Palestinians out altogether. "My father is from Ein Kerem,"[50] Elias told me. "We had a house there; we were very wealthy. When the war came, we fled, but my father stayed nearby to watch our fields and house. He was found by Israeli soldiers, shot, and put in jail for a year. Then they told him he could stay and work for them or he could leave. He's a simple man, not political. He left to find his family, and he found his wife and three children in Bethlehem. We've been there ever since. He lost so much — well, there's a war, so you lose what you have for five years, ten years — but look at what his children have lost, his grandchildren...." Elias still lives in Bethlehem. He invites me to visit, assures me there's no danger. I certainly will! He also points to the corner of the garden, where he has a barbecue, and invites me to have supper with him some evening.

The institute is housed in what I presume is an old Arab house (although not necessarily: some of the houses I would think were owned by Arabs before 1948 are part of the old "German colony" in this neighborhood).[51] I'd like to find out from Elias or someone else whether there's someone around who can give me a tour of the neighborhood and describe who lived here (or especially not so much here as in Baka) before 1948.

3:00. Just met with Howard Kaufman, an anthropologist at Hebrew University who — sometimes with his wife, Rachel Shalev-Kaufman, a sociologist — works on symbols of Israeli nationalism. I asked Howard whether anyone in the department had ever done work on Palestinians on the other side of the Green Line, and whether anyone seems to do work framed as ethnography of the Israeli-Palestinian cultural intersystem. Yes, to the first question; there had been someone in the department who worked on the structure of the Palestinian families in East Jerusalem. No, to the second. Most Israeli anthropologists still work on Edot Hamizrach;[52] most anthropologists working on Palestinians outside Israel don't want to have anything to do with Israeli scholars or scholarship. Howard says the Israel Anthropological Association has sometimes invited people from Bir Zeit to participate, and on a few oc-

---

50. Formerly a Palestinian village to the west of Jerusalem, Ein Kerem has now been incorporated into Jerusalem as an artists' colony and tourist center. One of the campuses of Hadassah Hospital is also at Ein Kerem.

51. The area was once largely populated by German Christians. Similarly, another small section nearby is still sometimes referred to as Moshava Yavanit, the Greek Colony. The American Colony Hotel on the other side of the Old City is named for what was once a neighborhood of American expatriates.

52. "Eastern" or "Sephardic" Jews, those from the Middle East and North Africa.

casions received acceptances, but they never actually made it. Howard has never met Riad Ghanem, and didn't know about his memorial book project.[53] (On the other hand, Bir Zeit doesn't want to touch Ahmed Abu Saleh's project — they don't want to be caught granting scholarly attention to Israel and Jews. The idea seems to be that accepting something as a legitimate topic for research is tantamount to granting it political legitimacy — an idea that echoes the debates about "political correctness" and "diversity" in America. Furthermore, there are an infinite number of roadblocks).

Howard said that he hasn't been in most of the West Bank for twenty years, and hasn't been in East Jerusalem since before the intifada began. The Jewish Quarter of the Old City seems to him to be an "abomination," and any Muslim or Christian coffeehouse is simply fraught with too many tensions and contradictions. When I mentioned Qetura and the deep identification of the people there with that particular place, even though it wasn't a historical or theological identification, he challenged me: "Don't you think they could develop the same attachment to the Negev?" — because, it turned out, he thought I was talking about an area across the Green Line. I had just before mentioned my trip to the Beit Shean Valley yesterday, and my feeling that it was hard to imagine Jewish settlers leaving there. He seemed reluctant to concede my impression of that deep attachment as long as he thought I was talking about an area across the Green Line.[54] He also mentioned that it was interesting that people in that region have never established graveyards,[55] which he interprets as a sign that they're not sure they're there permanently — but now I can't remember whether he was referring to the Arava or the area across the Green Line around the Dead Sea!

The sharpest anthropological critic of Israeli national symbolism doesn't know the Palestinian anthropologists, and they don't know him (although Riad and Chagit Katzev-Haft do know each other). On both sides there are

---

53. See the entry for July 1, immediately below.

54. The part of the Beit Shean Valley I had been to — the area around Mechola and Efraim's *he'achzut* — was across the Green Line, but the northern part of the valley is within pre-1967 Israel. Even though my project in this book is the explicit interrogation of notions of historical and territorial legitimacy, my account may also be colored by a tendency to take it as given that Jewish Israeli presence within the Green Line is legitimate, and anything on the other side illegitimate. Note above, in my entry for June 24, that when I was challenged by a resident of Qetura on the use of my terms "Israel and Palestine," I responded that I meant pre-1967 Israel, on one hand, and the Occupied Territories, on the other. Again, my enthusiasm for Qetura has partly to do with its character as a pioneering settlement "within Israel."

55. Evidently responding to a point that I had made (see above). Actually, although as stated above the Israeli government has not established graveyards in the Occupied Territories, settlers have established their own graveyards in their settlements. On the involvement of the state in cemetery practices elsewhere, see the chapter on mourning in my *Polish Jews in Paris* (Boyarin 1991a).

substantial reasons for this gulf. I'm in a position to have contacts on both "sides," even if my knowledge remains haphazard.[56] So I came away thinking that even if I can't do it thoroughly, it's worthwhile for me even to be raising the idea of an ethnography of Israel and Palestine.

• 6/28/91 •

I'll leave Emek Refaim in a few minutes for the American Colony, where Riad is picking me up at 4:00. This time I'm actually looking forward to being there, and I'll try to get there a bit early, sit and have a drink while I'm waiting. Ruth — dedicated to all the variety of folklore, local produce, and wild edible plants available — tells me, "If Riad offers you olive oil or anything else, take it!" She also tells me that a student of hers who happened to be visiting when I stopped by her place the other day was shocked to hear me casually discussing plans to go to East Jerusalem, even though I insist I'm not the macho, danger-loving kind of anthropologist.

• 7/1/91 •

After a fascinating, warm, and safe weekend in Riad's home village of Ar'ara, I'm nervous about writing up my notes: How rich is my memory really? How could my record possibly be adequate to my impressions?

Riad picked me up at the American Colony in a ten-year-old Mercedes, which, he later told me, had formerly served as a taxi. His sister-in-law, a woman wearing a Palestinian dress who didn't speak English, was in the front seat next to him, coming back from a visit in Ramallah. He explained to me that we were going to take a "scenic route" — the Allon Road along the less-inhabited heights of the West Bank, which marks the boundaries of the lands Israel would have kept according to the Allon Plan. Part of the reason that Riad wanted to take this road, rather than the straighter road down in the Jordan Valley, was that his car has Israeli plates, and is thus subject to stoning. Riad mentioned that he had taken that road the previous week, and I think he avoided it partly because he didn't want to expose me to any risk.

To get to the Allon Road, Riad drives out of East Jerusalem along Shmuel Hanagid, the road that goes out below French Hill. Coming this way, it seems much closer from the center of the city to the new Hyatt on French Hill

---

56. Perhaps marginal people are more inclined to see the "other" point of view because they are never fully at home with their own nominal collective identity. Again, insofar as I am doing Palestinian ethnography at all in this book, it is through an effort to imagine an internalized representation of that history based more on the fragments I "know" of that history and on my reactions *in situ* than on "oral history" or a synthesis of written accounts.

than when one goes around through the Jewish quarters on the heights. Then out past French Hill, past extensive Arab neighborhoods. I said to Riad that I had no idea East Jerusalem was this big, and he reminded me that most of it wasn't technically East Jerusalem at all, but a series of villages which had grown together but were still referred to by their separate names — Beit Hanina, and so on. What struck me, of course, was simply the existence of so many thousands of people living a short walk away from the roads I had ridden on dozens of times without ever imagining their presence — merely wondering whether the few houses visible from the bus leading to Mount Scopus were in fact Arab houses.

The landscape the Allon Road passes through, heading north by northeast, is quite different from the utterly bare hills the road to Jericho and the Dead Sea travels through. These hills are dry, but they have soil, not just rock. Some of the hills have small Palestinian villages on top of them, usually at some distance from the road. Occasionally there are small plowed fields on a patch of relatively flat ground near the road, or a small olive grove, or a flock of goats or sheep passing by; to me, such agriculture in an unwelcoming landscape has always been extremely moving.

I ask Riad whether any of the refugees from 1948 might have moved to villages such as these. He corrects me: no, the poorer ones went to refugee camps, and the wealthier ones either left Palestine entirely or found places in the larger towns. Gradually, he says, people are also leaving the refugee camps as they are able to afford to.

One of the villages we pass by is Mikhmas. Riad mentions that on the three road signs at various places mentioning this village, its name in Arabic is misspelled three different ways — largely because of the difference in Arabic between the aspirated *h* and the soft *kh*, a difference which doesn't exist in Hebrew and therefore confused Israelis. This leads him to the topic of the undercover Israeli army squads in the territories which have been pretending to be *shebaab*:[57] one can often tell when they're the ones who have written Hamas slogans on walls, because they spell it as "Khamas." More important, Riad is convinced that they are responsible for some of the killings of "collaborators" — a charge that is plausible but hard to prove or disprove, since such killings are always carried out by young men with their faces masked.[58]

Eventually the road begins to pass by a few Jewish settlements, includ-

---

57. The Palestinian youth who have been the main "troops" of the intifada.
58. Riad was right, as subsequently documented: "In order to conceal their identity, soldiers in the undercover units use diverse disguises (traditional Arab clothing, 'uniforms' of the various masked groups...)" (Yashuvi 1992: 13). See the brush with Israeli soldiers related by Elias, the caretaker at the Shalom Hartman Institute, contained in my journal entry for the evening of July 18.

ing Maaleh Efraim and Gitit. Both of them are agricultural settlements. Riad gives me clues to determining whether a particular patch of farmland is Palestinian or Jewish: first, Jewish farmland is irrigated, Palestinian land is not; and second, in the relatively rare situations where Palestinians have retained substantial fields on flat land, their fields are broken into small strips marked off by rows of stones, which show how land has been divided among successive generations of brothers. (Again the notion that the Jewish/Zionist ethos of collectivity and collective ownership of and belonging to the entire country, as contrasted with Palestinian familialism and localism, was an important factor in relative ability to mobilize effectively in the struggle over the land.)

Eventually we passed through a place called Jiftlik (the name is Turkish), a green oasis, stunning and unexpected in that landscape, with a small stream running through it, though as far as I could tell not much of a village relative to the amount of water available. Here the Allon Road ends, and Riad turned right, following the road that leads out of the hills back to Mechola. We passed a few more Jewish settlements — Beqa'ot and Ro'i — both utilizing a respectable amount of decent farmland, which Riad said he assumes was confiscated; it is hard to imagine this land was uncultivated before the Jewish settlers arrived.[59] Then we went past an army base — presumably the command center for my nephew Efraim's *he'achzut*, and hence the place where his case to be released to travel to the United States will have to be pleaded (today is just about the deadline for getting the decision reversed).[60]

•

Turning off the road to Safed, we drive through the mountains past Arab "villages" whose size surprises me: 'Eilabun, and then Riad's village of Ar'ara, which Riad tells me has thirteen or fourteen thousand people, although my *Carta's Official Guide*, edition 1986, says there are only eight thousand. (The *Guide* is also out of date in its discussions of some Jewish settlements; it says

---

59. Hard for whom to imagine? Presumably it would not be hard, even today, for many Zionists to imagine this was "barren land" before the Jewish settlers arrived! The notion of Jews settling empty land as part of the Zionist project continues to be reproduced in mass journalism. An article by Clyde Haberman in the *New York Times* of November 7, 1993, describes the sacrifices Israeli settlers on the Golan would have to make if the land were ceded back to Syria — primarily the sacrifice of successful vineyards. The text of the article is utterly silent about anyone or anything except "Syria" that might have an interest in the Israelis leaving the Golan. The photograph accompanying the article shows "workers" tending grapevines. The workers are evidently local Druze women, but how many readers of the *Times* would realize that?

60. Israeli Defense Force soldiers whose parents have been abroad for at least six months are entitled to a brief leave abroad once during their tour of duty, which usually lasts three years. In this case, there was some question as to whether Daniel had in fact been away from Israel for a full six months.

that Kibbutz Gezer is still occupied only by temporary "caretaker" groups, whereas Elissa and I have friends who've been living there permanently for about ten years now.) The *Guide* is entirely unhelpful regarding the history of Ar'ara as an Arab town, simply telling me that it is one and then proceeding for a paragraph about its ancient Jewish history; it was the home of Rabbi Jochanan ben Zakkai and Rabbi Hanina ben Dosi, two of the prominent figures of the Talmud. Riad isn't sure how long Arab Ar'ara has been around, either, but the Ghanem "clan" — whom he estimates now number at least three thousand — trace themselves back six or seven generations to a common ancestor who lived in the town.

We reach Ar'ara close to 7:00, about half an hour before Shabbat begins. I spend a pleasant and quiet Shabbat within the charmed confines of the Ghanems' house and garden, eating a kosher steak which Riad's American wife, Marilyn, has gone out of her way to find for me, and which I am both too gracious and too greedy to refuse, even though the "three weeks" have already begun,[61] and on Saturday night I note down several keynotes for writing up today, in no particular order.

I noticed a book sitting on the kitchen table: *Roots of Peace,* by Dr. Joseph Levy (check?), with a foreword by the minister of education, Zevulun Hammer of the National Religious Party. It's a collection of short portraits of admirable individuals who live in the Galilee area, and is intended as a supplementary reader for high school English students. The first story is about a boy named Yossi in Kiryat Shemona: his good deed is to run around his town after school, bringing good news about the health and safety of soldiers from the town fighting in "Operation Peace in the Galilee." He goes to a certain family, and there's a three-year-old girl there along with her mother, who gives him an eraser as a present in thanks for the good news he's brought about her father. I paraphrase: "Yossi understood that the gift was highly symbolic. It stood for the men who were doing their best to erase the enemy." Yossi understands that the war is for the safety of the people in the Galilee: "Now they could celebrate freely just like people in Herzlia and Tel Aviv." And he feels a sudden rush of camaraderie with all of his people, "as if the whole country were one large army." Now these struck me as contradictory statements: on the one hand, there's the claim to have increased the security of the border regions, and, on the other hand, there's the feeling that the whole country is enrolled in a collective military venture. I can see how they

---

61. A bit of mistakenly overinterpreted Judaism here. The three weeks mark the time from the breach of the walls of Jerusalem until the Ninth of Av, the anniversary of the destruction of the Temple in Jerusalem. From the First of Av until the Ninth (though not, as suggested here, throughout the full preceding three weeks), observant Jews observe various signs of mourning, one of which is not eating meat except on the Sabbath.

would go together, though: there's security if everyone is involved. See the exhaustive Alkali Hebrew-English dictionary, which contains two proverbs in the Hebrew, which translate roughly as "Trouble shared is trouble halved" and "That many suffer is comfort to a fool." I'm not sure this is directly analogous, but somehow, in addition to my critical eye for the contradiction, I can see how this kind of model would work for some people.

But not for all of the people the reader is intended for. One of those thanked in the acknowledgments is the superintendent of schools for the area which includes Ar'ara, a local Arab. When I asked Riad about the reader, he explained that it was for use in Marilyn's English classes in the town high school! I was shocked: I said that Arab kids would hardly be expected to learn English well from a book which overtly excluded them in this way. And Riad added that maybe they would learn English, but since there was a clear distinction between good Jews and bad Arabs in the book, they might accept the clear distinction and identify sharply with the Arabs — reverse the stereotype but reproduce the dichotomy, as it were.

Later, when I had some time to talk to Marilyn, I asked her about the book. She explained that in fact she doesn't use it, despite intense pressure from the superintendent to do so. "He told us he had this great book, so I asked him to bring a copy so I could see it. He photocopied one relatively inoffensive article, and then I ordered copies for the whole class, and when it arrived I realized I couldn't use it."

Riad's garden: Riad's share of the family land inherited, along with his three brothers and his five sisters as well (Did they get any land? I doubt it), is close to an acre. There's a relatively new, one-story house on it, and a substantial garden, half of which is given over to a young mixed fruit orchard. The house forms an "L" around a small lawn, very neatly tended by seventeen-year-old Hisham and fifteen-year-old Ali under Riad's weekend direction. Between the house and the new orchard is a somewhat more crowded area with young fruit trees as well, watered with an elaborate system of "drip" hoses Israeli style. Bougainvillea and other spectacular flowers cover the hedge between the lawn and the orchard. In the back is a sort of rock garden, with various plants including enough rosemary for the entire Galilee, mint, and other herbs. Riad spends most of his weekend time gardening with the help of the two boys, and the work pays off. This seems to be Riad's defiant little patch of Palestinian agriculture; perhaps it also reminds him of the years he spent living with Marilyn as a graduate student in Hawaii.

Ali's English reminds me very much of Efraim's: both tend to speak in bursts of intensity, slow beginnings of sentences moving to quick endings. I wonder whether there's something shared about the intonation patterns of Arabic and Hebrew that would make two people who came here as small kids, with one parent a native speaker of English, sound so similar, or maybe I was just being sentimental.

I asked Riad why he, too (not only the Israeli government), calls a place as large as Ar'ara a village. He explained that in Arabic, there's no word for a "town," for an intermediary settlement between a village and a city. Also, he said, as large as it is, Ar'ara is still organized like a village, growing out on the hillsides piecemeal, where families own land (and, Marilyn told me later, where zoning permits them to build, although some houses are built illegally), the streets narrow and winding and unnamed, and the parts of the village still divided according to clan. Later I asked Riad how he would direct someone to his house, since there are no street names and no grid. He said, "I would tell them to come to the entrance to the village and ask for Riad Ghanem — they might need to know a bit more about me, like my father's name, but they'd be directed to the Ghanem part of the village, and eventually they'd find me." So that's what makes the place a village, too.

I asked Riad why the people in Ar'ara and the surrounding region stayed in 1948. He approved of the way I asked the question: he agrees that the proper question is why some of the Palestinians stayed, not why most left. And his basic answer is that there was less pressure from the soon-to-be Israelis for the people of the hilly portions of the Galilee to leave. Most of the villages that were abandoned or destroyed are in the coastal plain or in other fertile valleys; it's clear that this was the land the Jewish population was mostly interested in (see Atran 1989). Riad is very skeptical of the repeated insistence in Benny Morris's book that there was no overall plan for the dispossession of the Palestinians: he thinks it's quite clear what the Jewish planners had in mind.[62]

• 7/2/91 •

Later, on Sunday, I asked Riad about the percentage of Arabs in Israeli universities. He told me it was probably about proportional to their percentage of the population, "although if you wanted to break it down by branches, you'd probably find something there." I didn't note his response at all at first, feeling slightly guilty that I wasn't noting something that reflected fairly well on Israeli society: nondiscrimination against Arabs in higher education. (I

---

62. The article by Atran referred to in the journal details what Atran calls "the surrogate colonization of Palestine" — the purchases, legal maneuvers, and interventions with the British mandate authorities on the part of the Jewish Agency that helped pass much of the land of Palestine into Jewish hands before the 1948 war (Atran 1989). The book by Benny Morris is the first major study by an Israeli scholar of the mass dispossession of Palestinians in the course of that war (Morris 1987).

know that Arabs have difficulty getting into certain fields, for example, at places like the Technion.) What this means, however, is that there are a high number of university graduates and more who live in places like Ar'ara and remain professionally unemployed.[63]

•

Along the road toward Akko, we passed a row of sabra plants and then a moshav which Riad told me was the site of Mahmoud Darwish's home village. On the right, in the valley, there were some substantial fields with Palestinians doing hand field work, and without the telltale rows of stones Riad had taught me about on Friday. Riad explained that this land was controlled by the "office of absentee property," which was set up after 1948 to administer the property of people who fled and — in effect — who weren't allowed to come back. Some of this land has been given or is assigned to Jewish farming settlements, but some of it also is leased back by Arabs, and such was the case in the fields we were driving past.

Not only fields. Riad told me of a village (name?) where the people left, but didn't go very far. [Some of?] the houses in the village were then assigned by the Israeli government to Bedouins from the area. Eventually the people started coming back to their village, but they didn't get their homes back. Instead they were allowed to lease homes and fields belonging to the village, but except for one family, the property they have been able to lease is not their own. So in effect they're "refugees" on their own land.

Riad told me that people from several villages in the area wound up in Nazareth as a result of the 1948 war. They've settled in distinctive neighborhoods on the hillsides facing the villages that they had left, and the pattern of extending development shows a "reach" toward their original villages — literally, that the newer houses tend to be closer to the village of origin.

I mentioned the village of 'Ein Hod to Riad. I know it because when we came in 1986 for my nephew Avner's bar mitzvah, the entire family came there to spend a few days at a religious guest house, and I learned the story of this village close to the coast near Haifa: it was abandoned in 1948, but the houses weren't destroyed. Today it's an artists' colony — most of the stuff seemed to me to be upper-middle brow.[64] On the next hill or so above 'Ein

---

63. It also means that the Arab high schools in Israel have an extraordinarily well-educated teaching cadre, a matter of considerable local pride.

64. As if this were subtly damning, which is how I intended it when I wrote it. The implication here is that a bad conscience will produce bad art — a crude expression of a thesis about the relation between art and politics in Israel developed by Avishai Margalit (Margalit 1988). My judgment of the art seems to confirm from another direction Riad's moral questioning of the new occupants' "colony." If I had deemed the art at 'Ein Hod to be of superior quality, innovative, and daring — would that have made the dispossession seem any more bearable?

Hod is the moshav, Nir Etzion, which has the guest house. Another hill or two beyond, and visible from some of the cottages at the end of Nir Etzion, is a sparkling new little village with a mosque. I had known that this village was started by Arabs from 'Ein Hod, and I knew that the people there were "squatters," still struggling to make themselves legal.

Riad had more to tell me. One of the memorial books he's written is about 'Ein Hod.[65] This surprised me: somehow the prototype I had imagined was of a place where the entire village was destroyed physically and all the people dispersed. But, he pointed out to me quite soundly, there is no "prototype" — if you look at them carefully, all the villages have a different story. Anyway, the story of the village is this: one man from 'Ein Hod had flocks which he kept in caves, and he wanted to be near them, so he stayed close by. Riad met him once in 1969, before he died. Now there are about 150 people in the new village, and they're all descended from him (down to great-grandchildren, I imagine).[66] For many years, in order to get into the new village, one had to be let in by someone from Nir Etzion; Riad doesn't know if that's still the case. The man who's the "spokesman" for the village, who directs their political campaign for legalization, is named Ahmed Hammoudi.[67] Riad says if I want to talk to him, I can use Riad's name, and it will be a good recommendation, even though Ahmed Hammoudi wasn't too happy about some of the internal disputes Riad recorded in the book about 'Ein Hod. Riad isn't entirely dispassionate in discussing 'Ein Hod:[68] "These are artists; they're supposed to be sensitive people. Don't they know that they're living in the homes that belong to the people who come to do their gardening [some of the people from the new village work in the old 'Ein Hod]. How must it feel for someone to come and work at his father's house and see a naked statue in the yard? (I remember the naked statue from my walk through 'Ein Hod.) Remember that to Palestinian villagers, their house and their fields were practically their whole world, the ground of their whole sense of identity. When they lost that, they lost practically everything they were."

More on Israeli-Palestinian academic relations, or lack of same. Tel Aviv University (the Jaffee Center?) recently sponsored a conference called "Di-

---

65. See Slyomovics 1994.

66. There is a very biblical sort of quality to this ancestor-tale: the cave, the flocks, the single patriarch.... The image also reminds me of the story of Tsupu, solitary female survivor of the decimation of the California coast Miwok Indians under Spanish rule. She walked fifty miles north into the Kashaya Pomo territory and married Tom Smith, a Kashaya man. Their descendants reconstituted the Coast Miwok tribe (Greg Sarris, personal communication).

67. The new 'Ein-Hod was one of three previously "unrecognized" villages that were granted official recognition by the Israeli minister of the interior, Mr. Deri of the Oriental Orthodox Shas Party, in 1992.

68. Referring here to the older village, which is now an Israeli artists' colony.

lemmas of Palestinian Society," or something along those lines. They asked Riad to be a respondent on one of the panels. Since it matters what one says in such a situation, he asked to be sent the papers in advance. He didn't receive them, so he didn't go.[69]

About 6:00 on Sunday it was time to go. Riad decided to take the old highway through the coast plain between Hadera and Tel Aviv — possibly because it was getting dark and he didn't want to take the lonely hill road, partly to show me around the country some more, partly because it's not much longer anyhow. It is a hell of a lot less picturesque: there are a lot of people living along this coastal strip, and relatively a lot of relatively ugly industry, and it's hot, and there's a lot of traffic on the highway. So I was relieved when we reached the main road from Tel Aviv to Jerusalem, and puzzled when we turned off it again onto a side road marked "Ashkelon" going to the right. We turned left. I asked Riad why we were taking this road, and he said he thought it was faster. Then he told me it was the old Latrun Road. It was dark by now, and all I could tell of the area we were passing through was that it was hilly and not too densely populated. Then we passed a gas station, and I was surprised to see that virtually all of the signs on it were in Arabic. Riad said that was normal: after all, we were in the West Bank. I was startled, still thinking of the West Bank as "a place you don't go to," to the extent that it didn't occur to me that we were outside the Green Line. My first thought, not consciously summoned but already ironic as it came to me, was, "So this is Palestine!"

A few minutes later we had a frightening moment: suddenly, along the dark road, there was an Israeli army truck on one side and an army jeep on the other, and four soldiers standing halfway out in the road who barely moved back in time as Riad barely saw them in time and drove around them without stopping. Riad was puzzled: it clearly hadn't been a formal roadblock. (Even though Riad has Israeli plates and would be let through, there wasn't enough warning for someone with West Bank plates, if they had wanted to stop someone.) Maybe it was a roadblock just coming down or going up. In any case, it was a close call.

By this point Riad had explained to me that his oldest daughter, Nadia, who is finishing her studies at Hebrew University, was now at their rented house in Ramallah. He wanted to stop by there to drop off his niece, who had come to Ramallah with us, because he didn't like the idea of Nadia being in the house alone. So I got my first view of Ramallah. At night it looked nice — a lot like a very large and wealthy version of a Palestinian village, with

---

69. See the notes on the meeting with Howard Kaufman above, where he remarks that people from Bir Zeit have been invited to Israeli academic meetings but failed to appear.

plenty of green, but with some new apartment houses on the outskirts. The "downtown" area looked familiar from slides I had seen, taken by American peaceniks who'd been on delegations to the territories in the course of the intifada: quite urban, no trees, the buildings uniformly about four stories high, but not on a grid, curving with the streets. There wasn't a soul outside. We barely passed another car. Riad said people are simply too scared to go out at night.

In a minute we reached the Ghanems' house — right next door to the police station. To reach it Riad had to get out and open a gate in a large new fence. He explained that the police had come to the landlady and told her that stones had been thrown from the lawn, and either they would cut down the big trees facing the street or she would put in the fence. Once through the fence, we drove along a substantial driveway behind houses on a larger street, to Riad's house, which looked quite modern and pleasant inside. The television was on, the sound turned down; it was obviously Jordan TV, since the subtitles were in Arabic only, and a show about America — maybe Florida — cows and then a smiling yachtsman. Nadia greeted me much less shyly than her brothers, and asked me if I was connected with Hebrew University.

Once I realized Riad was planning to go home and then take me back to Jerusalem after doing so much driving in one day, I said I could go back in a taxi, or else sleep over and go by taxi the next morning. There were no taxis, and evidently Riad didn't want to have to worry about my safety in Ramallah, because he took me back as far as French Hill — gee whiz, it took about five minutes, the cities are so close.

Yesterday morning I spoke to Ahmed Abu Saleh, to confirm my appointment with him and some of his friends from Bir Zeit for tomorrow, Wednesday. He told me that my taxi to El Bireh might cost an extra shekel or two, because the main road between Ramallah and El Bireh is closed off. He also said I'd have to go back to Jerusalem by 5:00, because Ramallah is under a 7:00 curfew for traffic. Now was that true on Sunday as well? Presumably. Did Riad not know about it because it had been announced after 3:00 Friday, when he left for the north? Possibly. (How are these intermittent curfews and road closings publicized?) Why did he drive into Ramallah so late, why did he drive back out with me so late? I don't know.[70]

I told Riad about the session I've organized for the AAA[71] this fall, taking off from Benedict Anderson's *Imagined Communities*.[72] He hadn't heard of the

---

70. Presumably Riad wasn't worried about the curfews because of his Israeli license plates.
71. American Anthropological Association.
72. This book, which has been reissued in a revised and updated second edition, has proven an enormous stimulus to anthropological work on the cultures of nationalism (Anderson 1991).

book, but was quite taken with the notion of national identity as a project. "If the Palestinians don't wind up with at least part of the land," he reflected, "they're certainly going to need somebody to imagine a collective identity for them."

Today, walking to Givat Ram to sign up for the pool, remembering how big the university campus is and how nice the sports facilities are, thinking, "Gee, this is all for me" — I'm the kind of person they made this place for, that is, a Jew. If I wanted to I suppose I could get a job here, I don't know.... In the physical education building, there's a wall plaque with photographs and articles about American Jewish sports heroes, and oh yes, there's the Howard and [his wife's name] Cosell physical education center (not the exact name, but part of the gym complex named for Howard Cosell).

• 7/3/91 •

Coming back, I noticed a place on Jaffa Road called "Olam Keyser" — The Caesar Club, perhaps named after Caesar's Palace in Las Vegas. What an ironic celebration of the people who defeated the previous Jewish commonwealth.

A sign on a small truck: *"Kol basar,"* "All flesh," a reference to the line from the grace after meals, *"Hu noten lechem lekol basar,"* "He gives bread (sustenance) to all flesh." But I don't think this was a bread truck, rather a meat-dealer. Again Israeli cleverness making commercial slogans out of traditional references, but kind of a weird switch here, turning the idea of creaturely dependence on divine provision into the idea of meat.

• 7/4/91 •

Caption on a postcard I just sent: "The Western Wall covered in snow." If you look at the picture, however, you see the Dome of the Rock prominently behind it. The photographer didn't even try to get an angle which downplayed the Dome of the Rock; the caption is sufficient to tell you that the Wall is the important thing. It reminds me of a recent *Smithsonian Magazine* article about Ferdinand Magellan, which describes the memorial at the site where he was killed. On one side it talks about the Spanish explorer Ferdinand Magellan, who was senselessly killed at this site when he first landed in the Philippines. On the other side it talks about the Filipino hero Lapu Lapu, who defended his people against Magellan's attempt to conquer them. The article is accompanied by an engraving of the scene of the death of Magellan, which has a caption basically saying, "Magellan was senselessly killed by Filipino natives who didn't want to be subject to the Spanish king" — certainly an incoherent sentence, but doubtless what gets reinforced as always is the old message that Magellan's death was "senseless." The analogy seems powerful to me between the postcard and the magazine: you're shown both perspectives, but you're directed which one to adopt.[73]

So now on to yesterday, my recollection perhaps just a bit fuzzy because I'm a little short on sleep and had gone swimming at Givat Ram for the first time just before going to see Ahmed in El-Bireh. I hustled myself over to the Damascus Gate by 12:30, found a taxi that was going to El-Bireh, got in, and waited for it to fill up. The man sitting next to me in the taxi had some cookies and offered me one, which I accepted. Taxi traffic was clearly slow: it took about fifteen minutes for ours to fill up. Eventually we set off, as usual on the new road straight out through French Hill, and I realized the big new building in East Jerusalem I'd wondered about was police headquarters — for the whole city, I presume. Passing the Hyatt again, I realized I'm still puzzled why they put it there — it's closer to the city than I thought, but who's going to go through East Jerusalem to "the city" now? What I wonder is whether they had some future political/geographic development of the city in mind when they built the hotel there, or whether they just made a mistake, or whether I'm missing something. Maybe I'll try to find out.

---

73. The relevant passage in the article I was citing from memory describes the two inscriptions as follows: "The one on the monument's eastern side — the side that pedant geographers will recognize as marginally nearer to the Spanish Main — records the event as a European tragedy. 'Here on 27th April 1521 the great Portuguese navigator Hernando de Magallanes, in the service of the King of Spain, was slain by native Filipinos....' On the other side, by contrast, it is seen as an Oriental triumph — a heroic blow struck for Philippine nationalism. 'Here on this spot the great chieftain Lapu Lapu repelled an attack by Ferdinand Magellan, killing him and sending his forces away....' Baring [the name of the guard at the monument] points to the latter and roars with laughter. 'This is the real story. This is the one we Filipinos like to hear!'" (Winchester 1991: 94). The superscripted caption to the reproduction of the engraving reads: "Tragic death of Magellan occurred on the island of Mactan in a senseless battle with spear-wielding tribesmen who did not want to become Christian or acknowledge the power of the King of Spain" (95). The rhetorical balance seems tipped toward Magellan's side here. It was *his* death that was tragic, not that of the anonymous "spear-wielding tribesmen." Stretching a point, one might claim that the judgment of "senselessness" applies both to Christians and to "tribesmen" here, but that is mere pious clucking: what battle is sensible? In any case, although we do tend more and more to couple the words "senseless" and "tragic," the latter term bears a fading connotation of great and noble destiny that would tend to make any tragic death meaningful, not senseless (see also Obeyesekere 1992). Furthermore, since the caption enumerates the "tribesmen's" motives and not those of Magellan, it suggests that they were the senseless ones. Since I too would not like to acknowledge the power of the king of Spain or become Christian, their motivations seem entirely self-explanatory and reasonable (see Rafael 1993). In any case, the entire article is about Magellan, not about native Filipino resistance. Flipping through the pages of this magazine in a doctor's office, however, the average American twelve-year-old would more likely come away remembering the caption and, perhaps, Magellan's name than the more ambivalent text. She or he would not, that is, be likely to come away with the "real" story.

One of the stores we pass on the main road out is the Nashashibi Supermarket (the sign's in English — I can't read Arabic that fast). The Nashashibis were a rival family of the Husseinis in pre-1948 Palestinian society, but their particular brand of nationalist politics lost out (Kayyali 1978). I guess they're fairly successful in Jordan now; I met a Nashashibi in Washington a couple of years ago who was the Jordanian ambassador to Italy. It's easy to imagine an alternative history in which the Nashashibis would have owned a chain of huge supermarkets, and so on. This somehow didn't seem to befit their aristocratic history.

I really liked being in the Palestinian taxi. I felt positively triumphant looking at the big new houses people were building, a sign that they weren't disappearing from this land yet. And I felt a great relief at finally going there, to this place that had seemed so important and yet so inaccessible to me until now — I mean the Palestinian world, inside.

El-Bireh — the part of it that I walked through with Ahmed, the part that includes his house, Um Sabri's house, and In'ash el-Usra — feels somehow more expansive than Ar'ara. The houses are more substantial, and there's more space between them. Of course the gardens are not as lush as they are in parts of Jewish Jerusalem — either because Palestinians aren't used to irrigation or because they aren't allowed to [use it], I don't know. But many of the yards are plowed, fenced in with substantial stone fences, and some of them are set off into separate terraced plots, all of which gives the impression of reminding the viewer that this too was an agricultural village fairly recently. The streets are also laid out on more of a grid than in Ar'ara, but it still doesn't feel like you're in the middle of a city.

In'ash el-Usra itself is a substantial institution. (I've been imagining it for years, ever since I heard about the place from Um Sabri's niece, Samiha Abdel-Kadir, an activist in New York and a friend of ours. I always imagined the place smaller and more run down than it is, and set in a much more humble and dusty hilltop village.) The driver left me off at the main entrance, as I asked him to; it cost me five shekels instead of the usual two for getting on or off anywhere along his usual route. As I entered, about half a dozen young Palestinian women, some of them wearing the plain grey dress and white head covering that seems to be replacing the older embroidered dresses for many Palestinian women, came out. The place seemed fairly busy. Ahmed came out and showed me into his simple medical office; we passed a small auditorium and various other offices.

Then we went to Ahmed's house for lunch. Here again I was confronted with the contrast between my imagination and what I saw: for some reason I had assumed Ahmed was unmarried — I think it has something to do with the fact that he doesn't have a telephone at his place. (He told me later that people in the territories have to apply to the civil authority and wait five years for a telephone.) He introduced me to his two daughters: one seven, I forget her name, and the second three and a half, named Rabab. He calls Rabab his "Ashkenazi" daughter because she's so headstrong and aggressive: in fact while we were there she kept lifting the sleeve of his short-sleeved shirt and slapping it as hard as she could. It seemed to me she was pretending to give him shots, since he's a doctor?

Walking back around the walls, a plaque which puzzled me, right next to the New Gate. The text, transliterated, says, "*Bema'aracha shel lochamei hahagana haetz'el vehaleh'i al shachror ir david biy' tamuz tashach — 17/17/49 nifrats shaar ze al yiday chayalei hairgun hatsvai haleumi shehkimu rosh-gesher betoch hair haatika.*"[74] What's strange about it is at the top is the figure of a forearm holding a rifle, and the slogan (one word on either side of the figure), "*Rak kach.*"[75] There's no indication of who put the plaque there or allowed it to be put there, but it certainly looks permanent. Was "*Rak kach*" the slogan of the Irgun before Kahane picked it up? (Before I found out how *kach* was spelled, I always thought that Kahane's party was the "take" party.) [Fn. 7/5: I ask my office-mate at the institute, Moshe Livni, where this slogan came from. He asks David Noam, across the hall, who says it was the slogan of Etsel, the Irgun. Moshe explains to me that David's father was in the Irgun, and was exiled to Eritrea. A reminder to me of something that no one talks about very much these days, the importance of the struggle against the British to the Israeli idea of being a national liberation movement (see above, on Mavo Hama'avak). I explain to David that I thought *kach* meant "take," and he says the theme of "taking" is national (take a present, take this, take that; the only question is how to take).]

A taped note: an Israeli tour guide with a group of about forty or fifty, I presume they're Americans, at the Jaffa Gate about to go straight in through the main street of the *shuk*,[76] and she's saying, "Please don't stop, please stay all together. I know it's very tempting, but it's not safe, and we're on a schedule. I promise you you'll have an opportunity to shop." So, this situation horrifies me,[77] and it must really drive the storekeepers crazy.

---

74. "By an alliance of the fighters of the Hagana, the Irgun, and Lehi for the liberation of the City of David on the 10th of Tammuz, *tashach* — July 17, 1949, this gate was opened by soldiers of the Irgun who established a bridgehead inside the Old City." The transliteration here as elsewhere in "My Trip to Israel" is approximate.

75. "Only thus," the slogan of the Irgun.

76. The Arab market (*suk* in Arabic; I use the cognate Hebrew term here).

77. Perhaps at this moment it was the guide's attitude that I reacted to, which would be consistent with the blatant moralism of much of this journal. In hindsight, I imagine she was only being responsible. Nevertheless, this example of the *enforced* separation of Palestinians

Full name of the Cosell gym (see above) is the Howard and Mary Edith Cosell Center for Physical Education, Leisure and Health Promotion.

• 7/5/91 •

Last night I reached one of the contacts Naftali Gertner had given me — a friend named Rebecca Nayshtot, a former co-worker of his at a New York law firm who's been here not that long, I think she said with her husband, who's also a lawyer. She was very friendly, and we talked on the phone for about an hour, her kids being asleep and her husband still at work. They're both clerking for lawyers in Tel Aviv, which is a *stage*[78] they have to go through before they can be admitted to the bar here. When I told Rebecca what I was doing, she asked whether I thought there was any hope for peace here. I told her the Berlin Wall had come down[79] and Nelson Mandela was negotiating with the president of South Africa, but on the other hand there's Northern Ireland, and it's not clear whether our situation here is as hopeless as that one. She responded to that — she'd never thought much about Ireland, but then she was talking to a British friend, and she realized how similar the tactics there were to the deceitful and manipulative tactics of the PLO I thought to myself, "Uh-oh, I'm going to have to be careful with this one." But gradually she got the idea that I'm a peacenik — I told her, for instance, that Naftali and I disagree a lot about politics and philosophy, but we get along well nevertheless. And she was genuinely quite interested in my views. I told her I had spent a very pleasant weekend in an Arab village in the north — I mentioned that these "villages" often have well over ten thousand residents, and that seemed to intrigue her. I carefully explained that I was trying to talk to many different kinds of people, and she asked whether I was calling her because she was one of the people I wanted to write about (more or less). I told her that was part of why I called. She said, "Well, have you learned anything interesting from this conversation?" I said, "Well, I learned that you don't trust the PLO." She responded, "You could have guessed that, since I'm a religious Jew from New York." Then she asked me what I thought the root of the problem was, and I said that I think a lot of it has to do with the fact that Israelis don't want to or can't acknowledge the dispossession of the Palestinians. She said, "Isn't

---

from both Israeli Jews and foreign tourists is a clear and indeed horrifying example of the way differences and conflicts are perpetuated through reiteration.

78. The French word for a set term of training; roughly, an internship.

79. I found the analogy to the fall of the Berlin Wall apt on several occasions in the fall of 1993, when asked my opinion about the Israel-PLO agreement: in both cases few people had anticipated that the dramatic event would come so quickly, but as with the fall of the Berlin Wall as well, there were likely to be shocking and murderous consequences that no one had anticipated either.

it their fault for running away?" I told her that I thought the Palestinians had behaved as any civilian population would, especially when they were "encouraged" to do so by the Israelis. She said she'd heard lots of stories of Jews telling the Palestinians to stay, and I said I'd also heard there were cases of that, especially where leftist kibbutzim made a point of having good relations with their Arab neighbors. But I also told her about Riad's (I didn't use his name) opinion that mostly Arabs stayed in places where the Jews hadn't made control a high priority — that is, in the hills — and I pointed out to her that even today most of the Arabs live in hilly areas, and the Jews got all the good valley land. I also told her that I thought this, rather than anti-Semitism per se, was the root of the Palestinians' hostility to Israel (while I agreed with her point that the Arab governments have manipulated the Palestinian issue for their own purposes). She didn't really challenge me, which makes me suspect that here's someone who hasn't thought about the issue a great deal, doesn't have a tremendous amount invested in denying the Palestinian experience, is not a racist, hasn't heard views like mine before, and is therefore open to them.

Somewhere in the conversation I mentioned that although I'm a peacenik, I'm also a religious Jew, and this is a nice place to be a religious Jew in some ways. She wasn't quite buying it: she's very bothered by the degree of mistrust and the fine distinctions that are made between different levels of religiosity here. On the other hand, she's working in an office where there aren't any religious people, and she finds some of the same gratifying and tolerant curiosity about her beliefs and her way of life that she enjoyed among her co-workers in New York. I tell her that "as an anthropologist" I very much appreciate any situation in which people are offered a chance to recognize and question their own stereotypes.[80]

I try to find nice things I can say about everybody here or about the place which don't deny politics and won't offend anybody, so at one point when she was saying how difficult it must be for me to be here for so long without my family, I said that the fact that everyone is so hospitable here makes it easier. She said, "Does that mean you want to come for a Shabbes?" I got just the tiniest bit embarrassed, because I'd thought to myself in passing that I might convey the hint that way. But obviously she wasn't simply teasing me — she said she'd love to see another American (there are Americans in Ramot where they're living, but...). I said yes, I would like to, and when I figured out how my schedule for July looked I would call back to arrange it.

---

80. Of course some of the "stereotypes" being questioned here are my own. I assumed that Israel as a religious experience was something she and I would agree on, but being more involved in religious Jewish life in Israel than I, she was less inclined to make a conventional gesture of that kind. Furthermore, as a Jerusalemite working in Tel Aviv, she herself was able to mobilize a diasporic model of mutually enriching difference.

Rebecca didn't give any hint that she regrets having made the move to Israel, but there are certain things she finds difficult, professionally most of all, based on what she said last night. There are very few women established in law practices right now. There are a lot of women in law school or just coming in, but the ones who are established are at the stage of saying, "We did it the hard way, you'll have to do it the hard way too," whereas in America they're a generation further on, beginning to realize that women might want to have children as well as a career. Also it's difficult for her that her children come home from school at 1:00. I said that obviously the people that decide these things don't expect her to be working, and she agreed. Also she shares my wonder at where all the money for all this construction and the expensive apartments that people continue to buy comes from — the main concern then seems to be how to make a living in Israel when prices are not really lower than American ones and salaries are much lower.

• 7/7/91 •

I spent several hours on Shabbes afternoon talking with my friend Charles Waters. I think I could do a fairly incisive book about Israel based solely on interviews with him, although he's fairly fond of stretched analogies and formulations which are primarily meant to be provocative.

Charles told me three good stories.

1. In Nazareth one Saturday. Charles's parents live there, and in addition to the Arabs shopping there, many people from Nazareth Illit — Russian and Rumanians, most of whom aren't religious — come to Nazareth to shop. A car pulls up to a crosswalk, barely stopping in time, and a man in a kaffiyeh with a mustache looks at the car and scolds, "Shabbes! Shabbes!"

2. On reserve duty in Bet Sahur, Charles does KP. (Charles mentioned what a revelation it was to him to go to a wealthy town like Bet Sahur after doing duty in Gaza; he told me he has a recurrent dream in which he's walking through a town like Nablus, seeing lots of new Malibu-style houses with luxuriant landscaping, and people who look like George Hamilton inside them. This after I told Charles and his wife, Sandy, how much I enjoyed seeing the new houses on the way to El-Bireh.) This is the one time a soldier is allowed to be without his rifle.[81] There are a group of Palestinians nearby, waiting to deal with the authorities about getting drivers' licenses, and so on, and one of them suddenly calls out to Charles, "Soldier! Where's your rifle?!"[82]

---

81. That is, when he's doing kitchen work.

82. This was in Hebrew, of course; the young Palestinian was, so to speak, impersonating an officer.

3. One day last summer the solar water heater on the roof of Charles's house burst. A disaster: water is pouring into the upstairs neighbors' apartment.... Charles called the plumber, a Palestinian who lives in a village called Azariya, and meanwhile went up on the roof to try to start fixing the problem. As he's working in the heat, sweat all over him, the plumber suddenly shows up and says cheerfully, "Can I help you?" They work together for about two hours, eventually get the problem fixed. They go downstairs into the house, Charles pours cold water, then makes coffee. They're sitting around making idle conversation, and after a brief silence, the plumber says in Hebrew, "You know, this house used to belong to my grandfather." Charles is struck dumb, and then the plumber laughs and says, "Ha, I got you! I got you!" (Charles and I both agree that this story reflects a tremendous amount of trust and intimacy — to be able to joke about something as sacred as a lost house, in the middle of the intifada.)

Charles showed me *Davar Acher*,[83] the four-page satirical supplement to the "new" *Davar*. They have about a page of headlines, making fun of the left and the right: "Abie Nathan isn't alone in his willingness to pay the full price for peace. Many of his comrades on the left are also willing for him to pay the full price."[84] "Government of Israel announces that it will stop the settlement policy as soon as another way to block the peace process can be found." The editor of this section also has a satirical TV program. Recently he picked up on a statement by Yuval Ne'eman[85] that Israel can live for another one hundred years without peace. "Yes," he said, "we can live without peace. The only problem is that goyim keep starting wars and Jews die in them." Then he started singing "We can live for another hundred years without peace" as an Ashkenazi *nigun*,[86] and got the whole studio audience to sing along. [9/7: thinking about this again — what's frightening is not only the costs and the death and the anxiety that a vision like Ne'eman's implies, but also the tremendous social conformity, the tremendous need to always maintain the strictest boundary controls on both sides.] Now this would be a good person

---

83. *Davar* can mean "word" or "thing" and is the name of the Labor Party's daily newspaper; *acher* is Hebrew for "other." *Davar acher* is a traditional Jewish euphemism for the forbidden and abominable pork, so the temptation is irresistible to say that *Davar Acher* pokes fun at the sacred cows of Israeli public culture.

84. Abie Nathan is a veteran and highly individualist Israeli peace activist, notable among other things for maintaining a decades-long pirate radio station called "The Voice of Peace," which broadcasts from a boat in the Mediterranean. At this time he was well into a hunger strike protesting the law forbidding contacts between Israeli citizens and the PLO.

85. A prominent physicist, minister of science in the Likud government, and erstwhile leader of the right-wing Tehiya Party.

86. Melody, usually religious.

to speak to[87] — Does he see himself as providing a safety valve or actually trying to awaken some kind of political consciousness?

This morning, Sunday, I went to meet my friend Naftali Gertner's mother, Rivka. She too wondered whether I was finding Palestinians to speak to, and I assured her that I was. She mentioned that she had taken an Arabic class at Hebrew University once, and on a few occasions her class was combined with a class of Arabs studying Hebrew. She says she used to be on friendly speaking terms with several Arabs — such as the person who washes the floors in her building — but since the intifada began he hardly speaks to her. "There was a trip to Neve Shalom.[88] I didn't go, but my friend who went says it doesn't really work — the Arabs still prefer to be with Arabs and the Jews are still Jews." "I can tell you that all the Arabs hate Jews, and even the Jews who speak Arabic hate Arabs." This is from someone who, I think, is not a racist, yet there's still the perception of an unbridgeable and hostile gulf between two categories of people. The language of "hatred" is particularly striking. What does it mean — that every time a Jew or an Arab sees each other, they feel the emotion of hatred? That all Jews or Arabs *say* they hate each other? That the respective words "Jew" and "Arab" call forth Pavlovian conditioned reflexes of the emotion of hatred? I suspect that this language of "hatred" is something like the baldest way to put a claim that it is unrealistic to expect Arabs and Jews to live together — as the reference to Neve Shalom supports.

• 7/8/91 •

Terri Khoury gave me the name of a geographer at Bir Zeit who may be able to help me understand this better on the ground. (I just tried one of the numbers Terri gave me for him. A woman answered, and I said in English, "I'd like to speak to Rifaat Abdel Malek." She said, *"Ani lo midaberet arabish — russish, yiddish...."*[89] So I explained to her who I was looking for, and she simply said, "No, I don't know him." Wrong number, evidently. I try the other number she gave me, and the man who answers says after hesitating, "He is not here. Would you like to speak to his frau — his wife?"[90] Anyway she says Rifaat is in America for the summer. I'll call him back in September.

•

---

87. I mean the editor of *Davar Acher*, not Yuval Ne'eman.
88. A small community designed as a model for cooperative living between Arabs and Jews.
89. "I don't speak Arabic — Russian, Yiddish...." Evidently the woman who answered when I called the wrong number was a recent Russian immigrant who heard me pronounce an Arabic name and assumed I was speaking Arabic.
90. Many Israeli Arabs go to Germany for their higher education.

Here at Givat Ram,[91] there's a bus stop sign which says "Katamon" and "Gonen" — both names, the old one which is still used and the new official one on the map. Yesterday in my daily conversation with Elias he mentioned how upsetting it is that the Jews insisted on changing the names of all the places here, when the Arabs had been content to maintain the same old names for hundreds of years. He also started talking about the issue of respect for grave sites — he grew up near Rachel's Tomb, always knew what it was and always stayed away from it; there was something holy and mysterious about it to him. He also says that the Western Wall and Rachel's Tomb could have been destroyed, but they never were. If some graveyards were destroyed, it was not because of [general, cultural] lack of reverence, but because such things happen anywhere. This is an issue I may take up further with Elias, since desecration of "Jewish holy sites" is a key part of the justification of maintaining control over East Jerusalem and the West Bank — or was when such control was more under debate. [As I'm typing this up, my office-mate, Moshe Livni, steps out to look for a Tanakh; out of all of my brother's rabbinic arcana in this office, there's no Bible. When he comes back, I ask him, "Did you have to go to Mount Sinai to find it?" He says, "Almost — the trouble is we don't know where Mount Sinai is. It's not important." Me: "So how come it's so important where Rachel's Tomb is, where Machpelah[92] is?" He: "I didn't say it's important. I think it's no accident that we don't have an exact place or a date for the giving of the Torah, and we don't know where Moses is buried. The only holy place is Jerusalem, and that's because that's where the Temple is and you can eat *kodshim*[93] there. But it seems that people need holy places."]

• 7/9/91 •

I'm starting finally to read *Fieldnotes* through now, and enjoying it so far. It encourages me to go ahead and record — safely here, because I've promised myself I can edit what I want to — how I backed into doing this fieldwork in the first place. I applied for fieldwork money as an afterthought, because Stuart Schaar said it was essential to this kind of project, not because I had any clear idea about what the fieldwork would consist of. I'm doing the fieldwork at the end for two reasons. The first is personal — I hoped Elissa would be able to study more and hence be ready to do her own research by now,

---

91. The campus of the Hebrew University, which includes the physical science faculties and the sports facilities; I was there for the pool. For most intents and purposes it is now the "older" university campus, the new one being the campus on Mount Scopus, which was reoccupied after the 1967 war.

92. The tomb of the patriarchs at Hebron.

93. Foods earmarked for consumption on pilgrimages to the Temple according to biblical law.

and anyway once she got sick there was no question of my going off before I had to. The second was principled: because of the premises of my project — that this is a contest for history, not only space, and hence a critical attitude toward the primacy of spatial identification was called for — I wanted to resist the whole mystique of "being there."[94] In addition, if I'm somewhat diffident about being here now, it's largely because I'd rather not be here by myself, without my family; one is supposed to regard fieldwork as almost a holy time, the time of inspiration, gathering mana[95] to be applied back at the university. (Moti referred to my time here as my "pilgrimage," and in a way that's quite appropriate.)[96] But I know I'm here because I need the money, in addition to whatever I or anybody else learns from my time here.

•

I just met for an hour with Judy Levi, another of the small handful of Orthodox radicals here in Jerusalem — Shari Brown[97] is another, my brother was one until he left — who teaches music at Givat Ram. Judy was eager to meet me and very friendly. She said that my brother had given her something of mine to read about "layers of memory" — I can't imagine now what it was[98] — just before she and Danny had gone to participate in the church service during the tax strike at Bet Sahour. They put Danny and Judy up front, as honored guests — I imagine because there were a number of Jews there, but because it was a religious service religious Jews were especially valued.[99] When the priests came around with the incense, Judy panicked. The memory/historical associations were too powerful — it made her think of the Inquisition and the whole history of Christian oppression of Jews. Then she remembered what I had written about "layers of memory" (again, ?), and she was able to calm down.

---

94. See, in addition to the recent critical literature on rhetorics of authority in ethnography (for example, Clifford and Marcus 1986; Fabian 1983, 1990), other work on dimensionality that I carried out simultaneously with this project (J. Boyarin 1992; J. Boyarin, ed., 1994).

95. Joel Bauman, reading these notes, suggests adding a second n to this word, which reminds me of the pun I obviously intended.

96. An ironic pilgrimage, perhaps, though the borders of conviction and irony are nowhere to be found. In any case an argument might be made that "My Trip to Israel" is actually a bid for an American identity, an inscription in a tradition of antiepiphanic journey-to-Jerusalem travelogues that Emily Budick has identified in authors from Mark Twain to Saul Bellow (Budick 1989). I would hope not, for Budick's paper was one of the rare arguments that I have heard that suggest that Jewish Israel, too, might well be considered as a colony. If there is an overarching allegory to "My Trip to Israel" on the basis of which such an argument could be made, it can only be made on the basis of this *book* that I am still writing.

97. A classicist and translator, active with the Alternative Information Center.

98. Probably "Palestine and Jewish History."

99. Read, "They put Danny and Judy up front, as honored guests. Even though there were a number of Jews there, evidently since it was a religious service religious Jews were especially valued."

We both agreed that Givat Ram is a much pleasanter campus than Scopus — it's laid out among gardens with lots of outdoor pathways. Scopus for the most part is one big building, with the greenery, such as it is, being for people to look out at from inside. In short Scopus is fortresslike; quite possibly, since the campus was under Jordanian control from 1948 to 1967, it has been designed to be defensible. The cost in quality of life is readily apparent when it's contrasted with Givat Ram, even though Givat Ram is generally older. (A thought comes to me: Why did King Hussein get involved in the 1967 war at all? He must have known he wasn't likely to gain anything. He must have been under tremendous pressure from his own people and from the other Arab states, just as he was during the Gulf War this year.)

I actually regretted that I hadn't taped this conversation with Judy, because she put some of the current issues so sharply and provided a few new angles that I hadn't thought of before. But my technique of recording main notes to myself on tape and then writing them up soon after seems to be satisfactory. She seemed to assume I was going to interview her immediately — practically as soon as we sat down she said, (no I'm getting this wrong). [Anyway,] I said that I was trying to meet many different kinds of people here, so she said, "So I'm your native informant — or actually migrating informant."

•

Resting from note taking, I glance at the thousand or so volumes belonging to my brother which line the walls of this office. One, unusually popular for my brother's library, is Rabbi Hayim Halevy Donin's *To Be a Jew: A Guide to Jewish Observance in Contemporary Life* (New York: Basic Books, 1972). I flip it open, and find in the introduction:

> Zionism...was and is a struggle for national liberation and for the crystallization of a national identity on the part of a nation that had been forced to wander from country to country over the centuries.
> 
> The early settlers found a land that had been neglected through the centuries, abounding in malarial swamps and diseases. It was a barren land — of rock, sand, and desert. The few remaining Jewish communities were concentrated in the cities of Jerusalem, Hebron, Tiberias, and Safed. (14)[100]

• 7/10/91 •

Tucked away, semidiscretely, on the side of the entrance to the security office here at Givat Ram, there's a sign saying, "Givat Ram Security," with a drawing of a middle-aged woman with two large, drooping breasts, and the breasts are

---

100. Two things are remarkable about this quote: first, the notion that *crystallization* of a national identity is desirable (Who would really want to be part of a crystal?); and second, the association of an absence of Jews with barrenness.

half-surrounding the head of a man with a short beard who's smiling broadly. I guess that's another notion of *bitachon*, "security."

On page 32 of her essay in *Fieldnotes*, Jean Jackson says that some anthropologists might feel negative about fieldnotes because they represent a removal from lived reality, whereas anthropologists want to be "free, like the noble natives, to experience life directly with no interfering intermediaries. ...Of course, those anthropologists who believe that fieldnotes fairly unproblematically reflect reality do not feel this way at all." The passage shows Jackson reverting back to the "normative image" of fieldwork as being done among illiterates, whereas by now many anthropologists do fieldwork with people whose lives are already thoroughly bureaucratized or who live with texts all the time; some of them even do fieldwork with people who write books themselves (Friedlander, Lavie).[101] I want to see if anybody in this volume acknowledges fieldnotes and ethnography as a way of participating in a literate culture. I also note that Roger Sanjek's commentary essay assumes that fieldnotes contain information that exists nowhere else in written or other publicly available form, and are precious for that reason. When he does refer to Boas as one of the few anthropologists who has done anything like really publish his fieldnotes, this is discussed as a case of completion, not a case of fragmentation, as I see mine.

•

Straight transcription of today's taped notes:

I have an appointment in East Jerusalem at 11:00 with Omar Medina, an acquaintance of Danny's, and I realize I'm going to be leaving my *shiur*[102] in the Jewish Quarter, walking back out the Jaffa Gate all the way around past the Damascus Gate to Salah el-Din, which is quite a detour, kind of a sad shlep. My morning routine provisionally is shul, an hour or so of work at the Hartman Institute, and then coming to the Old City for my Talmud class.[103] Well unfortunately there's really no way to get from Emek Refaim to the Jaffa Gate,[104] so I have to walk up this big hill and I guess it's every day I'm being

---

101. Friedlander 1990; Lavie 1992. See also Herzfeld 1993b; Fischer and Abadi 1990.

102. My regular religious study session.

103. After contacting a friend from the Lower East Side whom I had met while studying at the local yeshiva there in the mid-1980s, he invited me to join his study sessions with a young rabbi, also American born. These sessions were held at a small yeshiva called Yeshivat Hacohanim, which, like the much more famous Ateret Hacohanim, is devoted to those portions of the Torah and Talmud dealing with priestly responsibilities and Temple rites, but whose constituents, unlike those of Ateret Hacohanim, are willing to wait for the restoration of the Temple until the divinely appointed time. During the several sessions I actually attended we studied the tractate Yoma of the Babylonian Talmud, which deals with the Temple ritual on Yom Kippur.

104. By bus, that is.

*oleh regel* to Yerushalayim!¹⁰⁵ Andy tells me it's a lot better to take the 18 bus to Yaffa Street.

In the Old City particularly, I catch little tidbits of tour guides' explanation, with a mixture of greed and...reluctance. Kind of like sweets when they're around and I'm trying to diet. I'd love to have the information, but I'm not willing to get it that way, and I'm not willing to spend the money.

All the Arab bus companies are local, for each town. Unlike Egged, which is national and a cooperative. I've been waiting for twenty minutes at the sign that says the 23 bus to Scopus stops here on Salah e-Din. Haven't seen an Egged bus and I haven't seen any Israelis, except for an army truck that drove by here a few minutes ago. It's nice standing here, but I'm getting thirsty. I'll give it another ten minutes, just as an experiment.

The difference in the buses is enough explanation of why the Palestinians want their own state.¹⁰⁶

Another army truck goes by, squawking cars out its way.

At the post office at the end of Salah e-Din, a security guard tells two soldiers in a jeep that five *shebab* (the word he uses) are hanging out on the porch. A soldier comes up, checks their identity cards, and sends them off the porch.

A bus trying to get past a truck on Salah e-Din, which is not a very wide street. Soldiers kind of hanging around in the middle of it, acting vaguely bossy, not accomplishing much. Finally about four or five young Palestinian guys come and bounce a parked car until they can move it a few inches, and then the bus gets through.

I've been into the post office, and it's 12:30 and I still haven't seen the 23 bus. I think it just doesn't run here anymore, but I'm going to ask people. I'm going to forget about going to the university today. No — first I'm going to ask Omar Medina if he thinks it's safe for me to walk through Wadi Joz.

The smell of *nana*,¹⁰⁷ and the smell of cardamom, and the smell of diesel fuel.

There's the Palestine Press Service — big sign. A muezzin's call, not from a minaret but from a speaker on a rooftop.

---

105. That is, going up on foot to Jerusalem, the term used for the three annual festivals during which sacrifices were made when the Temples stood.

106. In other situations of systematic discrimination, of course, the demand on the part of the disadvantaged group is for inclusion and equality rather than separation and independence. Hence this kind of everyday, material discrepancy in the quality of life does not adequately explain a move for statehood. Yet, given the evident unwillingness of the majority of Israelis to consider inclusion and equality, statehood must seem to many Palestinians the only possible means toward achieving equable conditions, aside from any considerations of ideology, pride, or even collective identity.

107. Mint.

A whole network of little shoestring offices — human rights, early childhood resource, press centers, no bigger than the little peace groups in New York City. I ask a woman — I think an American woman — at PHRIC,[108] who's the receptionist, whether the 23 bus still runs. She says it runs every half hour — I must have just missed it. I asked her if it's safe for me to walk up Wadi Joz to Scopus. She checks out the bags I'm carrying to make sure there's no Hebrew on them. Of course there's not, I'm carrying a Met Life bag with Snoopy on it. She warns me it's a long walk. Well, that's my job, and it's certainly safer than walking through Bushwick.[109]

A long loop, a road along a hill in East Jerusalem; some wonderful houses right here, as fine as the ones in Baka, a few at least. Palm trees, bougainvillea; not much of that.

El-Aqsa Taxi.

From Wadi Joz the Scopus building does look rather fortresslike, although not offensive per se. It's not ugly.

Climbing up out of Wadi Joz is the hard part; here are some grapes on a bower at an entrance way, starting to turn purple.

Top of the hill is quite barren. On the building at the very top there's a menorah, looks like it's about three feet high and ten feet wide; not lit up right now, of course.

And then you get to the top of the hill, and of course, you can't get there from here. There's a lovely forest of olive trees, very carefully pruned and so forth, at the top of the hill. I can't even tell from here whether I'm actually below the buildings of Scopus or to the left of them, but there's a big barbed-wire fence and I'm going to have to walk down and around to get back there — back to the Hyatt, I think.

Flashback: Elissa had told me that Omar Medina[110] was a black Palestinian, and for some reason I always imagined him with, uh... oh, I'm stopping here because there's a couple of Palestinian kids about fifty yards ahead of me and I want to let them get ahead, nervous for some reason. Not nervous, I'm just being cautious, and I feel silly about that. I had imagined Omar with very fine features and shiny skin and a kaffiyeh. I think I was thinking about a black

---

108. The Palestine Human Rights Information Center.

109. Bushwick is a poor, largely African-American neighborhood in Brooklyn. Though all I intended here was a reminder that dangers are minimized by familiarity and exaggerated by strangeness, still the reference strikes me now as offensive, embarrassing, and in fact vaguely racist — partly because I have *never* walked through Bushwick and hence shouldn't presume to compare it to East Jerusalem.

110. Omar Medina is a Palestinian political activist who spent many years in Israeli jails and, at the time of this writing, was running an independent press service. His ancestors were Ethiopian Christians who emigrated to Palestine long before the establishment of the Jewish state.

Bedouin, I don't know why. He's kind of stocky, could pass for an American black, the way he looks. I don't know.

•

Yes — oh, yes — a flash of realization. From here I can see it. I'm halfway up the Boulevard of the Remnants of Mount Scopus — Shderot Shayeret Har Hatsofim. I look down to the Mosque of Omar, and I look all around, and I get it. *Yerushalayim horim soviv law* — Jerusalem is surrounded by hills. And as Omar Medina said, and as Greta Grünfeld also noted, we're almost completely surrounded now.

And now I'm at the beginning of the campus — hurray for Captain Spalding, the African explorer.

It's nice and cool and flat in here.

Tsvi Ben-Zev is dead. There — there — there's an announcement outside the Truman Institute. The funeral was three days ago in Haifa. He must have died in Canada. He was my age. I only found out because I came here to look for him. I wasn't surprised that he wasn't in his office. I don't understand.

Ronit at the department says it's not our Tsvi Ben-Zev. It's another one, also quite young, an archaeologist, however.

On the way back, the 28 bus from Har Hatsofim to swim at Givat Ram, this classic settler gets on, wearing pin-striped shirt, dark pants, two kids. The man is blond, short blond hair, long blond beard, largish knitted yarmulke, and a pistol stuck in the back of his belt. And as I think to myself I want to record this but can't till I get off, I'm reading Jim Clifford's essay in *Fieldnotes* about how everything we think of as worthwhile noting down is already prefigured.

Comment to Clifford, p. 65.[111] Charles says that in Hebrew going into the fieldwork is *laredet leshetach*, going down into the area; presumably then, to process the results of fieldwork is to raise them up, to spiritualize them, or as Clifford might also say, to allegorize them.

Another thought about East Jerusalem: How often are anthropologists in situations where they fervently wish to be perceived as tourists?

Question: If East Jerusalem is part of Israel, why are soldiers patrolling there?

---

111. "In various Western discourses 'field' is associated with agriculture, property, combat, and a 'feminine' place for ploughing, penetration, exploration, and improvement. The notion that one's empirical, practical activity unfolds in such a space has been shared by naturalists, geologists, archaeologists, ethnographers, missionaries, and military officers" (Clifford 1990: 65).

• 7/11/91 •

From Lederman's essay in *Fieldnotes*, p. 75: "The special value of fieldnotes is their capacity to unsettle, to cause a repositioning of existing boundaries and centers." Is that what I'm doing vis-à-vis my own previous theoretical positions, or am I mostly shoring up what I already see as formulations which transgress existing boundaries?[112]

• 7/14/91 •

Tape notes: Friday afternoon, off to Tekoa.[113] Shoshana seemed delighted — and perhaps even a bit surprised — when I told her I'd like to come out for the entire Shabbat. When I first met her, at a conference in Berkeley this spring, she told me where she lived and immediately said, "You wouldn't want to come there" — because it's across the Green Line and because my brother when he lived here, for a year or two before he left to teach in Berkeley,[114] refused to cross the Green Line unless he was invited by Palestinians. Despite their very different feelings toward the gentile world, my brother and Shoshana found each other as allies when she studied with him at Bar-Ilan University, and he helped her overcome resistance to become the first woman to earn a Ph.D. in Talmud there.

There are only two buses out on Fridays, one at 12:30 and one at 2:00. At the Central Bus Station, only six people get on, and I assume that's all there are going to be for this ride. On the back of the driver's petition,[115] there's a little sticker for an organization called Efrat (Aguda l'edud yeluda — Association for the Encouragement of Childbirth); it says, "Children — the treasure of the family; security [?] for the state; the future of the people." More people get on in front of the Bank Hapoalim Building farther down Rechov Yafo. One woman is reading a Russian newspaper. Stops on King

---

112. This query to myself might need retranslation. There is a certain amount of ethnography relevant to theoretical formulations that could serve them as ornamentation (like grace notes in music perhaps, or the extra lines added to certain letters in the Torah). In this case ethnography would be effectively reinforcing those general formulations rather than challenging them with the contingency of particular situations, as Lederman claims fieldnotes do. Inherent in my antiobjectivist stance is the implication that it is impossible to determine to what extent I have been trying to *use* or gain *insights* from cultural studies in order to gain new insights on Israel and Palestine and to what extent I've simply been trying to introduce the question of Israel and Palestine into the discourse of cultural studies.

113. An ideologically oriented West Bank settlement near Bethlehem.

114. Previously my brother's family had lived in a suburb of the southern city of Beersheba for over ten years, during which time they — like virtually every other Israeli Jew who traveled between Jerusalem and the Negev — regularly took the bus that ran through the West Bank between Jerusalem and Beersheba.

115. Obviously I had politics on my mind as I read this. Please read "partition."

George also. This is definitely not a *frum*[116] crowd. Bus sets off down Derekh Hevron. One woman is reading Kate Simon's *Bronx Primitive*. All of a sudden we're out of the city, in the middle of olive groves that look like Palestine.

When we turn off the main road there's a small army post, and a soldier with a field telephone and a rifle sits in the front seat. We'll be accompanied apparently by an army jeep in front of the bus. We wait; it pulls in front of us and we take off slowly. Is that Bethlehem across the hill to our right? Hebron? I don't know. It's so close to Jerusalem. After about a kilometer the jeep stops, then takes off. There's another army truck; the bus driver has to tell them he's going to Tekoa, and we take off. A few Bedouin tents in the valley; elaborate terracing on some of the hillsides; new houses. Through a crossroads in the middle of the village; a roadblock; we pass through. Next to the village an army camp called Machane Shdema. Another army jeep pulls in front of us. Jesus, what a wild commute. On the second jeep facing us, a soldier with a helmet facing toward us, maybe twenty yards ahead. Small Palestinian houses scattered widely on each hilltop. Very, very bare. An incredible landscape; minaret on top of one of them. Small new orchard. Plowed fields. Radio station playing nothing but American oldies from the 1950s. Valley an incredibly delicate... incredibly delicate landscape.[117] Young orchards, plowed but unirrigated fields, making use of the little water that's available. And then further out more rugged hills, utterly barren, nothing living on them.

We're in the middle of a village. I don't know what the name of it is. I didn't notice a sign. But I wish I was staying here. These villages are incredibly dramatic, partly because they're less crowded and also drier than the villages in the Galilee look. This is one of the most anthropological-looking landscapes I've ever been through. Incredibly[118] exotic to me.

Now we're going past excavations. I guess it's Herodion, since I've seen signs for Herodion all along. The excavated ancient columns nearest the road have graffiti on them.

Toward another valley, fields and orchards. What I mean by delicate agriculture — it's not intensive, it doesn't look crowded.

*There's* a settlement on the next hillside; you can tell from a distance the way the houses are crowded together, the red sort of villa roofs they all have.

Tiny hilltop settlement, a couple of dozen mobile homes. This has obviously

---

116. "Pious" or traditionally observant.
117. On the common use in America of the term "incredible": we often use its adverbial form casually, as a mere synonym for "very," but as in this case also for situations where we want to convey an emotional response we have no words for. Here I remember feeling stymied in particular by the failure of anthropologists to receive explicit training in landscape writing — or at any rate, by the fact that in my previous fieldwork I had rarely encountered a landscape that seemed to demand such an eloquent description.
118. See? Four "incredibles" in two paragraphs.

been here a few years, because of the small trees and shrubs. It's called El David. The Israeli flag flying in a brisk breeze at the entrance is ragged at the edges.

We're descending now into this gracious and bare valley — sparse anyhow — and I suspect that the settlement with the red roofs is going to be Tekoa after all. Yup. Sure isn't real big. It's not on the highest hill, but it sort of looks over the whole valley I've just been trying rather unsuccessfully to describe.

Off tape: Shoshana's husband, Aharon, meets me at the bus. I've met almost all the rest of his family — his brother Zev, an epidemiologist who's lived in Britain and now is married to a non-Jewish woman and lives in Boston; another brother named Geishen, who's studied in the States for a number of years as well; and his parents — his father's a biologist at Hebrew University, and his parents just started a two-year sabbatical in the States. Aharon takes me to their house, in the next-to-newest strip of houses in the settlement. (They call it a *yishuv*, which certainly means "settlement.") Their house has no landscaping. We enter through the sliding glass door of the living room, although there are also a couple of regular doors — the one to the kitchen, which is sometimes used, having an arrangement of large stones instead of proper steps. The Evenes' house right now is just four rooms on one floor — a decent-sized kitchen, a living room about the same size, and two bedrooms. One of the bedrooms is shared by their two boys, Amnon (three and a half) and Oz (two years, three months). There's a wooden area in the ceiling in the center of their house, and when I go next door, to the house that's empty for the weekend where I'll be sleeping the night, I see that a second floor has been added; going up a fairly new but rather creaky staircase I see a bedroom for the parents and a smaller room that's used as a study by the father, who's studying for a doctorate in Jewish thought at Tel Aviv University. The books are almost all in Hebrew and on subjects of Jewish thought and modern philosophy, ranging from Amos Funkenstein to Buber to Rambam and the traditional *sfarim*.[119]

Aharon has recently received official *smicha*[120] from the government religious bodies after finishing a prescribed course of study at an advanced

---

119. *Sfarim* (which can simply mean "books" in general in contemporary Israeli Hebrew) here refers broadly to rabbinic literature in philosophy, commentary, practical rulings, ethics, and the like. Amos Funkenstein is a contemporary historian of science and of Jewish thought, currently teaching at the University of California at Berkeley. Martin Buber was a twentieth-century German Jewish philosopher, writer, and Zionist. Rambam (the name comes from the initial letters of the name Reb Moshe ben Maimon) is Maimonides, the medieval Jewish philosopher, codifier, and physician. All of these figures fall within the broad field of *machshava yehudit*, or "Jewish thought," which is an established academic field in Israel.

120. Rabbinic ordination.

yeshiva, and is now pursuing a doctorate in Jewish studies at Hebrew University. Shoshana tells me that especially for her, but also for Aharon, part of the problem working with people at the university is a very different way of relating to language. When Aharon told his adviser that he wanted to work on a certain theme in Jewish thought, his adviser asked him whether he wanted to go into it before the *Gesher Hachayim* (The bridge of life) or after it. Now, obviously, although I never heard of it, the *Gesher Hachayim* is the name of a certain later rabbinic text; and although I'd never heard it used as a phrase before (except for Rabbi Nachman's song, "The whole wide world is a very narrow bridge"), it's obviously used as an expression to indicate the transitoriness of this world.[121] So to Aharon, when the professor asked that question, it was as if he was asking whether Aharon intended to do this study in this life or in the world to come. But the force of the expression itself didn't seem to enter his mind, only the technical, cataloguable referent — the book in the library.

I arrived at about 3:00 on Friday afternoon with several hours until nightfall and the beginning of Shabbat. During the afternoon Aharon received a telephone call from a woman — presumably in Tekoa — asking for a judgment about religious law. She's very pregnant, going to deliver soon, and she was wondering whether she has to fast on Tisha B'Av.[122] Apparently she does, and she doesn't want to, so she was really trying to find a way to get around it, but with no luck.

As a first reaction, in terms of the investment made at Tekoa, I could see the place being given up if necessary (in contrast to what I wrote about the Beit Shean Valley near Efraim's *he'achzut* a few weeks ago).

Taped notes again: Returning [Saturday night] we have a jeep in front of us and a jeep behind. The one behind us has a side spotlight, which is trained on individual Palestinian houses as we pass by, and then briefly illuminates the fortress of Herodion,[123] and a few minutes later shows me a minaret. As we get under way, a young man with a substantial ponytail and a yarmulke walks

---

121. Actually, it has been used as the title of several works over the last centuries, all dealing with Jewish religious laws surrounding death. "The bridge of life" here is a euphemism. According to my colleague Sylvie Anne Goldberg, the "bridge" indicates a view of death as passage between this world and the next — but, given the kabbalistic origins of the earliest volumes with this title, it must be understood as a bridge that goes both ways (personal communication; see also S. A. Goldberg 1989). Although this sense of the "bridge" is not quite the same as that in Rabbi Nachman's song, the sense of passage and the otherworldly goal are common to both of them.

122. The Ninth of Av, in Jewish tradition the date of the destruction of the Temple in Jerusalem.

123. According to the *Carta* guide, "Named after King Herod who built a fortress on summit and a settlement at its foot.... After great Revolt against Rome was quelled in 70 C.E., the fort served as a refuge for fighters who fled from Jerusalem, until it too fell — like Masada

toward the back of the bus where there's a light on, says *tefilat haderech*,[124] and goes back to his seat. Almost immediately after we turn back onto the main road, we see the lights of Jerusalem already — Gilo off to the immediate left, the Hilton unmistakable in the distance.

•

Various items recollected after Shabbat (during which, of course, I took no notes).

Shoshana's feelings about the Hartman Institute: when I arrived here Shoshana was just finishing up a year working at the institute. She tells me she felt very out of place here, among all these people who basically believe in liberal pluralism and tolerance — she calls it "a dictatorship of pluralism." She doesn't even think the people here were interested in trying to understand her personal attempt to recover the intense striving for divinity that she senses in the rabbis, up to the Geonic period — after which, she claims, there already began the separation between the "secular" and the "religious" aspects of Judaism, in itself therefore a process of secularization. What Shoshana sees in a figure like Rabbi Akiba, and in the other rabbis, especially as they are described in the midrash, is an attempt to capture the fragments of divinity that are present in the words of the Torah, to *become that* through their study of the Torah. And the kind of laid-back tolerance and objectivistic, scholarly attitude she finds at a place like Hartman seems to her utterly to vitiate that vital sense of a lost, authentically Jewish passion for God.

The settlement as it presently exists is laid out on two peaks of the same hill, with a small depression between them. The oldest parts of the settlement are at opposite ends of the two hills. On one, there's a cluster of concrete structures that look like mobile homes; these are the temporary housing, where prospective new residents usually live for a year, very inexpensively, before they decide whether to buy or not (and presumably also before they are formally accepted or not). There are some youngish trees on this part of the settlement, and plenty of grass and shrubs, although not elegantly landscaped. The synagogue — Young Israel of Tekoa,[125] as a matter of fact — is located here as well. At the other end of Tekoa is the oldest and fanciest-looking neighborhood of houses, which tend to be rather bigger and more custom-designed than the newer ones. They also have better gardens, with some

---

six months later. During the Bar Kokhba war, the fortress was used by rebels." There are more recent ruins as well (Carta 1986: 187).

124. Prayers for safety recited before beginning a dangerous journey.

125. Young Israel is the name of a network of mostly Modern Orthodox synagogues, established in 1912 to promote Orthodox Judaism in the United States. Hence, although by no means indicating that most or all of the residents of Tekoa are from the United States, the name of the synagogue indicates U.S. affiliation and sponsorship.

fairly mature trees, grape vines, and so forth. At the edge of this neighborhood is a small library building, in the garden of which are planted trees with the "seven varieties" of fruits of the Land of Israel which have particular religious significance, all of which are available for anyone who lives in Tekoa to take in order to teach the children. The people who live here are older, professional people.

The impression the whole place gives is that of a quickly growing and prosperous kibbutz. The original *garin*, or nucleus (Efraim's group is also called a *garin*, because in principle they're all expected to settle on a kibbutz together when they're done with the army, although most of them certainly won't), was made up of a combination of Americans and Russians. By now the population seems quite mixed — some Israelis, I heard one family speaking French.... Not quite everyone works in the city. There's a modest vineyard, which several families own and work in partnership. There's also a goat dairy downhill (and presumably also downwind) to the east; the milk from the goats is turned into cheese. There's also a family that has an educational software company — they manufacture, for instance, a program that teaches children how to read Hebrew. One of the houses has a curiously shaped top floor, kind of oblong like a ship; the roof contains an experimental wind-electric generating station. The family received money from someone in Germany to set up this experiment. Shoshana tells me that one time the lights went out in her home on Shabbat, and they had a very hard time figuring out what to do until someone remembered that there was a goy at Tekoa just then. They weren't allowed to directly ask him to turn the lights on, but he quickly figured out that they wanted him to be the *shabbes goy*, and he was delighted to be of service.[126]

There's no rush to get through the *kabbalat shabbat*[127] prayers at Tekoa — no reason to hurry, the day will be long enough. Before *maariv*[128] the rabbi gives a short lesson on the avoidance of slandering a fellow Jew. He introduces it with a comparison between two kinds of *shmira*:[129] Hashomer, the (antireligious and socialist or Marxist, though he doesn't say this) group that

---

126. In Jewish law, a Jew is not permitted directly to ask a Gentile to do something for the Jew that Jews are forbidden to do for themselves. Nevertheless, in many traditional diasporic Jewish communities, services such as lighting a fire on Sabbath mornings have been routinely performed by a Gentile, for this reason called a *shabbes goy* in Yiddish. (See also the entry in "My Trip to Israel" for October 1.) Symptomatic of the vastly different modality of even "Orthodox" Jewish life in a place like Tekoa, it was evidently extraordinary to find a Gentile available when one was needed.
127. "Welcoming the Sabbath," a series of psalms and hymns inserted before the evening prayers on Friday.
128. The evening service proper.
129. "Watching" or "guarding."

did so much to establish the original Jewish presence in the land in this century; and *Shmirat Halashon,* the book of the Chofets Chaim about the terrible sin of slander and the collective harm it causes the Jewish people. To my pleasure, I find I understand what the rabbi is saying — in an animated, clear, loud, and percussive, but not very fast, way — and Aharon explains to me later that the rabbi tends to keep his public lessons fairly simple, as I find confirmed later in the Shabbat.

Through the windows of the simple synagogue building I watch the fairly rapid progress of the color sequence of the sunset sky — from bright orange to red to purple, I think — just the same sight I saw through the much smaller window of a Persian synagogue in downtown Jerusalem about three weeks previously. I watch Rabbi Kertser (Kutsher? Katzer?), a man with medium-length straight *peyos*[130] and longish, light-brown beard going to gray, focusing with enthusiasm on *lecha dodi,*[131] spreading out his hands at the verse "spread out left and right," looking away from me toward the dusk. And as the night comes on, more and more lights appear on the far ridge. At first I think to myself that there are more people living around this little valley than I thought, but later Shoshana explains to me that those are the lights of Bethlehem, which, because of the slow ride to Tekoa and the winding road getting there, I had assumed was much farther away.

On Shabbat morning, as we walked toward the synagogue, I asked Aharon the name of the village directly in front of us and nearest to the settlement, with a minaret helping to make it seem more concentrated and permanent than the other clusters of houses surrounding the little valley. "Tekoa," Aharon said. At first I thought he hadn't understood me, and then I thought he was teasing me, but that's the name of the Arab village — or maybe it's something more like "Tuqua." "That's the original Tekoa," Aharon said. "Amos lived there." (After this conversation, I have the idea of getting to the village of Tuqua and trying to find out what people there have to say about Tekoa.) Later, on a late afternoon walk, Shoshana and Aharon mention the rabbi's insistence that Rabbi Shim'on ben Yochai also came from this Tekoa, although they say it's absolutely clear that he came from a village of the same name in the Galilee. "Patriotism," I say. No, they insist — the rabbi feels no need to prove that Yehuda[132] is part of Erets Yisrael. I say, no, I meant he's just boosting his town. The vineyards of the Arab village reach almost as far as the new settlement. I wondered briefly how the land had been acquired by the Israeli government, but didn't ask anybody there.

---

130. Sidelocks.
131. "Come, My Beloved," the high point of the *kabbalat shabbat* service.
132. Judea.

Every Shabbat morning after the services (which begin at 8:00 and are done by around 10:00), there's a lesson in the Torah portion of the week, which members of the congregation sign up to present. Shoshana tells me that she has given the *drasha,* and that the rabbi had no objections to it. Today, however, the rabbi himself gives the *drasha* — I think in substitute for someone who's not doing it for some reason that's not clear to me. Fortunately for me, the subject of this week's Torah reading — *matot-masa'i* — is substantially the process of entering the land, and hence the rabbi goes into a discussion of the question of the various borders for the land that are discussed at various times: How do the sages resolve the contradictions between the vast area promised to Abraham (from the Nile to the Euphrates), and the smaller area described (to Moses?)? Essentially, the answer is that the lands of the seven peoples (sometimes six) are given to the people immediately upon coming into the land, while the lands of the other three (the lands of ten peoples are promised to Abraham) are a promise for the World to Come. There's a debate among the rabbis about where the lands of those three peoples are — some say the land of the Nabateans (which presumably includes the Arava, not part of what's usually thought of as historical Erets Yisrael), some saying to the east, one of them mentioning "Cartagena" (which the rabbi insists is Carthage in Tunisia,[133] while a member of the congregation thinks it must mean the original city in Lebanon). Then the big question of the northern limits, simply designated in our portion of the Torah as "Har Hohar" — sort of meaning "The Big Mountain." Some opinions place this at the top of Lebanon, where Syria and Turkey meet, which would mean that all of Lebanon is in fact part of Erets Yisrael. Some, on the other hand, place it at a mountain in the middle of Lebanon, where the Canaanites were known to have an altar. And this indicates to the rabbi the symbolic significance that the borders of Judaism are the borders of idol worship; that Judaism lies between the "snow mountain" (*har hasheleg*) of philosophy (I don't think he indicated where that might be located) and the "fire mountain" of idolatry. Aharon interjects, "There are less mystical opinions about where the northern limit is," and the rabbi counters, "There are more mystical opinions as well!"

The rabbi has been informed about my visit, and I'm invited to his house for *seuda shlishit.*[134] Aharon walks me over about 6:30, and I find the rabbi sitting on his "back porch," underneath a metal framework that as of now is only very partially covered by a grape vine, overlooking the bare hills facing east toward the Jordan River — an incredible view, the opposite one from the view toward Bethlehem. (Shoshana says some people in Tekoa claim to

---

133. Thus extending Jewish territorial ambitions in a highly unorthodox direction.

134. The "third meal" on Saturday afternoon, designed to fulfill the injunction to enjoy three festive meals in the course of each Sabbath.

be able to see the Dead Sea.) (On the next hill now, in fact, there are a number of small concrete houses which, when they are completed, will be the first permanent houses of the new site of El David. These houses, which don't have the same European-style red roofs as the houses of Tekoa, don't look much different from the similar Palestinian houses close by, except that they're laid out more closely and more regularly.) About six of the rabbi's children — ranging from a young woman of perhaps seventeen, to a two- or three-year-old girl — wander in and out the open door, while one of the boys — Shivi? — keeps climbing around the metal latticework. In addition to his wife, the only people sitting and listening at this point are a fellow a few years older than me, who doesn't say anything, and an interesting couple — she with her head covered, very pregnant (in Hebrew the verb is *leha'er*, to become a mountain),[135] and wearing pants; he with thinning blond hair, barefoot, no shoes. The rabbi is reading from the *Talmudic Encyclopedia*, various items: about the virtue of this small country, that within such a small space everything is found: valleys, mountains, springs...; his wife interjects, "But we don't have a *yam*," a sea of our own.[136] He comes back, "Yes, we have the Dead Sea," but she's not satisfied with that. The last point he comes to is the names of the land — usually it's called Erets Canaan, and it's not until Ezekiel that, twice, the name "Erets Yisrael" is regularly used, although by the time of the Mishna and the Gemara the term Erets Yisrael is constantly used.[137]

After a while, the rabbi stopped, and asked me a little bit about what I was doing here. By now I felt fairly comfortable saying in Hebrew that I was working on the subject of collective identity and the Israeli-Palestinian conflict, but mostly I was just going around Jerusalem and around the country talking to people. He didn't object to my description of the project, except to correct me when I said I was talking both to Palestinians... (How did I say it, "around here"? I certainly didn't say in the "territories...") and to "the Arabs of the Land of Israel," as the government puts it. He said, "All of it's the Land of Israel; you mean the Arabs of the State of Israel."[138] OK. Other than that,

---

135. Actually *leharot*.
136. She either forgot about or discounted the Mediterranean here.
137. The Mishna and the Gemara together comprise the Talmud; the period referred to here is thus roughly the first through sixth centuries C.E.
138. The semiofficial phrase is actually Araviyey Erets Yisrael, meaning "The Arabs of the Land of Israel." Since I was the one who made the initial distinction between Palestinians and those living in the "Land of Israel," it is hardly surprising that he would feel compelled to remind me that the State of Israel was not the entire Land of Israel. If I did in fact use the term "Palestinians" at all, as I report here, I was in any case resisting the basic thrust of the official term, which has the effect of denying the specific ties between Palestinian identity and the land. I probably could have said "and also to Arab citizens," but anthropologists frequently make such mistakes as they try to adjust their own categories to those they expect their interlocutors to employ.

he was simply surprised at how general my project was, sensing correctly that it's much more general than the usual field project in anthropology. When I mentioned that I'd been in Ar'ara, the rabbi surprised me by saying that he knew the town — he'd spent several days there once, studying the Qur'an in a *khevruta*[139] with a man named Ali Samir.

During the "third meal," the rabbi teaches a few items from another book, called *People of the Bible* (*Ishei Hatanakh*), focusing on the figure of Joshua. He reads a midrash: Why was Joshua called *bin Nun*, son of a fish? (*Nun* means "fish" in Aramaic.) Answer: Joshua's parents tried unsuccessfully for a long time to have a child, and finally their prayers were answered and his mother became pregnant. His father continued praying, although his mother said it was no longer necessary, and eventually the father explained he'd had a dream that his son would be his hangman. They put the baby into an ark when he was born, and he was found by Pharaoh's family (daughter?) and raised in Pharaoh's house. Eventually Joshua became a hangman; his father somehow sinned against Pharaoh, and was brought before Joshua, who in fact hung him. This is a very interesting story, the rabbi commented — there are motifs similar to the story of Moses in it, but also similarities to the Oedipus story.

After the meal — cold breaded fish, fried cabbage, tomato and cucumber salad, reheated noodles, rice — that's somewhat more substantial than those I'm used to at my Lower East Side synagogue, the rabbi invited me to lead the *bentshing*. Rightly perceiving that he enjoys a little bit of cultural variety, I started off the way Rabbi Singer does, in Yiddish: "*Hert tsi, raboysey mir veln bentshn,*"[140] and was rewarded with a smile from the rabbi.

Then it was time for *maariv*, and as the rabbi and I hurried to the synagogue, we admired the new crescent moon. I asked him if they would be saying *kidush levana*[141] tonight, and he replied that even by the Ashkenazi tradition, which is to wait until three days after the New Moon, it wasn't time yet. But I got him talking about the moon — he wondered how it had become the Islamic symbol, and also noted that it's quite traditional for Israel to be identified with the moon,[142] and Rome with the sun.

---

139. This term denotes intense study — usually of Jewish religious texts — with a partner.

140. *Bentshn* is Yiddish for reciting any blessing, here specifically the blessings recited after a meal including bread. The term derives from the Latin *benedicere*. The formula "*Raboysey mir veln bentshn*" (Gentlemen, we will now recite the blessing), here with the added exhortation "*Hert tsi*" (Listen!), is used to gather everyone's attention and thus assure a quorum for the recitation of the prayer.

141. The sanctification of the new moon, recited once each month at the conclusion of the Sabbath, provided the moon is visible.

142. The text for the ceremony of *kiddush levana*, the sanctification of the new moon, makes this association explicit: "To the moon He said that it should renew itself as a crown

• 7/15/91 •

Tekoa still: Shoshana is not sure she and her family are going to stay in Tekoa; she's not happy with the school there. The population of Tekoa, unusual for a small settlement, is a mix of religious and secular Jews. The school is designed to accommodate both, and she finds it ends up providing neither perspective, nor does it provide enough educational substance — "They teach values instead." (It seemed to me that there was more of a religious presence, however. Thus when the boys and girls arrived for the evening service in their blue and white uniforms of Bnei Akiva,[143] Shoshana explained to me that a number of children from "secular" families participate in Bnei Akiva as well.) Nevertheless, the disputes in Tekoa aren't along religious lines — she doesn't specify, but I suppose she means they're about philosophy of education instead. For Amnon, who's almost four, she finds the *gan*[144] inadequate enough that this year they took him in to go to school in Jerusalem every day.

So Shoshana and Aharon clearly aren't ideologically committed to living in the "territories" or in "Judea"; what Shoshana stresses more than anything else as what attracts her to the place is rather the mix of religious and non-religious people, which permits her to develop and express her Judaism in her own individualistic way, without the sense of suffocating conformity that she feels in a typical Orthodox neighborhood like Bayit veGan.[145] I guess they're trying to make up their minds this summer so that they'll know where the children are going to go to school in the fall, because several times Shoshana stressed to me that they might be living somewhere else next time I come to visit them.

This certainly doesn't mean that Shoshana is indifferent to the question of where she lives. When she came to America for the conference this spring,[146] she was uncomfortable. The worst problem was not knowing what she could eat and what she couldn't. (Shoshana and Aharon are certainly stricter than I am, and doubtless somewhat stricter than my brother as well in matters of kashrut.) But she doesn't see what makes this country special for the type of Israeli who "just happens to be born here," and doesn't have any particular

---

of splendor for those borne [by Him] from the womb, those who are destined to renew themselves like it" (Scherman 1985: 648).

143. "Children of Akiva," the youth movement of the Mizrachi religious Zionist organization.

144. Nursery school or kindergarten.

145. A neighborhood of Jerusalem within the Green Line, toward the western part of the city, occupied largely by "black hat," or traditionalist, rather than "knitted-*kippa*," or Modern Orthodox, Jews.

146. A conference in April 1991 called "People of the Body/People of the Book," sponsored by the Jewish Studies programs at the University of California at Berkeley and at Stanford University.

Jewish education or sensibility. In fact, citing the example of Aharon's family, she assumes that eventually most of them will leave the country — "Why stay in a place where you're likely to get stabbed by an Arab just because you're Jewish, if being Jewish doesn't mean much of anything to you?" On the other hand, she sees the arrival of the Russians as an act of divine providence — if it weren't for such Jewish infusions, she could imagine this whole state becoming a relic, and nothing left behind but the same population of utterly devoted Jews who have always stayed in this land.

Shoshana says that raising children at Tekoa is very much like raising children on a kibbutz. Walking back and forth between the synagogue and Shoshana and Aharon's house, at the other end of the settlement, the two kids are continually being misplaced — they've wandered off with a friend, they've gone to the playground behind the synagogue. On Friday night we looked around for the older one, Amnon, and eventually found him waiting for us at home already. But generally when Shoshana is at home, she likes to keep the boys close to her, unlike other families where the kids wander freely around the settlement. This causes problems of safety, Shoshana points out: people's cars and houses are left open, kids can get in and hurt themselves. There was an incident in one settlement where two small children got into a car, closed the doors, and eventually died of exposure.

Another thing that draws Shoshana and Aharon to Tekoa is the unusual percentage of educated and professional people there — there are a number of professors, a couple of professional musicians, a psychologist, and so on.

On Friday night as we passed by a small parking lot in one of the neighborhoods, Aharon walked over to inspect a car whose rear right window was apparently rolled down, and the little window behind it shattered. A rock had been thrown at the car on Thursday. A pregnant woman from Tekoa was hurt by the rock. Shoshana thought she was in the hospital, though Aharon assured her that the woman was home. (Waiting for the bus Saturday night, they pointed her out to me, standing talking to some people, with a Band-Aid on her cheek.) Shoshana added: "And I drive back and forth at night all the time." I wasn't sure I saw this, but it seemed to me that when they can, cars join the caravan with the bus and the army jeep. The buses and some people's cars have shatterproof plastic windshields and windows, but Shoshana and Aharon's car doesn't.

The bus back to Jerusalem didn't leave until a few hours after the end of Shabbat — it pulled into Tekoa first at 10:30, but then made a circuit of a few more nearby settlements before it came back and headed for Jerusalem. Shoshana engaged me during these two or three hours in a rather challenging discussion, half in Hebrew and half in English, about the bases of my claim that in my theoretical work, what I'm trying to do is to articulate my Jewish identity and my human identity. How do I know that what I'm opposing to "human identity" is "Jewish"? It seemed to her that what I study is not so much Judaism as what people called Jews happen to think and believe, and that, like the people at Hebrew University, like the Wissenschaft des Judentums[147] crowd (in fact like the Rambam[148] as well, although Shoshana is obviously very conflicted about her criticisms of him: How can she accept him as a religious legal authority and then deny him intellectually?), most of what I do even when I'm talking about Jews is not particularly "Jewish." So I told her my standard story about being at Reed College and coming to consciousness of how much I'd been already shaped by my Jewishness,[149] but she still wasn't satisfied: What was the content of it? I told her that I was baffled and dissatisfied with the abstract idealism of the standard education, the notion that there was a world of ideas and analysis separate from history, from experience — that I believed that language and matter are all part of one world, and that this seems to me to be a Jewish idea. She agreed with that; a sense of the mystical character of language in constituting the world is very much part of her search for authentic Jewish experience; but still she persisted: How did I know that this wasn't perhaps a modern form of paganism? I turned the tables and asked her how she knew her own sensibilities were "Jewish." She replied, quite sensibly, that all of her education had been Jewish, just as her son, not four years old yet, will be starting to learn the weekly Torah portion in school next year. (Shoshana's mother is from Egypt; her father's mother was from Morocco, her father's father from Persia. Her father's father was apparently quite a kabbalist, participating in ceremonies at the kabbalist synagogue in Machane Yehuda, and so on. But the children know very little about it, partly because such things are not really to be spoken of; discretion is part of the whole aesthetic. One story she did tell me, however: he was part of an *aliya*[150] from Persia that came on horses and donkeys. He paid the donkey drivers extra money so that they would stop on Shabbat. Friday evening came, they were in the middle of a wilderness, and the drivers refused to lose a day of work. He said, "In that case we'll all just get off the donkeys and stay here," which the Jews did, while the donkey drivers continued. Just after nightfall, after Shabbat ended, the donkey drivers returned; the central donkey in the caravan had bolted, and they had only just found him, so in fact they were unable to continue without the Jews on the Shabbat. A folklorist from Hebrew University had collected some stories about Shoshana's grand-

---

147. The nineteenth-century "Science of Judaism" school of research, centered in Germany.
148. Maimonides.
149. Documented in J. Boyarin 1988: 58–60.
150. Here, a group migration to the Land of Israel.

father from her father, written an M.A. thesis which won a prize, and invited Shoshana's rather bemused father to the ceremony.)

What I think Shoshana wanted from me is not so much any renunciation of my own path as perhaps a bit less of a defensive framework — she challenged me especially on the idea that Judaism is simply a social construction (I didn't say that, but she correctly sensed that that's more or less my working assumption). She would like more Jews to be digging deeper to re-create an authentic Judaism, as she sees herself doing.

Immediately after my class, I set off for Beit Sahour to meet Hatem Asmari, whom several people — Terri Khoury, Lyla Shoukri, Chagit Katzev-Haft — have recommended to me as one of the most respected and thoroughthinking Palestinian intellectuals. He's instructed me first to take a taxi to Bethlehem, and then get onto the bus to Beit Sahour; I'm still not sure why he didn't tell me just to get onto the bus to Beit Sahour, although it seems clear that what he told me to do is considerably more comfortable and maybe even faster. The taxi costs a shekel and a half, the bus half a shekel.

• 7/16/91 •

Yesterday — after writing that first paragraph about Beit Sahour — I took a monumental day trip to Safed, which I'll write up shortly, based on my taped notes. We got back close to midnight, so I didn't even try to wake up early today — besides, my regular schedule, such as it is, is off because there's no Talmud class in the Old City on Tuesdays (Andy has to work), and I can't go swimming because of the Nine Days before Tisha B'Av. So I finally got up after the second train of the day — this one presumably arriving from Tel Aviv — going down the tracks behind Ruth's house passed at 7:40.[151] I was in the middle of an elaborate dream in which I was sitting and arguing with Abed Shahin[152] from the Palestine Aid Society about the best way to fight the American occupation [that's what I said in the tape] — heh heh, the

---

151. I had by this time moved from Yemin Moshe to Baka'a, but for some reason didn't think the move worthy of recording in my journal. It is not quite accurate to suggest, as I did in the introduction, that I was primarily dependent on "the kindness of strangers"; rather, I was dependent on the hospitality of friends and relatives. This has of necessity been a theme in my ethnographic practice among Jews from the beginning, from Paris to the Lower East Side and Jerusalem. Trained in a generation already questioning the epistemology that valued cultural distance prior to fieldwork, I have employed a logic of fieldwork that has always been built around a prior social/genealogical connection. My ethnography is thus both an investigation and a perpetuation of "Jewish geography" (D. Boyarin and J. Boyarin 1993; J. Boyarin, ed., 1994).

152. The organizer of the New York chapter of one of the Palestinian solidarity organizations, with whom I occasionally worked in my capacity as a member of the International Jewish Peace Union.

Israeli occupation — from America. I was proposing an elaborate scheme of boycotting any Israeli products that come from across the Green Line [for a while an Israeli organization called Twenty-First Year, whose explicit purpose was to refuse to benefit from the occupation, tried this; they haven't existed for about a year at this point, when the occupation is in its twenty-fifth year], and realizing that this was an extremely complicated thing to try to do.

•

Back to Beit Sahour: on the way out, along the same road — Derekh Hevron — which I'd gone out and come back in on to Tekoa, just past the Gilo intersection, I notice that all the buses and taxis are being pulled over and the passengers are having their papers checked. Coming back from Beit Sahour, I'm in one of those taxis that's stopped, and I realize that it's only the people with green plates from the territories who are being pulled over; those with yellow plates drive on past. I ask the driver of the taxi if it's like this every day, and he says it is. Since I'm sitting in the front seat next to the driver, the soldier leans in and asks me first — for my papers, or where I'm from — in Arabic, of course. I listen to him twice, and then for once do the right thing: I say in English, "I don't understand what you're saying." The taxi driver tells the soldier that I'm a tourist, and the soldier accepts the explanation, while everyone else's papers are being checked; one man says he's from Ramallah, and (I think) that his wife just gave birth and he's going to see her in the hospital. The whole procedure, of course, is irritating and demeaning, but I'm somewhat immune to it not only because I'm an outsider, but because I feel comfortable at being on the "right side" of this particular bit of degradation (see notes on Na'aran following). Gilo, on the opposite (west) side of this road from Bethlehem and Beit Sahour, seems (sorry for the anthropomorphism) to be reaching awfully close; but from my few forays into Palestinian towns and my attempts to understand the geography better, I don't yet understand the articles I've read about plans to develop Jewish neighborhoods in what the Israelis call "Jerusalem" that will cut off Bethlehem and Beit Sahour from Ramallah.[153]

Coming into Bethlehem, I realized that what I could see from Tekoa was probably only the last and probably newest hillside of houses; it feels like a city, even though it's on steep hills and not laid out on a grid. There are several long, low, fairly unattractive buildings that are billed as tourist/shopping centers, though today (again, maybe because it's Sunday) they're closed altogether. On the roofs of a couple of low commercial buildings, there are Israeli

---

153. A map of projected housing units in East Jerusalem for homeless Israelis and Soviet immigrants, published in *Ha'aretz* on November 7, 1990, notably shows a planned seven thousand new units in the north, toward Ramallah, and four thousand in Har Homa to the south (anonymous 1990: 12).

army tents — an incongruous site, as if conquering Bedouins had swept into the town and continued to live their own way.

Just in time I tell the driver I want to be let off next to the bus to Beit Sahour, and he shows me where to wait. One of the young men — *shebab* I suppose — waiting for the bus is wearing a Wildwood, New Jersey, T-shirt. Soon the bus comes — it's more than a van but less than a full bus, seats about twenty I suppose — and goes just a short way into Beit Sahour, which by now has grown to the point where there's no open country between the two towns. Hatem Asmari isn't there when I step off (when I meet him, he explains that he waited until 11:30 — just a few minutes before I arrived — and then left because I hadn't called to confirm. Nor had I taken into account that Sunday isn't a work day in Beit Sahour, a largely Christian town). A young man named Issa Jabari is waiting there for a group from Belgium to arrive. He waits with me for Hatem to come back, and after about twenty minutes I suggest we could try calling, which involves a walk through the old part of the town (narrow streets, archways; Hatem later says "old town" means anywhere between two and four hundred years old), down into a valley and a little bit up the other side, and then, because the post office is closed on Sunday, into the AbuSada part of town, where new and prosperous-looking houses are built on what used to be agricultural fields. I explain to Issa that I live in an apartment, and that there aren't any private houses in the part of New York where I live; the land alone would cost hundreds of thousands of dollars. "Here we own the land," he says; but he does complain about the unemployment and other problems. He has just graduated from high school, and is waiting for what he calls applications from several universities in the United States, which he thinks will permit him to study there this fall — I don't know whether he means acceptances, or whether he thinks applications are all he needs; but he does know that he'll have to work while he's there, and that he needs a sponsor to get a visa in any case. Before we arrive at his house — where he'll introduce me to his father and give me some Coke before taking me next door to his uncle's house to try to make a phone call there — he invites me to sleep over at his family's house any time.

I have a brief conversation with Issa's father, in Arabic and in English, in the course of which Issa's father makes it clear that it would be nice if Issa had someone in New York who would sponsor him and help him go to school there, but I, embarrassed, say that he would really have to work through Palestinian networks — New York is a very hard and expensive city, and I wouldn't know how to help Issa find work, and so on. They drop it, and we go to the uncle's house. Several people are sitting around in the kitchen of this large and unfinished home. There's no answer at Hatem's home, and the office number turns out to be a wrong number twice, though I've reached it before. Issa says he'll ask his father to take us to Hatem's office in his car, which I'm grateful for (how they found out where it was I don't know). There's no one at the office, but at the bakery downstairs where two young men are packing pita into plastic bags, they direct us next door to his home, where his mother, wife, and baby son invite me in. Hatem had told me that if for some reason he wasn't waiting for me, people would know how to find him; but still it was kind of Issa and his father to help me, especially after I'd basically given them the brush-off on their request for help in America.

The baby, maybe a year old maybe less but big, let me hold him, do "baby lifts" and amuse him, and tried to get at my glasses while Hatem's wife, Nadia, called Hatem and I waited for him to arrive, which he did after a few minutes: medium height, youngish-looking, but greying yet I think not much older than me, with short hair and a trim beard. When I told Hatem that this was my first time in Beit Sahour but that my brother had been here for the famous prayer service, he said, "Ah, I was in jail then." Later it came out that he[154] was the main author of the incredibly eloquent one-page statement "from the people of Beit Sahour to the peace-loving people in Israel" that was gotten out of Beit Sahour during the tax strike/Israeli siege and read by my brother on Israeli TV[155] (get a copy of this and append it).[156] The Israelis kept him at the police station from 8:00 A.M. to 8:00 P.M. every day, and then let him go home only when there was curfew, but somehow, with the help of Israeli friends,[157] they got the statement written. Hatem was detained because of alleged "underground activities," but he has never been formally charged.

We drive through the village a short way, and pull up in front of a lovely, sort of Malibu-style house[158] — two levels kind of set into the hillside, reddish-brown rather than the usual white concrete or stone, with a sloping roof — as Hatem explains, "I'm visiting with a few friends here." In fact it's

---

154. Hatem, not Daniel.
155. In fact, as my brother corrects the account, it was shown on Jordanian and Syrian television. Airwaves being no respecter of state boundaries, the footage was certainly seen by many Arabic speakers inside Israel as well.
156. See the entry above for June 26, 1991.
157. Primarily Judy Levi.
158. The source of this image is, patently, the dream of Charles Waters that I report above (in the entry for July 7): there, not his *description* of Beit Sahour but a dream association intended to highlight the contrast between Beit Sahour and Gaza. This is an unusually clear example of the way prior sets of rhetorics and available images help to structure and inform accounts of new places, a process that has been extraordinarily well documented in recent accounts of the colonial encounter in Latin America (see, for example, González Echevarría 1987; Greenblatt 1991; O'Gorman 1961; Rabasa 1993). Now, in February 1994, I have an image in my memory of what this particular house looked like, but only the vaguest notion of what a "Malibu-style house" might look like. This should serve as a reminder (and it *is* needed, repeatedly) that what's written on paper is not a perfect mapping of the images in a writer's mind.

quite a party, maybe thirty people including kids, most of them intellectuals, community activists, people from the university. The party is being given in honor of a couple of Americans who've been working as the Mennonite staff in East Jerusalem for the last five years, obviously working closely with people in Beit Sahour and with the Rapprochement Center which Hatem seems to be the host of, and are about to return to live in Indiana. The couple who are replacing them are there as well, having just arrived after two years' working with Father Elias Chacour in Ibillin. The host of the party, Abu Hamid, is a consulting contractor, as I'm informed by his son Hamid, who's just graduated from Valparaiso University in Indiana[159] with a degree in engineering (with the Russians and the Palestinians, this country must have the highest per capita ratio of engineers in the world). People are sitting on a concrete patio under the back, downhill side of the house, which faces a garden including a lush grape arbor and several young fruit trees, again facing a hillside and houses spread out on the other side. And lo and behold, at the side of the house there's a small swimming pool filled with kids — maybe ten feet wide by twenty-five, but deep enough to dive at one end. An elderly woman from Belgium remarks that this is the first time in "twenty-two years [living? visiting?] in Palestine" that she's seen a Palestinian swimming pool, and the woman who's standing with us watching the men and boys in the pool (some of the men eventually got in, but none of the adult women did) says that there are four or five in Beit-Sahour, "but remember this is the top of Palestinian society; they don't have swimming pools in refugee camps." She also mentions that before the intifada, they used to go to Israeli pools to swim, but they don't any more. (Useful to bear this in mind when I react to the absence of Arabs with the analogy of apartheid — some of the "separation" comes from the Palestinian side as well.) (Thinking of what has changed since the intifada, I remember the last time I was in Israel, in February of 1988, Sandy Brisker's wife, Beth, telling me about the mixed theater group she'd been running with Arab girls from Beit Safafa and Jewish girls from Jerusalem, and that it had been getting harder recently. I remember thinking that it was a sort of "liberal" thing — trying to show that people can get along without facing the really difficult political challenge — and in retrospect now I appreciate that kind of effort much more.) (The same woman said that at about any point, half of the town is "inside" and the other half is working "outside" — many in the States, but, surprisingly enough to me, she said they have a lot of people in Honduras as well.)[160]

---

159. Presumably because Valparaiso University is a Christian institution, a number of students from Beit Sahour have gone there.

160. "Inside" here means in Palestine; "outside" refers to the Palestinian Diaspora.

Everyone at the party speaks English well, and there's a lot of English around, since not only I, but also the people who work for the Mennonites, don't seem to be exactly fluent in Arabic. I participate in bits of various conversations: one is between me and Hatem, though it's not entirely successful because what I have to say to him is very theoretical and political, and we're in the midst of a congenial party. When I get to my point about Israelis not understanding what Palestinians are so angry about because they don't recognize the dispossession of the Palestinians, Hatem challenges me: Do they really not know, or do they actually know and they're content with the knowledge?[161] Talking this note into my tape recorder, a part of a verse from the daily morning service pops into my head: *"Hen heim yodu vey'vorchu,"* "They know and they bless...."[162] I mention to Hatem that I had been in Tekoa the previous day, and he mentions Rabbi Kutsher and says — I think — that Rabbi Kutsher is friendly with some people in Beit Sahour. On the other hand, he says, "We've had trouble with Tekoa — well, with one man in Tekoa. One day he came out with a rifle and shot a young boy who was sitting in his house[163] right in the head, and the boy died immediately. The man claimed there were some stones in the road, but some Palestinians went and they didn't see anything. He just wanted to kill somebody. He was arrested, and I think they locked him up for forty-eight hours, or something like that." Nobody mentioned this incident to me in Tekoa.

•

By about 3:00 the party was breaking up and it was time to head back to Jerusalem. Hatem drove me to the bus, which this time was empty except for me and a young blind man. The driver, a middle-aged man wearing a kaffiyeh, let the young blind man off just a hundred meters or so from the bus stop, and refused to accept the half-shekel fare from him. Hearing the way I pronounced "Bet-Lechem," the driver insisted on speaking Hebrew to me, though I said I wanted to speak Arabic. He knew Hebrew because he had

---

161. Over the last decade or so, and particularly since the beginning of the intifada, there has been a substantial debate in academic and intellectual circles over the "revisionist" historiography of the 1948 war and the immediate postwar years, sparked in particular by books written by Benny Morris (1987) and Tom Segev (1986). Certainly this should not be represented as a "national" recognition of the dispossession of the Palestinians, but it does represent a significant challenge to established Zionist historiography for those who explicitly concern themselves with such matters.

162. In fact, the inflected form *yodu* in this passage is derived from the infinitive *lehodot*, "to praise," and not from *lada'at*, "to know"; the phrase means "they thank and they bless." "They" here refers to the vital organs, the spirit and the tongue of God's creatures. It appears in the prayer that begins with *"Nishmas kol chay,"* "The spirit of all living things," in the Sabbath and festival service (Scherman 1985: 439). If my Hebrew had been better I would less likely have made this bitter association.

163. That is, the boy was sitting in the boy's own house.

worked for Egged for six years in the garage. He told me that the young man had been standing on the street in East Jerusalem, and had been shot in the head; the bullet went in here — he pointed near his temple — and went out the other side, and everyone was amazed that he survived.

On Monday morning here at Hartman, my office-mate, Moshe, is speculating on whom I'll find on a tour to the Ari's[164] grave run by the municipality — poor Sephardim, he guesses. Those waiting anxiously where the bus was parked on Strauss when I got there around 10:15 turned out to be what I noted as "an incredibly ordinary-looking bunch of Jews, mostly middle-aged or elderly. Not quite all of them religious, even; a couple of men with *kipas*. A woman and her husband or her father speaking French." The employee of the Torah Department — an unpretentious fellow named Lieberman, in his fifties — called out the names of those registered as they came on one by one, to make sure everybody was there. The bus belongs to the Mate Benyamin Development Company — so obviously it is not the case, as I assumed when I noticed such a bus for the first time about four weeks ago, that they are used exclusively for transportation to and around the various portions of the territories (there's also a Gush Etzion Development Company) with their own local councils. The guide, named Gavriel, was a trim, slight man with no beard and a knitted yarmulke; he was from (I think I heard correctly) a Persian Jewish family.

• 7/17/91 •

As the bus took off on Monday morning, the guide, Gavriel, read the aggadah[165] about Rabbi Akiva and the foxes in Jerusalem,[166] and said that he

---

164. Along with Joseph Caro, the most famous of the sixteenth-century kabbalists of Safed, and therefore revered as a saint up to the present.

165. A genre of rabbinic narrative, contained in the Talmud and in separate collections, relating to points in Jewish law and history.

166. "Once again they [Rabban Gamaliel, R. Eleazar b. 'Azariah, R. Joshua, and R. Akiba] were coming up to Jerusalem together, and just as they came to Mount Scopus they saw a fox emerging from the Holy of Holies. They began to weep and R. Akiba seemed happy. 'Why are you happy?' they said to him. He said: 'Why are you weeping?' They said to him: 'A place of which it was once said, *And the common man that draws near shall be put to death*, has become the haunt of foxes, and should we not weep?' He said to them: 'That is why I am happy, for it is written, *And I will take to Me faithful witnesses to record, Uriah the priest and Zechariah the son of Jeberechiah*. Now what connection has this Uriah the priest with Zechariah? Uriah lived during the time of the First Temple, while Zechariah lived during the Second Temple; but the Holy Writ linked the [later] prophecy of Zechariah with the [earlier] prophecy of Uriah. In the prophecy of Uriah it is written, *Therefore shall Zion for your sake be ploughed as a field etc.* In Zechariah it is written, *Thus saith the Lord of Hosts, Old men and old women shall yet sit in the broad places of Jerusalem*. So long as Uriah's prophecy had not been fulfilled, I worried that Zechariah's prophecy might not be fulfilled; now that Uriah's prophecy has been fulfilled, it is

hoped that after seeing the remains of the various Jewish communities and visiting the graves of the holy men in Safed, we would feel one-sixtieth of what the other rabbis felt when Rabbi Akiva explained his laughter and they replied, "Rabbi, you have comforted us." At the time I didn't really understand the connection, but thinking back on the whole day, it's fairly clear[167] that Gavriel was stressing throughout how much we had gained back of our former glory in the course of the past forty years, and — perhaps — he was saying that simply in being able to travel through and see the remains of that glory and the rebuilding of places like Capernaum (which, he said, Jesus had cursed and said would be wasted and never reinhabited), we were being given an indication of the final redemption to come.

As we descend through the hills from Jerusalem, the guide is talking about the ancient history of the place, and someone calls from the back, "The new housing on the hill is more important!" — a place called Mitspe Navo, part of Maalei Adumim perhaps? The guide maintains a running commentary; maybe by now I'm actually catching the gist but not the details, which would indicate a little bit of progress[168] in the past month. As we get to the bottom of the hills, I realize that we've been on the same road to Jericho that I've described before, but I really didn't recognize it until now, probably because the guide was describing so many details that I didn't see the impression of general desert I'd gotten before. He especially stressed the strategic importance of certain narrow passes, both during ancient wars (for example, during the Roman wars, in the time of the Hasmoneans, when the Greeks tried to get through them to Jerusalem) and during the 1948 war, when Jordanian troops tried to get past them. But even though I knew we would be passing through Jericho, that wasn't enough to make me see the same road I'd been on before.

As we drive through Jericho, the guide explains in detail the system of water distribution both in the ancient town and up until recent times. Since the water came from a central source and went through canals from there, the authority over the source was a very important position, which was given to a man with seniority and high reputation — hence the spring was called 'En Sultan. On my first trip through, with Avner to visit Efraim, I'd noticed that one of the small refugee camps in the area was called 'En Sultan, but the guide didn't mention anything about any refugee camps.

The first stop was at a synagogue at a place called Na'aran, just outside

---

quite certain that Zechariah's prophecy also will be fulfilled.' They said to him: 'Akiba, you have comforted us! Akiba, you have comforted us!'" (Babylonian Talmud, Makkot 24A, B; translation based on that in Epstein, ed., 1935: 174–75).

167. I have no reason to second-guess this interpretation now, but be wary whenever an ethnographer or other critic resorts to such hortatory phrases as "it's clear that" or "doubtless."

168. In my Hebrew comprehension.

modern Jericho, from the sixth or seventh century. To get to it, we first drove in a little way to a Palestinian day resort — a place with palm trees painted blue and green on the bottom of their trunks, a snack bar, picnic benches, and a complex system of narrow canals leading rushing water toward a small artificial waterfall and toward two small swimming pools, in which a few boys were splashing around in their clothes. The place wasn't crowded, although there were a few Palestinian families there. Our group seemed utterly incongruous there, buying ice cream, going to the bathroom, walking around a little bit. I felt like an occupier, like I was intruding on these people's little place of refuge, although there was no indication of overt hostility, and the people running the snack bar were probably glad of the little bit of business they got from us. Still the feeling I had — no way to say to these people, "I wish this really were your country" — was more or less the opposite of my satisfaction at being challenged by the soldier like everyone else in the taxi the day before.

Past the resort, we climb a bit along a well-maintained path, through banana groves (there seem to be a lot of them in Jericho), toward the cliffs which look very much like those behind Qetura.[169] The remains of the synagogue are on a relatively high spot, whether because the place was deliberately chosen as a building site or because it's a *tel*[170] I don't know. The place was discovered when a Turkish shell fell here in 1917. It was excavated, then covered over again, and accidentally rediscovered by an Israeli soldier in 1970. All that remains are somewhat more than half of a fairly large floor made out of small mosaic tiles, with decorations including a couple of birds at the entrance way and what some people speculate is a representation of Daniel in the lion's den. The importance of the place as Gavriel presents it is the indication of a large and wealthy Jewish community here centuries after the destruction of the Second Temple. The wealth is confirmed especially by an inscription which credits one Pinchas with having donated the entire mosaic floor. And as Gavriel points out, if there was such a big synagogue here there must have been others — because every Jew has one synagogue he goes to, and one he doesn't go to (see Kugelmass's book on Intervale).[171]

Gavriel points out the mountains of Gilboa to the west and the mountains of Gilead to the right, "where Jacob fled when he left his father-in-law Laban."

---

169. These cliffs are in fact a northern continuation of the hills behind Qetura; both form the western border of the Great Rift Valley.
170. A mound covering an archaeological site.
171. There is a standard joke about the Jew stranded on a desert island who gives a tour to his rescuer. When they reach the second synagogue on the island, the rescuer naturally asks the Jew why, if he's all alone, there are two synagogues. "Oh, that!" replies the Jew: "That's the synagogue I don't go to!" The punch line is used as a chapter title in the book by my colleague Jack Kugelmass, *The Miracle of Intervale Avenue*, about the last functioning synagogue in the South Bronx (Kugelmass 1986).

He describes in detail Saul's last, tragic battle, pressed against the mountains of Gilboa, and points out that even though God promised the land to us, it took a lot of fighting to actually get it. "So once again applying to our days, we are — what are we complaining about? The State of Israel was established in 1948, and *baruch hashem*, thanks God, whatever we had to go through, right now we are the sovereigns in Erets Yisrael."

South of the Kinneret, we enter into a narrow valley above a small river which I first think is the Jordan, but which is in fact the Yarmuk, separating Jordan on the opposite side from what was until 1967 Syria, on this side. The valley is dramatic; on the Jordanian side, on somewhat gentler slopes, there's lovely agriculture which reminds me of the valley below Tekoa. Although I can't see it, Gavriel explains that most of the water of the Yarmuk is diverted at this point on the Jordanian side, and then descends through a carrier, pulled along by gravity, to irrigate the substantial agricultural settlements and villages (which I had already remarked on during my first trip through the Jordan Valley) almost as far as Jericho on the Jordanian side.

From the side of this valley, we begin a tortuous ascent up a steep slope along one of the scariest roads I've ever traveled — let alone on a full-sized, fully loaded bus — through what Gavriel calls the Syrian Maginot Line, with minefields and bunkers on both sides of the road. At one point the driver has trouble making a hairpin turn — the bottom of the bus scrapes the road, and he has to back up a few feet. Fortunately I'm not sitting at the back of the bus, but I'm quite frightened as it is — the feeling that one man's competence is all that's separating us from a deadly roll down a mountainside. People at the back of the bus were shouting to him, "Enough! Enough!" and indeed it's hard to know how he can tell exactly how far back he can go; on such a slope the bus is always going to roll back a few feet before it can go forward at all. As I did once on a small plane in a thunderstorm, I just closed my eyes and breathed deeply, and eventually the driver made the turn. We were climbing the Golan Heights the back way, and Gavriel didn't miss the chance to point out how much harder it had been for the Israeli soldiers who had conquered this plateau in 1967.

And then we were on top: first through a newly planted forest, and then rolling through an area of flat plains with large fields of hay, sunflowers, corn, and the like, which almost looked as though it could have been one of the dryer areas of the Great Plains. We pulled off the road on the lands of Kibbutz Mavo Hama, got off the bus, and stepped into a high wind a few feet from the edge of the cliff. A single artillery gun commemorates the fact that the Syrians held this high point until 1967. Immediately below us are En Gev and the other kibbutzim on the eastern shore of the Kinneret, then the lake itself, and the mountains of the Galilee, with Mount Tabor a distinctive peak in the distance. As Gavriel says, "This is a view you don't usually get to see." Once again he gives a brief talk about how exposed the settlements around Kinneret were before 1967, but here he spends more time talking about the original Deganya, the first kibbutz, on the shores of the Kinneret ("sixty boys and one girl"), and how difficult the health conditions were — when children were born they were sent away and not brought back until they'd grown up somewhat. "Ladies and gentlemen, I don't want to talk about politics, but we have to realize what a tremendous debt we owe these people" — this perhaps an oblique reference to the recent Rabbi Peretz affair.[172] In fact every time he talks about the significance of the borders for security purposes, based on their history in this century, he prefaces the comments with the disclaimer that he's not talking about politics; this of course means he's about to make a political point.

When I got on the bus in the morning, I had some choice of where to sit, and I chose [the seat next to] a small, elderly man with a pleasant, unpretentious face and a nice, trimmed beard, guessing correctly that he wasn't Ashkenazi.[173] We exchanged a few words during the trip, but nothing in detail; when I asked him where he was from, he said, "Jerusalem," even though I suspected he had been born in another country. But we got to talk a little more when we finally made a lunch break at En Gev around 4:30. They've built a little promenade next to the Kinneret, and when I said it was beautiful there, he said, "I know the place. I worked here building shelters after 1967. I was a metalworker." His name is Rahamim, after one of the Ari's students, and he lives quite close to me in Baka'a, although he's been there a lot longer than I have — since 1948, in fact, the year he arrived with his wife and his parents (during the war). So he was one of the original Jewish inhabitants of the abandoned Arab houses,[174] at a time when there weren't any cars in the area, let alone buses. I asked him where he was from in Morocco, and he said,

---

172. Rabbi Peretz, who had broken away from the Orthodox Sephardi Shas Party in 1988, had made bitter public statements that reflected general Sephardi Orthodox anger about their perceived mistreatment during the absorption process in the first decades of the state, particularly at the hands of secular Zionist kibbutzim. This in turn led to a spirited and outraged defense of the heritage and present role of the kibbutzim in Israeli life (see Willis 1992). Here, addressing a generally Orthodox (though not necessarily "Sephardi") audience, the guide was in fact reasserting the value of that heritage.

173. My clues included the fact that he was quite short, dark-skinned and wore a Basque beret.

174. The words "original" and "abandoned" here are both charged with connotations of propriety — that someone was an "original" inhabitant tends, on one hand, to occlude the memory of the previous residents and, on the other, to question the legitimacy of the "gentrifying" Jewish newcomers of the last two decades, most of them Ashkenazi Jews. To refer to a house as "abandoned" obscures the danger or threat of violence that caused the pre-1948 owners to flee, as well as the new state power that forbade them from reclaiming homes they never abandoned in memory.

"You wouldn't have heard of it." I insisted, and he named the place; I hadn't heard of it quite, but it begins with a *T*. He asked if I'd heard of Baba Sali; I said yes, and he told me that his father had studied with Baba Sali. When his father was already his age (late sixties — Rahamim was twenty-five or so when he arrived in Israel), he and his wife still had no children. So he asked Baba Sali's father for a blessing, and Baba Sali's father said, "There will be children around your table," after which they actually did have children.

We drove along the northwest shore of Kinneret, over the narrow Jordan stream which held a couple of kayakers, through an area where rows of sabra plants and large ruined stone fences are clear evidence of Palestinian agriculture. As we begin to climb through the hills, Gavriel points out Kfar Nachum and other ancient sites in this area which is so sacred to Christians, and as I wrote above, emphasizes that after so many centuries of Christian domination, these are once again Jewish communities. Eventually we climb high enough to catch a view of Safed across the valley: it seems incongruous, a city in the middle of the hills, especially with a number of substantial new apartment buildings on the lower slopes. What is that city doing there? It's hard to imagine it ever having had a commercial or agricultural base. How could ten thousand Arabs have been living there before 1948?[175] How did they earn their livings? Presumably they weren't supported by philanthropists, like the Jews.

There's a stop in Safed before we get to the Ari,[176] this one once again devoted to the war in 1948, when there were two thousand mostly elderly Jews in the city and ten thousand Arabs. At the highest point inside the city, a beautiful garden has been planted, with intricate winding walkways up to a viewing platform and a memorial obelisk at the top devoted to the fighters who fell there. Jewish units from a nearby kibbutz made it through to the city and, as Gavriel put it, "managed to kick out the Arabs." In gratitude the rabbis of the city ordered the residents to desecrate the Sabbath to care for the Jewish soldiers who had come to rescue them.

Finally we wind around to the cemetery; it's well after 8:00 by this time, and the sun is starting to go down. The cemetery is on a stony, steep hillside, and like the Muslim cemetery in the middle of Jerusalem I described a few weeks ago, the graves are not dug into the ground but [or maybe they are built into the ground but are also][177] built out of stone and laid out on the

---

175. Yet the figure does not seem too high. Benny Morris gives two estimates for the Arab population of Safad in 1948: "about 9,500" (Morris 1987: 21) and "10–12,000 Arabs," along with "1,500 Jews" (102).

176. That is, the grave of the Ari.

177. An American Jewish friend whose father's grave on the Mount of Olives near Jerusalem is of the same style assures me that the graves are dug into the ground.

surface. Some of the newest ones also have vertical stones at the head with inscriptions, some of these in styles reminiscent of modern Western gravestones, but still with the concrete framework above the surface. We all — including several fairly elderly people, who must be at least as tired as I am by this point — climb up a rough, stony path a hundred fifty meters or so, past Reb Joseph Caro's grave,[178] to a place where lights have been strung up, there's a flat area, and perhaps a couple of dozen men, mostly Hasidim, are already saying Psalms. We stay there for about fifteen minutes, some of the women from our group straying onto the wrong side of the curtain, to the annoyance of some of the Hasidim present. Leafing through the Psalms, since I don't have any particular favorites and don't know if there are any in particular that one is supposed to read on this occasion, I come to the Twenty-third Psalm, which Rabbi Singer sings every Shabbes after *shalosh seudes,* and despite the power of the scene around me, the ancient dress several of the men are wearing, and the sense of awareness of being in the same place that the dead had lived in, of being in their presence (which I hadn't felt at Meron at all), and comparing his Yiddishkeit to this, I'd take Shabbes afternoon at Rabbi Singer's shul over the Ari's grave any day.

Before piling back on the bus, the men say *maariv* at the entrance to the cemetery — one of them hasn't come in, because he's a *kohen.*[179] By this point, Lieberman and several of the other men are speaking Yiddish to each other, which no one had been doing in the morning.

The day wasn't what I had expected. I could have lived without that hair-raising moment on the road going up to the Golan, although I'm glad to have seen the view from the top. I also thought we'd spend more time in Safed itself, so that I would be doing more "observation" of the pilgrimages. The overall theme of the day seemed to be much more the Jewish presence in the north and east of the land, in ancient times and in the present, and the importance of the "current" borders — up to the Jordan, including the Golan Heights — to the *kiyum,* the continued existence and safety of the state and people of Israel. As far as connections to Judaism go, an anecdote Gavriel told about the Ari (which I had heard before), perhaps sums it up: one Friday afternoon the Ari said to his disciples, "Let's go to Jerusalem for the Shabbat." Half of his disciples immediately agreed, while the rest doubted. Disappointed, the Ari said that if everyone had really believed it was possible, they could

---

178. Along with the Ari, the most famous of the sixteenth-century Safed kabbalists and the author of the *Shulkhan Arukh,* considered the single most authoritative guide to Orthodox Jewish practical law.

179. Men descended from the priestly clans in the biblical period are forbidden from entering cemeteries, which bear ritually polluting effects in the system of purity and defilement associated with the Temple.

have brought the Messiah then and there. And, Gavriel concluded, this shows you the power of people who devote themselves fully to an ideal. Well, that's not what it teaches me — what it teaches me is that people like to tell stories about other people's great faith. But somehow in Gavriel's narrative it became blended with the rescue and conquest of Safed in 1948, and so the message of the whole day was: we've been around for a long time, we're doing pretty well, and we can look forward to even better as long as we remain united and vigilant. I was impressed by the lessons about "Israel's security needs" — given the present situation of unremitting hostility, on a day-to-day basis it seems just as well for ordinary Israelis to have the Jordan Valley patrolled and the Golan Heights under Israeli control.[180] But aside from the question of how substantial this "security" really is, the whole premise falls apart if we assume that the hostility is not eternal and inevitable: in narratives like Gavriel's, being embattled seems constitutive of the Jewish people.

•

About 5:00 P.M. Raphael Korn, one of the administrators at Hartman, is apologizing to one of the fellows here for the fact that he couldn't make a scheduled meeting. Something to do with Elias — his car was pulled over, a soldier slapped him a few times, Raphael had to go somewhere with Elias, to complain about the soldier, to speak to Elias Freij, the mayor of Bethlehem, the soldier was a little tough guy in sneakers, they're getting nastier and nastier all the time.... I didn't get the whole story, most of it was in Hebrew and I didn't want to ask Raphael to repeat it. It felt like one of my dreams, especially because I placed it in my imagination at the spot where the cars with green license plates are pulled over coming into Jerusalem. I didn't like the thought of Elias being slapped at all.

Realizing that I'm closing in on myself a little too much, I make arrangements to go to Kfar Qara to see Fawzi and Aisha next week. Aisha answers; she sounds tired — she gave birth by C-section two weeks ago, which is part of why I hesitated to go so soon — and as I try to ask for Fawzi in Arabic, she recognizes that it's me. I'll have to bring them some sort of baby present, I realize.

• 7/18/91 •

This morning my longest Arabic conversation/lesson with Elias yet, which I'm glad of, given what I heard about what happened to him yesterday. So far he hasn't repeated the invitation to his home in Bethlehem, but what he's giving me already is more than generous.

---

180. Huh! The guide got to me more than I would have imagined.

## My Trip to Israel, Continued

• 7/18/91, evening. •

A little while ago I met Elias in the garden, and had my second Arabic lesson of the day. I asked him why he was here so late, and he said, "Where should I go?" He explained to me that his family is in Jordan, with his wife's parents. So he spends a lot of time here, where he feels safe; even when his family's here, he spends long days here. He told me, without my asking, what had happened to him yesterday: he was pulled over on the highway near Bethlehem by some soldiers, who told him to get out of his car (many cars have been confiscated lately). (Here Elias explained that he'd broken the doors on his car, so that they couldn't be opened from the inside? the outside? I didn't understand exactly why.)[181] They made him lie face down on the ground, then ordered him to get back in the car and start it, then get back on the ground again, and thus several times. Eventually he objected, telling them, OK, just take the car (as he says has happened to him a number of times: "If I worked in Bethlehem, they might stop me every two or three hours. When the soldiers take people's cars, they drive them over rocks and frequently damage them"). A soldier made him lie down on the ground, and started hitting him. Then they made him get back in the car, took his papers, and told him to drive his car to the military governor's headquarters; the little soldier yelled at him, "Drive straight to the headquarters, and if you damage your car, I'll kill you." Instead he drove straight to the institute, where at a certain point during the day he wept instead of going crazy, as he says. Eventually Raphael and another man from the institute went to the military headquarters and helped him get his papers back. Elias is very pessimistic: the Palestinians are always making terrible political mistakes, and the Israelis are getting crueler all the time.

The moon is waxing again.

No Talmud class today, because our teacher is at a bar mitzvah, so I get to spend about an hour and a half with Riah at his shop.[182] He says many of the merchants have gone abroad, to the United States, to Jordan, to Egypt.... Riah himself thinks about the possibility of going to Egypt. He has uncles there, and his grandfather and both of his parents were born in Cairo. His father would like to move back there. Two years ago his father bought a store there; it's closed right now, because there's nobody from the family to run it. If any of the young men who are under thirty-five go to Cairo, they probably won't be allowed back in. Riah is over thirty-five, but if he goes

---

181. "In order to conceal their identity, soldiers in the undercover units use diverse disguises.... For transportation they use cars belonging to residents of the territories, bearing local license plates, which have been confiscated by the army" (Yashuvi 1992: 13). Breaking the handles on the inside would make it difficult for the squads to jump out of the cars and carry out their missions.

182. A merchant in the Old City and friend of Elissa's; see entry for June 12.

alone, then he leaves his whole family behind. If he takes his family, then he has four sons who can't go to public school; they'd have to go to private school, where the tuition alone is four thousand dollars a year, plus transportation and so forth. So he can't afford to go to Cairo, though he'd like to. It's a beautiful city, and one can do business there, because even though there are a lot of very poor people, there are a lot of very rich people too. He would use the store either as a supermarket or for children's clothes.

Riah explained to me in some detail how he came to have a lot of family in Egypt. In 1910 or 1911 his grandfather was born, as the twelfth child in the family after eleven daughters. When his grandfather was six, both of his parents died, and he was sent to live with relatives in Cairo. ("In those days, it was all part of Turkey, so it was easy to move back and forth. You could travel to Cairo either by camel or by railroad; there was a railroad station right outside the Jaffa Gate,[183] and you could go to Cairo from there.") In 1942 one of Riah's grandmother's sisters died, leaving three very young children; before she died, she asked Riah's grandmother to give her thirteen-year-old daughter to her husband to raise the children. Riah's grandfather was very unhappy with this; he loved his daughter very much, and said she was too young. When Riah's grandmother insisted, his grandfather said, "If she's moving back to Jerusalem to get married, we'll all move back to Jerusalem." That's how the whole family, including Riah's father and mother,[184] came back to Jerusalem, leaving one uncle in Cairo.

• 7/21/91 •

I spent Friday afternoon with Moti,[185] first at the trendy Kaffit (Moti calls it a "Ratz cafe")[186] on Emek Refaim, then on the roof of his small house at the end of the Katamonim, almost in Beit Safafa. Here, as I mentioned above, Moti stresses that Arabs and Jews live in virtual proximity, and it's almost

---

183. Evidently the railroad station that is still there and functioning, actually at the end of Baka'a going toward the Jaffa Gate.
184. Presumably they were already married.
185. A history teacher and Ph.D. candidate in Jewish history at Tel Aviv University.
186. Ratz, called in English the Citizens' Rights Movement, is a secularist Israeli political party generally supportive of Israeli-Palestinian reconciliation. Its constituency is heavily weighted toward well-educated, middle-class, secular Zionist Ashkenazi Jews. They are commonly devoted to European elite culture, hostile toward what they call religious coercion, and sometimes resented for an alleged air of superiority vis-à-vis Mizrachi Jews. The individualist ethos that informs Ratz positions, a recent and new development out of the collectivism marking the classical period of prestate and early Israeli Zionism, is tied to its supporters' identity as "postcultural citizens." This identity is implicitly understood as the culmination of a developmental process whereby people "grow increasingly cultured until they reach that postcultural point where they become transparent to 'us'" (Rosaldo 1988: 80).

the only place in Jerusalem where they do; and to him, the culture of the Jews from Arab countries fits in with the Palestinian culture. From his roof, there's a view of the crowded housing down the slope to Beit Safafa, which was a divided village — half in Israel, half in Jordan — from 1948 to 1967. To the left, one can see the road leading toward Bethlehem; straight ahead on the next ridge, the massive cluster of apartment buildings called Gilo; in the valley toward the right, the Jerusalem sports stadium; and above and beyond the stadium, the wooded, as yet undeveloped hills surrounding Bet Hakerem. Moti confirmed Charles's assertion that Jerusalem is a relatively poor city, pointing out that apartments in a place like Gilo start at only about forty thousand dollars: "The land was stolen, the labor is cheap...." Tel Aviv, by contrast, is a rich city, he says — there's a lot of industry there, high-tech...

Friday night I was invited to Judy Levi's for dinner. She lives in East Talpiot, where I'd never been, and she insisted the easiest way for me to get there would be to go the end of the Tayelet[187] and have someone from her family meet me there. It was about 8:15, dusk, as I walked out onto the Tayelet, and the view down the hill, in the valley, and up the next slopes toward Mount Scopus and the Mount of Olives, with the lights of the Arab houses scattered on the slopes, struck me as one of the most beautiful things I've ever seen in my life. The Tayelet is also nice because there aren't many tourists there — it's fairly new, and I guess the word hasn't really gotten around yet. Toward the left of this view is the Old City, with the Mosque of Omar of course the most prominent landmark; and if you aren't careful to keep your eyes right, it's very easy to take in the Hilton in the same gaze. Later, at Shabbes lunch, Sandy's wife, Beth, told me that Sandy (a jazz guitarist) had played at the restaurant at the end of the Tayelet on Friday afternoon, and her four-year-old, Uri, looking past the band toward the Old City, had asked, "Ima, is that a map?"

• 

Talking with Charles at his house yesterday afternoon, I tried out my point about the Israeli need to repress the dispossession of the Palestinians, and how much that costs. He made an opposite point, which I find quite acute: any peace settlement that can be contemplated now will require a mutual agreement to forget — the Israelis will have to agree to stop reminding the Palestinians what a stupid mistake they made not accepting partition in 1947; and the Palestinians will have to stop reminding the Israelis that what they've been doing in the Occupied Territories since 1967 is the same thing they did in 1948. "And then maybe, after a number of years, they'll be able to start talking about those things again."

---

187. See entry for June 16.

## • 7/22/91 •

I come and go at Hartman fairly early and late, although not consistently, and Elias seems to be here early and late, nor does his car move from its spot. Yesterday I came out of the office with half an hour to go before the fast ended,[188] and sat talking with him a little longer than our usual passing Arabic lesson. I asked him whether the main building of the institute was a pre-1948 Arab house. It certainly looks like one, but it also looks like it's been renovated, and it's so big I guess I couldn't quite imagine it as a house. It was, of course. Elias told me that around the time he started to work here, some ten years ago (I think he's been with the institute as long as it's been in this building), one day he saw a man standing in front of the building with his American wife, weeping; he said everything looked just at it had before his family had lost it, when he was a child. There were two rose bushes in front that he remembered planting. (One has since been destroyed by a truck which ran over it. Elias carefully nurtures the second one.) In 1948, his father leased the house to the Czechoslovakian government as their embassy, trying to maintain possession of the house that way. But in 1967, when Czechoslovakia broke diplomatic relations with Israel, the Israeli government confiscated the building.[189]

Elias says that there probably isn't anyone who could tell me who all the old houses in Katamon and Baka'a belonged to. They weren't old neighborhoods — people started to move here around the turn of the century. Elias says the houses were widely spread apart (although on Derekh Bet-Lekhem, for instance, they seem to me to be closer together; it makes sense that that area would have been built up first). People didn't necessarily know all of their neighbors, the way people do in a village. He, anyway, knows four or five of the houses in this area.

Charles was complaining to me yesterday about some of the bizarre laws here, such as the one that says the government can confiscate your garden, build a road on it, and charge you for improvements. That almost happened a few years ago, with a plan to more than double the width of Yehuda Street, to make it a feeder road for Derekh Hevron, which has become a major highway, especially for settlers from the south. This came about shortly after Land Day, when Charles had been very impressed by a speech Mohammed Darawshe[190] made, saying people shouldn't think of Land Day as simply an Arab issue,

---

188. The fast of Tisha B'Av.
189. The mother of a schoolmate of Jonah's in New York comes from a prominent Iraqi Jewish family. Her mother's family home in Baghdad became the French embassy after the majority of the Jews left Iraq. Watching TV footage of Baghdad as it was being bombed during the Gulf War, the grandmother suddenly called out, "That's our house!"
190. One of the Arab members of the Knesset.

but as a question of civil rights — a struggle to prevent the government from arbitrary confiscation of land.

I got onto the subject of hospitality; Charles and Sandy agree that everybody here is generally a lot more hospitable than people from New York, partly because people here spend a lot more time talking to each other. So Charles told me another story: his mother works as a social worker in the Nazareth area. One of her colleagues is a woman from Ramallah who's married to a man from Nazareth. One day she complained to Charles's mother that before 1967 hospitality meant that when people came to your house, you had to offer them coffee and a piece of cake, but ever since they've been exposed to the Israelis, you have to empty out your whole refrigerator when people come over!

It seemed to me that, on a very different level than the T-shirt here that says "Israel is real," Charles keeps making a point of bringing home to me the lesson that things go on here based on people's lives here, not based on Marxist analyses from America. He's not especially defensive, I suppose he's just trying to challenge me with his pungent illustrations and contradictions; but there does also seem to be something of the concern to rhetorically establish the autonomous reality of this place vis-à-vis the mind of America.

• 7/24/91 •

When I visited Charles on Saturday afternoon, he told me a cute story about his five-year-old, Yonah. Yonah was looking at something once, and asked Charles, "Aba, is that a *kinor?*"[191] Charles patiently said, "How would you say that in English?" Yonah replied, *"Kinor"* — with the flat vowel and *r* of English. I remarked that telling the story is good practice in Hebrew *r*'s for Charles. I'm reminded of it because the first of my taped notes from Kfar Qara has me pronouncing Ar'ara as if it were Ahari — the combination of the ayin and the double rolled *r* is simply beyond me. Anyway, Kfar Qara appears much more spread out than Ar'ara, even though in both villages the oldest part is the most crowded. The hills are gentler here as well, so that from various points you can see good portions of the village spread out on the surrounding hills. Fawzi and Aisha's house isn't at an especially high point, but it has a good view of the next couple of hills. In the evening I noticed an interesting pattern of lines — the clothesline at the side of their lawn, dipping slightly; close to it in my line of sight, a hillside still in Kfar Qara, with the usual apparently haphazard arrangement of lights coming from various houses; farther off, more visible as the night grew dark, an ordered row

---

191. Violin, in Hebrew.

of brighter, yellowish lights on the slightly curved ridge of the next hill. Fawzi explained that the farthest lights were those of a moshav — "They put Israelis there to guard over us. Isn't that thoughtful of them?" (Army jeeps occasionally patrol the village as well.)

There are about ten thousand people in Kfar Qara, which makes it a little bit smaller than Ar'ara, but still bigger than it looks from the Wadi 'Ara Highway — where all you see are a number of houses that spill out over the first row of hills. Apparently also the clans aren't as neatly clumped together in Kfar Qara, partly because they run out of land and then parts of the family buy land and build houses elsewhere in the village; presumably there's some pattern here that would interest a social anthropologist.

In any case the Abu Ahmeds aren't a particularly large "clan," although Fawzi's grandfather was, Fawzi says, one of the richest men in the village, owning about ten thousand dunams (a dunam is much less than an acre, I don't know exactly how much) of land before 1948. At some point during the war, Fawzi says, a number of people in the village were killed, and the rest fled the village — Fawzi's family went to relatives in, I think he said, Nazareth. They returned after several months, but all of the family's land except for two thousand dunams was confiscated by the Israelis, who gave them about five dollars per dunam as recompense.

Now land in the village is extremely expensive. There's a parcel of ten dunams that someone wants to sell for eighty thousand dollars. Fawzi wants my brother to buy the land with him, which Fawzi is convinced he can then sell for twelve thousand dollars or so per dunam. Although most of the people in the town earn their living from agriculture, obviously as the population grows and everybody wants their own houses, there's less and less land available for farming.

Some of the houses going up are quite impressive.[192] One of the fanciest ones — situated on a hillside, with floodlights in the evening making it even more conspicuous — belongs to a man who owns a cement-block factory in town. Some of the new houses have three floors and ten rooms or so. There

---

192. Palestinians, both Israeli citizens and those living under occupation, often invest a large proportion of their resources in their houses. There are a number of reasons for this, including restrictions on buying land or establishing businesses, their heavy involvement in the construction industry (to some extent as contractors, and especially as laborers), and the value of the house as a symbol of permanent residence. On one occasion one of my Palestinian-American graduate student friends went on a tour of a number of settlements conducted by the Palestine Human Rights Information Center. They met with one of the settlers' representatives, who asked rhetorically, "When was the last time you saw a Palestinian house more than ten years old?" — thus managing to suggest that Palestinians were newly arrived in the land themselves and also prospering from the Israeli presence. A sharp answer, of course, would have been, "When I was in Baka'a."

is no standard design, although cement is the usual building material, and certain curves and shapes are characteristic. While some of the houses are more or less rectangular, even many of the simplest ones are built one flight off the ground (presumably so that they'll be cooler, and the technique is effective). There are however no architects; people hire engineers to draw the plans for their houses. People also go deeply into debt to pay for their houses; it would be interesting to know the terms.

Within the last dozen years or so, Fawzi, his brother Rauf (the oldest), and a third brother, Ali, have all married and built houses for their families adjacent to each other, but at some distance from their parents' house, which is in the relatively older (mid-century) part of the village. It's obviously especially nice for the cousins, who move freely to and from each other's yards; next to Rauf's house there's a big sandy area with a little merry-go-round. Rauf's house is one story, raised off the ground; Ali's is two stories, but rather plain in design; Fawzi and Aisha's (now look at me, I'm talking about Rauf and Ali, and I don't even know their wives' names) is not elevated, but at the right places in the house (such as the room where I slept), there's still a fine breeze. I've never been inside their parents' house (perhaps the living room), but it is pleasant to sit in front in the late afternoon, on cane stools, near Fawzi's mother, who wears a traditional Palestinian dress and sits on a jacket spread out on the bare ground, and respond to Fawzi's father's question about my father's health (my whole family has visited here at various times) that he is well, thank God (now — I didn't mention that he had been sick recently). Bleating comes from the blind side of their house; Fawzi took me to see the six sheep in a small pen who fled to the back of the pen at our approach. Well, why shouldn't they be afraid — Fawzi told me he had taken one of them and slaughtered it a few weeks ago for the festival of the slaughter.[193] We went back and sipped coffee for a few more minutes in the shade of some old pine trees, and I looked at the pattern of their roots in the bare and dusty soil.

Fawzi spoke at length of his and Aisha's fantasy trip to America, which they've been planning for many years — but the more children they have, the more expensive a trip they're contemplating. He brought out a booklet of guided tours on the West Coast for Hebrew speakers, from three to seven days. I wonder whether they actually would take such tours (I advised them to stay in the Bay Area, rent a car, and take day trips instead) with an Israeli group, and what their experience would be like if they did. We agreed that if they do make it, they can certainly spend a few days staying with us in New York (although I warned them it would be crowded), and they could probably

---

193. *Id ul-daha*, better translated as the festival of the sacrifice, commemorating the story of Abraham's sacrifice as recounted in the Qur'an.

stay with my parents in New Jersey for a few days (although I warned them my father gets tired when there's a lot of commotion around). Fawzi told me quite plainly, and sensibly I think, that if he comes so far as a guest, he doesn't expect that his hosts will go off to work and leave him to explore New York alone — that he'll really have a host and a guide for a few days. I told him that made sense, although for some people it's hard to just take a few days off.

They're feeling less and less comfortable with Israelis now; sometimes, Aisha says, they feel like they could explode, which is part of why they dream of getting away, at least for a while. Aisha says she doesn't even like to travel around Israel anymore, not even to Hadera (where, as an English teacher named Salim from Kfar Qara had assured me on the taxi ride from Hadera to the village, Arabs and Jews get along together well, and people come in sometimes just to spend time in a city).

•

There was a guest at lunch the first day — Abu Hisham, whom Ruth had told me beforehand was very interested in meeting me. He's an engineer, and as I found out at lunch the next day, has a house worthy of it, not the fanciest in the village; but graciously centered on a second story, with a large central hallway that efficiently circulates a cooling breeze to the living room, which is furnished with a combination of overstuffed armchairs and low foam cushions (where I preferred to sit, "Arab style" as someone put it; how many chances do I get?). Abu Hisham may have forgotten exactly who I was, or maybe he was feigning when he asked if I knew Danny (as everyone in the village calls my brother, though respectfully; Fawzi's parents sometimes call my brother Professor Danny). I said, yes, and did he perhaps know the Abu Ahmed family from Kfar Qara? When he found out I was an anthropologist, Abu Hisham wondered whether I was concentrating on folklore or social organization, and offered to show me a couple of books — a fat book about anthropology in Arabic; a translation into Hebrew of a nineteenth-century study of "everyday life in Palestine"; a book, which I did see yesterday after lunch, about "people and their land," basically documenting the rural Palestinian methods of farming and processing various agricultural products.

•

Yesterday, as I said, Fawzi and I were invited to Abu Hisham's house for lunch, which was indeed a feast — again chicken-vegetable soup and roast chicken, which Umm Hisham had stuffed with rice and giblets; meatballs; a plate of chopped meat cooked with tomato sauce; and wonderful vine leaves. We ate in the dining room, which, unlike the dining area at Fawzi's house (where the dining room table is moved from the kitchen into the dining area for fancy events), is furnished with low cushions and the food is set out on cloths on the floor. Abu Hisham's younger brother (name?) and his teenage daughter (who speaks English quite well) joined us, as did a young German woman named Greta, who's spending five weeks in the village as the guest of a man named Shafiq, who also came, and with whom I had a long conversation after lunch in German about American politics vis-à-vis the Middle East. None of us pretends to understand it. Sitting on the floor in the living room, looking out at space and then the next hill, which gives the main story of Abu Hisham's house the pleasant feeling of being suspended above the ground, I suddenly had an image of sitting on the floor two days before in the Ramban synagogue here in Baka'a, in mourning for the Temple. When did Jews get the idea that sitting on the floor was a sign of mourning?

• 

On the #18 bus back to Baka'a, I realize I'm sitting behind Mordechai Bar-On,[194] and ask him if I can talk to him sometime. He doesn't know who I am, probably doesn't recognize the name of IJPU[195] either, and wonders how he can help me in my research. No matter; he wasn't enthusiastic, but I got his telephone number anyway. Meanwhile there are two men, one sitting next to me and one sitting next to him, Jews having a conversation in Arabic. The guy sitting next to him is sitting sideways, with his rear end squeezing Bar-On next to the wall. Eventually Bar-On says, "I see that you must love me, because you're sitting so close to me." The guy gets up, walks around, and sits down facing the other way, and asks: "Now I don't love you?"

• 7/25 •

Anyway, I saw a relatively large collection of leftist intellectuals, including a number of Israeli Palestinians, on Tuesday night, at the old meeting room/theater (who owns it?) called Tsavta.[196] The room seats maybe eighty, and it was about two-thirds full. People ranged, I'd say, from their twenties through their fifties, and I don't think anybody was a newcomer to politics. Men vastly outproportioned women. Only two women spoke during the whole evening. The purpose was to begin a discussion about the feasibility of starting a new movement or party including both Arabs and Jews. Moti sort of chaired the meeting, but Walid Masalha[197] set the tone and was clearly the focus of it, although he clearly wasn't giving a lecture. His opening comments, however,

---

194. A former general in the Israeli army, former Knesset member, and leader of Peace Now.
195. The International Jewish Peace Union, which worked for Israeli-Palestinian reconciliation by promoting the establishment of a Palestinian state and in which I was active at the time.
196. The name means "team" or "association." The hall is owned by the Labor Party.
197. Professor of philosophy at Bir Zeit University, fellow of the Van Leer Institute in Jerusalem, and erstwhile activist in the Israeli Communist Party.

made me look forward very much to meeting him on Monday afternoon — especially his statement that a new group had to look beyond the borders of Israel and the territories, and think about the situation of this country within the Middle East, and to talk about the politics of the Middle East in general: surprisingly, a very new idea, I think, which is an indication of how limited the mental boundaries of even leftists here have been.[198] He also made it clear that he was through with Marxist-Leninist purity, and that we have to find new ways to cooperate with diverse ideas; and that as far as equality goes, the important and difficult thing was to find ways for people to be different and still equal. A number of very interesting issues were raised relating to states, borders, and identity. One of the Israeli Palestinians (Walid is, I think, from East Jerusalem) said that he was tired of groups like the Progressive List for Peace[199] that said one thing to Jews and another thing to Arabs: there has to be one line for everybody, or else the politics end up being divergent. (Alex interjected, "That's Lenin!" which made me think of the dispute between Lenin and the bund back in 1903....)[200] Toufiq, an activist intellectual from Kfar Qara (later when I mentioned I'd just been there visiting Fawzi and Aisha, he said, "Oh yes, they've become religious, haven't they?"), said he didn't want to be in another Arab-Jewish or Jewish-Arab organization: he wanted an organization that agreed on a set of principles and didn't try to legislate its ethnic composition. Someone (Alex, but not just him, other people as well) spoke about the slogan of Israel as "the state of all its citizens" — which Mohammed Miari[201] tried to decree his allegiance to in the Knesset a few years back, and wasn't permitted to (the members of Knesset have to declare their allegiance to Israel as the state of the Jewish people). A man named Shim'on (who Moti later said to me is a half-Zionist) said that we should have a party for... what was the exact wording? I don't remember, but the idea was for all the people of the country of Israel. A couple of the Palestinians didn't accept that, insisting that they will never be Israelis and we have to acknowledge that there are two peoples here. One of the Israelis

---

198. This idea might have been resisted because the left has insisted for decades that the heart of the "conflict" is the situation of the Palestinians, rather than state relations between "Israel" and "the Arabs."

199. A joint Arab-Jewish electoral list that ran on a platform calling for the establishment of a Palestinian state alongside Israel and that once had representatives in the Knesset.

200. The failure adequately to address the national question in Leninist theory can be traced back to the second congress of the Russian Social Democratic Party in 1903. At that meeting, the Jewish Workers' Bund — an organization established in 1897, which eventually enjoyed the loyalty of large segments of the East European Jewish working class and intelligentsia — put forward a platform based on national-cultural autonomy for the various nationalities in the Russian Empire. Lenin, insisting on centralism, won the day, and the Bund representatives withdrew from the congress.

201. Former Knesset member representing the Progressive List for Peace.

spoke about abrogating the Law of Return, to which Walid eventually replied that he wasn't against the right of anybody to immigrate here, what he's opposed to is forcing anybody to immigrate here (so what will he say about the Palestinian right of return?). A woman named Chana Hacohen complained that she hadn't heard anybody talking about what the main program of such an organization should be, which is social problems in Arab society; this infuriated Toufiq, who interrupted her, shouting that maybe she should be more concerned with confronting Shamir and Raful[202] instead. (Moti later said to me that, on the one hand, Chana's point is that it's paternalistic to simply accept that "their culture" is like that — problems like physical attacks and even murder of unmarried daughters who become pregnant, which my sister-in-law Ruth had also mentioned to me, but, on the other hand, Toufiq is perfectly aware of these issues and confronts them all the time at home.) Toward the end, Alex raised the point that the borders of the state might well have to be a topic for discussion — at the beginning of the intifada people thought, "Well there will be a Palestinian state and that's it," but now we have to take into consideration that the territories are effectively part of Israel; furthermore, there's a lack of fit between the theme of "Israel as the state of all its citizens" and the theme of "two states for two peoples" (which everybody agreed is inadequate, not surprising since the Palestinians there were Israelis who don't want to be shut out of Israel just because there might be a Palestinian state). Various people spoke about shared humanistic values, but Walid took care to point out, citing Leibowitz, that these are matters of faith with us, separate from the objective discourse of "science." Nobody said a word about Oriental Jews, nobody said a word about disarmament, and although everyone agreed that equality for women is a basic platform, nobody censured Toufiq for jumping down Chana's throat. Moti gave me a ride home, and asked me what I thought: it seemed to him there's a possibility of something developing here. I told him that raising new ideas is itself helpful: "When you're at your weakest, the smartest thing you can do is start having an intelligent discussion about why you're so weak."

The meeting brought out some of the peculiar contradictions of political action in this context: the borders of the polity are both highly artificial and very much under contention (thus, as well, there was no discussion of the possibility and difficulty of including people from the territories in such an organization), and it is not at all clear what vision of *ethnic* and *territorial* representation such an organization should or would want to take. Furthermore, I think that everybody assumes they're going to be appealing to a minority of leftist intellectuals and Arabs who are alienated from the state; what I

---

202. Rafael Eitan, from the right-wing Tsomet Party.

didn't hear, again, was the beginning of a discussion about why leftist principles don't appeal to "ordinary" citizens.[203] But the initial assumption that there are many issues to be discussed and that the process of debate takes precedence over the struggle for power at this point gave me some hope that these issues might in fact be developed further.

• 7/26/91 •

The more times I travel back and forth along the Jerusalem–Tel Aviv Highway, the more clearly I see the traces of the artificial (I suppose "manmade" would be technically accurate here, but I'm shrinking from it as sexist all the same) terracing on the hillsides — places where there are just the ruins of stone walls, places where the terraces are intact but the fields are not in use, a few places where the terraced fields are still in use. The most spectacular of the latter is to the left (south) coming down from Jerusalem, at 'En Hemed or Beit Nekofa — it's a bit hard to tell the name of that village from the road signs or the map. In at least one place where the natural striation of the rock was relatively stable, it has humanly produced rock walls on top of it, so there the distinction that worried me the day I first came up, about which was natural and which was a trace of Palestinian settlement (which, in fact, reflected my worry about my own biases — I didn't want to sound like a jerk talking about abandoned Palestinian fields which were actually just "undeveloped" mountainsides), was dissolved. Presumably if there were places where the natural striation was adequate to provide terracing, then they just used that.

Trying to figure out exactly where on the map these spectacular still-used terraces are, I think the village might actually be 'En Raza. I don't know. In any case I notice on the other side of the road, still quite close to the highway, the name of Qatana. I had heard of Qatana, but somehow imagined it to be quite distant. It came up in the following context: five years ago, when Elissa and I were here with Jonah for Avner's bar mitzvah, we went to visit Father Chacour in Ibillin. He described to us various of his militant nonviolent actions. One of them involved young olive trees from Qatana, which had been uprooted by the occupation authorities and confiscated. Eventually a number of them (I don't know how they were identified) reappeared in the new Martin Luther King Garden, part of the Liberty Bell Garden. Father Chacour took a group of young people to the garden where they had been planted (the

---

203. Moti, one of the organizers of this meeting, has begun to articulate in writing a Benjaminian "politics of tradition" that would work with the resources of difference and memory, rather than simply overcome them (Raz-Krakotzkin 1993).

night before the dedication?), and had them tie a ribbon around each of the trees, saying "Take me back to Qatana."

• 7/28/91 •

Ramot[204] now covers two large hills directly west of the northern part of Jerusalem. Rebecca and Roger live in Ramot A, the older part of this suburb, [a suburb] which is in fact still part of the Jerusalem municipality and which (as I presume not too many people spend much time thinking about) is across the Green Line as well. The homes in their part of Ramot are built perhaps six to a building, "terraced" up the steep hillside, so that many of them are only accessible by a number of steps — a problem for young families with small children, which characterizes most of the Modern Orthodox neighborhood where the Nayshtots are living for now.

They've only been there since October, and just signed a lease for another year, but have no idea whether they're going to stay permanently. Roger had come on an exploratory trip arranged by the Orthodox Aliyah movement (did he call it Tehila?), over a year ago, when their youngest daughter, Davida (now fifteen months old and absolutely lovely), was practically a newborn. He brought back videotapes of various places the group of prospective immigrants had been taken to as potential places to live. As Rebecca put it, she thought the videotape was showing her what it was really like, but coming here and being here was so different.... From their balcony a broad sweep of the western part of the city is visible, from the Hilton to the south to the tower on Scopus in the northeast. Slightly to the left is another large hill, as yet undeveloped; the two slopes of this hill are neatly framed, on the right by the Scopus tower and on the left by a minaret. To the left are the Arab villages along the road to Ramallah.

Roger and I go to the synagogue for Kabbalat Shabbat; it's a fairly large building, with certainly over one hundred men present, about half-filling it I think. The style of services is quite similar to that in Tekoa, although maybe a little bit quicker. At one point I looked out through one of the narrow windows in the front of the synagogue and saw a huge, full orange moon just rising over the bare hill; at that point in its cycle, if you look closely, you can actually see it fully emerging and then growing more and more distant from a line between my sight and the earth. This morning when I came out to the synagogue in Baka'a, the moon was still fairly high in the opposite side of the sky; it's amazing that its position could shift so fast as to be vis-

---

204. This entry details the Sabbath I spent with the American couple in the suburb of Ramot, growing out of the telephone conversation I describe above, in the entry for July 7.

ible when it's first rising, and that it yet takes so many hours to cross the full sky.

Based on sketchy information, I'd have to say the knitted-*kipa* community at Ramot is officially more or less right-wing. In addition to Rebecca's general comments, this is based on three hints. (1) The rabbi, whom I met and then overheard at a kiddush after shul, was going over his sermon with some of the *balebatim*,[205] and remarked that he hadn't stated a position on politics, but just mentioned that the Bible talks about the conquest of the "territories which are under dispute right now"; but now he pointed out that the cities of refuge mentioned in the Bible were virtually all in Yehuda, Shomron, and the Golan (the last being especially under discussion these days, since there's a serious danger of negotiations between Israel and Syria, especially after the right-wing parties agreed not to pull out of the government coalition). (2) When Roger and I walked in a few minutes late to a Shabbes afternoon *gemara shiur*,[206] the discussion was about whether the *musaf*[207] service has any particular associations of *bekoshe*, of asking God for something, and someone briefly alluded to an opinion that it's a request for "Greater Israel." (3) Rebecca and Roger are both lawyers. Another friend of theirs in the neighborhood, an American named Reuven, gave the kiddush because he just finished his very first tour of army duty, of six weeks. There was brief talk about whether he'd want to do his *miluim*[208] service as an army lawyer. He said, "Someone has to defend those guys who throw the rocks," and then explained that he was joking — if anything he would be a prosecutor. Does the army in fact provide defense lawyers in cases like that?[209] Are defense lawyers allowed at all? (I'm alluding to so many cases we've heard about in the States where lawyers for people in the territories aren't allowed access to their clients or to the files on their clients. I don't get any hint that this is something that concerns lawyers such as these Americans in Ramot, or even that they're necessarily aware of.) Reuven also mentioned that one of his and Roger's (or Rebecca's?) classmates from law school is here, a Peace Now activist who works as a prosecutor when he's in the army because he believes that Palestinians should be fairly prosecuted and not abusively prosecuted. Rebecca said, "Well, that's not who I think should be a prosecutor!"

At this point it seems Rebecca and Roger are still frankly ambivalent about

---

205. Male heads of families.
206. Talmud study session.
207. The additional prayers recited on the Sabbath and festivals in recollection of the extra sacrifices brought on those days when the Temple stood.
208. Israel Defense Force reserve duty.
209. The answer is yes, but successful defenses are almost unheard of.

the choice they've made, although they don't admit regretting it and I presume they don't. Rebecca's unhappy about not having a free day off — going right back to work on Sunday is hard, especially with three kids. She and Roger don't know where they're going to be working once they finish their clerkships and are licensed to practice law in Israel, and she's very worried about their ability to buy a home (presumably an apartment — she doubts they'll ever have a backyard like she enjoyed in her parents' house in Queens when she grew up), given the Israeli mortgage system whereby, as Zev[210] had just explained to me, the principal can and usually does go up.

They had the Friday *Jerusalem Post;* I hardly see any newspapers here, because the *Post* has been discredited since it was sold to...Robert Maxwell (and rightly discredited I think after reading it this weekend), and I haven't invested time or money in trying to work through any of the Hebrew newspapers. But there were a couple of items of interest to my interests. One was in Rabbi Riskin's "Shabbat Shalom" feature, a commentary on the weekly Torah portion, in the course of which he managed to include a reference to the pioneering Jewish settlers of this country, without whom the swamps of Petach Tikwa would still be swamps, and it wouldn't be called Petach Tiqwa — a lovely illustration of the use of synechdoche (or is it metonymy?)[211] to reinforce a selective and tendentious account of history. The other was in a column criticizing a recent *New York Times Magazine* cover story on the Palestinians by Judith Miller, which talked, according to this *Post* column, about the 5 million Palestinians and the Jews who had displaced them from their land. The column claimed in return that, in effect, the 450,000 Palestinian refugees had "escaped" from a "mostly barren" land. An interesting point: the two ways the land is described in Zionist myth before the arrival of the Jews are as "barren" and "swampy": this suggests a structuralist analysis, which I will probably never seriously engage in, that the land has to be controlled by Jews in order for the distribution of water to be in a state of proper balance. There was also an article discussing the recent murder of the head of the Arab hospital in Jenin and the murder of an Arab worker in a small town, presumably because he had a Jewish wife. Regarding the hospital administrator, it said that he had been so afraid of being attacked as a "collaborator" that he went to Amman and

---

210. An Israeli educator and writer whom I had just visited at his apartment in Tel Aviv.
211. Actually, it is *synecdoche* — according to *Webster's Unabridged:* "in rhetoric, a figure of speech, by which the whole of a thing is put for a part, or a part for the whole." Here, the early Zionist colony of Petach Tiqwa, and the ground, said to be previously neglected, on which it was built, are taken as a synecdoche for all the Land of Israel before Zionist settlement. Thus the redemptive, developmental aspect of Zionist "pioneering" is highlighted and the displacement of Palestinian Arabs occluded.

got a certificate from the PLO to the contrary. Then the editorial generalized these two cases as evidence of the "PLO-Hamas" reign of terror, without remarking on the evident contradiction between this man's certificate from the PLO and the claim that he had been attacked by the PLO. Or do they mean that it's a reign of terror *between* the PLO and Hamas? Possibly, but presumably clarity on such issues isn't important for the *Post*'s editorial writers: as long as you can reiterate the claim that there's no one to talk to, you've done your job. On the other hand, the Friday *Post Magazine* carried a substantial article sympathetically recording the claims of Haifa Arabs that they are discriminated against, especially in areas such as housing.

• 8/1/91 •

Flashback to Rebecca and Roger Nayshtot: at one point, talking about the various American products she misses, Rebecca pulled out from the freezer a half-gallon carton of fresh-squeezed (NOT from concentrate) Tropicana orange juice, which she says she's saving for the moment when she and Roger finish their respective *stages* (they use the French word here), their internships, and get their licenses to practice law. I find it striking how, at this point early in their "absorption" and settling into Israel, she (especially, I think, although in their descriptions of the process of moving here they both emphasize that he was the more skeptical and reluctant one in general) is so attached to small items of American material culture — Celestial Seasonings herb tea was absolutely the right gift for her, although there are herb teas made here that seem perfectly good. Whatever their reasons for moving here, they certainly weren't what we would usually call "materialistic" ones.

While doing this work at Scopus, I run into Kobi Arnon, who tells me that Ahmed Abu Saleh is meeting with Ronald Perahiye-Bloom at Beit Maiersdorf, the faculty club, so I go to join them. Ruhama Hertz is there as well; the four of us strategize about a speaking tour of the United States for Ahmed and (probably) Kobi rather than Ronald this fall or winter, since Kobi will be teaching at San Diego in the fall semester. Meanwhile Chagit comes in, and we get copies of the California document from her;[212] she didn't

---

212. Kobi Arnon is an anthropologist at Hebrew University; Ronald Perahiye-Bloom is a professor of history there. Ruhama Hertz is professor of Jewish studies at Case Western Reserve University. Chagit Katzev-Haft is a folklorist at Hebrew University. The document in question, a blueprint of steps toward Israeli-Palestinian peace, was produced by a committee of Israelis and Palestinians at a conference in California sponsored by the Beyond War organization;

know we were all going to be there either, so it's a fortuitous meeting all around.

I hadn't understood that Ahmed can't come into Jerusalem. He doesn't have a pass. It costs 350 shekels to get one, and he already owes his lawyer 350 shekels as it is. Ronald is going to try to get another lawyer to help Ahmed get a pass as a physician. Ronald comments that the whole system of grades for Palestinians to get passes to come into Jerusalem is reminiscent of the situation in Prussia at the time of Mendelssohn, when Jews were divided into fourteen categories for purposes of travel privileges. The analogy is particularly poignant since Ronald is a professor of, among other things, German Jewish history, and Ahmed himself spent a number of years studying in Germany, which is one source of his interest in Jewish history (and also helps explain his friendship with Greta, I imagine).

Ahmed is looking forward to my brother's coming, and plans to set up a meeting hopefully with Samir Turki[213] — Kassis and a few others as well. Chagit tells us that in California, she gave a copy of Ahmed's research center proposal to Nabil Shaath,[214] whose first response was, "Oh yes, we have a number of such joint research centers." Chagit pointed out to him that this was a Palestinian project, not a joint one.

Leaving Scopus together with Ronald and Ahmed, we're joined by Stephen Fogel,[215] who's visiting Ronald, and by Stephen's son, who's just had his bar mitzvah and is wearing a *kipa,* which Stephen doesn't. Ronald has to drive Ahmed back past the checkpoint between Jerusalem and Ramallah; it seems there's always a checkpoint coming into Jerusalem, although now there isn't one going out. The "dangerous stretch," as Ahmed calls it, is just past Pisgat Ze'ev and Newe Yaakov, which I realize I hadn't noticed before on my times on this road. They're actually "settlements," although they look simply like new Jewish neighborhoods, like French Hill for instance. They're placed right in the middle of Arab neighborhoods.

Ahmed stresses that if he tours America, he also wants the chance to meet Palestinian intellectuals and promote his own project. If he gets some money, he says, he's not going to build a house like all the other Arabs — he's just going to sit in a room for six months and read and write and translate. I give him a copy of Zev Efrat's book, and he's interested in it but doesn't know when he'll get to it.

Apparently Um Sabri was interviewed on Israeli TV the other night about

---

it received the endorsement of the PLO and was remarkable, among other things, for its mention of the then-current wave of stabbings of Israelis inside the Green Line.

213. A prominent Palestinian sociologist on the faculty of Bir Zeit University.
214. A leading political adviser within the PLO.
215. Professor of Jewish studies at the University of Chicago.

her reactions to the peace-talk discussions (flash: today's headlines, August 1, bear the news that after the Bush-Gorbachev summit in Moscow, they announced there will be a peace conference in October, and Baker is coming here to get Shamir's response). She must have been very negative; Ahmed is quite unhappy with what she said, and gives me the impression that his relations with her are worse than ever. It's alright for some of the leaders to be "tough," as he and I both describe her, but he points out that it's irresponsible for leaders to give the impression that the people should hold out for more than they can possibly obtain. Ahmed is also eager to come to the United States because he feels he desperately needs a vacation; he hasn't had one in four years, and Um Sabri absolutely will not permit him a vacation. She says, "We have to die for our people." How she reminds me of Samiha!

Ahmed is from Tulkarm. He says if he can get a day off and if his friend who has a car is free, he might be able to take me there one day, and he also offers to spend a full day with me and Danny in Ramallah; he'll take me to a refugee camp outside Ramallah if we can work it out (I'm sure he has good contacts since he's an M.D.).

We dropped off Ahmed safely, then Ronald made a rather hairy U-turn in front of an Egged bus, and drove back past where all the cars with blue license plates were being stopped coming into Jerusalem. I think I noticed Pisgat Ze'ev partly because Najwa had mentioned to me that where her aunt is — either living now or about to move — is just past Pisgat Ze'ev, and since Najwa will have to get into West Jerusalem frequently, it matters whether she'll be inside the checkpoint or not. On the other hand, if she buys a car and she can get one with yellow license plates, she'll be OK inside the checkpoint....

These last taped notes (which I expand on and edit when I type them up at the computer) were recorded in the garden at the Van Leer Institute, a sort of liberal think tank here that looks like it could well be in suburban Maryland. By 3:15 Walid Masalha hadn't shown up, and I decided to take off for home, grab my things, and make the 5:00 bus to Qetura.

•

I never marked before the numerous little stone markers all the way up the Arava Road: some a small pyramid, some merely a stack of four or five stones on top of each other, some with found objects (a tire) integrated into the design, some including or consisting of inscriptions in Hebrew or English. Certainly the essay "The Presence of the Dead"[216] helps me to see this, as does being on this road once again and looking for things I haven't noticed before. Could they possibly commemorate battles along the Arava Road? I don't remember having heard of any, but what do I know about the history of wars in

---

216. Handelman and Shamgar-Handelman 1991.

158 My Trip to Israel, Continued

Israel? Could they commemorate traffic accidents — I know there are plenty of those on this road. (I conceive the idea of doing a John McPhee–style story about the Arava.)

• 8/2/91 •

Last night after swimming a mile for the first time since I've been here, I decided to do a bit of shopping at Mahane Yehuda.[217] Wandering back and forth comparing prices on mixed nuts to bring to the place I've been invited for supper tonight, I noticed a small boy who'd obviously been separated from whoever was taking care of him. I took his hand, and he immediately stopped crying, which intrigued me already. He wouldn't say his name. I called out a few times to see if anybody within hearing distance was looking for him, but no one responded. Then the owner of one of the stalls told me to take him to a police station nearby, which turned out to be upstairs in one of the side streets — intriguing, to be inside the market for a change. I knocked on the one door where I saw a light, but the woman inside said, "There are no police here. Go home." I persisted: I had a lost child with me. Eventually she made me understand that the police station was across the "hall" (not covered, not inside the building) and there was no one there. By this time I had a perhaps thirteen-year-old girl accompanying me and trying to help — she reminded me of Zoe Goldberg.[218] I went back to the stall where I'd found the kid. There an elderly man with a Mizrachi-style beret like the one I wear took an interest, saying the same thing had happened the day before. He picked the kid up, gave him a cookie, and started working on getting his name. Just then somebody noticed a couple of Mishmar HaGvul[219] soldiers on patrol coming our way. One of the soldiers immediately took the child in his arms, and that was the end of my story, except for the ironic reflection: Mishmar HaGvul has such a bad reputation among people concerned about the brutality with which the intifada has been put down, and here they were helping to rescue a child whom, had he been on the other side of... the border (*mishmar hagvul*) and in a tense situation, they might well have shot at.

---

217. Mahane Yehuda, the open market in West Jerusalem, is one of the oldest and generally one of the poorest neighborhoods in that part of the city. Its stalls, which sell meat, fruit, vegetables, canned goods, and dry goods, are located on the ground floor of what are mostly pedestrian streets. Above the shops and behind them, in the interior of the buildings, there are residences. Thus immediately below, when I refer to going "inside," I mean these dwellings that few shoppers and virtually no tourists ever have reason or opportunity to enter.

218. A neighbor in New York.

219. "Border Patrol," an Israeli army unit that has long been assigned much of the routine police work both in Jerusalem and in the Occupied Territories, thus obtaining a general reputation for brutality among Israeli leftists and among Palestinians.

• 8/4/91 •

For me, Shabbes is the hardest day, the day when everybody's supposed to be at home with their families, and I'm an anomalous and uneligible bachelor. Which is not to gainsay all the warm invitations I've enjoyed.

One anecdote from hanging out with Charles last night, pursuing questions of space and collective identity together: at the beginning of the intifada, the normal complement of three hundred Israeli policemen in East Jerusalem were backed up by fifteen hundred soldiers. Charles spent one tour of duty patrolling there. The police were very glad to have the soldiers around, and one of the policemen chatted Charles's unit up by asking all of them where they were from (since it's a unit of older *olim*). He got to the Ethiopian in the group last, asked the guy where he was from, and the Ethiopian answered, "Sweden."

I was invited (along with Avner, who didn't come) to the Katzevs[220] for Shabbes lunch again. The guests this time were more enjoyable — this fellow Binyomin, who had sardonic Litvak sensibilities (especially vis-à-vis the singing of Shabbes *nigunim* to modern tunes) which were very sympathetic to my own; and also a family named Mintz from Los Angeles, South Africans who've been in California about fifteen years. The paterfamilias was witty without quite being obnoxious, irreverent of liberal pieties without quite being snotty. He told a story about a black accountant who'd worked for him. First he complained that this man couldn't spell "Wednesday" or "February," and sniffed that it would be unheard of for a CPA in South Africa to be unable to spell those words. (I wonder how many black CPAs there are in South Africa.) Then he said the guy had come in one day wearing a gold chain with a pendant showing Africa in outline. He asked the guy, "How come you're wearing that?" The guy said, "I'm a child of Africa." He said, "Have you ever been to Africa?" The guy said, "No." He said, "Have your parents ever been to Africa?" The guy said, "No." He said, "*I'm* a child of Africa. I was born in Africa and my parents were born in Africa." The guy said, "Your color's wrong." He said, "They bleached me for three weeks before I left Africa."

What do I make of this story? It was funny as he told it. I could get huffy and analyze the difference between leaving voluntarily and having one's ancestors shipped out. But I prefer to leave it at the level of irony here — especially because of the curious juxtaposition it offers to the rhetorics of "belonging" to this land on the part of Zionists and Palestinians. Najwa told me, for the second time, on Friday about an unpleasant encounter with an Israeli-American woman whom Virginia Domínguez[221] had introduced her to in the

---

220. American immigrants, friends of my brother and sister-in-law.
221. Najwa Abu el-Hakim, a Ph.D. student in anthropology at Duke University, was just

States, who, when told about Najwa's project, became very defensive and insisted, "It's *our* country." Now as Najwa points out, this was someone who had spent the first eighteen years of her life in America. So what is the analogy between the relative positions of Najwa, a Palestinian-American raised in Iran and Lebanon, and of this American-Israeli woman, on one hand, and Mintz and the black accountant, on the other? No, I don't want to trace it out. I want to leave those two relations in counterpoint, to disturb once again the assumption that in every colonial encounter it's easy to categorize some people as colonizers and others as colonized.

• 

Woman sitting in a wheelchair on a sidewalk on Rachel Immenu Street, smoking a cigarette and wearing a T-shirt that says, "I walked my feet off in Jerusalem."

• 8/6/91 •

Last night when I reached Moti he told me they'd been trying to reach me all day. There's a group going to Gaza for two days starting today, and they would have included me, but then they filled the space. A shame. But it would have been a conflict for me, since I started a four-week intensive Arabic course last night. I probably would have gone to Gaza, since I want to do it and since if I don't take Arabic now I'll save three hundred dollars, the total amount I've "saved" over my projected weekly budget since I got here.

On the other hand, let's consider for a minute what I could do if I really knew Arabic. I could apply for Middle East studies jobs. I could feel comfortable about the fact that I've already listed Arabic among my languages on my CV. Maybe I could even talk to people when I go to places like this refugee camp (which one is it going to be?). I could have answered in Arabic a few minutes ago when an elderly street sweeper asked me the time, instead of just showing him my watch; and when he thanked me with a warm *"Shukran"* and I shook his hand, I might even have been able to say, "You're welcome." I've certainly learned how to say "You're welcome" in previous Arabic classes, but when have I had any reason to say it to anybody in real life? Have I really never offered an Arabic speaker anything more than the time of day?

More than that, maybe, if I really knew Arabic, I could finally start to learn something more about the Arab world, beyond the question of how Pales-

---

beginning fieldwork toward her dissertation on archaeology as a component of Israeli national ideology. Virginia Domínguez was a member of the anthropology department at Duke at the time Najwa began her graduate studies.

tinian life impinges on Jewish history.[222] I could ponder and help respond to a question William Pfaff — whose writings in the *New Yorker* usually strike me as characteristic of an intelligent, old-line, unwarlike conservative — posed in a piece reprinted in yesterday's *Jerusalem Post:* even if some kind of a regional peace treaty ultimately comes out of the Gulf War, the suffering during the war, not just the money spent on it, must be calculated as part of its costs; and who will ever be able to say that it was worth it? For whom? For the Iraqi dead? Nevertheless the prospect of even a formal peace is so tantalizing: the idea, for instance, that the likelihood of Avner being in combat would be minimal. I have this utterly irrational sensation of empathy with Faisal Husseini (whom I've never met, though I was told to back in 1983 and certainly could have then) and Hanan Ashrawi (whom I met briefly about three years ago when we[223] sponsored her as a speaker in New York). The responsibility riding on them is astonishing. If as I hope they come out finding a way to participate in the conference (Faisal presumably can't, since he's from East Jerusalem), they (still, whoever they are) will be representing a suffering and murderously fragmented group of people who have not had the opportunity to choose their representatives by any semblance of democracy. What does Shamir want? To be able to go along with the Americans without losing his right wing? To avoid any symbolic concessions which would grant Palestinians legitimacy? To force the Palestinian representatives to fail to be representative? It's going to be a rocky period; but as I've been saying for years, it's when the Palestinians get their state that the shit will really hit the fan. The point being the necessity of remembering that even with statehood as a goal, the vision of an organization of polity beyond the state must not be suppressed entirely: the third way. And how, from the United States, could activists or intellectuals continue to be concerned in a responsible way with — for example — Iraq, without knowing infinitely more than we do? So hopefully investing the three hundred dollars and missing the trip to Gaza (which I missed regardless) may set me on the road to, as I've called it, "really learning Arabic."

The middle of the day yesterday saw me on a very different road, going to Hod Hasharon to visit for a few hours with Jonah's best friend, Arye, from nursery school and his parents. It's about halfway between the sea and the hills: again I'm struck by how prominent the hills are from the plain, and whereas over the last several years I've gotten quite rightly disgusted with the "eleven-mile-wide" argument[224] for keeping the "West Bank" (as Nancy did refer to it yesterday), being down there in the valley makes me think once

---

222. A question elaborated on in the earlier "Palestine and Jewish History" essay. That it does so impinge is the starting point of this entire investigation.
223. The New York chapter of the International Jewish Peace Union.
224. The observation that Israel inside the Green Line is, at its latitudinal and population

more of the simplistic truth of the necessity of being able to see a situation from different perspectives. Literally: look from down in the valley and think that you wouldn't want hostile cannon aimed at your city from the hills; look down from the hills (well, assuming you're a Palestinian and not a suburban settler in Ariel) and resent the fact that the people who stole the valley forty years ago are now bossing you around up in the hills.

• 7/8/91 •

Across the street from the Binyanei Ha'ooma,[225] there are some older, smaller, almost hidden buildings which are still apparently used as government offices. At the entrance to them there's a hand-painted sign saying *"misadat hastatistika."*[226]

• 8/10/91 •

Avner's back for Shabbat.[227] So far he's pretty cheerful (I imagine he'd remain pretty cheerful under virtually any circumstances). He says that the guys from Hartman and the other *bnei yeshivot*[228] are treated very well — all the other guys who didn't come in with groups of friends have to stand at attention from time to time, etc., but the officers just told the *bnei yeshivot* what they had to do and not to get into trouble. Avner expects to get into the *sayeret tsanchanim*, the elite group among the paratroopers. They got spiels from all the units, who are all competing for the "best" recruits. The antiaircraft units are part of the air force, which has a general reputation for being snobbish and relatively easy, and is considered undesirable on that account. So the officer who gave the spiel for the antiaircraft units gave a speech where he said things like, "It's very hard work, the conditions are lousy, you don't get much to eat," and so on — trying to convince the kids that it was "really shitty" as Avner puts it, and therefore make it a more socially attractive choice. So Avner and his friends were watching the whole thing, kibitzing, and laughing. Meanwhile the sergeant for the paratroopers was thrilled when Avner said he'd passed the test for the commandos (which he can't be in because his eyesight isn't good enough), and practically guaranteed Avner that he'd get in. The gem that Avner gave me was that this morning all of the new recruits

---

center around Tel Aviv, only eleven miles wide at its narrowest point and therefore extremely vulnerable to attack from the hills of the West Bank.
225. National Theater.
226. The Restaurant of Statistics.
227. A few days after being inducted into the army.
228. Yeshiva students — here, those entering the army.

were taken out to sit in the hot sun and wait for hours while their numbers were called and they were sent to the various units they're being assigned to (his group, the *bnei yeshivot*, weren't called today; at 10:30 they got their passes to go home for Shabbat). This ritual is called — guess what — the *shuk avadim*, the slave market, the same name as is used for and possibly even named after the places where Palestinian men from the territories come in and wait to be picked up for day labor. I told Avner, "That's going in my diary," and he said, "Of course, why do you think I told you? I'm going to tell you a lot of good stuff about the army."

• 8/13/91 •

In the morning we took a private taxi from Kfar Qara to Rotem.[229] The driver/owner of the taxi has a regular gig during the school year — he takes three children from a nearby kibbutz into Tel Aviv to a special school, then works Tel Aviv as a regular taxi while they're in school, and then brings them home.

The route we followed generally retraced the way I had come up to the Galilee with Riad several weeks before, except for a cutoff from the 'Ara Road (toward Afula it's called the Ruler Road, because it's ten kilometers without a curve, and as Dan adds, there's a hole [Afula] at the end of it)[230] through the Jezreel Valley — which looks like just about the richest agricultural land in the country. I asked the driver whether there had been Arab villages in the region we were passing through, and he said there weren't many, although there were Bedouins. Then we came to a point where the road wound down a bit farther with a spectacular view of the northern Beit Shean Valley, with sparkling bits that I thought were lakes but must have been fish ponds. Here — at the point where the two valleys are contingent — the driver pointed out the ruins of a village called Zar'in, now a pile of stones.[231] I said it looked like a *tel*, and lo and behold, fifty meters farther on there was an archaeological dig! Presumably the village had been directly on top of the *tel*, and now that there are no people there, it's diggable.... I'll have to tell Najwa about it, maybe she'll get the story for me. I thought of what you would say

---

229. This was at the end of a second visit to Kfar Qara, which Dan and I made together.

230. Afula is one of the "development towns" that were spread around the country in the first decades after the establishment of the state, many of which are still populated primarily by poorer Jews from Middle Eastern or North African backgrounds (now often along with more recent Soviet or Ethiopian immigrants), so my brother's crack is actually derogatory.

231. Nothing in this region with this spelling appears in *All That Remains*, the encyclopedia of Palestinian villages destroyed or abandoned in 1948 (Khalidi, ed., 1992), although there's a Zir'in near Jenin.

in Yiddish about this: *"Funem dorf iz a tel gevorn."*[232] Danny had just gotten through saying that the Jezreel Valley is his favorite part of the country, and now he said he would never be able to enjoy it the same way again; he said we should write a *kine*, a Tisha B'Av lamentation for the four hundred Arab villages destroyed in 1948.

Shortly after we come back onto the main Beit Shean–Jericho Highway from the side road which passes several kibbutzim, the driver points out the exact spot where the border had been until 1967. I don't know why it wasn't clearer to me before (although it seems closer to Mehola than the woman from the settlement had stated when I came through with the tour group): the pattern of land use changes dramatically. The fields are smaller (although still symmetrical and not tiny), there are more stones, the plowing seems perhaps shallower, there are people in the fields and not just sprinklers, the hills behind the valley are bare (no JNF forests here), there are a couple of small Palestinian villages, or maybe one village in several clusters of houses; name of the village is 'Adala, something like that.

•

Efraim took us to see the chicken coop (remember Dan hadn't been here before). I wanted him to tell Dan the story about counting chickens when they were sold to the Arabs, because I wanted to explain to him that I didn't think it was just a case of cross-cultural mistrust. Dan knew the story. He said he'd related it to our father and to Sam Tarnow — two ex–chicken farmers themselves — and they confirmed that that's exactly what happens whenever you sell chickens. They remembered one man in particular (with a Slavic-Jewish name which Dan didn't remember exactly) whom you had to watch like a hawk because he would always grab more chickens at a time than he was supposed to.

• 8/14/91 •

There's an abandoned village halfway down a steep hillside to the left just as you're coming into Jerusalem. Danny says there's a restaurant there that you can only get to by car. My question: Why did they leave the houses standing there (a decision that presumably is remade every day)? Does that land somehow still belong to the office of the custodian of absentee property? It's not important: it wouldn't stop them from destroying the houses. Those abandoned houses there mean something, and it's not obvious what, since

---

232. Literally, "The village became a *tel*"; but in Yiddish, "*Vern a tel*" means to be ruined or destroyed in general, as in the folk song "Di Grine Kuzine" (My immigrant cousin), in which "the cousin" describes how she arrives in America fresh and lively but after a few years "*Fun ir iz a tel gevorn*" — she has been ruined.

presumably nobody with authority wants people like me to be reminded of the fact that Arabs used to live here.[233]

•

Yesterday afternoon instead of our usual Arabic class, we had a class trip to Abu Ghosh, an Arab village below Jerusalem on the Tel Aviv Road which is famous as a "friendly" village which has always gotten along well with the Israeli government.[234] It's also evidently a model village — one member of our group mentioned that the last time she'd been there, there was a group of *olim hadashim*, new immigrants, who were being shown "how the Arabs live." According to our host there — Abu Ismail, a man who works at the Italian consulate in East Jerusalem — the village was founded by a Muslim from the Caucasus who came here seven hundred years ago, found water, stayed there, and married a Yemenite woman; and there are four families in the village, which are descended from his four children.

The village is extraordinarily beautiful, built as it is on two steep hillsides, the streets as narrow, steep, and curved as those of Ar'ara, but the earth seeming somehow better-watered and more fertile. According to Abu Ismail, this is apparently the site of the ancient Kiryat 'Anavim,[235] after which a nearby kibbutz is named, and the grapes of Abu Ghosh which we tasted were delicious.[236]

When we arrived at the middle of the village, Dr. Aziz split us up into groups and sent us off with three boys who turned out to be Ismail's brothers — he assigned us to find Abu Ismail's house by asking people along the way, a bit sneaky because only by asking Abbas, the brother who accompanied my group, did I figure out that Abu Ismail was also Abbas's father. (This exercise — finding a house in the village by asking for it — is consistent with Riad's answer to me when I asked how I would find his house from the entrance to 'Arrabi.) No matter. Along the way Abbas asked me if we'd like to see the church at the top of the highest hill, I said "Why not?" so I think almost the whole group of students wound up with a brief tour of the church and an explanation in English by an elderly nun from the Sisters of St. Joseph. She explained to us that this was the site where the Ark of the Covenant had stayed for eight years after being retrieved from the Philistines, before being

---

233. See "Ruins, Mounting toward Jerusalem," the last chapter of this book.

234. Although in the early, heady days of the intifada there were incidents of stone throwing and the like even in Abu Ghosh.

235. Grape Village.

236. By mentioning in the same sentence the grapes of Abu Ghosh and the ancient name of "Grape Village," I here reinforce the identification of contemporary Palestinians with ancient Israelites. This is particularly ironic given the specific and well-known history of the immigration to Palestine that led to the founding of Abu Ghosh.

brought to Jerusalem (that's a part of Jewish "history" I'm completely ignorant of).[237] She also showed us the special icon at the left in the front of the church, which showed Jesus and Mary being borne to Jerusalem instead of the ark, with David looking on and admiring them. She also told us that her order had been the first group of missionary nuns in the Middle East, going against the French proverb which says that a woman should have *"un mari ou un mur."*[238]

From the hill where the church is located there's a fantastic view back to Jerusalem — toward the right, some Jewish settlements on the other side of the main road; straight ahead, the highway and the Hilton; and, again a bit to the right and farther off (I think), the tower at Mount Scopus. Another view again of the hills surrounding Jerusalem — but this time with a better sense of their current settlement.

At the (back) entrance to the village, just at the bottom of the church hill, is a weathered sign saying in English, "Border of the tribe of Benjamin during the period of the time of the Judges." On the hill opposite the church is a rival occupancy of a high place — a small permanent Israeli army installation. Between the church and Abu Ismail's house is a day-care center with a sign saying it was sponsored by Na'amat — Pioneer Women.

Soon we are all gathered at Abu Ismail's house. It's three stories high — bigger than Abu Hisham's house in Kfar Qara — and the little party (about thirty people altogether, including his family) is held in a large, empty room with a sort of stucco-concrete ceiling on the top floor. There's a large balcony just outside, which has much of the same view as the top of the church hill. (There's another church in the town as well, but virtually no Christians live in Abu Ghosh now.) Abu Ismail tells us about the village in some detail. Someone asks him about marriages, and he says that dowries are becoming less universal, and that whereas most marriages used to be within the village, since 1967 a lot of people have been marrying people from Jerusalem and the West Bank. When I ask him what happened to the village in 1948, he says, "Ah, that's the hard question," but the basic answer is that Yitskhak

---

237. According to the account in 1 Samuel, the Philistines voluntarily relinquished the ark, which caused great destruction while they kept it. They first returned it to the border city of Bet Shemesh, where 50,070 Israelite men were smitten "because they had gazed upon the ark of the Lord" (1 Samuel 7:19). The people of Bet Shemesh in turn passed the ark on to the people of Kiryat Yearim, where it was evidently safer: "And it came to pass, from the day that the ark abode in Kiryat Yearim, that the time was long; for it was twenty years; and all the house of Israel yearned after the Lord." Kiryat Yearim is in fact quite close to Kiryat 'Anavim/Abu Ghosh. I have no explanation for the discrepancy between the "eight years" I report the nun as referring to and the twenty years referred to in the biblical account.

238. Evidently meaning "a husband or a cloister" (literally, a husband or a wall): these nuns, that is, were not confined in either fashion.

Navon was the local military commander, protected the village, and urged the people to stay. As to the relations of the people in the village to the Israelis, on one hand, and to their fellow Arabs, on the other (this last a matter of some dispute, the female teacher of the elementary class somewhat teasingly insisting that the people in Abu Ghosh aren't really Arabs),[239] he explains that there could be two brothers, one of whom is peaceful and one of whom is a troublemaker — making political/historical differences into a matter of accidents of character. But he also adds that the people of Abu Ghosh see themselves as a "bridge" between Israelis and Arabs.

After perhaps three-quarters of an hour of this, Ismail starts playing music on a small electric organ — "Yamaha" in English and Arabic — backed up first by a canned rhythm track and then by a full complement of "music minus one." The music is Arab pop instrumental, not *dabka*,[240] until the end — but it's got a good beat and you can dance to it, and I wind up as one of few dancers, "really getting into it" as we used to say, lifting my arms and shaking them, shaking my hips.... I don't know what you call that. They loved it when I took off my yarmulke and started waving it around while I danced. I also don't know in what situations men or women would dance like that together or separately (at weddings? Fawzi's youngest brother will be married soon, and I very much hope to be invited), which inhibits me at first — but within limits what's appropriate here, or rather what's "authentic," is itself an inappropriate question. When I'm exhausted I step out onto the balcony for cooler air and conversation with a journalist named John something from the Jerusalem *Post*, who's in my class, and an elderly man named Halil, whose grapes and plums I gather we've been eating. Halil mentions that before 1948 he worked in the German Colony as a cook for the British head of the YMCA — who left in 1948 of course.

•

Yesterday afternoon Dan and I went to El-Bireh to meet Ahmed and four of his friends. We wound up taking a "special" taxi to In'ash el-Usra, because the driver was tired of waiting around for passengers — it was 2:00 and all the stores had closed by 1:00, so no shoppers were going back from Jerusalem. The driver spoke Hebrew quite well, and we commiserated about the inability of people like Shamir to envision peace: as the driver said, then Palestinians could come back and start businesses, Israelis could do business with Palestine and all the Arab countries (they're so good in agriculture, so many specialists — this he pointed out).... In talking about the failure of most Israelis and Jews to "see" Palestinians, I talked about what it was like to replace the

---

239. Being descended, as Abu Ismail had explained, from Caucasian migrants.
240. The "traditional" Palestinian dance rhythm and steps.

figure of 1.5 million Palestinians with an image of these cities, all of these houses leading from Jerusalem to Ramallah — the places where real people live. He gave it a twist I didn't expect: there are 1.5 million people, and there aren't enough houses for them. Someone adds a room onto his house, and the authorities come along and tear it down. Fifteen people crammed into a tiny house in a refugee camp, with the bathtub in the room and the kitchen right next to it. A sense of tremendous injustice combined with a sense that peace is so possible and would be so beneficial even for his enemies. A taxi driver's rap: in New York they often speak the same way, talkative, sometimes racist or warlike, often down-to-earth, humane, and perceptive. But in any case not the conciliatory line of someone in the job of making Palestinians sound reasonable.

Ahmed introduced Dan to his two daughters, and again referred to Rabab as "we call this one our Ashkenazi daughter" and the other "we call this one our Sephardi daughter," although this time he pointed out that the older one was born in Germany and Rabab in Palestine. He understands the irony of that, but more interesting than his sophistication is the implicit notion that colonialism and simple bad manners are connected to Europe, politeness and hospitality to the Mediterranean.

I didn't even get all of the names of Ahmed's friends: Said, Mushar(?), a physics professor, and one other. A long conversation, and here I'll only have fragments from it. Toward the beginning I was trying to explain to the physics professor my ideas about the archaeology of notions of time and space as separate dimensions. I kept getting vaguer and vaguer, thinking that what he wanted from me was precision about my methodological approach to studying the theoretical issues on the ground. It wasn't that at all; finally he said, "But these ideas seem to leave us with nothing except for the here and now." What he was concerned about was the legitimacy of his memories of the home he left in 1948 (I didn't ask where it was). I have no insight as to why what I said left him that impression; it's very clear to me, and the subsequent dialogue confirmed, that what lay behind it in general is the feeling that it's not enough for the Israelis that the Palestinians say they're willing to compromise, to grant the Israelis title to their, the Palestinians', homeland; that what the Israelis demand is that the Palestinians also renounce their memories.[241] My

---

241. The Israeli writer Anton Shammas responded to the Israel-PLO agreement of September 1993 in terms that articulate this feeling as a fait accompli: "For all those Palestinians who, in the last 45 years, kept hoping that their displacement and exile were a grave injustice that somehow would be acknowledged and rectified, it's time now to master the art of forgetting.... It will be painful for them to forget because theirs is an oral history of pain.... And as the Israelis, in their euphoria over the signing of the declaration, are preparing to write the definitive history of the conflict now that it has been 'resolved,' the Palestinians will have also to get used to the fact that their past will be written by those who

brother and I hastened to assure him that we appreciate very well the power of memory.[242]

We get into a taxi — two shekels a head, going to Jerusalem — and Dan remarks again after we get out that just by entering a Palestinian taxi, there's a sense of acceptance that comes from the driver and the other passengers: there's no evident feeling that we don't belong with them. If we're willing to join them and ride with them, we're not categorical "settlers" (we're not wearing yarmulkes, of course, but together I don't think anybody would fail to realize that we are Jews). We pass the first checkpoint; a young soldier waves us past, and the driver does the minislalom past the barrels set up in the street. I joke to the driver: *"Hada walad hilu"* (He's a nice boy); our "luck" doesn't hold, though; there's a second checkpoint, and the taxi is waved over and here (unlike the time I came back from Beit Sahour) we're all told to get out. The young blond Mishmar Hagvulnik asks first for Dan's papers, in Hebrew. He looks at them, and asks Dan where he's from: "America." "What are you doing here?" "Visiting." "Where do you live?" "California." "How come it says New Jersey?" [It says New Jersey's where he was born, asshole, but that's not what Dan says:] "I moved." "You like Atlantic City?" Coldly: "I've never been there."[243] End of interrogation. Mine is a simple glance at the passport. The other soldier says we can go back in the car, but blondy says, "No they can't. If you can be nasty, so can I." A couple of minutes later we're allowed in, and gradually our legs stop trembling. Dan mutters something about Mishmar HaGvul being "guard dogs," although later in the evening he talks about other soldiers doing the same job who are much more polite. But you know what it's like? For me it's like when I was a kid and had just moved to a new town, and as an outsider — a new kid, a Jew, a reader, not a fighter — somehow the other kids constantly had to challenge, to threaten me, to assert their authority. Some nineteen-year-old Israeli kid is making me feel that way again: imagine if I had never been able to escape

---

have expelled them in the past.... And in their dreams they will see, among other images of their lost past, the map that the United Nations drew on Nov. 29, 1947, giving them an hourglass-shaped state, which they refused.... A key to a house in Yafa, then, is bound to become a collector's item that opens no door, a threatless tool of the imagination" (Shammas 1993: 33).

242. Presumably I had been talking about memory as a social construction of the present. This could be taken to suggest that all collective memory, including that of a people struggling for recognition, is merely an illusion with no real standing as a basis for claims in the present. This interpretation of social construction would indeed seem to leave memory at the mercy of hegemony, and it is true enough that when academic scholars speak of the "politics of memory," they generally seem to have in mind rhetorics of the present about the past, rather than claims grounded in past experience per se. I discuss this conundrum in an essay entitled "Space, Time, and the Politics of Memory" (1994c).

243. Daniel Boyarin notes, "In fact I said, 'I'm not talking with you.'"

that situation, and it makes it easier to imagine some of what inspired the first Zionists, some of what some Israelis are still afraid of returning to today, and what legions of Palestinians experience every day of their lives, not only in Israel and the "Occupied Territories." Then the other passengers (young men; the one young religious woman wasn't made to get out), then eventually the driver. The driver tells us in English: "They asked where you came from. I told them you came to the taxi station. They asked what you were doing, I told them I didn't know. The soldier yelled at me for not showing him my passport, but he didn't ask me to show him my passport. They get cars and houses, we get nothing. A taxi from Hebron gets permission to drive between Hebron and Tel Aviv; Ramallah–Tel Aviv; Hebron–Jerusalem, and that's it."

• 8/15/91 •

A meeting with Hatem and his friend Yasir (who said very little) and Dan this morning at their Rapprochement Center in Beit Sahour. I taped part of Hatem's discussion both of his period of administrative detention and of his notions about how the Palestinians can handle this difficult situation they're in right now, and I hope to transcribe that on Sunday.

I started taping when Hatem was in the middle of a story about the first big visit to Beit Sahour by a group of seventy or eighty mostly religious Israelis. Their arrival was timed for just before Shabbat, to make it too late for the military authorities to order the Israelis to go home. In the evening everyone ate supper and visited at the homes of the people they were staying with, and in the morning the whole group together with their hosts proceeded to the Shepherd's Field. At that point the local army decided that it was a closed military zone and the Israelis had to go. But they refused: it was Shabbat! It was a contest between Rabin and God, Hatem says. The captain didn't know what to do. Bigger and bigger officers kept coming. Here's the tape; I'll transcribe on Sunday, it's time to shower for Shabbes, but I've got my transcriber set up already.

• 8/18/91 •

"They complain that we teach our children to throw stones. But we don't teach our children to throw stones. One night in February 1989, about 1:30, after midnight, the *muhabbarat* (what are they called?) — intelligence officers — came and knocked on my door. The officer told me to come with him. I said, 'OK, just give me two minutes to go into my bedroom and put my clothes on, and please be quiet, so you won't wake up my two-year-old son.'

I went into my bedroom and started changing out of my pajamas, and then two or three of the *muhabbarat* came in and started yelling and banging on the walls. So my son woke up and asked me why the *yahud*[244] were here, and I went in and told him that I was just going outside with them for a little while. I thought he went back to sleep, but he didn't; when they wanted to take me outside he was in the corridor with me, standing between my legs and shouting at them, 'Leave my father alone! Don't take my father!' When they took me outside, the officer asked me why I teach my children to hate Jews [not these words exactly; wish I had it more precisely here].[245] I told him I didn't teach him anything like that. The truth is he taught it to our children. And the settlers teach their children to hate us; he comes to us and teaches our children to hate him, but we don't go to the settlements and teach their children to hate us. This is a true story, February 1, 1989."

About the disco,[246] which for some reason I'm apprehensive about trying to describe: Efraim led us to a place called the Underground, right across the street from the big new ugly building with the Bank Hapoalim in it at Kikar Tsion. The place was jammed with kids who looked like they were all between nineteen and twenty-two, and most of them were wearing white T-shirts, and most of the girls (the ones I noticed anyway) were skinny and had long really curly hair. Here and there on the side of the room couples were making out. By that time in the evening I was quite aware that I was enjoying the noise and the crowding — touching young healthy bodies wherever I turned. They had loud, piped-in music in the outer room and a video screen showing old Tom and Jerry cartoons. Buying drinks and getting our hands stamped entitled us to go inside and down to the disco room — stuffed with maybe two hundred people, done up sort of like a cave as a lot of discos I think are, incredibly hot, God forbid they should ever have a fire there, it would be worse than the Happy Land Social Club disaster. Randi and Efraim immediately found a space at the other end of the room, sort of off to the side, where there was more room for dancing. I stood near the entrance at the top of a series of wide stairs drinking my J & B and just watching the crowd of young people (I'm not quite old enough to call them kids yet), entranced by the sensual exuberance of the music and the bodies, thinking briefly (what a trite thought, this is standard intifada documentary stuff) that all of this stuff always goes on whatever else is going on — and thinking that perhaps because nearly all of the music is American, the kids might look a little different but

---

244. Jews.
245. Why don't I have the precise words? This purports to be a tape transcript, but I have not kept the tape, and I have no explanation for the imprecision.
246. During my brother's two-week stay back in Jerusalem, my sister-in-law Randi came to Jerusalem from Qetura, and she, my nephew Efraim, and I went dancing.

otherwise the scene is interchangeable. Randi came up and showed me where she and Efraim were, but I shrugged her off; I thought I was going to leave. I finished my drink, found them, started dancing, and kept dancing until we all left together at 3:00 in the morning. I shouted the words of the songs I knew (not too many; most were new stuff I didn't recognize), and sort of acted them out as I danced. Several times I laughed loudly while I danced. I kicked my legs high, and I swung my arms low, and I shook my hips, and I leaned so far back that I almost fell down, and at one point I started turning slowly and turned about fifteen times with my glasses off, thinking wow so this is how the world looks when it's spinning around you, and when I stopped I couldn't stand up straight for a little while and felt a little nauseous and Efraim was worried about me and asked if I needed to go outside for air or have some water, but I sat down and my head was OK and I started dancing again. We were all sweating like horses; the kind of thing where someone hands you an ice cube, you rub it on your arms and neck and chest and it cools you down a little bit, it's not a shock at all, and after a few seconds it's melted. Well, I didn't dance all the time: twice I announced I was leaving and made it to the end of the disco. Was this another time that I felt younger, like when Dan and I were stopped with the taxi coming back from Ramallah or when we were at Moti's?[247] I don't think so, I think it was better than even when I was a teenager and I danced a lot — because I think I dance better now, but also because the internal voice that always used to separate some conscious "me" from the body that was moving is less obtrusive now. Anyway as I wrote just above, I felt like the dance had exorcised my discombobulation at this looming interruption of my work, this very different challenge facing me for the next two weeks.[248] And I was glad of the chance to be with Efraim like that, someone whom I've never felt close to like I'm starting to now — I told him afterword that I much prefer thinking of him and Avner as cousins than as my nephews.

---

247. An evening left out of this published version, during which Daniel and I, along with Moti, Alex, and Chagit Katzev-Haft, sat around the kitchen table drinking wine for hours in an intellectual bullshit session, something I haven't had many chances to do since college (see Moffatt 1987).

248. A close friend from New York, now living in London with her new husband and their baby, had called Elissa to say that her husband had been diagnosed with Huntington's disease. My offer to come to London for two weeks while he was in the hospital, to keep her company and help with the baby, was accepted. The break was a difficult one for me, and it was especially hard to return to Jerusalem alone at the end of my stay in London: I felt I'd made it halfway home to my family and then been forced to turn around and go back again. Indeed, the vast bulk of my journal comes from the period before I went to London; afterward, with just two months to go before I was set to return to New York, I was more concerned with keeping myself comfortable.

• 8/19/91 •

HA:[249] "God said that they're not allowed to go, and Rabin said yes. And finally they couldn't do it."

JB: "And if they put them on busses and they go back through an Orthodox neighborhood, people might throw stones!"

HA: "And finally they said, 'Look, OK, we won't be capable of evacuating you, we will confine you somewhere until sunset. So they ordered them to go back to the place where they were sitting at the beginning and that they shouldn't mix up with Palestinians until sunset. But they couldn't actually observe that, you know. They just gave the orders and they couldn't follow it up, so they just withdrew. And we continued the event until sunset, and finally they were taken back to Jerusalem."

DB: "The little moments of victory..."

JB: "They provide a lot of fuel to keep going."

DB: "I think that for me that Mass in Beit Sahour in the church was — you know I'm also an Orthodox Jew and this was one of the greatest religious moments of my life."

HA: "I wish I have been here."

DB: "When the old mufti of Jerusalem came in with all the Muslims — up till that moment there were the Catholics and the other, the Orthodox Christians, and the few Jews that were here, and the mufti was trying to get in all day. And they'd been blocking him. And he made wonderful speeches on television about being blocked. Then they brought him in around the back over the hills and brought him into Beit Sahour. He came into the church with all of the Muslims of Beit Sahour and everybody in church stood up and cheered. And it was a redemptive moment, it was a vision of some kind of— altogether, the priest spoke about the Holocaust, spoke about the Holocaust of the Jews and the Holocaust of the Palestinians, and just every — like a flash of a possibility of redemption, what human beings could be."

GA: "Yeah, I wish I was there. I was in Ketziot[250] at the time."

DB: "On vacation in the south."

• 8/20/91 •

"...Arrested for four times. The most painful was when I was held for eight days in the arrestment procedure. You know I'll be sitting in front of the room with an officer for about twelve hours. You know, I wouldn't have food. I

---

249. The transcription of the interview with Hatem Asmari resumes here.
250. An Israeli mass detention camp where Palestinian men active in the intifada were held, often without trial, under "administrative detention."

can't move or fiddle around. I can't go to the toilet. And I'm there for no purpose, just sitting. Finally I started bringing my food with me, I started bringing some books to read, and I had big fights with them to take that right for myself. On one occasion they were sort of laughing at me; you know one officer was laughing and the other one was sitting beside me chatting with me, sort of inviting me that I should convince the Beit Sahourians not to do it, they should pay their taxes. And when the other officer passed there the first one told him, 'Look, this guy is hungry, you don't bring him food.' This guy told him, 'Well, he can't go to the *sherutim*.'[251] At that time the guy didn't know that I understand Hebrew, so I had a big fight with him, we almost sort of quarreled with hands. And afterwards I started enjoying the company of others, you know, many people started joining me in this procedure, so it was a bit easier. One guy included was a very old person from Deheisheh refugee camp; he's about seventy-five to eighty years old. They accused his child of throwing stones. This child is nine years old. I think not his child, the child of his son, and his son was killed, so they sort of picked him up. Now they wanted him to pay a fine. [I remember listening to this part of the story, looking out past the window of the Rapprochement Center to the next distant hill from Beit Sahour, which has a narrow modern rode cut into its side; a 'settler's road,' I imagine — JB.] Now this guy was not even capable of feeding himself and his family, so to pay a few hundred shekels fine was the last thing that he thought about in his whole life. So he told the officer, 'You have two options: either arrest the kid or arrest me. Even if you search my family or all my property you won't find two hundred shekels.' So they wanted to punish him, so they started forcing him to come daily from 8:00 to 8:00 also. And I learned a lot from that guy. At that time I was actually reading through that book about the Palestinian refugee problem, 19 — "

JB: "Benny Morris's book?"

GA: "Yeah. I was reading through that book, I used to take him with me. And that guy was a witness, he was there at that time, and I started asking him about things I read through the book. And he started telling me stories about that time that couldn't be included actually in such textbooks. And really it was an education for me to sit with this guy and to learn from him. You know he was a very simple guy, he was a religious man, but he was open-minded. I was also reading through another book called *The First Three Minutes*, which is a book by a professor in physics talking about astronomy and this idea of a big bang at the creation of the world, and so on. Now part of the people there asked me so that we could spend the time, that when I read

---

251. Toilet.

something I should try to explain it. And I was stuck there, you know. I tried to explain how the universe sort of exploded randomly with a big explosion and that it's expanding all over...."

DB: "Don't you realize you were committing a serious crime?"

JB: "Education, the universities are closed..."

GA: "No, it wasn't a crime for the officers only, it was a crime in front of this old guy. You know it didn't fit with his mind. He said, 'Look, guy. For the whole past period I respected you. Now it is unfortunate that...' I was forced to apologize to him. I said, 'Look, I'm not telling you my beliefs. I'm just trying to explain what's in this book.' Oh my God. Now this guy's in the hospital actually, he's in a very serious condition, he has cancer. I talked to him in el-Mokassed Hospital at one point. You know, I feel attached to this guy actually. I spent about six days with him. Finally it's part of my life, I just can't forget about him."

[In the next taped section, Hatem is explaining what Palestinians used to think about Zionist history, and how their notions of the Israeli collective have changed.]

GA: "[We used to think that] Jews were trapped by the Zionists, and the moment they discover the kind of trap they were in or that they were deceived, the moment they discover it they will leave immediately. And when you follow up, never Palestinians were thinking that there is more than a cheat, more than a lie behind the motives of these Jews coming to this land. I think we lost out of that. What we lost is that we didn't realize that we are facing a community that is maybe as committed as us to the idea of being here, to the extent of fighting, losing their lives; we thought the Zionist movement had bluffed them, they were you know, just routed to this place by... they are not really rooted here, but this is a sort of conspiracy, and they were trapped, and we got used to a strategy that, 'Look, it's easy — the moment we convince them that this is a real trap, they are not related to this area and therefore they'll just leave.' To build a large part of your strategy for a long time on such assumptions, and finally after forty years to realize that you were wrong on the basic assumption, and that's why I think it's partially responsible how the Palestinians did lose the struggle. I think they have lost good opportunities to compromise at some point, if they have realized that..."[252]

---

252. In this sense it may be compared to the assumption of liberal and socialist Zionists that the local Arabs would essentially welcome their presence because of the benefits of modernity the European Zionists brought with them, and perhaps as well to the rhetorical claims often made by Zionists that "Arabs" should be at home in any of the Arab states.

## • 9/6/91 •

I made it to the Yesh Gvul pre–Women in Black[253] vigil for the first time today. Sam Englander[254] was there handing out leaflets, and Shimon Ostrowsky[255] told me he wants to organize an informal discussion about the political situation after the collapse of the Soviet Union. More important, I actually got up and held a sign saying, *"Hakibush mashkhit! Yesh gvul!"*[256] I got two reactions. One was from an older American man, who looked at me silently for a few seconds, and then said, "Take off the yarmulke!" He didn't shout, but I was so embarrassed; I didn't say a thing. I can't even explain well why.[257] The second was an Israeli woman, later middle-aged, who started asking me, "What does that mean, 'The occupation kills'?[258] What occupation? What do you want us to return? The cave at Machpelah? The Golan Heights?" Surprising myself, I had some answers for her, even though I didn't catch every word she said. If she didn't want to "return" anything, then "Maybe we should make them citizens. That's a different solution." She agreed that might be a solution. "What about Jerusalem?" she asked. I said Jerusalem has to be discussed, and I said the Golan represents a genuine security issue.... I did my best, but my answers aren't what interested me, upon reflection. In responding to her, I had used the first-person plural: "Maybe *we*

---

253. Yesh Gvul (There is a Limit, or There is a Border) is the organization that supports Israeli soldiers — mostly reservists — who refuse service in the Occupied Territories. Women in Black is an organization that has held weekly vigils protesting the occupation in various spots around the country for several years. The Jerusalem vigil is held every Friday from 1:00 to 2:00 P.M. at Kikar Tsarfat (Paris Square). It is preceded by a weekly Yesh Gvul demonstration, which among other things helps to secure the square for the Women in Black to come later and keeps the right-wing counterdemonstrators (who are also there every week) across the street.

254. An American immigrant writer and tour guide.

255. An American-born administrator at the School for Overseas Students at the Hebrew University and a veteran Israeli leftist.

256. "Occupation corrupts! There's a limit!" The slogan *"Yesh gvul"* here implies both "There's a border" (that is, a border to "Israel proper" beyond which the Israeli military has no business maintaining an extended occupation) and "There's a limit" (that is, a moral boundary beyond which unconscionable acts cannot be justified on the grounds of "security").

257. To this man, the yarmulke evidently was supposed to mean that its wearer was a loyal Jew. My demonstrating against the occupation must have meant to him that I failed to acknowledge either the paramount importance of protecting Jewish lives or the right and duty of Jews to possess and occupy all of the Land of Israel. Furthermore, it is often assumed that the generally empathic, "rights"-oriented politics informing Yesh Gvul and the Women in Black are necessarily associated with secularist universalism. Therefore, he may have reacted to the yarmulke on my head in that context as a bad-faith usurpation. My own unease with his vehement reaction may suggest that I sense myself indeed to be a better human than I am a Jew.

258. As noted above, *"Hakibush mashkhit"* actually means "The occupation corrupts." I doubtless translated *mashkhit* as "kills" because it sounds like *shkhita,* meaning "slaughter."

should make them citizens." And when she asked me whom the occupation kills, I said, "Both us and them." She said it wasn't killing her, so a young woman passing by joked to me, "Your sign should say the occupation kills — except for her!" But I was caught up at the easy way my rhetoric shifted, literally, into a discourse of "us and them" — different, certainly, from the implicit "us or them," if you're not with us you're against us, of the man who had told me to take off my yarmulke, but a stance almost impossible to avoid in a situation like that. What the woman was objecting to was the generality of our slogans, as if they were frozen into a ritual without recognition of nuance; she said she was "for compromise."

• 9/7/91 •

Thinking further about my conversation with the sixtyish woman at the Yesh Gvul demonstration yesterday: first of all, she said that she had fought in '48. Part of her complaint was, "What is the *kibush*? What borders are you talking about? '67? '48? Jerusalem? Hebron? Gush Etsion? Kastel?" Kastel seems to be the key here, really. If '67 was a conquest, then what was '48? In a way, her complaint was analogous to Riad Ghanem's view that settling for a separate Palestinian ministate is hardly worth all of this suffering and dying. To simply say that "conquest" is wrong put into question everything that she had fought for when she was younger — this, as she made clear when she told Steve that she was for territorial compromise, is a separate issue from the commitment to Erets Yisrael Hashleyma.[259] To her, I suppose, our imposition of an arbitrary formula was as much (or more) of a betrayal than the Israeli government's refusal to consider anything but its own maximal stance — she had fought for something that we were willing to forgo in favor of a formula.

Charles told me about a story Chana Hacohen told about herself at a party in the neighborhood. She had asked somebody what the verb *lezaken* means, because she kept hearing men in the street shouting, *"Al tezaken."* What they were actually saying, of course, was *"Alte zakhen,"* "old things," which they buy and resell. This is a classic nostalgia figure of immigrant Jewish life, both here and in America — the *alte zakhen* man, but only in Israel do people of my generation still remember him, generally as an old Ashkenazi Jew. The day after Charles told me this story I heard a young man in the street with the same cry I'd heard the day before, only now I understood it for the first time: *"Zakhe-e-e-n! Al-te zakhe-e-e-n!"* And another man the next day... And I don't think they were Yiddish speakers either; the phrase removed from its

---

259. Greater Israel.

original language has taken on its own character in Hebrew.[260] This marginal profession, then, has been maintained and been passed on, along with its characteristic announcement, to a different immigrant ethnic group.

• 9/12/91 •

This morning, as I write, there's another *alte zakhen* in the street — calling his call, no one coming out in this poor neighborhood; maybe they did all their cleaning and throwing away before Rosh Hashanah. One of the ways the phrase becomes strange is that in Yiddish the words would be stressed on the first syllable, whereas these guys stress the second, so that it sounds like "Altie zakhi-i-i-n." As he calls and walks and sits and rests and waits, operatic-style *chazanut*[261] is being played in the building across the street; the *alte zakhen*'s hawking and coughing are amplified and echoed across the walls of these long, low buildings.

• 9/15/91 •

I actually found out about this latest visit to Ramye — a small "Bedouin" (that's what they are called and call themselves, but I don't know what it means) village of seventeen nuclear families, ninety-six people in all (not my census; these are the numbers agreed on by the residents and activists supporting them) next to the economically and socially healthy and rapidly expanding development town of Carmiel in the Galilee, which I've written about above in describing my visit to Ar'ara — from Sam Englander, at the Yesh Gvul vigil last Friday. Basically the story is that Ramye is one of perhaps 120 "unrecognized" Arab villages in Israel — that is, one of those villages which was not included in the official 1965 census of Israel, and which hence fall entirely outside the governmental guidelines for residence, utility services, and building permits. 'Ein Hod, which I also wrote about after my weekend in Ar'ara, is another; two men from 'Ein Hod seem to be among the leaders of an umbrella organization called the Committee of the Forty, which is trying to agitate on behalf of all the unrecognized villages. In April, the people of Ramye received an eviction notice. (Along with an offer of apartments elsewhere? Carmiel has grown very close to Ramye; there are plans to build thousands more new units there [everything is talked about as if it's for Russian *olim*, but generally there's a perennial housing shortage in Israel], and the one hundred dunams of Ramye are presumably to be incorporated into

---

260. I can't say now at exactly what point I realized that, of course, these people were Palestinians.

261. Cantorial music.

Carmiel and built on. Thus one of the lines in the announcement calling for a "day of solidarity with the residents of the Arab village of Ramye" states, "We are opposed to the cynical use of 'public need' in order to justify the expulsion of the children of one people from their homes and land in order to settle children of another people in their place." I haven't gotten a clear story about what compensation, in terms of other places to live or payment, they've been offered, although people from Ramye whom we spoke to said the money they've been offered is ludicrous.) The effective date is tomorrow, September 16; my thirty-fifty birthday and two days before Yom Kippur. Perhaps today the lawyer for the families of Ramye will manage to obtain a restraining order, and the issue will drag on.[262] Anyway, the people from Derekh Hanitzotz — one of the splinter Trotskyist organizations here, competitors of Matzpen, the group Alex and Moti (I think) belong to[263] — have been organizing solidarity for Ramye, deciding that there's a limit inside the Green Line as well: a good strategy, since it's much easier to actually get people to sites marked for confiscation inside the Green Line, where areas can't simply be declared "closed military zones" at the government's will. Someone — Derekh Hanitzotz is coordinating with the Committee of the Forty and also with the Va'ad HaMagaz(?),[264] a more established Arab-Israeli political umbrella — decided that the activity this time would be a symbolic tree planting. I decided to go, but since it was to be on Shabbat, I had to go up on Friday afternoon. Fortunately, on Thursday afternoon at the church service for peace, I found two more people — both American immigrants, Ana Fruchter and Susannah Levi (the latter a former national cochair of NJA,[265] just arrived here three weeks ago to live) — who were also willing to come and spend the whole Shabbat.

There was a complicated interaction getting onto the bus for Haifa (where we would change for a bus for Carmiel) — some confusion about a woman with a small child. Perhaps she had brought a large bill and had to go back to the ticket window, or she hadn't paid enough for her ticket. She bulled past us as we waited to get onto the bus, and the driver and super-

---

262. As of February 1994, the residents of Ramye were still living there. Evidently a deal had been struck whereby, in exchange for their electoral support of the mayor, he was to have Ramye incorporated as a neighborhood within Carmiel.

263. In fact, Moti is not a member of Matzpen, nor do the Derekh Hanitzotz group identify themselves as Trotskyist. The name means "the way of the spark," an illusion to Lenin's newspaper *Iskra* (The Spark).

264. Queries to various activists on the Ramye issue in February 1994 produced absolutely no recognition of this organization as I have named it, but early in March, Daniel Boyarin happened to hear a reference to the Vaadat Ham'akav ("Follow-up" or "Oversight Committee"), an umbrella group representing all of the Arab municipalities.

265. New Jewish Agenda, a multi-issue U.S. organization active primarily during the 1980s.

visor let her on. But she still owed three shekels. The supervisor resolved it by taking my fifteen-shekel ticket for Haifa from the driver, giving me her twelve-shekel ticket, and having her give me three shekels. No one collected the three shekels from me, so I made three shekels on the deal. Very confusing.

Ana, Susannah, and I arrived at Carmiel about 4:30, an hour before candle-lighting time. We'd received the vaguest instructions from the organizers about how to find Ramye — "Walk across Carmiel to the west side, where there are new buildings that aren't completed, follow the dirt path over the hill" — and wisely decided to try to get a taxi to take us across Carmiel, although we were uncertain what to ask for. The "other side of Carmiel" is getting bigger all the time. Fortunately, all of the taxi drivers waiting at the stand were Arabs, and even more fortunately one of them knew where Ramye was, and realized we weren't talking about Rame, another larger village near Carmiel. He thought, however, that there weren't more than two families living there, and when he dropped us off by a dirt path at the edge of Carmiel we understood why. There we were walking down a hillside, carrying a bouquet of flowers into nowhere as far as we could tell — I said it was like something out of a Bunuel movie — when we saw the ruins of a couple of shacks, and then noticed a small concrete structure with a woman standing in the doorway. She was middle-aged, thick, her head covered with a scarf, barefoot, with a large and welcoming smile, and she invited us in, gave us coffee and cola and peaches, apologizing that she wasn't more prepared because she didn't know we were coming, and that the cola wasn't cold because she has no electricity to run a refrigerator. The house seemed indeed very bare: a few wicker stools, a few sleeping mats... a daughter, perhaps twelve years old, with reddish-brown hair who spoke Hebrew to us at the points where I had to admit I didn't understand the woman's Arabic (I didn't understand most of it). But I did catch that she had had ten daughters and then a son, and stopped; and that seven, I think, of her children were alive (presumably mostly grown and moved out). What do I remember of what I understood of what she told us? "Where are we going to go?" "Al kul hal elhamdulila."[266] "Ahlan wesahlan,"[267] over and over. After about twenty minutes Ana — especially concerned that we arrive at Ramye in time to get settled before Shabbat — got me to impress upon her that we had to continue, and she walked with us a couple of hundred meters along another dirt path to the main village.

The first house we came to was that of Tarik, one of the elder householders

---

266. Whatever happens, thanks to God.
267. Welcome.

in the village — a grandfather with, I think, three sons married and living in Ramye, and two daughters married and living in Ibillin, though those from Ibillin had come for the weekend. I'm pretty sure by now that the organizers didn't let anyone in Ramye know we were coming, but of course (Bedouin hospitality! I counted on it) Tarik and his family acted like we were expected,[268] and sat us down on plastic chairs on the concrete platform under the grape arbor which provides shade in front of their tin house. Now I want to say this is a house, not a shack: it looks like what you'd call a shack from outside, but inside it's divided into rooms (the living room has two armchairs and two couches), has a concrete floor, and so on, and Tarik says he would have built a concrete house if he could have gotten a permit for it.[269] We noticed immediately that we were given cold soda here, and the family explained that they have a generator which provides electricity. We also noticed a large, metal tank on wheels, which this family and some of the others (though not all in Ramye) hitch to a tractor and take down to buy water from the national water authority.

What did they give us for supper? They understood we would eat no meat; I'm sure they weren't planning to eat any meat anyway. But whatever they ate — for supper on Friday, breakfast the next morning, or supper before we left — they fed us separately, and I only realized that now. Tomatoes and cucumbers (store-bought, because their growing season had just ended due to a lack of water); *labane*[270] made from their own goats' milk; greasy french fries; humus; horribly sweet soft drinks.[271] Also at various times during our stay, grapes from their arbor, almonds from their tree, stale sunflower seeds, and peanuts.

What did Tarik and his children, and the other people of Ramye, say about their situation? That they were all related to each other; that there were in fact seven brothers and their families living there; that their grandparents were both buried there; that they were sure that Arabs and Jews could live together and had to live together; that Jewish immigrants were unwill-

---

268. This sounds off to me: somehow it sounds as if all of the political activity aimed at securing the rights of the people of Ramye to their lands were done *to* or *for* them by others. The reason they were not surprised to see us come was that they had been involved in the planning of the next day's event and because other Israeli Jews had stayed over at Ramye for varying periods as part of the solidarity effort.

269. David Harvey, expanding on comments by Gaston Bachelard, writes that "the space which is paramount for memory is the house — 'one of the greatest powers of integration of the thoughts, memories and dreams of mankind.' For it is within that space that we learned how to dream and imagine" (Harvey 1989: 217, quoting Bachelard 1964).

270. A distinctive Middle Eastern yogurt.

271. Lest this sound ungrateful, please add "wonderfully" before "greasy french fries." But I stick by the description of the Arab-made sodas that I've had here and in other communities as, to a middle-class American taste, almost unbearably sugary as well as flat.

ing or incapable of doing the hard physical labor that they are employed to do in Carmiel; that they were willing to share their land, but not to give it all up.

Did you accept all this as truth? I did, and Ana and Susannah certainly seemed to. We were very impressed by the facts that they were seriously farming (although the men had jobs in Carmiel as well); that they were living in whatever houses they had been permitted to build, that they had found ways to get electricity and water for themselves; by the contrast between their homes spread out on their land, and the impression of a crowded spillage created by the clump of new villas a couple of hundred meters distant, representing the farthest reach of Carmiel toward Ramye (Susannah remarked that it was strange because they were built like private houses but had none of the space around them that we expect private houses to enjoy); by Tarik's statement that the Jews evidently fear all Arabs as if they were wild wolves living on top of the mountains, waiting to come down and kill baby goats; by their hospitality. On the phone this morning Elissa, who's done much work to publicize the case of Ramye in North America, told me my brother doesn't want to work on the case because some of the Derekh Hanitzotz people had told him that some of the people in Ramye are just in it for the money.[272] My attitude after spending a night there is, So what? Let them get a lot of money for their land, if that's what they want; just don't let it be confiscated in the name of the sole and collective good of "the Jewish people."

What was on TV, when they switched it on (to the Israeli Hebrew government channel, not to an Arabic channel that came on first — perhaps for our benefit, though we'd said we didn't want to watch TV on Friday night) in the living room, all the adults crowded together as the three of us grew sleepier? Long news features, one showing clips of President Bush at his news conference insisting on the four-month delay in the loan guarantees; another going on at length about the popularity of kibbutz tourism, including a close-up of a guest trying out attaching milking pumps to the udders of a kibbutz cow.

Why didn't I mention lunch on Saturday? Saturday morning was long for

---

272. This sentence illustrates well the danger of "telephone ethnography": not just of reporting telephone conversations as fact but more generally of failing to recognize the distortions in transmission of oral communication, as in the children's whispering game of telephone. Upon reading the journal, Daniel Boyarin noted: "Not accurate at all. I said that questions had been raised by Matzpen people as to how the Ramye activity was impacting on the Committee of Forty and the general effort to win recognition for the villages. I think I was wrong nevertheless." The Committee of Forty is an umbrella organization representing all of the officially "unrecognized" Arab and Bedouin communities in the State of Israel, of which there are actually many more than forty.

us, waking up at 6:00 and waiting for people to arrive around 11:00, so we took a walk around the fields of the village. We found out, as best we could determine, that Ramye means a "plateau"; and indeed there's a surprisingly large stretch of flat land not in a valley but among larger hills there, and real plowed fields upon it. When we came to the edge of this plowed area, to the expanse of wild land strewn with huge rocks, we understood a bit better the work that had gone into clearing those fields. We walked to where the hill did slope down, and where there are newer, smaller, rockier, and more tentative fields. We came to a concrete platform, which we at first thought was the foundation of a new house, but then realized was the top of a cistern, and we stretched out on it to sunbathe and to stare out at this astonishing stark view for a few minutes. Then we saw a figure walking up the hill, wiry, his head covered in a small, white cloth, not really what I'd call a kaffiyeh. As he reached the cistern, we recognized a man who'd visited Tarik's family the night before (his name is Ibrahim), and we also saw a herd of goats following him. He pulled the cover of the cistern aside and began drawing buckets of water to fill half-barrels and water the goats. Ana wanted to lift several [filled] buckets..., and I did a couple as well, while he watched us and I joked about Tom Sawyer and the whitewashing of the fence. When the goats had enough water (they started and sneezed when water was splashed over them; some had sticks tied through their mouths, to prevent them from nursing), Ibrahim invited us back up the hill to his house for coffee. We sat in the "living room" (presumably a sleeping room as well; we'd slept on foam mattresses on the floor of the living room in Tarik's house), and drank coffee, and soon a sixtyish woman wearing sensible Western shoes and a Western but old-fashioned dress came in. She spoke excellent Hebrew, spoke Arabic assertively to Ibrahim's wife ("Bring the women here! I have to speak to the women"), told us she was from Nazareth, and when I asked whether she was with any organization, told us she worked with the Union of Democratic Women (which means she's a Communist Party organizer), Women in Black, Reshet, WILPF,[273] and so on. She refused fruit and bread, complaining that her bad teeth wouldn't let her chew them (though she had to argue). She graciously translated Ibrahim's Arabic into Hebrew for us, summarizing that everything he said was aimed at his insistence that they could and were willing to live together with the Jews. But she repeated several times, without apparent success, that she wanted to see the women and that the women had to get involved in the struggle for the land. We, after initially refusing, accepted a bit of food, which turned out

---

273. Communist-affiliated organizations in many countries use the term "democratic" in their names. Women in Black is described briefly in a footnote to the entry for September 6. Reshet is an Israeli feminist network for peace and dialogue with Palestinian women. WILPF is the Women's International League for Peace and Freedom.

to be homemade bread (not what I think of as pita, closer to what I could call a *pletsl*)[274] spread with olive oil, lemon juice, and *zatar*[275] — at that moment one of the most delicious things I could remember ever having eaten. When we finished, we went outside with Miriam Karim (for that was the name of this lovely, assertive, and aristocratic woman from Nazareth), where there was a tree waiting to be planted by us. I dug a bit with an old-fashioned pick, Miriam finished, and a photographer took a picture of Susannah and Miriam leaning over the little olive sapling, with Ibrahim's wife standing behind, a bit uncertainly.

How much more is there to tell? There were about two hundred people present. Naomi Ben Ariel, from Derekh Hanitzotz (the name means "The Way of the Spark" — remember Lenin's *Iskra*?),[276] introduced herself and asked me if I would say a few words, to represent the international support on this case. I went after a number of other speakers, including MK Mohammed Miari[277] and an Arab MK from Hadash and a speaker from Peace Now, who spoke flatly and longer than anyone else. I started out in Hebrew and continued longer than I expected in Hebrew: "I've finally gotten the chance to plant a tree in the Holy Land [appreciative laughter]. For this I thank the activists of the peace movement and the residents of Ramye. And I'm ready to say '*shehekhiyanu*,' even though planting is forbidden on Shabbat. [At this point Miari, sitting at the front of the audience facing me, interjects: '*Pikuach nefesh!*'][278] Exactly, but why? Last night I slept here [scattered applause]! I ate *labne* made from these people's goats, I ate grapes from their vines, I ate bread

---

274. A round, chewy, flat, but leavened loaf. The classic *bialystoker pletsl* I refer to here is still available at various bakeries on the Lower East Side.

275. *Zatar*, a kind of wild thyme or oregano, has become an important symbol of Palestinian collective identity for several reasons: because of its pungent and distinctive flavor; because of its tenacious and "indigenous" growth on the hills of Palestine; and because Israeli conservation officials enforce a ban on its harvest as an endangered wild herb.

276. The name of the original Leninist newspaper means "The Spark."

277. Miari represented a party called the Progressive List for Peace, a joint Jewish-Arab list that campaigned on a platform calling for the establishment of a Palestinian state alongside Israel. The party never had more than two representatives in the 120-member Knesset and as of early 1994 hardly exists on the Israeli political scene.

278. In English translation, the blessing of *shehekhiyanu* reads, "Blessed are You, Hashem, our God, King of the universe, Who has kept us alive, sustained us, and brought us to this season." According to the *Complete ArtScroll Siddur*, this blessing is said upon "(a) eating seasonal fruits of a new season for the first time; (b) purchasing a new garment...; (c) performance of a seasonal *mitzvah* [commandment]; or (d) deriving significant benefit from an event" (Scherman, ed., 1985: 287). Whether or not planting a tree as part of a political demonstration would call for such a blessing is not obvious. *Pikuach nefesh* refers to the principle that actions prohibited on the Sabbath may be done in vital emergencies. Even if this particular act were permitted on the Sabbath in a case of vital emergency, as Mr. Miari suggested, it would not then entail a blessing, since the performance of a commandment that entails committing a forbidden act is not considered a *mitzvah* at all.

made from their wheat. These people *live* from this land! And I understood another thing — why the government wants this land. It's good land! The people here have made it good — taken out the stones to make fields, and planted trees." Then I switched to English, to say that since the government of Israel spoke in the name of all Jews, it was my responsibility to speak out when it is acting unjustly; and that being in Ramye gave me strength to go back and keep struggling in America. Several people congratulated me, and I jokingly complained to Miari that he'd stolen my line. An Arab reporter for *Ha'aretz* from Haifa interviewed me and took my picture, which made me flattered and nervous — it wasn't very *shabbesdik*[279] at all, really; what if I get exposed as a phony religious Jew in public?

The buses left at 3:00, too early for the three of us to ride back with them. Around 6:00 we were fed supper again, and one of the sons or sons-in-law of Tarik asked us how the afternoon program went; he'd been in the fields all afternoon. But he told us he was at the site of the public meeting in the morning, and that he'd dug one of the large pits there. He told us the pits were there to show that that's where the people of Ramye want to be buried, in case the bulldozers come... a way, I explained to Susannah later on the bus going home, of saying, "Over our dead bodies." I hope it doesn't come to that. We don't really know when we'll know, unless and until the people sign a deal and move, or unless some Kafkaesque final court decides they're legal after all.

We're driven back to the bus station in Carmiel (people in Ramye have cars, yes), slowly along a perhaps one-kilometer dirt road to another new end of the development town, and the young man giving us a ride points to new apartment buildings and says, "We're building those." On the dirt road we stop to let a boy with perhaps a dozen cows from Ramye pass; they're being taken to water, presumably because it's too hard or expensive to bring the water to them. We get to the bus stop, where I *shmuez*[280] briefly (practically my first conversation in Yiddish since I've been here) with an elderly man who says he's from Prague and has been hired as a *chazan* for a synagogue in Carmiel. The Haifa bus comes, and we trek back to Jerusalem in unairconditioned discomfort.

• 9/16/91 •

My thirty-fifth birthday and the date of the eviction order for Ramye, unless there was a stay yesterday. Immediately after writing my notes yesterday, I

---

279. Appropriate behavior for a religious Jew on the Sabbath.
280. Chat or converse (Yiddish).

walked up toward Derekh Hevron, stopping at Charles and Sandy's house to tell someone where I was going ("You're spending the night there? Watch your ass!" says Sandy), change my shirt, make a phone call to tell Moti I won't be able to come see his new baby that evening.[281] I get on the bus that goes to Bethlehem and Beit Sahour — the directions that Said, my contact from the Bethlehem Press Service, has given me to get to his office were about as useful as the directions Yitzkhak Ben Ariel gave me to get to Ramye from the bus station in Carmiel. So I get off somewhere on the road through Bethlehem to Bet Sahour, and wander into a safe-looking and prosperous store called "Habash Home Appliances" (sign in English). The boss's friend and his wife — elderly people, a slight man wearing sunglasses and his wife, with black hair, in a blue and white print dress, they could have been Polish Jews in Paris — help figure out where I should be going (Said said "El Matbasa Square" several times, but somehow I wrote down "El Makdasa"), and get me onto the minibus that goes to that part of Bethlehem. Once again, I'm impressed by the size of the city; how many people who've never been there read "Bethlehem" and still think of a village?

I find the office and meet Said, a man perhaps my age with a round face and much humor. Meanwhile Khalid[282] has been replaced by a new colleague of Said's, and while I wait I talk with this new colleague. He asks me what I think about the anthropology of the people here. I try to explain my idea that Israel/Palestine is "one system," and he disagrees: the most important thing in anthropology is the family structure, right? (What do I know about family structures?) And the Palestinians, with their large extended families, have a very different family structure from the Israelis. Anyway, he continues, the Israelis are so diverse, depending on the different countries they come from. He thinks that the Moroccan Jews, for instance, who are so downtrodden, would mostly leave Israel if they could — although he acknowledges that the longer they stay here, the more they become integrated into the infrastructure, the more they come to belong to Israeli society.

Said tells me my contact, Rashad (Rashid?), will meet me at the gate to Deheisheh. Is ten shekels too much for me to pay for the taxi? OK, he'll arrange with the driver for me to pay five shekels. The driver is waiting downstairs, but there are others in the taxi as well — I'm sure I'm paying more than they are. Well, what the hell, if Said is getting this guy a couple of extra shekels, I'm not paying Said for his help. The driver lets me off across the street from a gate in a long, high fence, bordering the highway for several hundred me-

---

281. This entry records the one time I actually visited a Palestinian refugee camp — Deheisheh, near Bethlehem.

282. A journalist whom I had previously met and who also worked at the Bethlehem Press Service.

ters(?). The gate is actually a turnstile, not the kind one could possibly jump but the kind with three or four rows of perhaps twenty one-inch metal bars, each about eighteen inches long and set several inches apart, which move in one direction past a single barrier, so you can only go through the turnstile one way. (Rashid tells me later that there's also an automobile entrance all the way on the other side of the camp.) There is no guard at the gate, and later I am told that right now the army isn't patrolling inside the camp much — though the military headquarters are clearly visible on the hill above the camp.

Rashid is waiting for me just outside the gate: he's a good-looking young man in his early twenties who speaks English fairly well but hesitantly. We walk past the UNRWA[283] clinic just next to the gate, and straight up the hill perhaps a hundred yards to his family's house (his mother is still alive; his father died of a blood cancer about fifteen years ago). I'm pleasantly surprised: there's a small garden, and the newer top floor of the house has a typical Palestinian living room, with largish windows, tile floor, and overstuffed chairs and couch. Rashid shows me photographs of his father — a handsome, middle-aged man with a mustache, though the photograph looks as if it's been painted — and of his mother at perhaps fifty, in three-quarter profile with a shawl over her head, her nose prominent and her smile proud, one of the most beautiful photographic portraits I have ever seen — I'd like to include it in my book. Rashid introduces me to his older sister (name?) who, it turns out, is a fieldworker for El Haq; I'm gratified to learn that she knows about the Human Rights Rapid Response Network[284] which Elissa runs. I tell her that I was pleased to see this decent house — my image of a refugee camp, aside from those I brought with me, comes from what I saw outside Jericho from the bus. She agrees that those are miserably poor places. [I'm not doing this well; I'm in a rush, I want to go swimming before Rachel[285] comes; I missed swimming yesterday and the pool will be closed tomorrow, *erev*[286] Yom Kippur.]

Let me interrupt this flat narrative: Deheisheh didn't feel right. It's not supposed to feel right, I suppose, but for me it was also because I really wasn't sure what I was doing there. When I was in Ar'ara or Kfar Qara (What's the connection, really, other than that they're all places where Arab Palestinians

---

283. United Nations Relief and Works Agency.
284. El Haq, originally named Law in the Service of Man, is perhaps the oldest human rights law organization in the Occupied Territories. The Human Rights Rapid Response Network was set up to focus each month on a different Palestinian or Israeli human rights issue and to send monthly telexes to the appropriate authorities in the name of each person who agreed to subscribe to the network.
285. An American-Israeli friend from New York.
286. The "eve" or day before Yom Kippur.

live?) I was a guest; in Ramye I was in solidarity. In Deheisheh I felt like I was slumming — and when Rashid took me to see people's houses, he was puzzled that I didn't know exactly what I wanted to say to the people.[287] He took me to three houses, in fact. The first was their immediate neighbors' — people, I think, from Rashid's parents' village (Sifla did he say? and I didn't catch exactly where inside the Green Line it was), with whom Rashid's family is still obviously quite friendly. We got there by climbing steps onto the roof of Rashid's house, going down a few more steps, and stepping over the head of the neighboring family's goat onto their patio. In this part of Deheisheh at least, even the poorer houses are not just adobe or tin; the floors are concrete at least, if not tiled. Here I was introduced to Um Shaker, a seventy-year-old mother of eleven children ("*Alla yihalillek yahom!*"[288] I think to interject, and that much at least of my Arabic she understands and is pleased) and grandmother of perhaps forty more — she is quite articulate though I am not equally comprehending of her Arabic. Rashid translates for me: Jews can come here from Russia or anywhere and settle anywhere they want in this country, but an Arab can't even come from Jordan. One of her sons or grandsons, who accompanies us to the other two houses, explains that he wants to marry a woman who lives in Jordan, but can't afford the high fee the Israelis charge for that privilege. I enjoy being in Um Shaker's company, and after we visit the other two houses (I'm getting to them) we come back to her home and she feeds me, Rashid, and her son/grandson a copious supper of *maghlube*[289] (right, that's what Wafa made last week, and now I connect Wafa's translation of it as "upside-down" with the word I learned in Arabic for "the loser" of a war).

The second house we visit is the poorest one I've seen: a concrete floor, much simpler furniture, two adolescent boys who don't really have anything to say or are too shy to say it, a younger mother who is a widow... I ask

---

287. As a student of sociology, Rashid doubtless (and reasonably) expected me to have some sort of questionnaire along, or at least a fairly clear notion of the information I wanted to elicit: all I clearly wanted was to know what it felt like to "be there," if even for a short time. Part of my uncertainty also came from the fact that my chain of contacts was here stretched further than at almost any other point during my entire trip to Israel: from my Palestinian friends in New York to an intermediate contact to the Bethlehem Press Service to Rashid.... In fact an Israeli anthropologist named Maya Rosenfeld was doing fieldwork for her dissertation at Deheisheh at this time.

288. May God preserve them for you!

289. A beef stew. For some reason, I didn't record the best part of this visit (aside from the food itself) in my notes: the *maghlube* was served on a large platter. Everyone except me ate directly from the platter, with large spoons. I was given my own plate, and when I finished it, Um Shaker heaped my plate again. My distress was evident because Rashid (remember, a sociology student) looked at me and laughed as he said, "You think you have to finish everything on your plate, don't you!"

where her family is from — a village between Ramle and Jaffa; she was very young when they left, and she doesn't know exactly where it was. She has some memories of the place. She hasn't been back to see it. I tell her that when I was a child, my parents were *fellahin*[290] (it feels a bit chutzpadik[291] to use that word, but I don't know how to say "chicken farmers" in Arabic any differently), and that we lost our house to the government as well. There's no comparison, and then again there is.[292]

The third house is also poorer and more cramped than Rashid's family's. It's down a narrow, dark alley, which reminds me that I was fortunate to come at a time when there was no 8:00–6:00 nighttime curfew; for an entire year the people of Deheisheh couldn't go out at night. Here there are about fifteen people standing and sitting at the entranceway, some watching a TV that's been set up on a chair outside. We go into the small living room and are greeted by a slight, middle-aged man. Here again there are overstuffed armchairs, a color TV, a large "box" cassette player, and also an armoire with a large number of china coffee cups, and so on. I see this room and a kitchen; the man tells us that there are two rooms in his house, one the UN built and one which he built, and eleven people live in the house. He's not working now: he doesn't have a pass to come into Israel. He looks through all his documents, I think for an address of someone he knows in America to show me, but doesn't find it. We leave after a few minutes, and on our way out, there's an altercation; I catch the words, *"Hamse shekel biddi yah!"* (I want the five shekels!). Rashid tells me don't worry, it's just a crazy guy, and as I cower to the side of the alley he takes my arm and walks me safely past the pushing. He tries to explain the problem to me, but I don't quite get the story: this family we were visiting own a store, someone owed them fifteen shekels, that

---

290. Peasants (Arabic).
291. Nervy (Yiddish).
292. I was born into a community of Jewish chicken farmers in central New Jersey, but by the early 1960s, when I was a young child, it had become almost impossible to earn a living running a family chicken farm, and the community had largely disintegrated. In the mid-1960s the State of New Jersey bought our farm and all of the surrounding land, planning to build a reservoir. The reservoir was finally built a few years ago. In the summer of 1993, when my sister Sandy and I walked the five-mile perimeter trail of the reservoir, we identified our old farm by the apple tree that had once stood in our backyard and that was still producing a large crop of small, tart fruit. On Labor Day weekend I went back with Jonah (by then age seven) to pick some of the fruit for pies, but we were chased away by a park ranger who, upon listening to my explanation that this had once been our farm, woodenly insisted, "Well, it's state land now, and you can't pick fruit here." He did let us keep the few dozen apples we had already gathered off the ground. Inevitably I was reminded of a story the Israeli journalist Dani Rubinstein tells in his book *The People of Nowhere*, about seeing a group of Palestinians gathered at the median strip on the Jerusalem–Tel Aviv Highway. When he stopped and asked why they were there, they explained that the olive trees there had once belonged to them, and they still liked to come back to harvest the fruit (Rubinstein 1991).

someone sent this crazy young man to buy cigarettes, he handed the store owner ten shekels, and he took it in repayment of the debt without giving the crazy guy the cigarettes.

Later, after supper at Um Shaker's, we go back to Rashid's house, and Said and a few friends are waiting to visit. Rashid tells the story in Arabic, and Said, teasingly testing me, asks me to explain to him what happened. I give my version but don't get the part about the five shekels. Said explains: the cigarettes cost five shekels; the five that was supposed to be in change was a "tip" for this crazy young man, "a fortune for him," as Said says, and now he wanted "his" five shekels from the storekeepers. "It's all because of the occupation," Said says jokingly: "You know, whatever the problem that we have is we know the reason beforehand: it's the occupation!" Rashid isn't so amused; he asks rhetorically, "So how come the Israelis gave this crazy guy a green permit [What exactly does that entail?]?" Said spoke of the frustration of waiting, not being free to move ("You can take off your [yarmulke] and come to East Jerusalem, but I can't change my [obviously Palestinian] face and come to West Jerusalem" [Said just got a pass last week]). Shortly Said and his friend get up, saying to me, "Jonathan, you are tired; but we are more tired."

• 9/19/91 •

Instead of going to shul yesterday,[293] I ended up spending the day talking with Charles. He does most of the talking. We reminisced about college a lot, but of the things he was saying about his experience in Israel, the most significant here for me seems to be what he said about his army service. It began with his statement that here in the Middle East, symbols are extremely important to many people, more than they seem to be to him. I said, "Yeah, like the Wall really doesn't mean anything in particular to me." He was thinking about going to jail rather than serving in the territories, however, and for the second time since I've been here spoke at length about why he goes where he's told to go. So far he's managed to avoid actually doing guard duty, and since his first tour of duty in the territories (in Jabaliya),[294] he says that the only direct contact he's had with Palestinians was the time he was guarding inside the base in Beit Sahour and he helped a small child get his sheep extricated from the fence.

But the story that stays in my mind was about his tour of duty in East Jerusalem early in the intifada. His unit was assigned to go on patrol with

---

293. Yom Kippur.
294. A refugee camp in Gaza.

guys from Mishmar HaGvul who'd just been sent up from Gaza, and as older and wiser reservists, their main task was to keep the Magavnikim[295] in line: "The rules are different in Jerusalem. It's all politics. One person killed in Jerusalem is the same as a hundred people killed in Gaza." He did his best to make sure he was always sent out with a fellow named Graham, a non-Jewish son of an English coal miner who fell in love with a kibbutznik and moved here. One time they were on patrol with a Magavnik as usual, and the Magavnik decided to stop a nineteen-year-old Palestinian and demand his papers. He made the Palestinian stand up against the wall, and then pretended that he was about to kick him in the crotch, so that the Palestinian crouched down to protect himself; then he shouted, "Stand up straight!" He repeated this about three times, until Graham shouted at the Magavnik in Hebrew, "Stop it! That's enough! Leave him alone!" The Magavnik, who outranked Charles and Graham, was astonished, let the guy go, and then started threatening to have Graham court-martialed. Charles started talking to the Magavnik: "Look, right here you outrank us, but I'm a lot older than you. I'm going to be out of here in two months, and you're going to be out of here in two years, and you're going to have to live the rest of your life. You said you want to become a policeman when you get out of here. If you bring charges against us, we'll have to bring countercharges against you for brutality. And it doesn't matter whether you're convicted or not. They don't like to take former Magavnikim into the police because of this kind of thing. You don't really want to make a case out of it, do you?" and thus defused the issue. Now, Charles says, "Sometimes I think I'm just being rational and sometimes I think I'm just a chicken. Never mind jail; sometimes I want to point my gun at these guys and shoot them. Anyway, just to refuse service in the territories isn't the important thing; it's after they've made you do horrible things and then they ask you to go again, and you refuse then, that's when it's an important statement. Is it better to guard prisoners in Tel Aviv than to hide inside a base in Beit Sahour? But anyway — Graham's way of dealing with the situation was to burst out and protest, like the son of a coal miner, never mind what would happen afterward, and my way was to talk myself out of the situation. So where's the pure morality? One thing that's clear to me is that the skills that are most useful to me here are the same skills that I learned growing up as a Jew among goyim." By the way, after thinking it over I've decided to reject the interpretation that Charles was implicitly following the "decent people should serve in the territories to curb the brutal tendencies of other soldiers" line here.

---

295. Mishmar HaGvul — the Border Guards (see entry for August 2).

Another Jerusalem story Charles told: one time he was on patrol with a Magavnik who was a permanent soldier—did the work because the overtime pay was good, in other words effectively a professional policeman. Suddenly a small Palestinian boy came running up, tugging the policeman's leg and calling, "Rafael! Rafael!" The child lived near Ateret Kohanim,[296] and several yeshiva boys from Ateret Kohanim decided to come into the house with their deed to the property and occupy it, even though the case was still in court and the family had won a restraining order. Rafael came in, looked at both pieces of paper, and said to the yeshiva boys, "It doesn't matter what I think, the law is on their side right now, and I have to keep the law. You're going to have to leave."

•

I felt so down just before Yom Kippur, after spending the day putting together applications for jobs I think I'm not at all likely to get. I explained it to Charles as a feeling of having had my identity pulled in so many different directions while I've been here that it's thoroughly dissolved by now, and the exhaustion that comes from that strain. Of course I'm thinking about Judy Butler's book[297]—if gender is thoroughly constructed, then certainly ethnicity as well, and when you're deliberately putting yourself into situations where the props of that identity are constantly being called into question, it's got to get shaky.

• 9/20/91 •

A strange conversation with Moti last night: we were both very sluggish, and yet still trying to be abstractly intelligent.

I confided to Moti my repeated experiences of being slighted by young Mizrachi Jewish kids. Like the time I had to get past somebody to get off the bus, said *"Slicha"*[298] in my obvious American accent, and got in response

---

296. A yeshiva in East Jerusalem that specializes in the preparation of Jewish men enjoying the hereditary status of *kohen* (priest) for service in the rebuilt Temple (that is, the Third Temple) and that is regarded as a center of anti-Arab, militant, or aggressive activity aimed at the reestablishment of absolute Jewish dominion over all of Jerusalem and the Land of Israel.

297. I was then reading for the first time Judith Butler's *Gender Trouble: Feminism and the Subversion of Identity*. Contrary to the implication of this sentence, Butler takes pains to explain that because an identity effect such as gender or ethnicity is *constructed*, that does not mean it is not *real*. In *Gender Trouble* and her more recent *Bodies That Matter*, Butler explores precisely the shaping of real genders through repeated "performances" of gender-appropriate behavior and acutely analyzes the way deviance *within* given cultural paradigms both shows up this process of shaping and offers clues toward reflexive reshaping of identities (Butler 1990, 1993; see also J. Boyarin 1995). See my comments on Gregory Bateson in the introduction to this book.

298. Excuse me (Hebrew).

a joking, "Yes, of course." This happens a few times, and you get to feel that they don't want you here. Moti's response: "They make you feel like a Jew."[299] Exactly — and one of the most difficult things here is to feel both guilty and excluded "as a Jew."

• 10/1/91 •

I broke off from struggling with my paper about 7:30 Thursday evening.

---

299. That is, like a lower-case "jew" (see Lyotard 1990), an outsider who *doesn't belong here*.

# 4

# In Search of "Israeli Identity": Anecdotes and Afterthoughts

The sharpening in recent years of the conflict between Israeli Jews and Palestinian Arabs should not be taken as evidence that the two identities are fixed or frozen irrevocably into what are sometimes called "tribalist" positions. I'd like to give a few pointed examples of the way these ethnic boundaries are rhetorically reshaped, reinvented, and often subverted as well. Beyond the case discussed here, my suggestion is that if national identities are imagined with a good deal of self-consciousness, people might learn to imagine their collectives in ways that are less dependent on exclusion and, beyond tolerance, actively rely on cultural symbiosis.

Zionism was born as one proposed solution to the predicament of Jewish identity and Jewish existence in late nineteenth-century Europe. These were two identical but not overlapping problems. Some Zionists were more concerned with a reinvigoration of Jewish culture that would help ensure the continuity of a voluntarily distinctive Jewish collective in the modern period. Others were convinced that a Jewish homeland or state was the only way the physical safety and continuity of Jewish lives could be assured. In any case, most versions of Zionism entailed the vision of a new kind of Jew. Max Nordau, a popular Zionist lecturer and publicist, called them "muscle Jews" (see Gilman 1986).

The attempt to create a new, territorially based, collective Jewish identity in the Jewish State of Israel has drawn on multiple resources. One of these is a social-scientific apparatus unusually close to the centers of state power (Goldberg 1977); at the time when the new state was faced with the massive immigration of Jews from the Middle East and North Africa, a deliberate decision was taken to structure their absorption according to a model of assimilation rather than pluralism, and the consequences of that decision still affect Israeli politics.

A second such resource is the inculcation of "knowledge of the land" as a fundamental of early childhood education (Benvenisti 1986), continuing through participation in youth movements and through army service. This aspect of Israeli culture is grounded in the early Zionist belief that Diaspora Jews suffered from their estrangement from nature and that reconnection with the geography of the ancient homeland would revitalize both Jewish bodies and Jewish culture. The effort to "know the land" as an active, transformative process is also evident in the profusion of new, Hebrew-sounding names given to localities and natural features, especially after the forming of the state. It is continued in expeditions organized by bodies as different as the Society for the Protection of Nature in Israel and the Department for Torah Culture of the Torah Branch of the Jerusalem Municipality.

A third resource in creating the sense of a cohesive Israeli Jewish polity that belongs on its land is a continuing discourse on identity as a theme in everyday middle and upper-brow culture — a topic carefully documented in Virginia Domínguez's book (1990) on Israeli national identity. The close attention paid to the "heritages" of the various groups among Israeli Jews — generally broken down either into nations of origin or into binary distinctions between "Ashkenazim" (those of European origin) and "Sephardim" (those of North African, Middle Eastern, or Indian origin) — helps to sustain an impression of rich variety and continued vitality within a Jewish collective whose external boundaries are nevertheless quite clear. Indeed, the rhetoric of Jewish peoplehood and of a binary opposition between Jews and Arabs is so powerful that even Israeli political dissenters have recourse to it when protesting discriminatory actions by the Israeli government. This was clear, for example, in a flyer put out by a radical Israeli political group to protest the confiscation of lands owned by Israeli Arabs that are to be used for housing for new Soviet Jewish immigrants. The flyer contained the statement, "We are opposed to the cynical use of 'public need' in order to justify the expulsion of the children of one people from their homes and land in order to settle children of another people in their place." This statement, by a group explicitly opposed to the very idea of a Jewish state, nevertheless underscores the consensus that Russian Jews have more in common with Israeli Jews than either have in common with Israeli Arabs.

By reinforcing the association between particular peoplehood and proper control of a given space, even this anti-Zionist claim tends ultimately to reinforce the basic Zionist formula "a land without people for a people without land," itself grounded in implicit colonial criteria for determining the presence of people on desired lands. But unlike the radical statement, the rhetorical efforts in the realms of mainstream social science, "knowledge of the land," and discourse on identity rely on the continued silencing of the displacement and exclusion of the Palestinians, most massively during the 1948 war but more generally as a part of Zionist history. The persistence and crystallization of Palestinian national identity make this silencing highly problematic.

The mutual violence attendant on the intifada produces among some Israelis the sense that the occupation of the West Bank and Gaza is ultimately untenable and among others the sense that Jews and Arabs truly cannot live together. It is not sufficient to attribute this growth in intolerance to a generalized growth of so-called fundamentalism in the Middle East, since much of the exclusionary discourse has nothing to do with religious fanaticism. Rather, as some of the leaders of the West Bank settlers' movement have claimed, their effort to acquire control over all of "the historical land of Israel" is the current manifestation of Zionism as an ongoing, struggling *project* — without which this central ideology loses a great deal of its centralizing, galvanizing force. For secular liberal Israelis raised on the notion of Zionism as a humane project of autonomous national regeneration, the occupation contributes to what may be described as a malaise or crisis in Israeli ideology. Not only this anthropologist but many Israelis who are opposed to the current territorialist and exclusivist drive are therefore currently in search of Israeli identity.

Yet beyond the level of official symbolic frameworks, some Israeli popular culture reflects the submerged presence of Palestinian Arabs. Much as Americans are accustomed to black street culture filtering through to hip, middle-class, white youth culture in the United States, Israeli Jewish youth — especially those about army age, between eighteen and twenty-one — use a number of Arabic expressions. A New Year's card sent to my nephew by one of his female friends when he had just begun basic training in the prestigious paratroopers' branch read, "*Dir balak* [Arabic for 'Watch out'] if I don't see you in two months with your paratrooper's red shoes on!" — a playful warning that he'd better do well in the army. In this case, the expression of being locally grounded blended with an entirely conventional stress on success in the military, another prime site of what is called *gibush*, the massive and deliberate structuring of social cohesion in Israel.

More commonly perhaps, Israeli culture represses the mutual influences between Jews and Arabs, inventing instead new meanings for tropes present in traditional Jewish culture. Several examples can be drawn from an ongoing, massive public relations campaign for public safety. The overall theme of the campaign is *khatima lekhayem* — signature for life. The phrase is drawn from the liturgy and folklore of the High Holy Days, when Jews wish each other that God may "sign" them in the book of life for a year of health and prosperity. Here it is the driver of the car bearing the bumper sticker with this slogan who is said to be "signing for life." Another borrowing from the textual tradition is, "*Venahagta lereyekha kemocha*"; *lenhog* means "to behave" or "to drive," so the phrase means, "You shall drive/behave toward your neighbor as toward yourself." In both of these examples, religious references are being extended into secular contexts, reinforcing the impression that a common Jewish identity suffices for all of the needs of a shared and responsible civil society. This is quite a different strategy from a conceivable but highly unlikely and actually nonexistent alternative of a bumper sticker saying, *"Dir balak* when you're driving!"

Not all of the slogans pertaining to traffic safety were endorsed and promoted by the Ministry of Transportation, however. One clever bumper sticker combined references to the Gulf War and to the high accident rate: *"Ani lo skad v'al tehi li patriot,"* or "I'm not a Scud, so don't be a Patriot!" This was in turn an ironic comment on a bumper sticker from the time of the war that said *"Kulanu patriotim"* — "We're all Patriots!" That slogan, which relied on awareness of the original meaning of the English word "patriot" and on the presence of the Patriot defensive missiles in recent Israeli experience, suggested once again that the unity and loyalty of Israeli Jews are the most important defensive weapons they have.

Finally, I offer a cartoon from the *Jerusalem Report* — the weekly started in protest over the takeover of the *Jerusalem Post* by the conservative newspaper magnate Robert Maxwell. The cartoon ironically points out the disjunction between the intense and violent efforts to repress Palestinian terrorism, and the much less stringent efforts to improve traffic safety, by facetiously suggesting that since automobile accidents cause twice as many deaths as guerrilla attacks in Israel each year, careless drivers and those who train them should be dealt with the way Palestinian terrorists are. Indeed, the hapless victims of the imagined ruthless campaign against dangerous drivers are this well-known cartoonist's familiar figures of put-upon, long-suffering, uncomprehending, ordinary Israeli citizens. The cartoon is perhaps an effective safety valve for those who believe that the specter of Palestinian terrorism is cynically manipulated anyway. But if it has any social effect, it will more likely be to make Israelis aware of the road-safety problem than of the systematic violation of Palestinian rights. Like the humorous and traditionalistic bumper stickers, the cartoon deals with a real and deadly problem. At the same time, all of these are both part of a search for normalcy and an allegory of war.

So far I have discussed symbols and strategies used in reinforcing the sense of a distinctive and unitary Israeli Jewish identity. Another place where the reflexive shaping of complex identity can be seen is in what I would like to call here the ironies of the Palestinian/Israeli interculture. Unlike the cartoons and bumper stickers of the Israeli traffic-safety campaign, I draw here rather on ephemeral bits of oral humor. In these anecdotes, dissident Israelis make unexpected analogies between their situation and the situation of Palestinians, while Palestinians are able to put themselves into the rhetorical position of speaking as Israeli Jews.

During my recent fieldwork, I visited a friend in an Israeli Arab village who teaches Hebrew in a local primary school. Wondering whether my wife, Elissa Sampson, would be coming to visit, he asked, *"Matay elissa ba'a le'erets haplaot?"* (When is Elissa coming to Wonderland?). This witticism displayed his familiarity with Western secular literate culture, through an Israeli looking glass. More significantly, it constituted a sardonic comment on the frequent depiction of Israel as a barren land where Jewish dedication has wrought wonders—a picture that erases the Arab presence he, by this pun, was ironically reasserting.

I have another friend who is a Palestinian physician, trained in Germany and currently working for a social-welfare institution on the West Bank. He has two daughters. The elder is quiet, gentle, sweet, and polite, and he calls her his "Sephardi" daughter. The younger is noisy, rambunctious, and likes to punch him in the shoulder, and he calls her his "Ashkenazi" daughter. Already this is a complex and sophisticated bit of humor. It implicitly endorses the dissenting Israeli view that values the supposedly "Mediterranean" values of hospitality and modesty over the supposedly "European" values of aggressive egoism. At the same time as the internal binary helping to structure the Israeli Jewish collective is borrowed, it is undermined here as well, for the doctor points out that the "Sephardic" elder daughter was born in Germany, the "Ashkenazi" younger daughter in the Middle East. And of course they are both born of the same parents, neither of them Jewish. Thus while the joke asserts that Palestinians are capable of recognizing the complexity of identity among Israeli Jews, it simultaneously subverts the idea that personal character can be ascribed in any determinate way to ethnic or geographical origin. This, by the way, is a man whose greatest ambition is to establish a Palestine center for Israel and Jewish studies.

An ironic identification of Jews with Palestinians is used by some Israelis to confront the prevalent rigorous separation between the two. Thus, at a Sabbath lunch with American Jewish friends, our hostess remarked that the intifada had come along just in time to prevent a civil war between traditionalist Orthodox Hasidim and secularist Israeli Jews. "Yes," another guest retorted facetiously, "the Hasidim had to stop throwing stones at cars driving past on the Sabbath because they were afraid if they didn't their houses would be blown up!" Months later, a member of the Hasidic community told me that the Sabbath stone-throwing demonstrations had indeed been stopped at the beginning of the intifada, at the request of the Jerusalem police commander, but he added: "Those Palestinians don't just run when the police come at them like our Hasidic guys do. They're taking revenge on the police for the way the police treated us when we demonstrated!"

It is true that, more often than they threw stones, the Hasidic demonstrators would shout "Shabbes! Shabbes!" to remind the drivers that they were desecrating the Sabbath. Such demonstrations only took place in parts of Israel where the religious population felt strong and competent enough to try to enforce Orthodox law in the public sphere. In other parts of the country, such as the Nazareth area, secular Jews benefit from the presence of nearby Arab communities to use Saturday as a shopping day. A friend of mine tells of going shopping in Nazareth one Saturday and crossing a busy highway with several other people. A car came toward the intersection very fast and barely managed to stop before the crosswalk. At that moment an Arab man wearing a kaffiyeh paused as he was crossing the street, shook his finger reprovingly at the driver of the car, and scolded, "Shabbes! Shabbes!" Note well that the identity momentarily borrowed here was not just generally "Israeli" but that of a very particular — and in some ways marginal — group among Jews in Israel.

This same Jewish friend of mine lives in a large and gracious house, originally owned by Arabs, in the Jerusalem neighborhood of Baka'a. Although many of the homes in this area were lived in by members of the Greek and German Christian communities during the period of the British mandate, such houses and more modest ones throughout the country are a staple of Palestinian memorial literature and folklore, a well-recognized emblem of Palestinian rootedness and the ramification of Palestinian society. One day my friend called his Palestinian plumber in to help fix a leak in their solar water heater. After they worked together for an hour or two and solved the problem, they went downstairs and my friend made coffee. They chatted for a while; then there was a significant pause, after which the plumber said in Hebrew, "You know, this was my grandfather's house." My friend's heart skipped a beat, until the plumber added triumphantly, "I got you! I got you that time!" It hadn't been his grandfather's house at all, though well it might have. Obviously he had fun being able to play such a joke on my friend. But what strikes me even more in this story is the level of shared assumptions and indeed the intimacy and trust required for such a painful topic to be available for a joke.

I've told too many stories, so I must jump to conclusions. The theme of the lost house stands for a shared experience of loss that is one of the major sources of Palestinian collective identity since 1948. Jewish history provides Israelis with plenty of arguments for the view that they are ultimately alone in the world and have no one to depend on except each other. Neither Palestinians nor Israelis will enjoy freedom from fear of the other — and thus the chance to make their own identities richer and more resilient — as long as they have not acknowledged each other's histories. Palestinians, virtually powerless in what has been construed as a struggle between two nations, have everything to gain from a greater understanding of the motivations and fantasies of their antagonistic Other. And for those who believe that long-term Israeli survival requires interaction with Palestinians rather than separation, a reconceptualization of Zionist history is required, such that the dispossession of the Palestinians can be acknowledged without the invalidation of the entire thrust of the Zionist project.

But it is fruitless simply to wait for those empathic projects to be undertaken on a grand scale. Rather, we should be looking more closely both at the way rhetorical power is deployed to patrol the margins of ethnic identity and at the way these two congealed and mutually exclusive identities are already momentarily, but regularly, thrown into question through the everyday workings of a reflexive and ironic dialogic imagination.

•

The above paper was read, verbatim, at two conventions in November, when I came back to the United States before returning to Jerusalem for a final week or so in early December. I read it first at a session I'd organized called "Imagining Other Communities: Collective Identity and Reflexive Discourse," for the annual meeting of the American Anthropological Association, in Chicago. The overall theme of the session was the claim that the production of national identities as a cultural project was not inconsistent with self-awareness on the part of its producers and — less certainly — that this combination might be a clue to the production of such collective identities in nonexclusivist ways. The discussants for that panel were Daniel Segal, an anthropologist specializing in nationalist rhetorics in Trinidad, and Benedict Anderson, author of a famous text on nations as "imagined communities" (Anderson 1991). The second reading, just two or three days later, was at an all-day session organized by Smadar Lavie and Ted Swedenburg (two fellow anthropologists) called "Eurocentrism and the Tropics of Middle Eastern Identity," part of the annual meeting of the Middle East Studies Association (MESA) in Washington, D.C. The general purpose of that session was to explore the ways that postmodern frames of reference intersect with postcolonial situations in the contemporary Middle East. There the two discussants were Barbara Harlow, author of a well-known and respected text on literature and resistance (1987), and the Israeli Palestinian Hebrew writer Anton Shammas.

The paper evoked remarkably differing responses at the two conventions. The night before I left New York for Chicago, one of the organizers of the MESA panel called me to say that Anton Shammas was "furious" at my paper. This left a cloud of guilty anxiety over my whole trip to Chicago and Washington. Nevertheless, the responses to my paper and the entire panel

I'd organized for the anthropology convention were generally encouraging. Segal, God bless him, praised the paper's nuanced sensibilities and enjoyed my anecdotes. Anderson, whose presence helped attract a gratifyingly large audience, wondered in response to the story about Charles's house whether the Palestinian plumber's practical joke was as benign in intention as my telling of it. A member of the audience presented himself as one of the "natives" I was presuming to speak for or about — an Israeli — but whatever criticisms of my paper he intended to ground in that assertion were inarticulate ones.

The reactions from the two respondents at the MESA panel were quite different. Barbara Harlow's strategy for handling the difficult task of organizing a coherent fifteen-minute response to a day-long set of papers was to range everything on a scale from "most political" to "most cultural." She placed my paper at the extremely cultural end, criticizing its evacuation of politics. She was especially annoyed by my reference to the "mutual violence attendant upon the intifada," quite understandably seeing it as a reduction of the situation to a quarrel between two equally empowered and equally wrong combatants. In vain, I fear, I tried to explain my intention: Israelis had certainly suffered from violence in the course of the intifada, and *if they wanted it to end,* they had a stake in attaining critical awareness into the blinders of their own ideology.

Somewhat to my relief, but still leaving me in suspense, Shammas's response to my paper as part of the whole panel hardly reflected "fury." Rather like Benedict Anderson, he did say that he thought my references to "intimacy and trust" in connection with the house story were far too rosy an interpretation and that the plumber's line could not have been quite so innocent. Also, he apparently thought that my discussion of Israeli army slang borrowed from Arabic was intended as an example of the kind of acknowledged and symbiotic intercultural dynamics I would like to see, whereas I had merely intended it as an example of the murky and tortured context in which such exchanges now usually take place. Over an excellent Middle Eastern dinner shared by most of the panelists at a Connecticut Avenue restaurant that evening, Shammas refused to add to his comments on my paper, though he promised to write a letter.

For whatever reason — simple overwork or some intention I could only guess at — that letter has never been sent, while I have continued to wonder what could have made Shammas "furious" (if indeed he was). I still wonder and worry, and not only because of my immense respect for Shammas's critical sensibilities. It is impossible for me to escape seeing his reaction as that of a generalized, stand-in "Palestinian" — one, moreover, whose reaction to my analysis counts *as if* it were the reaction of the person who originally had this interaction with Charles.[1] The cruelest interpretation of this vaguely communicated negative response that I can impose on myself now is that it represents a moment where an ethnographer identified with the "dominant" group, exultantly thinking he has identified a point of transcendence of domination — an empathic "moment of redemption" — is brought crashing down by the hint that what he has really done is unwittingly indulged in the arrogantly liberal self-delusion of the colonizer.

My response to this situation has been a careful rereading of the original paper, to sift for clues to its negative reception by Harlow and Shammas. Such clues are hardly lacking, and they begin with the simple fact that the paper was written "in the field." At the outset, as indicated by the journal entry to which I have tagged this extended critical interruption, I found the writing of the paper extremely difficult and was primarily concerned with finding enough material to make it last for the twenty minutes I would be allotted in which to read it. Smadar Lavie herself criticized the paper for being "untheorized," and indeed, I remarked to several friends in Jerusalem as I was writing it how difficult it was to shift from a straightforward journal to the very different discipline of writing a critical academic paper.

Perhaps because of my intended insistence on the mutual interpenetration of Israeli and Palestinian identities, the entire tone of the paper reads to me now as suggesting a great deal more parity than is warranted between the situations of those who bear those identities. My desire to illustrate some of the "ironies of the interculture" leaves me dealing with the problem at a strictly "cultural" level, as if such a thing existed. "Culture" and "irony" in our *culture* tend to signal lightness and mutability, as opposed to the weighty materiality of the factual, the historical, and the material. The very first paragraph already sounds remarkably insubstantial: if the problem is how people "imagine themselves," this could be taken to imply an evacuation of history as well as of power differentials. And in any case, it might plausibly be argued, an ironic stance is more likely to be the privilege of the colonizer. My own absence from the intercultural anecdotes presented emphasizes this patronizing sort of standing beyond or above the situation. Also patronizing is my comment "by the way" that Ahmed Abu Saleh wants to establish an academic center, a rhetorical pat on the head for being a good Palestinian. The pat phrases about "freedom from fear of the other" and acknowledging "each other's histories" are chillingly banal paraphrases of the kind of ideas articulated by Gregory Bateson that motivate this project and that I discuss in the

---

1. Nor am I the only Jew to respond to Shammas in this fashion. My colleague Sidra Ezrahi told me that, after spending a term as a guest scholar at the University of Michigan where Shammas teaches, she could no longer use the phrase "the Other Jerusalem" as a poetic allusion to Jerusalem's Jewish dead (personal communication).

introduction to this book. The statement that Palestinian nationalism makes the silencing of the Palestinian in Zionist historiography "problematic" might come across as a suggestion that everyone would have been better off without Palestinian nationalism, which was certainly not what I intended. In theoretical terms, the implied symmetry of the Arabic in army teenager slang and of the various examples of Arabs adopting Israeli Jewish identities leaves a confusion whether I'm talking about mutual perceptions by Others or a relationship between hegemonic and subaltern identities. My qualification that many of the homes in Baka'a had not been owned by Arabs before 1948 manages to imply that the "Arab house" is a post hoc Palestinian construction — that Palestinians took over the image of the Arab house, which really had belonged to other people: whereas what I intended was rather to avoid reifying everything in Jerusalem before 1948 as having been either "Jewish" or "Arab," thereby effacing an entire colonial/cosmopolitan past and reiterating the dichotomy I frankly seek to undermine. The closing, ringing endorsement of "reflexive and ironic dialogic imagination" again smacks too much of postmodern play, even as it stands as a prefiguration of a grander reconciliation. References to Israeli Jews, on the other hand, may be insufficiently ironized, such as my allusion to their search for Israeli identity. The quotation marks around this hackneyed phrase in my title evidently did not make it sufficiently clear that I know there's no self-sufficient, objectively existing *ding an sich* there that will someday be found. And if a "reconceptualization of Zionist history is required," then it is fair at least to ask, For whom and by whom? Believing, at least at the time I wrote this, that Israel's legitimation structure was not about to be dismantled, I meant to call pragmatically for its revision. But a refinement of an unjust doctrine is an ambiguous achievement at best.

Fulfilling stipulations of my fellowship and hoping to accomplish a few crucial pieces of fieldwork, I returned briefly to Jerusalem after the two conventions. I stayed at Charles and Sandy's house during that rainy December week, except for the one night in the Galilee described in this book's final pages. I told Charles about the mixed reaction to my paper and to the story about his house in particular, and in response he was kind enough to tell me a much more detailed version of the brief anecdote I presented in the paper. I taped the longer version, but while still in Jerusalem, mislaid the bag containing that tape, to my double distress: first at losing the important story it contained and second, as will be clearer, because if (as in my frightened imagining) it were found and listened to by the police, it could have harmed the plumber and made him an innocent victim of ethnography.

Jetting back to New York for the second time, I reconstructed the following notes on the longer version of the story Charles had just told me:

I show Charles what I had read at the conventions. First thing he says is that it wasn't an Arab house in the first place — it was a school. "A *gan yeladim*,"[2] Sandy specifies from the kitchen area. Charles also says that not only Arabs lived in Baka'a before 1948 — note some of the modern houses, especially close to Derekh Hevron. (I had assumed these were built after 1948. Fn.: Najwa's[3] grandfather — a dealer in rugs, who also had a restaurant in West Jerusalem — had a house somewhere along Derekh Hevron: interestingly enough, she's not sure where. When the family had to flee West Jerusalem, he had a shipment of rugs waiting for him in the port of Aqaba. But the receipt for the rugs had been left in the house in West Jerusalem, so someone had to steal "across" and retrieve the receipt. He was able to get the rugs and thus rebuild the family fortune.)

...Anyway — the architect who designed the renovating for the expanded apartment[4] is a Japanese who has been in Palestine for 20 years and lives in Azariya;[5] Charles doesn't know why. Sandy has known him for a long time. He brought in a Palestinian contractor (which, Charles says, already makes this unusual). The contractor hired various artisans, including the plumber, whose name is S. Now S.'s family is from the Old City. They still have their house there. Because of his Jerusalem residency, S. was able to get a job as a plumber for the Jerusalem municipality. He did the renovation work moonlighting — after his job, or perhaps calling in sick sometimes. He in fact lives outside of Jerusalem. Hence — Charles points out — in fact Charles's house could not have been S.'s grandfather's house, and the experience of S.'s family vis-à-vis the Israelis is quite different from that of Palestinians who lost homes in 1948. Charles knew this, but of course it didn't occur to him the moment S. said, "This was my grandfather's house." The telling of the story therefore also reveals differences among Palestinians.

Charles agrees that S. had the upper hand in this situation but laughed when I reported Ben Anderson's remark that the joke was "meaner" than I had made it out to be. Charles gave the following further contextualization: at the time of the story, the work in the house had been going on for two months. Charles was home most of that time. The one member of the construction group who hadn't been brought in by the contractor was the electrician, B., who was not well liked: he would (Charles reports) flash his blue identity card and say that the other guys from East Jerusalem were chumps for not having taken Israeli citizenship. Sometimes he would show up in a dress suit, drink coffee, and then announce that he couldn't work that day because he wasn't wearing work clothes. Eventually the contractor said that either B. would have to leave or he would leave. B. was dismissed, and Charles did the rest of the electrical work himself. Sometimes he would have lunch with the workmen, and then they would hold their conversations — consisting largely of el-Azariya gossip — in

---

2. Kindergarten.
3. My friend and colleague Najwa el-Hakim.
4. That is, Charles and Sandy's apartment was expanded to include a large part of the subdivided original house.
5. A village in the Occupied Territories, outside Jerusalem.

Hebrew. Charles says he thinks it was probably stranger for them to be gossiping in Hebrew than to have him around when they did it.

The plasterer was a slightly older man named Musa ("the only Palestinian I've ever met who gets heartburn from hummus," says Charles). Musa somehow found out that Charles's Hebrew name is Moshe and started calling him Musa as well.

The day the solar heater started leaking, Charles was especially anxious to avoid getting into a fight with the upstairs neighbor, whom he finds very quarrelsome and uncooperative. (One day this fall I was at the house when Charles and Sandy's new plumber, a recent American immigrant named Max Weiss, showed up. He came back a second later to report that the upstairs neighbor wouldn't let him in to do the work. Charles went to investigate, and she said, "I won't let an Arab into my house!") Charles had no idea whether or not S. would be coming that day (cf. the version as I told it at the AAA and MESA meetings). So when S. popped his head up onto the roof and asked, "*Tsarikh ezra?*"[6] he was like a good angel. At that point Charles started working as his assistant, handing him tools, etc. So (and this is my interpretation now), in a way, in addition to the "intimacy" I referred to in my earlier account — reinforced now by the information that they'd been working together for two months, and S. had had the chance to realize that, on the one hand, the story would work (Charles wouldn't say, "So what?") and, on the other hand, Charles wouldn't be angry — S. also "had the upper hand" because he'd just rescued Charles and Charles's house.

I asked Charles why he tells this story. Two reasons, he says: (*a*) it's very funny; (*b*) it shows neatly that relations between Palestinians and Jews on the ground are more complicated than people think. I ask him to speculate on why Shammas might have been upset and why I hesitate to tell this story to Palestinian friends. He speculates that it sounds like S. was being disloyal — like if a Jew were to tell an internally critical Jewish joke to a goy. "And then to have it told back to Jews by a goy!" I extend the analogy.

The next day, sitting in Beit Maiersdorf with Najwa and her friend Saleh, a graduate student of criminology from Lydda, I tell them the story in the course of narrating my adventures in the United States. They laugh, but not uproariously.

•

Where does this leave the story in its multiple layers? I've identified weaknesses in the paper as I originally presented it and suggested some of the reasons for those weaknesses. In particular, I can absorb Shammas's and Anderson's comments that the story is not as innocuous as I make it seem in the earlier presentation. I myself, of course, don't regard the pained memory of the real loss on which the plumber's joke was based as being innocuous, either — although I do insist that such loss does not produce unambiguous, clearly differentiated, good-guy and bad-guy dichotomies. I can also see more

---

6. "Need help?" (in Hebrew).

clearly now than when I first wrote the paper that the central position of the story about Charles's house presents him as my model of a "good Israeli," the reflexive, ironic one, the civilized and educated kind... who get the Arab houses in Baka'a. Perhaps the extra contextualization of Charles's contacts with the Palestinian workmen adds some credibility to my claim that there was some barbed transcendence of defensively guarded identities here. In any case I will not let the story go. Certainly its end has not been told. I still *need* that story and, particularly with this (still-partial, one-sided) elaboration of it, offer it here again for other, contentious readings.

# 5

# Enough Already with My Trip to Israel

• 10/1/91 •

I broke off from struggling with my paper about 7:30 Thursday evening, because I'd promised Yosef Shtrigler that I'd come to the Simchas Beis Hashoeva one night during the intermediate days of Sukkot.[1] Yosef was out when I arrived on time at 8:30: he'd been to a *shmues*[2] given by the Rosh Yeshiva. Meanwhile I sat in the sukkah and ate a large, greasy, thin, and delicious potato latke made by Yosef's wife, and I listened in some astonishment to Zalmen and the younger boy playing and joking in Yiddish. Zalmen was imitating some older man: "Do you know how much 60 and 60 is? — Yes, 60 and 60 is 120 — Oh, what a clever child! Tomorrow I'll bring you a candy...." How astonishing to me to hear children, not only speaking Yiddish or studying Yiddish, but being wise guys and making fun of their elders in Yiddish! Also, on hearing that my name was not just Yoynesn but Yoynesn Ahron,[3] Zalmen pointed out correctly, "You're the *ushpizin*! Today's Ahron's *ushpizin*" (the prophet Aaron is the "special guest" invited to the sukkah on the fifth day of Sukkot).[4] When Yosef came in, Zalmen told him that I was the guest

---

1. This entry describes my visit to the traditionalist Orthodox neighborhood of Mea Shearim, in the company of a family I met through friends on the Lower East Side. The Simchas Beis Hashoeva (literally, celebration of the place where water is drawn for use in Temple rituals) is observed on the intermediate nights of Sukkot, one of the three ancient festivals of pilgrimage to Jerusalem, in honor of the rabbinic statement that "whoever has not seen the Simchas Beis Hashoeva has not seen a celebration in his life."

2. Here, referring to an informal sermon.

3. My Yiddish name; my full name in English is Jonathan Aaron Boyarin.

4. *Ushpizin* ("guests") refers here to a formula in Aramaic recited each night of Sukkot, each night inviting one of the seven "faithful shepherds" — Abraham, Isaac, Jacob, Moses, Aaron, Joseph, and King David — as guest of honor in every sukkah. To identify a living, speaking, visible guest with that night's *ushpizin* simultaneously honors the living guest and actualizes the presence of the *ushpizin*. Normally, if I think about my middle name at all I think of myself as being named after a brother who died young before I was born, or at most of our great-grandfather Reb Ahron Kravitz who lived, studied, and died in Lithuania. Clearly Yosef did not know beforehand that I would have the appropriate name for the night, but

Ahron, and Yosef acted very pleased: "We always try to have a guest with the name of the *ushpizin* on that night."

After Yosef came home, there was some consultation, after which it was decided that his wife would come along with us to watch the dancing for a while, and we waited for her to get changed and ready. Meanwhile Yosef told me about his trip to Hebron that day — he was astonished at the number of soldiers, both male and female, they had assembled to guard the Jewish visitors to the traditional gravesites. Clearly he thought the whole thing a bit overdone in terms of the military presence. I asked him whether there was a yeshiva in Hebron (wondering whether the Hebron Yeshiva had been reestablished there; I later found out, I don't think it was Yosef telling me that evening, that though there is a yeshiva there, the Hebron Yeshiva is in Jerusalem now). He told me there was, but he really couldn't imagine sitting and studying in such a tense and confrontational place. "Here in Jerusalem, everybody keeps to their own place more or less, but there..." He finds the Jewish settlement at Hebron to be a deliberate provocation of the goyim, of the kind that's prohibited by the Torah: he cited a verse which he translated as, "Don't start up with the goyim. OK, you could say they're like animals even, but it's stupid to start up with a dog, and they're living creatures, too. You come in and move in right next to people's homes, how do you expect them to react?" (I wish I had this one verbatim: both in terms of my paper about Jew/animal/human, and in terms of Marc Shell's claim about the space Judaism preserves for a legitimate human existence that is not Jewish,[5] Yosef's

---

the practice of inviting appropriately named guests each night is entirely plausible given the prevalence of certain names within the Hasidic community. More significantly, the heightening of given names as a constituent of panchronic personal identity is the virtual opposite of the generally modern — and specifically structuralist — postulate of the arbitrariness of names.

5. The paper of mine I refer to here, to which I gave the provocative title "That Jew's an Animal!" explored the suppression of the body in modern liberal discourse on Jewish culture as part of the emancipation insistence that Jews are first and foremost *men:* that is, that the overwhelming pressure to assert the equal humanity of Jews has led Jews and sympathetic non-Jews to suppress the organismic aspects of Jewish culture, as of all culture (J. Boyarin 1991b). The paper by Marc Shell basically contends that Christianity, in its universalist thrust, sees all persons as either Christians, potential Christians, or not fully human. On the other hand, Shell argues that the built-in particularism of Judaism allows an intermediate space where those who are not and never will be Jews can be acknowledged as human as well (Shell 1991). Yosef's pragmatic assertion — that even if one assumes *arguendo* that the Palestinians are like animals, they are deserving of the mercy due all God's creatures and should not be provoked — reveals, I think, an important caveat to Shell's essentially theoretical distinction: Jews in Diaspora have been effectively forced to acknowledge the "right to difference" of other humans, even if the particular formation of Jewish identity and theology predispose Judaism toward such an acknowledgment. Thus, power (and, I would suggest also, a construction of masculinity that is not dependent on dominance) is involved, along with theories of particular and universal authority. Note, however, that (at least in my reconstruction) Yosef returns to a reference to "moving in next to people's homes," thus suggesting that in his view, these

statement was fascinating. I've gotten lazy — haven't been recording notes lately, and now I regret it.)

There's some dancing at the Slonimer Yeshiva where Yosef studies, but Yosef dismissed it as weak and uninspired. The two best places to go, he informed me, are Karlin-Stolin and Toldos Aharon.[6] With him, a younger Hasidic guest, Yosef's wife, the two boys, and the older girls, we drove off in a borrowed car to Mea Shearim. Yosef looked at my sandals and said, "Oh, boy, are you going to regret those — your feet are going to get stepped on plenty, and some of these guys, when they jump, they come down really hard." As it turned out, I think I stepped on more toes than I got stepped on, so there! We walked in [to Karlin-Stolin] together, joined a line, and I lost Yosef and the boys after a few minutes, what with others breaking in and the one time I switched to a different section where the dancers seemed more lively. The *bes medresh*[7] is very crowded with dancers, so there has to be a certain pattern in order for everybody to be able to move. At Karlin they do it like this: everybody snaking in amongst each other. I don't know, I suppose there are a few beginnings and ends to the lines, but it almost seems as if it could be a single line without beginning or end, folded in upon itself any number of times. The result is that there are always two irregular, bending, and twisting lines of dancers facing each other closely but moving in opposite directions, coming within a foot or two of each other as the rhythm of the dance dictates that they step forward, then backing off a couple feet more distant. After a few minutes, you're facing the same people again, so that in the forty minutes or so that we were dancing I passed Yosef at least half a dozen times. The lines themselves are quite closely crowded, and holding the hand of the man in front of me and the man behind me, I was frequently pressing the small of the back of the man in front and the man behind was doing the same to me. The rhythm and repetition are hypnotic, and the homoerotic intensity of hundreds of men stomping and swaying so closely together (thrusting forward to each other, then moving back) is astonishing. It was fortunate that we had set a time limit for the dancing (Yosef's wife needed to go back home with the kids, and I had left my bag in the car), because my left knee was getting sore from the repetitive stamping.

Yosef drove me part of the way down Mea Shearim Street — very crowded, with traffic moving slowly — toward the Toldos Aharon Yeshiva. I made my way inside, pushing past crowds of men going into the sukkah with plastic

---

neighbors are in fact *people* — which stands perhaps as evidence for Shell's positive argument about Jews and other differences.

6. All three mentioned in these two sentences are Hasidic groups with their own institutions, including yeshivot.

7. Literally, "study house"; the main communal study hall of the yeshiva.

cups of some cold drink, smaller crowds considering the tapes for sale of Simchas Beis Hashoeva [recordings] and clustered around the table at the entrance to the yeshiva where lottery tickets (I think) for fund-raising for the yeshiva were being sold. I stood on the side for a while, watching the dance, considering how to join in while clutching my bag (the spring holding the leather shoulder strap hooked on broke last week) — how could I dance with only one hand? And as I stood, a line of about thirty young boys formed around me (as if I were a pearl inside their oyster) and began dancing, their hands on the shoulders of the boy in front of me.[8] That's how they dance at Toldos Aharon: every man with both hands on the shoulder of the one in front of him, in a circle, so that the entire floor of the *bes medresh* is covered with concentric circles of dancers — a giant, slowly revolving wheel made up of hundreds of lumbering dancers.... I joined in, simply using one hand instead of two, and found that though I started at the edge, after a few minutes my circle was much closer toward the middle. Most of the dancers were Hasidic, but only in the very central circles were nearly all of the dancers wearing the Toldos Aharon striped *kapotes*.[9] I couldn't help thinking of some Buddhist concept of a "great wheel of life," and of the contrast in styles between the Karliner interweaving snake and the Toldos Aharon circle.

[I'm writing in the office at Hartman again. There's a noisy family or two in the apartment building opposite the window; sometimes they have loud business phone conversations out on the balcony. Lately some kid's been playing his drum set and heavy metal music; right now it's "Smoke on the Water." Incredibly irritating to be distracted by that in Israel, although Ruth did mention to me that Deep Purple is coming to play in Israel (are they still alive?).]

Friday at 1:00 I set off for another Shabbat in Ramye. (I don't have the pleasure from keeping this journal that I did at the beginning; I have a sense of winding down, even though what I saw and heard and learned this weekend was as interesting as anything else I've done.) I rode up on the bus with a fellow named Khanon Berlin(?), a nice, overweight, single, unpretentious lawyer from New York who's been here about seven years now. This time we were sleeping at Ban'e, the village down the hill from Ramye, across the road from Carmiel, since the action was a demonstration on the highway followed by a march up to Ramye and a rally there. We were met by Yitzkhak Ben Ariel and his friend Avshalom, both from Derekh Hanitzotz, the group which has

---

8. Read, "the boy in front of them." The description is confusing: How could a *line* form around me? My memory of this moment is no longer independent of this description. It seems likely that what I was trying to describe was actually the great circle (see the following notes) expanding outside of me and incorporating me, so that I was now inside it and willy-nilly became one of the dancers rather than a stationary obstacle.

9. The long gowns worn by traditionalist Hasidim.

been coordinating the Jewish side of the Ramye solidarity work, and driven, along with Sharon Brown and her twelve-year-old son, Gadi, the other religious Jews who had come up for the whole Shabbat, to the home of the head of the village council, whom we stayed with. Now this man, Ismail Hashmi, is a Communist (he's also the uncle of Ismail Hashmi, the famous actor, who lives nearby in the same village), as is 80 percent of the village. Now there are just a few things I want to record about Ban'e, not trying to be systematic or thorough.

1. The head of the village council, our host, is a physician. He worked for a time in Qiryat Shemona (as a Kupat Holim doctor, I presume). One of his patients was a young boy (Asaf?) from an Indian Jewish family. This boy's parents had been murdered in their home by an Arab when he was an infant, and he was raised by his aunt and uncle. The uncle was a member of Tehiya; the aunt was a member of Ratz.[10] Dr. Ismail, knowing the boy was an orphan and knowing the story, paid a lot of attention to him, visiting him from time to time and bringing him presents, and thus he became friendly with the aunt and uncle as well. He would have civil political arguments with the uncle. When the boy's bar mitzvah came, the aunt and uncle invited the doctor to come, but the uncle warned him that his friend, Rehavam Ze'evi,[11] would be coming as well. He decided, "In that case I won't come to the bar mitzvah. I'll come earlier, say hello, give the boy my present, and leave." The bar mitzvah was scheduled for 7:00. He arrived at 5:00, and who was sitting at the table but "Gandhi" and his wife. There was nothing to do but be introduced and sit down for a cup of coffee. "Hello, this is our doctor, Dr. Ismail Hashmi; this is our friend Rehavam Ze'evi and Mrs. Ze'evi [whatever her name is—J.B.]." When the doctor sat down, Gandhi said, "Here, I want you to see the present I got for the boy." He pushed it across the table, and the doctor realized it was the book he'd written, and responded, "Yes, I've read your book." Gandhi said, "Read the inscription." The inscription read: "Asaf — remember and do not forget. Revenge!"[12] The doctor said, "First of all, it won't work. I've

---

10. Tehiya was, until the 1992 elections, one of the far-right parties represented in the Knesset. Ratz, the Citizens' Rights Party, eventually joined with two other left-of-center parties to form the Meretz coalition in the 1992 elections.

11. Rehavam Ze'evi, popularly known throughout Israel as "Gandhi" because he was so thin as a young soldier in the prestate Palmach military organization, was at this time a leader in the far right-wing Moledet Party, calling for "transfer" or mass deportation of Palestinians from the West Bank in particular.

12. This vignette presents two opposed responses to the boy's situation as an orphan whose parents had been murdered by "the enemy." Dr. Hashmi presents himself as being kind to the boy, out of sympathy for an orphan, and also to avoid the boy's growing up with an image of all Arabs as murderously vicious. Ze'evi chooses rather to present the boy's history as a stark reminder of the brute realities of the situation and as an unanswered legacy that calls for acts of violence in return.

worked very hard to make this boy my friend, both because he's an orphan and because I want him to know that not all Arabs are murderers, and he knows that. Second of all, this is not an appropriate gift for a bar mitzvah boy — to remind him of such a terrible thing that happened in his childhood. Is 'revenge' the lesson for a bar mitzvah boy? Now, I'll show you what I got the boy" — and he pulled out a pen, marked "From your friend, Dr. Ismail." "With this he can create, maybe he'll write poems. This is the kind of thing you give as a bar mitzvah present." Gandhi was silent; Mrs. Ze'evi agreed that the pen was a more appropriate present. "And do you know why I'm here now?" the doctor added. "I'm here because I knew you were coming, and I didn't want to see you. But I came here, and you were here already, and it would have been impolite to refuse to sit and drink a cup of coffee. And now I'm leaving."[13]

2. A lot of the activists in the village — well, anyway a few Hashmis — have been professionally educated in Eastern Europe (Russia or Poland). Dr. Hashmi's deceased wife was Ukrainian. His close relative also living close by, who has a carpenter shop, thinks it was inappropriate for Dr. Hashmi to marry a European woman and bring her to the village: "It was hard for her and it was hard for us. If we wanted to go over and visit them, we had to make an appointment. We're not used to that; with us, if people drop by, even at midnight, they're always welcome guests. And she wasn't used to that. So why marry someone so different, when it's going to make it hard for everybody?"

3. In the evening — Friday evening — we walked a little bit further up the hill on which Ban'e (pop. about four thousand) is spread out to see part of a wedding celebration. Mostly loudspeaker repetitive-chant music, slow dancing, the women, with the groom in the middle turning slowly and awkwardly among them. Briefly, a slow *debka* line of young men, who urged me to join them, which I did. The village — actually the neighboring village of Deir el Asad — continues up the steep slope; there are many new houses. The bright spotlights onto the concrete area where the celebration was going on made it impossible to see the ground at the bottom of the houses farther up the hillside, so all we could see were the lights of the houses. It made it look like they were so many stars, or rather, like the houses were suspended from the sky.... Looking down, in the other direction, the close-by village of Majd

---

13. Dr. Hashmi's rebuke to "Gandhi" is thus twofold. On a more overt level, his gift encourages creativity rather than hatred. More subtly, whereas "Gandhi" unnecessarily provokes his inadvertent fellow guest (Dr. Hashmi) by showing him not only the book but the inscription, Dr. Hashmi points out he himself has refrained from similarly hostile behavior out of respect for their host. The story thus not only presents a contrast between the cultivation of interethnic friendship and the maintenance of vigilant, defensive ethnic boundaries but also underscores which party really knows and observes the etiquette of hospitality and guesthood.

el-Krum with its mosque, all tucked into a fold between two mountains, and much farther down and dimmer, the lights of Haifa by the sea, an hour away by bus.

4. "Shabbes goy"[14] — the term came up Friday evening, probably in connection with what Khanon and I could and could not do, and what others could or could not do for us on Shabbat. Yitzkhak mentioned that some Israeli Arab intellectual or writer had called Emil Habibi, mockingly, the "Shabbes goy," meaning that he was too accommodating to the Jews. The next morning at breakfast, on the patio of the mayor's house next to the small green lawn, overlooking the terrace of olive trees on the side of the house, after the hot milk his sister served us, I mentioned to the mayor that Khanon was hoping there'd be coffee, but didn't want to ask. I didn't even realize that the reason Khanon didn't ask was because he didn't want to ask someone to do something he couldn't do on Shabbat, but he explained that to Dr. Ismail, who responded that he was happy to do anything for us that we couldn't do ourselves on Shabbat. (Did I mention that when Chaya, Becky, and I slept in Ramye, Tarik's son, seeing that Chaya was having trouble lighting the Shabbat candles, lit them for her? None of us said anything.) "If you don't want to ask me to make coffee, what you can do is say loudly, 'I really don't want any coffee!' and then I'll know what to do" — which struck me as an amusingly rabbinic approach to this problem of halachic[15] etiquette.

5. After the march and the inevitable speeches in Ramye at the middle of the day (there were several hundred or a thousand people there this time, mostly Arabs, as was intended), Sharon, Gadi, Khanon, and I were invited to the home of Ibrahim, at the other edge of the village (across the fields) from Tarik's, where we had stayed last time. Ibrahim's wife is from Majd al-Krum — so apparently the exchanges don't go only one way. While we waited for him to come back to the house, she showed us the goats in their stall. We stared at the goats, and they stared at us; finally I joked in Hebrew, "It's the first time they've seen Jews!" And I added sotto voce to Sharon, "They probably think we have horns." Ibrahim came back, and we were served the usual meal (we'd had the same in Ban'e for supper the night before): tomatoes maybe, cucumbers and peppers, *labne*, fried eggs or omelettes, greasy and delicious french fries. Ibrahim talked a lot: he's quite articulate. He said that one of the things he liked about this whole fuss (to someone who asked whether the villagers were getting tired of all the strangers coming through) was that he was getting to meet so many new people. We asked precisely what the people of Ramye had so far been offered, and he said half a dunam per family, room

---

14. See the entry for July 14.
15. Jewish law.

for one *migrash* (compound), on land at Ban'e or Majd el-Krum — which means, presumably, "military reserve" land which the government at some point in the past confiscated from those villages. But that's not enough, he complained; he needs enough room for a house for each of his children when they grow up and start families of their own. If there's just half a dunum, where will his family live?

Later, in the car, Sharon remarked on this point he'd made: we, middle-class Jews, hardly expect that our children will live next to us! She's not planning to build a house for Gadi in her backyard. So the cultural expectations, the expectations of what's needed, are quite different. On the other hand, Sharon also pointed out, there aren't many places in Israel except for their native village where Arabs can settle in. In a new village, which would also be crowded anyway, they'd be outsiders for generations. And it's very difficult for Arabs to move onto any housing on land owned by the JNF.[16] The only other alternative is... to leave the country.

• 10/2/91 •

A few notes on what I've been calling here "Arab houses": many of them in Baka'a, Katamon, and Emek Refaim were, especially before 1948 and to a slight extent still now, owned actually by Armenians, Greeks, and Germans, a fact that's obvious from the names ("Moshava Germanit," still in use; "Moshava Yavanit," less obvious, but mentioned by Sam Englander as where he lives, and I noticed this morning an older building with a sign saying, "The Greek Community of Jerusalem"; also at the top of the hill, between Old Katamon and the Katamonim,[17] the church that presumably gives rise to the name of San Simon), but which I've been suppressing until now. Also, I wanted to note that many more of the old houses are getting second and third floors added onto them now, which, even when it's done in a relatively tasteful way, ruins their proportions and obscures their history.[18]

---

16. The vast majority of land within the State of Israel is owned by the Jewish National Fund, often parceled out in ninety-nine-year leases that are unavailable to Arab individuals or groups.

17. See the explanation of Katamon Tet in the entry for July 11.

18. This sentence beautifully gives the lie to all of my sophistication about rhetorics of ruination as of history. It suggests a curious linkage between the transitive verb "ruin," here implying a willful disregard of an original aesthetic unity in the process of modernization, and the production of that *thing* called "a ruin" that comes from neglect, abandonment, and mortal struggle for territory. Not that my dismissal of the additions as ruins is simply an inappropriate judgment from outside: it is fairly easy, I think, to imagine a pre-1948 owner of one of these homes returning and reacting to the changes in quite the same way: "They've ruined our house!" The history of these homes is treated here with the same implicit regard for a pristine originality as their proportions are: their real *history*, I'm implying, is the story of

Also about *"Avoda aravit,"* which I referred to in the first weeks of my journal as the headline of an article about an Arab restaurant that moved from Bethlehem to Jerusalem: the phrase isn't a takeoff on *avoda ivrit* (how many Israelis today even know what that means?), but on the slang term *avoda aravit*, which means "shoddy workmanship." I realized this yesterday when I told Ruth about Fawzi's line, *"Matay elissa ba'a le'erets haplaot?"*[19] and she in turn told me about the work Fawzi and his brothers had done on their parents' house when their parents went on hajj; showing it to Ruth, Fawzi and Aisha had joked, *"Avoda aravit!"*

This morning, going out of the *shikun* to cross the railroad tracks toward Emek Refaim, I saw my first stone-throwing incident. Three boys from the neighborhood — about twelve or fourteen — two of them walking after the third yelling at him, *"Ganav! Ganav!"*[20] while they threw stones at him and he back at them, keeping at a sufficient distance to make sure that if any of the stones were thrown accurately there'd still be time to dodge them.

• 10/7/91 •

Thursday evening came an event I'd been waiting for since before my fieldwork began: Avner's swearing-in at the Western Wall. I don't have more than fragmentary notes about it — I was both tired and generally out of sorts that evening, and I felt alienated virtually to the point of horror and nausea by the ceremony. But here's what I have.

Above the entranceway to the plaza in front of the Wall from the Old City are six huge flames, like great memorial candles. Ruth explained to me that they had been put up at Rabbi Goren's[21] initiative, even though making such additions without a permit in the Old City is illegal, and they were still there. After they were turned on, as it got dark, the letters *"yizkor"*[22] appeared in the spaces between the flames. Eyal Sivan[23] would have loved it.

As part of the swearing-in ceremony — the segment where each soldier in each company was being handed their paratrooper's pin, a Bible, and a gun, but not the red beret which they'll only receive at the end of basic training, by slightly older soldiers already wearing the red beret — there was a band that played three tunes. (The second two tunes I didn't recognize; the first

---

the people for whom they were built and to whom they still "really" belong. It might be more accurate to say that second and third stories were currently being added onto their history.

19. See above, p. 198.
20. Thief!
21. The former chief rabbi of the Israel Defense Forces who became the government-appointed chief rabbi of Jerusalem.
22. Remember (Hebrew).
23. Director of a documentary film called *Yizkor*.

one was the one about *"Kan noladati, kan noldu li yeladi,"*[24] which was a big hit this summer). They warmed up for a while before the ceremony began, as some soldiers were laying out the rifles in racks inside a roped-off section of the plaza (next to the Wall itself, a continual minyan is going on, trying to ignore this disruption). The bass player warmed up by playing a few times the opening riff to that obnoxious song by Queen, "Dum-dum-dum — another one bites the dust; dum-dum-dum — another one bites the dust," which Avner's friend Jessica, who'd come along to see him sworn in, thought was cool, though a different American friend of hers, here for a year on a USY[25] program, lightly noted that the sentiment was inappropriate for the occasion. Ruth points out a Yemenite mother passing by bearing a large branch of basil for good luck for her son. She's also amazed at the large number of religious family members here; in earlier years, she says, it was almost unheard of for a religious guy to volunteer for the paratroopers.[26] We hear faintly the muezzin's call while we're waiting. The organist, warming up, does a chorus of Billy Joel's "I Love You Just the Way You Are." Then he plays "Let It Be."

The ceremony for the most part, except for the actual oath of loyalty to the state and the army and to carry out orders to the point of death, which the soldiers respond to with a joint shout, "I swear!" consisted of the recruits being ordered at attention and at ease, as punctuation to brief speeches by the head of the paratroopers, the chief rabbi of the paratroopers (I think), and the head of the Central Region command. The first speech focused on the theme of *yizkor* — mentioning the Nazis, the Warsaw Ghetto fighters, all the soldiers who've died defending Israel, and the paratroopers who fought to take the Wall. The second speech was a reading from the first chapter of the book of Joshua, about coming in to inherit the land; no wonder these kids think Israel goes at least to the Jordan River, just look at that text (Ruth says they read the same text at Efraim's swearing-in, also at the Wall). The third speech focused on the fact that the paratroopers are an elite unit, the work is hard and dangerous, the state depends on the army as the basis of its existence, both militarily and diplomatically. Now at last there's a real chance of peace and the role of the Defense Forces is as important as ever. One of the speeches — also the third, I think — talked about the final blessing of Moses to the people, *"Chazak ve'amatz."* The first word, the speaker explained, refers

---

24. "Here I was born, here my children were born," the lyrics sung to a very assertive disco beat.

25. United Synagogue Youth, the youth organization of Conservative Judaism.

26. That is, the paratroopers were formerly constituted as a unit of the best "Israeli" youth — secular Zionists, mostly from Ashkenazi backgrounds and disproportionately children of the kibbutzim. The larger number of religious youth joining the paratroopers represents a diversification of army culture and not merely, as the text implies, greater patriotism on the part of religious Jewish Israelis.

to physical strength, the second to spiritual strength, and this is reflected in the gun and the Bible the soldiers were getting. He stressed the heritage of *am hasefer,* the people of the book.

I told Ruth later that it seemed to me to be a "powerful" ceremony. In reality it confused me utterly: it was repugnant, though I didn't want to repudiate Avner of course (Ruth said he didn't seem especially overwhelmed by the ceremony; afterwards she stressed that he's really miserable in the army, as it turns out).[27] I didn't understand quite why it upset me so. This may be intellectualizing too much, but it seemed to have something to do with the way all of the contradictions were blurred — the stress on the decency of *am hasefer,* neatly neutralized through a dichotomization between spirit and body, at the same time as the Bible is being recruited to reinforce loyalty and inspiration to a military organization; generally the sense that this was, even more perhaps than acts of brutality, the heart of the machine of state, the point of emotional recruitment. Perhaps this was why I added the following afternote to my trip to Ramye in the middle of the ceremony; or perhaps it was just that my attention wandered and I had my tape recorder out: Friday evening at Ramye, sitting around with Dr. Hashmi and Khanon and Yitzkhak and Avshalom, we were arguing about the 'Zionism is racism' formula. Dr. Hashmi was arguing for; Yitzkhak was trying to insist that the colonialist moment is much more central.[28] I tried to point out to Dr. Hashmi that he was insisting on 'racism' because he thought it was the worst word to condemn discrimination, and that if we demurred, it wasn't by way of excusing or mitigating. But he had a clinching argument: Why does Israel's land-control policy constitute *gezanut* (racism)? Because they uproot one *geza* (stalk, shoot),[29] and they plant another in its stead. A very Jewish, that is rabbinic, kind of argument."

---

27. My nephew subsequently was offered, and refused, entry to officer training school, which would have entailed an extra year of army duty. He eventually became a sergeant in charge of the basic training of new recruits, which helped to minimize the time he had to spend in the Occupied Territories. As of this writing (January 31, 1994) he is less than six months from completing his service and is relieved that he has never shot his gun at a human being.

28. Yitzkhak and Avshalom are members of Derekh Hanitzotz, the organization that began and coordinated much of the Israeli solidarity work in cooperation with the residents of Ramye.

29. According to Alcalay, "trunk, stem, shoot" (R. Alcalay 1965: 339). This dictionary helpfully cites a biblical usage of the word: *"Veyatsa khoter megez yeshay,"* "And there shall come forth a shoot out of the stock of Jesse" (Isaiah 11:1). The word *geza* thus also means people, ethnos, tribe, or lineage; hence the modern coinage of *gezanut* for racism. Rather than understanding the social meaning of the term as being derived from the botanical (such that we would say that the Hebrew term glossed as "tribe" is an analogical extension, a natural symbol, from the term for "shoot"), it is probably safest to understand the social and the botanical as having an equal semantic status in an ancient Hebrew cultural system that did

To Shilo[30] to see Ber Hirshkovitz on Friday. There are only two buses out there on Fridays, and they're basically empty, since everybody from Shilo who works in Jerusalem tries to avoid going in on Fridays. So the 7:00 A.M. bus — which leaves from the same spot, more or less, across from the Central Bus Station as the bus I took to Tekoa months ago, but then heads out in the opposite direction, north toward Ramallah rather than south toward Bethlehem — was filled mostly with soldiers, male and female. The bus takes off at the beep of the 7:00 A.M. news. I hadn't checked the map; I really didn't know where I was going. This is the first time I've been on the road to Ramallah in an Israeli vehicle. Yep, that old bus is going right through Ramallah. Well, not quite; it's turning right through El-Bireh, passing very close to Ahmed's house, then past the office of the Civil Administration of Judea and Samaria, where several soldiers, both male and female, get off. Immediately after that an army base where the rest of the soldiers get off. Then just into the settlement of Bet El. We pass a bus from the Khevra Petuach Matei Benyamin.[31] "Dangerous curves" indeed! (There used to be a popular T-shirt for teenage girls with a reproduction of that sign on it.)[32] Road off to the left leading to Nahaliel and Halamish.[33] Past the Bir-Zeit turnoff (I only recognize it because of the name of the university). It really doesn't look crowded at all, but how crowded could it be, how many people could a landscape like this support? Steep hillsides terraced with olives; as usual, the land under the olive trees is carefully plowed. There are two soldiers and me left on the bus at this point. Miles with no visible habitation; very little traffic on the road [I didn't yet realize this was the main road from Nablus to Ramallah]. Just the olive trees and the terraces, which are a combination of natural striation and human-constructed walls. The wadi opens up into a wider flat area with plowed fields; not irrigated apparently. Then the first village in several miles. And here's the Shilo turnoff, at a point where terrain, as I've said, becomes a little less hilly and there's more Palestinian houses and villages and fields. New roads being built, cutting right through the Palestinian fields. Shilo itself is well beyond that area just described near the road, climbing up a steep and otherwise quite barren hill.

---

not sharply differentiate among humans, animals, and plants as various fecund aspects of the divinely created world (see Eilberg-Schwartz 1990).

30. Shilo, similar to Tekoa in this respect, is one of the ideologically motivated and relatively isolated settlements on the West Bank.

31. Benjamin Region Development Corporation; see the entry for June 20.

32. I refer to a tourist item. The signs referred to say *"sevuvim mesukanim"* in Hebrew and "dangerous curves" in English. My paltry irony here refers to the hilly topography through which the West Bank roads curve, which makes driving through them doubly risky for anyone identified as Israeli.

33. I'm identifying them here by the Hebrew sound of their names as Jewish settlements.

(More notes after I met Ber, had a breakfast of granola, crackers with peanut butter, and coffee, and was taken around by him for an expert and well-rehearsed tour and history, including the approaches to Tel Shilo nearby:)

Ber's house is on the top of the hill, facing basically west [wrong: east] toward Jordan. An interruption as I'm taking notes: a jet flies by, invisible, and Ber comes over and says that during the war there were planes circling overhead twenty-four hours a day because this area directly faces western Iraq across Jordan, and the Scuds that came toward Tel Aviv came right over here. Ber feels anyhow that the question of security and the strategic importance of this region for Israel [are of primary importance?], and he can't see turning it over to the Palestinians unless it's possible to guarantee in some way that there won't be any Arab military presence here for the next fifteen years, which he doesn't think is possible. In fact he thinks the most likely eventuality is a major war which will determine the fate of this area. Anyway, the house facing west [wrong: east] toward Jordan at the top of the hill in the highest of the three neighborhoods in Shilo, the lowest being where the temporary housing is, and then on the top of that hill there's an area of nice houses, and a big Bet Knesset — supposedly in the shape of the *ohel mo'ed*[34] at Shilo — which cost an immense amount of money and isn't getting finished very quickly. The Hirshkovitzes live at the top of the hill partly as a result of a decision after a debate in the early 1980s between the expansionists and — what was the other word he used? — [homesteaders]. The expansionists wanted to secure the top of the hill, and sort of use this as a *mitspe*;[35] the others wanted to stay closer and maintain a strong sense of community. This came after Ber's explanation that they had settled on this hill because all the land around is owned and used by Arabs in the local village, and this hill was a Jordanian military base, so after the Israeli conquest by international law it belonged to Israel, so it was available for settlement — and not as I had assumed that it had been put up here as a *mitspe*. There are some agricultural lands that belong to Shilo; there's one orchard area, pretty much neglected, down the slope on this side that belonged to the village of [Qariot; check exact name on map] behind the west [east] side, that was given to Shilo by the *mukhtar*,[36] in connection with a rivalry with another family. There's another area on another side which belonged to the same small village; [it] was first confiscated by the Israeli government for military purposes and used as a shooting range, and then handed over to Shilo — the

---

34. The Tent of Meeting, which served as the pre-Temple Israelite sacred center.
35. A lookout post (see entry for June 25).
36. The village leader (Arabic).

community and some individuals in Shilo have planted orchards and vines on it. That's the only area that Ber finds problematic in terms of legitimacy of ownership.

There have been a lot of journalists up here; Ber refers to himself as having done anthropology up here for twenty years, which is how long he's been in Israel. He emphasized to me the sense that this is the cradle of Judaism, of the Jewish people, that the center of gravity certainly — the discrepancy between the historical area and the contemporary State of Israel.[37] And he feels it was a tremendous mistake on the part of the religious peace movement not to say quite clearly that this is the center for Judaism, this is the land for Judaism, and we are willing to sacrifice it to the Palestinians because they're living there and for the sake of peace. But for the religious Zionists [peace oriented] not to have talked about the importance of this territory and to leave that to Gush Emunim was a major mistake which has turned him off from the left, and has made him realize that aside from a shared concern for the humanity of the Palestinians, the vast gulf that separates him from, especially, the secular Israeli leftists leaves really no common ground. This was all in response to my volunteered statement that I've become aware that the demonization of settlers is a serious mistake on the part of the left.[38] Qariot is the name of the village to the west [east].

Ber is going to introduce me to Reb Volf, eighty-seven years old and a recent immigrant from the Soviet Union, bar mitzvahed before the revolution. Reb Volf is being reintroduced to Judaism; Ber tells me that the day after Rosh Hashanah, he realized that people were fasting, and he asked whether it was Yom Kippur.[39]

Ber is the son of Rabbi Meir Hirshkovitz, a famous "liberal" Orthodox rabbi. This came up in the context of a discussion about shared peoplehood between Israeli Jews and Jews elsewhere. Ber told me about an American Jewish Congress "dialogue" meeting where an Israeli woman had said that as far as she was concerned, the history of Israeli Jews was a separate one from that of other Jews. I told him I'd heard the same story from Ruhama Hertz. He remembered meeting her at that meeting, and telling her how much her father's work had meant to him, and inviting her to Shilo, which she ducked out of accepting. This brought us to the general topic of the refusal of leftists

---

37. Read, "He emphasized to me the sense that this is the cradle of Judaism, of the Jewish people, that there is a discrepancy between the historical area and the contemporary State of Israel."

38. Analogous, perhaps, to a widespread tendency to view Palestinian leftist or fundamentalist guerrillas as irrational fanatics.

39. The day after Rosh Hashanah, the Fast of Gedalya, is one of several annual historically based, dawn-to-dusk fast days in the Jewish calendar.

to come to visit settlers. When Ber taught at Pardes,[40] sometimes students would ask whether he'd be willing to teach in a Conservative or Reform synagogue. He said his father always would; he said that though he wouldn't pray with them, as far as he was concerned their prayers were heard by God. But these same students at Pardes refused to come into the territories.[41]

Later, Ber takes me over to meet Reb Volf and his wife, Dobe. Between Ber's house and Reb Volf's, there's a house that's very much in Palestinian style. Ber says, "You guessed it — that's a Yemenite family." But I certainly wouldn't have assumed that Yemenites would build like Palestinians....

There's no fence around Shilo [David Noam, who gave me Ber's name, suggested I ask about it]. It's a continuing issue of contention — the government wants them to have a fence, and they don't want to put one up (sign of their insistence that they belong there?).

Ber says that under David Levy as housing minister in the mid-1980s there was very little building here, since Levy spent most of his budget in the development towns which were his base. Just before Sharon came in this last time there was a little bit of construction, and now with Sharon in and the Soviets coming, there are a hundred new units going up in the neighborhood at the top of the hill.

I asked Ber whether he thinks that Shilo is really far out. He says that there are settlements in the Jenin-Tulkarm area which are more isolated from the Israeli superstructure. But people in mainstream, bourgeois Israeli society see a place like Shilo as being really far out. He sees it as being roughly in the situation that kibbutzim were in during the earlier periods, when the country was less populated and mass communications and mass transportation were less developed. Yes, also — basically Ber feels that when the new one hundred houses are built and there are families in them, and there certainly will be families in them, then the feeling of pioneering will be over. He says that before the intifada people didn't talk so much about what would happen in the eventuality of territorial compromise, what to do about the Arabs, what would be just — it only came out in periods of crisis. [There had, for instance,

---

40. A generally liberal institute of rabbinic studies in Jerusalem, one of the very few, for example, where men and women study together.

41. This pointed comparison rests on the presumed analogy between two differences of principle, one "religious" and the other "political." In both cases, Hirshkovitz suggests, the dilemma is whether to "stand on principle" by refusing to enter the space controlled by those with whom you differ, to hear them, and to address them in their own space. What presumably prevented the students at Pardes from coming to Shiloh was the conviction, shared by many liberal and leftist Israelis especially since the beginning of the intifada, that the Occupied Territories were essentially Palestinian land and therefore should not be entered without a Palestinian invitation. By setting up an analogy with a diasporic situation strictly between Jews (and not involving coercive violence in any respect; see the third footnote following this one), Hirshkowitz erases the Palestinian presence as a factor.

been] a debate whether to send a few families down to live in Yamit.[42] At that time there were only thirty-five families in Shilo, so it meant setting the development of the community back for a year or two. Since the intifada, he says, the sense of rootedness has increased. People feel that this is where they live, and it doesn't feel temporary anymore.

Ber also drew an analogy between the people at Shilo and the American Havura Movement[43] — very different forms and directions, but a similar impulse to communitarianism and an aversion to standard materialism. (Cf. Sandy Weitzer a week before, complaining that beards, long hair, and flannel had been taken by the settlers as symbols from "us." I'm sure even she realizes that many of the settlers are "us.")[44]

Something I want to take back to the States: the belief that demonizing settlers doesn't help us to help the situation.

I asked Ber about the big highway going through. He said that some land had been confiscated from Turmus 'Aiya. They also confiscated some land from Shilo. It's the highway to Eli, which is twice as big now as it was a year ago — or a lot bigger in any case, there's a lot of new construction — and which is intended to be sort of the metropolitan center for this area of settlements. And the new highway is also intended as part of the big new main road from Ramallah all the way up to Nablus and Jenin (in fact it will go all the way up to Afula).

Reb Volf and his wife seem very satisfied to be here. They say they're treated well, and people are very warm to them. They're the oldest people in Shilo. Why did they leave? Well, a lot of people were leaving and they didn't want to be left in Russia when there were no other Jews, and the doors were open — they didn't want to be left feeling like they were stuck and didn't get out when they could.

Through the hills here, starting just before Shilo, there are small fertile valleys scattered among the hills. Ber explains that they continue until the Emek Yizrael, and that this area hence constituted a border area between the Kingdom of Israel and the Kingdom of Judah, between the hill country and the valley country.

---

42. Yamit was a settlement in the Sinai, part of the region that was returned to Egypt in line with the Camp David agreements. The dismantling of Yamit was bitterly opposed by its residents and by many other Israelis.

43. *Havurot* are a particular type of Jewish religious and communal association inspired by the communalist spirit of the 1960s.

44. In this respect, the "ideological" settlements are also often portrayed as the true heirs of the original, self-sacrificing, idealistic kibbutz pioneers. Unlike American *havurot*, however, and unlike hippie communes in the United States in the 1960s, West Bank settlements depend for their existence on privileged ties to a state that controls the means of violence and directly uses violence to protect their presence.

[Going back] I get onto the bus that comes through, letting people off at Shilo on its way up to a new little settlement called Maalei Levonot, which will come back up to Shilo — but I just wanted to see. [Breathless, melodramatic tone]: The terracing... terracing here is astonishing! On this side, going up an incredible hillside to Maalei Levonot — which does have a fence around it. [Checking later, I see that Maalei Levonot is at least formally at least five years old, since it appears on my Carta map from 1986.]

Ber says the Arabs in this area moved in basically in the 1850s and 1860s, and they are refugees from Syria.

Ber can't imagine any settlers being allowed to stay in a Palestinian state or wanting to stay.

Ber would be happy to meet Un Najwa and to show her the *tel*.[45]

•

About 50 percent of the people in Shilo are employed locally. Many are in education, some at the yeshiva *hesder*[46] located in Shilo, some in primary schools which serve the area. The rest work in Jerusalem.

Ber also doesn't think that most of the settlers or the Israeli government really have a transfer plan particularly in mind — they're simply sort of bulling through in a style he explicitly traces back to Ben-Gurion (making reality conform eventually to your vision) and creating facts.

Interesting that Ber's sense of alienation from the Israeli secular left — because they don't acknowledge, it doesn't seem important to them in any case, or they're actively irritated by the importance of the West Bank hills, Judea, and Samaria, as the heartland of Judaism — coincides with his diminished sense that there's a possibility of giving up these territories in exchange for a real peace.

Ber's comment after my description of my two previous projects on Jewish memory: "Now you're doing the big one." Ber agrees that a synthetic ethnography of the Israeli-Palestinian conflict is virtually impossible, so my fragmentary, anecdotal approach is appropriate.

• 10/8/91 •

Sunday morning I, Najwa, Alex, Ian Bailey,[47] and a woman named Jean Rivers who teaches conflict resolution at a community college in California were

---

45. On Najwa el-Hakim, see the entry for August 4. I raised the possibility of her visiting Shilo on my own initiative, rather than at her request, and my mention of Ber's positive response is probably intended to show that he is open-minded and confident in his own articulation of his situation.

46. A religious yeshiva with links to the state, whose students serve in the army.

47. Alex is Alex Kracauer of the Alternative Information Center. Ian Bailey is a Canadian who at this time was doing human rights work for the Bir Zeit University community.

taken on a "settlement tour" by a man named Khalil (I don't even know his last name) who is the cartographer for the Arab Studies Society.[48] The area we concentrated on was near the Green Line on both sides, in the foothills area east of Kfar Sava and Netanya, up to and around Qalqilya, which is just across the Green Line, and Taibeh, which is just inside the Green Line.

The first stop was Re'ut, one of the places referred to as the "thirteen stars," a series of settlements, some already built, some under construction, and some planned, which will straddle the Green Line in this area. Re'ut is inside the Green Line. It looks like there are perhaps two thousand units already finished or under construction, relatively few of which are occupied so far. Behind, to the east, are the mountains of the West Bank; in front, to the west, is the coastal plain. You can see why an old-fashioned military strategist would want to control this area. A few hundred meters away is a slightly older settlement called Maccabeem, which is in a no-man's-land that between 1948 and 1967 belonged neither to Israel nor to Jordan. A few kilometers farther north are settlements across the Green Line. Khalil explained to us that, first of all, these settlements effectively push the "Green Line" farther to the east; and, more complexly, that they are part of the northern of two bands intended to separate the Arab population centers into three cantons. The southern band consists of Maalei Adumim and the planned developments continuing all the way down to Jericho in the east, which will isolate the Hebron region. So, although it was difficult throughout the day for us to get the general picture of Khalil's interpretation of the Israeli settlement strategy, I tried summarizing it this way: it's a threefold strategy. First, the two bands of settlement from west to east, one Maalei Adumim down to Jericho, and the second from Ariel on to the east, cutting the Arab population of the West Bank into three "cantons." Second, a line of settlements from north to south, moving the Green Line progressively east. And third, surrounding major cities, in particular Hebron, with settlements.

In the unfinished shopping center in Re'ut, there was a banner on one storefront saying *"Bet sefer lemusika Yamaha."*[49] There's also going to be a frozen yogurt store. There's a housewares and gift shop that's already open. The Supersol has an Ultra Slim-Fast display. Alex says that the prices for wine at the Supersol are cheaper than in Jerusalem. The signs are in Hebrew, English, and Russian.

When Ian asks Khalil what we should be doing politically now, Khalil points out that while 70 percent of the land on the West Bank has been

---

48. Run by Faisal Husseini, scion of one of the leading families in the Palestinian national movement, a prominent Palestinian spokesperson vis-à-vis the Israeli public and, especially since the Israeli-Palestinian negotiations began in late 1991, in international fora as well.

49. Yamaha Music School.

confiscated, only about 4 percent of that is actually being built on, and the cost of that construction so far is about 6.5 billion dollars. He says that if you want to make peace, the confiscation is not irreversible.

Khalil wants to take us to a settlement called Avnei Khefets, where, he says, Sharon has claimed that six hundred units are being put up, but all Khalil saw the last time he was there was forty units. Khalil seemed genuinely puzzled over why Sharon would want to inflate the claim — perhaps assuming that Sharon would rather minimize the extent of the settlement construction. We responded that (*a*) for internal consumption, Sharon is motivated to emphasize how much he's getting done, and (*b*) for external consumption, Sharon is motivated to present the settlement and annexation of the West Bank as a fait accompli.

In Cochav Yair, a large suburban settlement just inside the Green Line, I notice a series of streets named after regions — Hasharon, Hashfela, Hashomron[50] — and then I realize as we pull up to a sudden stop at the end of the town (across which is the Green Line, thus far and no more for this particular town) that we've been driving along Shderot Ha'arets.[51] Then I see another series of streets named after plants — Vered, Hadas....[52] So the significance of place-names here seems to be a combination of particularly Israeli references, with the kinds of categories for street names in different parts of a planned development that would be used in a new American development as well (where it might be states, women's names, presidents, trees...).

One of the villages we have to pass through to get to one of the settlements Khalil wants to show us is under curfew, so we have to take a smaller road around through the hills and through other villages. It's a strike day,[53] and we're even more conspicuous because both the car Alex is driving, and Ian's car, which I'm riding in, have yellow license plates. As we drive into the villages we get some hostile looks from groups of boys walking down the road, but we drive slowly and Khalil waves and speaks to everybody in Arabic. Most of the people either ignore us or return our greetings of *"Marhaba"* and *"Ahlan."* Here, especially given that no major roads have been put through and the small road we're on involves hairpin turns through dry hills which

---

50. Respectively, the central coastal region; the foothills of the Judean Hills; and the northern part of the West Bank, often called Samaria in Israel.
51. Nation Boulevard.
52. Rose and Myrtle.
53. Throughout the intifada, various Palestinian groupings called regular general strikes on different days of the week and months as a means of nonviolent protest and refusal to cooperate with the business as usual of Israeli occupation. The degree to which such strikes were observed in various parts of the Occupied Territories was taken as a mark of the relative strength of groups such as Fatah and Hamas, and varying degrees of intimidation were intermittently used to enforce the strikes.

remind me of Provence, I feel like I'm finally seeing the rural West Bank in a way I didn't even on the road to Shilo.

Outside a settlement across the Green Line called Tsofim, we pull off to check out the view, onto a dirt track leading to a small Bedouin settlement. These Bedouin, unlike the people in Ramye, really are living in tents.

We arrive at Avney Khefets [Fn.: the reference is to a passage in the Haftorah[54] for Parshat Noach,[55] from Isaiah]. It's a few kilometers in from Taibeh, on a very basic road. It's a very new settlement with only a couple of dozen families apparently living there; there are indeed only about forty trailers, and some of them are not occupied yet. To get in past the soldier on guard, Alex concocted a story about looking for a family of new Russian immigrants that we, the Americans, had known in Ulpan.[56] He gets into a conversation with the representative of the regional council who happens to be there, who goes and checks at the office to see if there's anybody by the name Alex gave, but is suspicious: "Are you sure you're not journalists?" Alex keeps up the bluff, asking whether there are any new settlements nearby where these people might be living. The man from the regional council asks Khalil where he's from, and he says he's from Jerusalem. Later Alex says that he told Alex, "I'm sure he's from a minority group." The whole thing made me feel distinctly uncomfortable; I hate this kind of deception, because it feels like someone is being humiliated, even if he doesn't know it.[57] We extricate ourselves, and coming out, the gate is blocked: a Mercedes with yellow plates and an Arab driver has gotten stuck in the ditch at the side of the road. We help push it out. Ian says he must be a collaborator; I suggest he's probably just a contractor. We agree that the difference isn't clear. On our way back out from Avney Khefets, we notice a couple of Israeli soldiers at a lookout point on the roof of a Palestinian house at the top of a hill next to the road, and a middle-aged woman entering the house. How does she feel about having them on her roof? How do they feel about being on her roof?

I ask Khalil about the very wealthy-looking village inside the Green Line we passed just before the turnoff for Avney Khefets. He and Alex tell me

---

54. The reading from the Prophets following the weekly Torah portion in the synagogue.
55. The second of the weekly Torah readings in the annual synagogue cycle.
56. An intensive Hebrew-language immersion program.
57. One of the official Israeli euphemisms for non-Jews in the State of Israel is "minority groups," which includes Arabs but also smaller ethnic communities such as the Circassians and Druze. The man from the regional council had no proper reason to be concerned with Khalil's nationality. Although I did not record it at the time, this man's skin was fairly dark, and I imagined him to be a Mizrachi Jew who had achieved a steady but unrewarding government post. Perhaps my discomfort with the game we played in deceiving him has to do with an exaggerated sympathy I somewhere acquired for people who are stuck in petty bureaucratic jobs and who adjust their horizons accordingly.

that in this village, Taibeh, and the nearby village of Tira, while all the men work outside, they also do intensive agriculture and make a lot of money from that, especially strawberries. Alex adds, and Khalil concurs, that the people from these two villages used to hire workers from Gaza, and certainly treated them no better than Israelis employers would have. They kept the Gazans in "caves," and forbade their children from speaking with them. Alex says they were treated like slaves; Khalil says no, they were treated like mosquitos. They also both say that Taibeh and Tira are centers of drug use and selling in Israel. Khalil says it's claimed that the drugs come through Gaza, but he thinks most of the smuggling is from Lebanon.

Taibeh is at the edge of the valley, and its land (such as has been retained in the ownership of the village) is rich bottomland. Obviously this is a place in the valley where people managed to stay in 1948 — an interesting footnote to my conversation with Riad when I was in Ar'ara.

Lunch in Tira, with a guy who, Alex tells me, was one of the first people sentenced to death in Israel for an attack on a bus in the late 1960s. He was in jail with an Israeli businessman who was convicted of massive fraud. The Israeli pleaded to be let out, claiming that he was going to be killed by this man who buys us lunch. Alex says that in order for Begin to get the Israeli out of jail, they faked a urine test saying that he had cancer. For what it's worth, Alex also says that the head of the village, who's a "collaborator," has officially been a member of the DFLP[58] for fifteen years — the deal was made that if he joined the DFLP on paper, they'd keep him in office. The government has just returned forty dunams of land to him, for forty years of good behavior.... Alex jokes that this must be the only place in Israel where high school kids drive their own cars! I smell some of the village's produce: a packing house full of the intoxicating and unmistakable smell of guavas. I buy a tray, maybe five kilos for eight shekels, one of which the sellers return to me. Ruth will maybe make guava jelly.

The Green Line seems much less present in the area around Qalqilya; we've been crisscrossing it all day. Ian tells me that though in principle, everyone in the West Bank needs a pass to go anywhere inside Israel, the police tend to be much stricter about this in the Jerusalem area than elsewhere in the country.

Najwa joins me in Ian's car for the ride back to Jerusalem: she finds Khalil informative and Alex full of wild stories, a real character, but Jean Rivers's horrified overreaction to every view of a new settlement becomes wearing. We get into a strange conversation about Osnat's[59] note to me about my

---

58. The Democratic Front for the Liberation of Palestine.
59. Osnat Cohen, an anthropologist at the University of California at Davis. When we

gushing over Qetura (I raised the issue). Najwa doesn't see my point about Qetura seeming less soiled with expropriation; it's part of Zionism, she says, part of taking over the land of another nation. I say, "Well, I guess I'm just making a distinction you're not making," but go on to try to explain myself some more: if anything, the problem with the agricultural development of the Arava is a question whether or not the ecology can support it, and anyhow I don't think people have ever thought of the Arava as part of Palestine, etc. A strange and awkward conversation, difficult to sum up.

• 10/16/91 •

Sitting under trees on the square at Dizengoff,[60] waiting to see whether the Agam fountain is really going to go into a show at 11:00 as the sign promises. It's perfectly cool in the shade, there are pigeons, a child chasing them, and I'm reading *The Accidental Tourist*. The jets of water in the fountain rise and fall to the rhythm of the music. It's cute.

"It was one of Macon's bad habits to start itching to go home too early. No matter how short a stay he'd planned, partway through he would decide that he had to leave, that he'd allowed himself far too much time, that everything truly necessary had already been accomplished — or almost everything, almost accomplished.... He always promised himself this wouldn't happen again, but somehow it always did" (*The Accidental Tourist*, p. 37).

• 10/17/91 •

Brief conversation with a street sweeper named Kobi, maybe forty years old, thin, medium height, short dark hair, blind in one eye. As I stroll by we catch each other's eye. He says, "*Ma nishma?*"[61] and we start talking. He gives me a cigarette. He asks me where I'm from, where I'm coming from; asks me whether I'm coming from the *mikvah*.[62] I don't know why, maybe because I'm wearing a yarmulke and I'm carrying a bag that looks like it would have things for the *mikvah*. I asked him where he was from, because he asked me where

---

had spoken in Jerusalem during the summer, I evidently enthused about Qetura. I also told Osnat about my visits to Ramye and my contacts for the visits there. Osnat wrote to thank me for helping her to visit Ramye and also mentioned that what I had said about the kibbutz made her uncomfortable.

60. All through the summer I had promised myself and several friends that at the end of the summer I would spend at least a week lying on the beach in Tel Aviv. The fact is that I had never felt comfortable in Tel Aviv before, especially in the humid midsummer heat. Around this time I finally went for a few days.

61. "What's new?" (Hebrew; a calque of the Yiddish "*Vos hert zikh*").

62. The ritual bath.

I was from, and I thought he was going to say Gaza. [I didn't really think so, that was just my hypothesis.] He said Tel Aviv; [apparently] he was Jewish in fact. He asked me who I was staying with, I told him friends I knew from New York. He asked me how I liked Israel, and I said, "Well, I don't really feel at home here with all the guns, all the soldiers...." Then I said, sort of by way of admission or something [call it better an attempt at cultural-relativist generosity], that there's a lot of murder in New York, there's a lot of drugs.... He asked me if I'd ever taken cocaine. I said, "No," which is not quite true. I said, "Marijuana — that's light...." He said, "I have marijuana here," pointing to his shoulder, and raised his T-shirt to reveal a little tattoo of a marijuana leaf, which he said he'd gotten in Holland. When I asked him his name he said "Kobi," and I told him my name was Yonatan. He said, "Oh, that's a beautiful name." I thanked him for the cigarette, he asked if I wanted another, I said, "No, thanks — *lehitraot*." What's this? There's no ethnographic information of substance in this paragraph, except that I had a gentle conversation with a street sweeper.

• 10/20/91 •

Yesterday morning the air was so clear that walking away from Yemin Moshe toward Baka'a,[63] for the very first time I could see past the ridge of hills on which Abu Dis lies all the way to the mountains on the east side of the Jordan River, the mountains of Jordan, seeing them clearly where there'd always been a haze before.... This morning it's wonderfully cool, like a mild autumn. I've got exactly three weeks left. So three weeks left: I can visualize my homecoming so intensely that it seems I could take a giant step across three weeks and be there, and then again it's astonishing that I still have to wait. And my eagerness to be home is starting to mix with nostalgia, which I feed with a determination to come back next summer with Elissa and Jonah, and a sense that Jerusalem will become a regular stopping place in my work much as Paris has. I feel half gone, and I don't feel the tremendous weight of the occupation the way I did all summer; and I feel a bit giddy and greedy and confused. I want all of the love at once.

• 10/30/91 •

Ten days since my last entry; it seems that I took my own self-imposed goal of three hundred pages quite seriously, since I virtually stopped writing once

---

63. Back in Jerusalem already, and living once again in the old apartment in Yemin Moshe where I had stayed at the beginning of my time in Jerusalem.

I reached it. And I'm more tired than anything of commenting on the note-taking process itself! But just once more... this afternoon on my way to Van Leer to meet Walid (surprise! he was there this time, and we had a great conversation for two hours, and we made a tentative appointment for him to come to dinner to meet Elissa in New York in two weeks, talk about space-time compression!),[64] I ran into the same Palestinian woman I write about on September 25, who got five shekels out of me. She didn't get anything out of me today; the weather's changed, it's "fall" (nobody seems to refer to it being fall here; the weather changed yesterday, it poured rain, and the wind blew all over the country — fantastic — and now everybody says it's winter all of a sudden), it feels like New York out, and I'm practically home; I wasn't feeling psychologically needy like I was that day and besides she wasn't carrying a basket on her head and she wasn't even wearing a Palestinian dress. So there!

Well, there's a twinge of regret that so much happens without being recorded, but so be it. As it happens, what gets me writing again now is a fax from Santa Cruz, with an invitation to a conference on "The Culture of Ruins." Actually they want me to talk about Masada and the Wall — well I've never been up Masada, and I don't know that much about the Wall. But I'm coming back in December anyway, so I'll spend a few more days here and do a bit more — thinking about it I realize I have a fair amount of material about "ruins" as it is (Randi with the Nabateans, the Torah Department tour with the fifth-century synagogue, the terraced hillsides); anyway I do want to try to get to Masada just so I can say I've been there, and maybe Najwa will come with me so it can be a bit of dialogic fieldwork,[65] and I just arranged for Riad to take me to some ruined Palestinian villages as we'd discussed in June, and I'd like to see 'Ein Hod, and I'd like to talk to Steven MacKern's friend the archaeologist from Haifa Adam Zertal.

---

64. The phrase is borrowed from David Harvey's book *The Condition of Postmodernity*. Harvey identifies a recurring process in capitalist development whereby new technical developments driven by the demand for capital accumulation produce radical and sudden diminutions of the time required to travel or communicate between various points. The effects of the most recent space-time compression entail elements such as mass airplane travel and the fax. Harvey sees them as marking a time that is distinctive in some ways, but — more than other analysts of postmodernity — he sees these as essentially continuous with modern capitalism. The effect on the "classic" distinction between field site and home research base is obvious, and the form of this book is part of the debate within anthropology on how to respond to the current compression.

The dinner did take place, but it was disappointing: Walid, who had come for a speaking engagement, was exhausted and out of sorts, and so was I.

65. How wonderfully crass this "arrangement" seems now! When I returned in December, Israel and Palestine had been visited by the worst rains in many years (after a long drought). The roads south were washed out, and it was impossible for Najwa and me to go to Masada together. As documented in the last chapter, we did go to Biram/Bir'im and to other ruined villages with Riad.

Meanwhile this, which I have to enter into my diary before it gets away entirely, and which will already go in molded toward the purposes of that presentation, and which as I say I probably wouldn't have "written up" at all without the invitation from Santa Cruz, which would have been a shame.

Last Tuesday (October 29) I traveled with Sam Englander for a day of touring with a group of American Protestants, mostly clergy and all prospective Holy Land tour leaders. We visited, uh, four or five sites: Nabi Samwel just north and west of Jerusalem, which Sam explained is the grave of the prophet Samuel according to an originally Christian tradition, but which now has a mosque with one grave of the prophet Samuel and a synagogue with another grave — Sam calls them First Samuel and Second Samuel, and which also (here's the hook to ruins) has one Palestinian house left of what was formerly a village on this site, a high hill overlooking ancient Gibeon (now the village of El Jib) with a commanding view back to Jerusalem and through the Judean plateau. I won't even try to reproduce Sam's masterful panoramic explanation of the various biblical sites visible from the spot, including Rama to the east, and so on.... Anyway Sam's explanation of the reason for the one Palestinian house still being there is that sometime in the 1970s, the Israelis came to demolish all the houses and expel the inhabitants into Jordan. Only one family was away visiting relatives near Nablus, and since it's illegal to demolish a house without informing the owners, this house was left standing, and subsequently the order to demolish was successfully defeated in court. So there you are. Ruins even when you aren't looking for them.

Next stop was Tel Bet Shean, very briefly; it remains mostly unexcavated. The Ark of the Covenant was brought to Bet Shean, according to the biblical story, by the Philistines, who realized that terrible things were happening to them anyplace where they kept it themselves. The "Jews" of Bet Shean had trouble with it themselves; seventy of them died from approaching it. It was then brought to Kiryat Yearim for eleven years (remember my description of my evening in Abu Ghosh, and the tour of the church?), before finally being brought to Jerusalem by David.

Now here comes a high point: Tel Maresha (Beit Guvrin), a site in the foothills (the *shfela*; Sam resisted translating this as "foothills" because of what he calls a natural "moat" separating it from the Judean mountains per se) of an ancient city which was destroyed by John Hyrkanus in 113 B.C.E. Maresha was, like other cities along valleys through the *shfela*, largely a strategic post guarding the way from the coast up through the valleys into the mountains — although, as Sam stressed throughout the day, the mountains rise so steeply and suddenly on every side except the north that the only time they were ever conquered from those sides was when there were collaborators already up in the hills; this insularity in the mountains, he insisted, has a lot to do with the conditions that enabled the formulation of ancient Judaism (so maybe his next book should be the social ecology of ancient Judaism?).[66] But Maresha was also a wealthy city; it derived its living largely from the export of olive oil to Egypt (where, apparently, it's too hot to grow olives well), and later on from the burning of limestone to make plaster — I don't think that was until Roman times. The limestone is very soft, which permits not only mining of it for burning for plaster (the area around Maresha is riddled with small mine shafts through the rock), but carving for all sorts of economic purposes, such that the basis of various family's sustenance is located literally underneath their houses. Five thousand people lived at Maresha; a great deal of the site remains to be excavated. But what has been excavated is fascinating. Thus, following Sam, our group came to the site of a two-story house with a number of rooms, which has been excavated (and restored?) to the point where you see the layout. Interesting enough. Then you go inside the house, and start walking down a staircase in the interior. You keep walking down! There's a huge, cylindrical cistern underneath this house — maybe ten meters deep by five wide, cut right into the limestone, which has now been thoroughly excavated. The stairs are a bit tricky, but basically by now they've been well prepared for people to walk down and through. Sam did stress that six soldiers had died (all at once?) exploring this before it was fixed up — just because the descent had been so treacherous (slipping and falling into the cistern). Also one archaeologist. Then directly from the bottom of the cistern you can now walk into the "basement" of another house, which was simply carved out for getting the limestone — in other words, there was a mine under the house! In a third place, you go down a set of steps to an elaborate underground olive press. Then, walking around the site (all this is at the bottom of the huge acropolis, which has not yet been excavated as far as I can tell), on the other side of the hill, you walk down into the "columbarium," a chamber in the form of a cross, perhaps twenty-five meters long, with a couple of side chambers, and with niches for two-thousand pigeons cut into the rock. Sam explains that there were debates for many years about the ancient purpose of this construction — were the doves grown for sacrifice in the temple, or what? Finally someone came up with an explanation which seems convincing: they were there for fertilizer. Apparently the pigeons would be brought inside and given

---

66. At this time he was putting the finishing touches on, and agonizing over the title of, *Confession from a Jericho Jail* (Langfur 1992), a highly readable and moving account in the form of a diary kept during his twenty-eight day stay in military jail for refusing to perform reserve army duty in the West Bank. In fact the book contains an extended discussion of Langfur's thesis that profound theological and social shifts were linked to the development of large cisterns for water storage, which reduced the ancient Israelites' dependence on the vagaries of the weather and helped enable the first stable, class-structured Israelite kingdom.

enough food for about two weeks, which was enough time for them to establish nests. Then the covers at ground level were opened, and the birds could fly out to feed, and come back to roost, meanwhile producing manure for fertilizer. The mundane purpose is an ironic counterpoint to the churchlike feel of the interior, deep, regular as it is, with lighting to make it even more impressive. While we were there, a single pigeon flew around the columbarium, as if to give a demonstration. To recapitulate, the themes I found most salient there for my purposes were the ways that this particular ecology and an appropriate technology had sustained a large community there in ancient times, the danger (although this mentioned only in passing) inherent in the process of domesticating an archaeological site, and the way the existence of these ancient communities tells us much about the ecological/strategic bases of Israelite ethnicity and religion.

Next stop on the day was Hirbat Medras, a *tel* which hasn't been excavated at all — except for tunnels under the unwalled town which, Sam explained, were built as part of the preparations for the Bar Kokhba rebellion against the Romans. Only about seven of the twenty-five people on the trip — all men, two of them being Sam and myself — rose to the challenge of actually crawling through these tunnels for a bit. The idea was that defenders could crawl out through the tunnels, and strike at the Romans who wouldn't know where they'd come from; and the tunnels were narrow enough so that presumably Romans in armor wouldn't be able to crawl back through them; and they're also warrens, such that you wouldn't be able to follow if you didn't know your way around them. Sam says these are only found in unwalled sites; why, neither he nor I could really figure out. Anyway the seven of us crawled through these tunnels for just a total of seventeen minutes (which included several minutes in one of the larger interior "halls" while one of the group tried to take a picture, and tried to make his flash work). This involved some tight squeezing — about ten feet where you had to just push through on your back, holding your arms on your stomach because there was no place else to put them, and another spot where you had to crawl through on your elbows. OK, no dramatic points here, just that it was a kind of "experiential" way of dealing with ruins, and we felt we'd earned the *shmutz* on our clothes by the time we got out. Earned it? The question is, what had we "produced"?

•

Important: after a week in which Randi seemed so tired and withdrawn into herself (bad foot, working in the packing plant, which she hates, doing extra milkings, who knows what else was going on), we finally went dancing in Eilat Saturday night. Pulling out of Ketura, we gave a lift to a member of the kibbutz — an American guy named Alon, who works half the week in Tel Aviv as an environmental lawyer. He talked about his appointment two days later[67] in favor of a recycling law for Israel. Then asked me about myself, and I mentioned I was going home shortly. "We didn't hook you this time, huh?" I said that I hadn't been here on a trial at all — I was planning to return all along. Later I said to Randi that I find it really irritating when people assume that I am or should be coming here to stay, assuming that this is where I belong. "It's like people assuming you're heterosexual," she came back, which was brilliant and I love her for it, and I may have more to say about this yet.

• 11/7/91 •

To Lifta with Ruth Selden yesterday. Ruth is a graduate student of Hebrew at Berkeley, and a fascinating person in her own right, but now I'm just writing for the sake of my presentation to the culture of ruins conference.

I believe I've remarked on Lifta before in this journal: the ruined/abandoned Arab village on the hillside to the left, just as you're entering Jerusalem. Since noticing it — maybe I never noticed it before this trip, in a way you have to be looking for it, as Moti remarked, most people probably don't see it at all — I've wondered at it, because it seems very unusual that the Israelis would leave a ruined/abandoned village as conspicuous as this one without either destroying it or renovating it. From the road it seemed even to me a very dreary place, the houses gray of course, built out of Jerusalem limestone and not cleaned for God knows how long. Apparently Lifta is in fact caught up in some sort of complicated long-term legal dispute, and that's why it's in this state. I'll try to track the story down more exactly; maybe Riad or Greg Rossman knows something. (Hard to concentrate even on writing notes now; David Hartman is holding forth to a seminar in the next room.) It may be that were it not for this dispute, Lifta would have been reinvested and renovated the way Ein Karem has, although it's on a steeper hillside. Anyway: the village was clearly a wealthy one; the houses are large, the walls massive, the lower basement floors seem quite ancient — at least of a style of arched and vaulted stone construction that seems like it could be thousands of years old. The wealthier houses have, on the upper floors, rooms perhaps fifteen meters long with vaulted ceilings five meters high or so. Some of the tiled floors remain, although some have already been stolen; in one house, where a pool of rainwater had collected, the rich colors of the floor tiles could be seen. The houses hug a steep hillside, as I've said, and are grouped on the two flanks of the hillside that come outward from a central narrow valley which contains a spring — Ma'ayan Niftoach, from which the fancy Mizrachi restaurant higher up the hill takes its name. (Carved into the rock above the

---

67. Insert, "to testify."

opening that leads back to the spring is the figure of a key, which must have some connection to the name of the spring.) The area around the spring itself seems to have been renovated by the Israelis; the opening in the rock leading back to the spring itself seems to have been carved out and shored up, the water flows into a couple of small pools, and the stone plaza and walkways around it seem to be too regular and too well-maintained to simply be a remain from pre-1948. Walking around, it's also clear that the structure of irrigation canals, terraces, and walkways, and perhaps even a sewage canal, was quite complex, and that whatever has been done by the Israelis if anything is not really in the way of "improvements." Also, the pool is evidently in some way used by Orthodox Jewish men — conceivably as a *mikvah*. When Ruth and I arrived, there were three men there; one clearly Jewish and Orthodox, closing up his pants, and two others whom we first took for Arabs, until they finished dressing as well. When we passed by on our way back up, there was a single Orthodox man there, eating lunch perhaps, also with his shirttails out however. You can see where the irrigation canals lead down from these pools to water the carefully terraced hillsides, and you can see the natural limestone terraces interacting with the humanly produced terraces. (N.B.: Sam Englander, in his rap as we were in fact passing by Lifta on the way from Nabi Samwel to our next stop on the day I toured with his group, explained that the limestone striation was the original inspiration for the careful culture of terracing — something I had begun to wonder about months ago.) Altogether, partly because of the spring and partly because of the rain this week, tramping through the tumbling terraces of this hillside didn't quite feel like Palestine because the vegetation, even if it was past its season, seemed too lush, and there were actually muddy spots.

Ruth and I went into a number of the houses; you can sit in an empty window frame, and look out over the whole valley toward Beit Iksa (check) at one end, parallel to the road leading toward Tel Aviv, and toward the right you can see Ramot: what an almost tacky contrast to even mention it.[68] Because of the steepness of the hillside, some of the houses are more than ten meters high in front. There's a lot of graffiti in many of the houses; I didn't record too much, in fact I didn't take any notes while I was there, because I was too moved by the place and by being there with Ruth: I did catch "*Begin*

---

68. "Tacky" because of the violent contrast presented by Ramot's crowded, identical, almost treeless, American-suburb style occupation of the facing hillside. The contrast is indeed dramatic, although of course a resident or developer of Ramot might well interpret it proudly, as a mark of Israeli industry and vitality. In the critical context of this book, the problem with such blatant examples of the gap between Palestinian "absence" and Israeli development is that they may feed into a numbing impression of a monotonous, worldwide evacuation of anamnestic difference in the face of aggressive and essentially undifferentiated global capital investment.

*melech yisrael"* and, above one doorway, a Jewish star with the slogan *"Am yisrael chai."*[69] Many of the houses have clearly been used by squatters; there are remains of fires or even piles of firewood in some of the old living rooms, and smoke holes in the top of the roof in the middle of these rooms. The holes are rough; I wonder whether they were there at all before the houses were abandoned, or whether they've been punched out later. Also many window frames and nooks in the walls have little bunches of flowers placed in them; they seemed very much like the flowers that one would place in a cemetery, and it wasn't clear to Ruth and me what they might signify.

There are young almond trees on some of the slopes; it didn't seem to me that they could be from before 1948. This is the season for the almonds, and I opened a couple. Unfortunately they were quite bitter, and on the other hand they left a strong aftertaste of marzipan — much more so than one gets from eating fresh commercial almonds. As we walked toward the houses in the second flank of the village — the side of the hill down from the highway — I heard a cough, looked about twenty meters away, and saw a gazelle. I didn't see it so clearly; Ruth said it must be a young one.

Ruth says that Lifta has continued to live quite a shadowy life over the years; on the way down through the path from the highway (by the way, a few of the houses nearest the top of the hill, that is, nearest the highway and the road to Ramot, have been renovated or have been lived in throughout; I've always been fascinated by the couple of houses that are inhabited just to the right of the highway past the gas stations, that seem to hang on the side of the hill in the middle of nowhere, unless you see from beneath that they're actually the top of Lifta), we passed an old man in classic homeless person's rags. She also said that when she'd been living in Israel a few years ago, she'd known a group of Argentineans who used to bring generators and hold wild parties until 4:00 A.M. with loud music and drugs, until the police found out about them and they found more remote ruins farther away.... Ruth also says there are crime stories set in Lifta.

What else? Well, as we were walking back up, we passed a group of middle-aged Russians with a guide walking down toward Lifta. But clearly it hasn't yet been transformed into a tourist site per se.

To summarize: if I talk about Lifta in my paper, I think I'll focus on the transformation in my perception, from curiosity about the houses on the side of the road, to seeing the collection of ghostly houses from the hillside and wondering about them (again, they don't cohere as a village until you're there, and from the highway you certainly don't get a sense of how impres-

---

69. Respectively meaning "Begin, king of Israel" and "The people of Israel live!"

sive the houses and the landscaping were), to going and imagining a rich life there as it may have been.

• 11/8/91 •

Going to the bank this morning to close out my account, I met Rahamim, the man I'd sat next to on the Torah Department tour back in July. He invited me to his house, and made me Tunisian-style tea with *sheba*. (At Ramye I thought it was the same thing as *miramiya*, but it's not; one of them at least is I think sage.)[70] He has the bottom floor of a large house, and the layout and furnishing of his home strike me as a curious combination of Paris Yiddish and classic Middle Eastern; quite respectable in any case. He asked me whether I'd been thinking about the question I'd asked him — namely, whether I knew someone for him to marry. This time I took his name, phone number, and address, and promised I'd ask around Naftali Street. Ruth will ask Berta, the woman at the *makolet*[71] who found Ruth this apartment. Anyway seeing Rahamim, whom I'd thought of several times, provided a nice looping kind of closure.

---

70. *Miramiya* is sage; *sheba* is absinthe.
71. Corner grocery store.

# 6

# Ruins, Mounting toward Jerusalem

> Where national memories are concerned, griefs are of more value than triumphs, for they impose duties, and require a common effort.
>
> ERNEST RENAN (1990: 19)
>
> •
>
> Certainty may be a need for a man, but in itself, it is only a vacant reply to a penultimate question, with the ultimate left in suspense.
> ...vacant like a lot on which no building will ever rise because it would immediately tumble to ruins.
>
> EDMOND JABÈS (1989: 17; ellipsis in original)

This chapter deals primarily with the heritage of Palestinian dispossession—a history that constitutes an unmasterable past (see Maier 1988), for Israeli Jews and for all Jews, insofar as they identify with the State of Israel. This past that is not yet mastered is not over. It is still happening. It is meet therefore that my text be less than masterful. I will not conceal the fact that my "activity is one of arranging" (Benjamin 1977: 179). Any such presentation is nothing more nor less than a fragment of a continuing discussion.

I begin then not with the destruction of the Second Temple in Jerusalem, not with the book of Lamentations, which mourns that destruction, but with a striking passage of metadiscourse contained in Eichah Rabbah, the rabbinic midrashic commentary on Lamentations, composed in Palestine roughly between the fifth and seventh centuries C.E. The midrash informs us as follows:

> Rabbi used to expound the verse "The Lord laid waste without pity" in twenty-four ways. R[eb] Yohanan could expound it in sixty. Could it be that R. Yohanan was greater than Rabbi! Rather, because Rabbi was closer in time to the Destruction of the Temple he would remember as he expounded and stop to weep and console himself; he would begin again only to weep, console himself, and halt. R. Yohanan, because he was not close in time to the Destruction of the Temple, was able to continue to expound without pause. (Solomon Buber edition, 1899, p. 100, translated by Mintz 1984: 50)

We, of course, are much further in time from that destruction than even R. Yohanan was. We can compensate for that somewhat and move immediately very close to the destruction in space. Not, surely, onto the Temple Mount itself, as some contemporary Jewish zealots would like, since that is now a Muslim holy site. We can in any case approach that venerated outer wall somewhat inaccurately referred to as the Western Wall of the Temple. Let us imagine ourselves there. We have made aliya! We have, in the words of the biblical phrase that is the source of the current Israeli Hebrew term for immigration to Israel, "gone up" to Jerusalem, to the pinnacle of Jewish pilgrimage, to Judaism's highest ruin.

That this relic is visitable at all by Jews or by visitors to Israel is itself, of course, a mark of Israel victorious in the 1967 war. I first visited the Wall as a child, coming to Israel for the first time, only a few days after the end of that war. I remember hardly anything except a large, dusty, raw plaza. Indeed, as I try to recall that early memory, it is twice overlaid: first, by the image of the stone-paved courtyard, the paved entranceway, and the security checks that stand in front of the Wall today; second, by the phantoms of the Arab houses that, I have since been told, were destroyed to make space for that very plaza.

During the months I spent in Jerusalem in 1991, I had the nagging sense that I should have visited the Wall more, knowing that it, and the Dome of the Rock that lies behind and above it, are the very epicenters of the contest between Jews and Arabs for memory and territory. Yet it confused and repelled me in a way that I will not detail further now — except to say that I feel there none of the "concentrated holiness" that attracts so many other Jews to the spot. I visited the Wall only twice during that year, in fact: once for a generally failed attempt by Israeli peace activists to organize a ritual commemoration of the massacre of Palestinian worshipers on the Temple Mount on October 8, 1990; the second time for my nephew's swearing-in as a member of the elite paratroopers' unit of the Israeli Defense Forces, held at the Wall partly because it was the paratroopers who captured the area around the Wall in 1967.[1]

---

1. Don Handelman has provided us with an exhaustive ethnographic description of a similar ceremony, emphasizing that this monument serves as an effective prop for inculcating a sense of unity among Israeli citizens: "Throughout the [remembrance] ceremony [at the Wall] there is the decisive symbolic equation between 'oneness' and unity. Therefore there is little or no recognition of horizontal variation within categories of persons or symbols.... The version of moral and social order that is presented through this ceremony is marked by a sparseness and singularity of roles and symbols, by a homogeneity of membership, by a single-mindedness of intention, and by a oneness of being — of everything in its place, in a continuous hierarchy of heritage and legacy. An extremely holistic unity, in which each component imparts its sense of purpose to the one beneath, with little strain, competition, or conflict" (Handelman 1991: 210–11). The Wall did not suddenly become a political focus with the victory in 1967 or even with its loss to Jewish access in 1948. For the Wall as a site of political contention within the

I could find more to say about the wall in this chapter. But if — as I began just now — we ignore the journey from Ben-Gurion Airport and begin by facing the Western Wall, we thereby reinforce the obfuscation of another set of ruins available to the perceptive viewer from the highway leading up from Tel Aviv to Jerusalem. Where the most famous Jewish ruins in Israel — the Western Wall and Masada — are monumental relics of ancient Jewish state power, these Palestinian ruins, which easily blend into the landscape, stand as witness to domesticity and to local communal life (see Shammas 1989). This difference between national-monumental ruins and communal-domestic ones is compounded by the fact that the former are ancient, the latter virtually contemporary by comparison. The contest between these two different landscapes of commemoration is especially dramatic where they constitute chronotopes in collision. Thus the Dome of the Rock, still physically intact and in use, can nevertheless be spoken of as a relic of the long period of Muslim Arab hegemony. It sits on top of the site, and therefore presumably above the very ruins, of the Second Temple — excavation of which many Jews would consider sacrilege.

As the midrash suggests, some of the sting of loss represented by ruins may be diminished over the years. Nevertheless, although physical erosion takes place, old ruins don't just fade away; there is no external force called time that heals all wounds or effaces every trace. On the contrary, the rhetoric of ruins is a perfect example of the way destruction and loss are *created*. This is evidenced not by a "reversibility" in the process of creation and destruction but rather by a multiplicity of frames and effects that confounds the linearity that is still our first, unreflective assumption. Thus ancient ruins are subject in different ways to participatory immersion. This was brought home to me at a site called Hirbat Madras, a partially excavated Jewish settlement dating from the period of the disastrous Bar-Kokhba revolt against the Romans. In preparation for the rebellion, a honeycomb of narrow tunnels was dug out, enabling the residents of the town to slip out at night and conduct guerrilla — or should I say "terrorist" — attacks against the occupiers. Venturesome tourists visiting the site today can crawl through a portion of these tunnels themselves, experiencing the constriction of siege if not the desperate desire to shake off the oppressor. Thus the ancient ruins of Hirbat Madras envelope or incorporate the intrepid visitor.

More commonly the remains of former inhabitants — whether ancient or

---

Jewish community of Jerusalem in the nineteenth century, see Halper 1991: 104, 136; for its role in interethnic politics at the same period, see ibid: 35. For an indication of the potent symbolism of pilgrimage and restoration of the Temple in Israeli popular culture, listen to the song "Hilloula" on the best-selling tape *Masala*, by the group bearing the name Ha'etnix.

recent — are themselves incorporated within new architectures.[2] They need not of course be ruins. Thus the village of 'Ein Karem, outside Jerusalem, is now a lush and expensive center for tourists and artists. So is the former Arab village of 'Ein Hod south of Haifa, distinctive because descendants of some of the former residents of the village now live just two hills over, in a new village with the same name that has yet to be recognized by the Israeli government. The wealthy Jerusalem neighborhood of Baka'a, before 1948 ethnically mixed but predominantly Arab, is now a desirable address for Jewish Jerusalemites from Western countries. Buildings of Deir Yassin near 'Ein Karem, the site of a famous massacre by Menahem Begin's forces in 1948, are now incorporated into a mental hospital. It is easy to imagine some Palestinian version of *One Flew over the Cuckoo's Nest* set in Deir Yassin.

Ancient ruins incorporating tourists who arrive by jet. Relics of medieval empire on top of ruins of an ancient commonwealth, the site of murderous struggles today. Abandoned, evacuated houses left intact, coming into the hands of new residents from far away. All these reminders work against the tendency to assume that if, as Walter Benjamin wrote early in his career, "in the ruin history has physically merged into the setting" (Benjamin 1977: 177–78, cited in Crapanzano 1991), then this merging must be a "natural" process. The process that Benjamin notes is not only confirmed but aesthetically and morally endorsed in an essay by Georg Simmel, who assumes a priori an absolute dichotomy between nature and spirit. When a building becomes a ruin,

> the balance between nature and spirit, which the building manifested, shifts in favor of nature. This shift becomes a cosmic tragedy which, so we feel, makes every ruin an object infused with our nostalgia; for now the decay appears as nature's revenge for the spirit's having violated it by making a form in its own image....
> 
> For this reason, a good many Roman ruins, however interesting they may be otherwise, lack the specific fascination of the ruin — to the extent, that is, to which one notices in them the destruction *by man*; for this contradicts the contrast between human work and the effect of *nature* on which rests the significance of the ruin as such. (Simmel 1959)

Simmel insists that violence contradicts the meaning of the ruin — whereas it is almost always either overt violence, the imperiousness of a politico-economic system, or a disastrous shift in the resource base that initiates the process of ruination. This tendency to naturalize the process of ruination can and often does serve the state, as I will discuss at the end. It is hard to resist

---

2. For a discussion of the incorporation of Tenochtitlán into Mexico City, see Rabasa 1990.

rhetorically, and I will indulge it at first, only to break with it partially at the end of this text.

So if I focus the rest of this chapter on the ruins of pre-1948 Palestinian life in Israel, it is partly to confront the legacy of violence that ruins safeguard. But I am wary lest such a move smack of a too-easy appropriation of the mantle of the Other or the authoritative voice *for* (not of) the oppressed. The shift to a discussion of Palestinian ruins carries its own rhetorical dangers of naturalization, as does my framing of this paper within a Jewish hermeneutic, rather than an autonomous Palestinian, Muslim, or Arab tradition of commemoration. This chapter has been formulated within the context of a larger study of the critical challenge posed to Jewish collective identity by the formation and persistence of Palestinian collective identity. Hence, despite brief references to Palestinian colleagues toward the end, my main strategy is to record my own growing critical awareness. My attention to Palestinian ruins is both an extension of my work on Jewish memory and an attempt to assure myself that my own ambivalence toward the Jewish state is not just a phantasmatic personal quirk.

Is the dialogic model of fieldwork appropriate to an encounter with such ruins? Is a "dialogue" with ruins possible at all? Even my idea that the stone remains of prewar Palestinian life can be made to speak is a reference back to a Jewish source: a volume of photographs of synagogues and Jewish cemeteries in Poland published after World War II and titled in Yiddish *Shteyner dertseyln* — Stones retell (Gostynsky 1973). To the extent that we confront the Other only in relics, we are cast back even more on our own codes than in conversation with another living person. Which cannot gainsay the *desire* at least for autonomous communication reflected in a painful recognition of ruins.

We engage such theoretical aporiae best when we allow them to sharpen our work, to make us approach if not overcome the communicative barriers identified in theory and in personal encounters. Rather than "settle" the question of dialogue with ruins, it may be helpful to document a series of such encounters with ruins of pre-1948 Palestinian life that are visible from the modern Tel Aviv–Jerusalem Highway, thereby making explicit the notion of recursive difference implicit in my title. I hope thereby to suggest something about the way in which ruins either remain part of the background or alternatively come to the forefront of consciousness — a coming to consciousness that is always incomplete and to which the best response might be a straightforward acknowledgment of provisionality, against the comprehension and closure still expected of scholarly criticism.

The stretch I will be visiting and revisiting here begins at the place called in Arabic Bab-el-Wad and in Hebrew Sha'ar ha-Gay, both meaning "the gate to the valley." From this spot the new four-lane highway winds upward for perhaps fifteen miles before reaching the edge of Jerusalem, the first several miles through a narrow and steep pass.

Again, of my first visit to Israel in 1967, all I remember is what was doubtless pointed out to me: the hulks of armored cars on the side of the highway, relics of the battle for access to Jerusalem during the 1948 war. In several trips during the past years, I have noticed that these wrecks are periodically painted with rust-free paint, precisely to prevent their merging back into the landscape.

On later visits, I began to discern the remains of agricultural terracing on the dry, steep slopes of the wadi. Toward these I experienced an inchoate, doubtless romanticized nostalgia — precisely the kind of response to ruins evoked by Simmel, but already mixed with a vague need to distinguish them from the landscape. Then, during my extended stay in 1991, as I took the bus back and forth between Tel Aviv and Jerusalem, these terraces began to come into sharper focus for me. On July 26 I wrote in my journal:

> The more times I travel back and forth along the Jerusalem–Tel Aviv Highway, the more clearly I see the traces of the artificial... terracing on the hillsides — places where there are just the ruins of stone walls, places where the terraces are intact but the fields are not in use, a few places where the terraced fields are still in use.... In at least one place where the natural striation of the rock was relatively stable, it has humanly produced rock walls on top of it, so there the distinction that worried me the day I first came up, about which was natural and which was a trace of Palestinian settlement (which, in fact, reflected my worry about my own biases — I didn't want to sound like a jerk talking about abandoned Palestinian fields which were actually just "undeveloped" mountainsides), was dissolved. Presumably if there were places where the natural striation was adequate to provide terracing, then they just used that.

Here the problem is fairly straightforward: the built terraces had originally been inspired by, and served to extend and reinforce, limestone striations that themselves formed a kind of terracing. Until I understood that, I constantly worried whether I was looking at a geological formation and reading into it a history of settlement and expulsion that was not proper to it — or whether I was looking at the ruins of a humanly produced landscape and seeing it as ahistorical, as a pile of rock devoid of human agency. When I understood better the relation among the stone structure of the mountain, the effort that had gone into making its slopes tillable, and the deterioration resulting from the absence of those who had once kept the terraces in order, my guilty consciousness was relieved; but the horror itself was none the less.

Terraced hillsides are not the only remains of earlier settlement that can be seen from the Jerusalem–Tel Aviv Highway. Just outside of Jerusalem the hills fall away to the north, and I was always struck by the steep slopes descending both right next to the road and in front to the left, as if protecting the entrance to the new city. I wondered as well for years at the few houses hugging the slope hard by the highway, which are inhabited but obviously predate the Israeli state. It was not until I began my formal fieldwork this year — already looking out for traces in the landscape — that I realized these few houses were only the uppermost of a large number of gray, empty houses scattered along those two slopes. I couldn't understand why they were left there, empty, like a memorial to the vanished Palestinians at the entrance to the Jewish city. Why had they been neither destroyed nor renovated?

The place is called Lifta (Ignatius 1982; Khalidi, ed., 1992). It has not yet been incorporated into Jerusalem, cut off as it is by two highways from the rest of the city. I finally visited there in the beginning of November, only several days before I was to return to New York City and my family. I was first amazed by how wealthy the village had evidently been. These were not the monochrome-gray hovels they appeared to be from the highway, but substantial homes, several with large upper rooms covered by high, vaulted ceilings, lower levels, and storage basements, all open to the mountainside. Most of them had once had the magnificent tile floors that characterize Arab homes in this region. Many of the floor tiles had been stolen. Those that were covered in dust revealed none of their brilliance. Only those floors that lay under shallow pools of water from recent rains shone proudly. One reason for the wealth of the village was evident even before descending toward the houses: a spring that runs constantly out of the mountainside, at the intersection of the two slopes along which Lifta was built. A small pool at the mouth of the spring appears to have been restored rather recently, and traces of the irrigation system that led from the spring to the pool remain.

My companion/guide — also an American Jew — and I scrambled all through the abandoned village, wondering at a deer that betrayed its presence by sneezing and at the evidently young almond trees that, as I learned later, propagate themselves once they've been planted at a certain spot. The interiors of several of the houses revealed that squatters had lived there recently: there were fireplaces at the center of former living rooms and storm candles in window frames. My companion told me stories about wild parties thrown at Lifta by Argentinean immigrant hippies, and later I learned that members of the so-called Jewish underground had hidden out there from the Israeli police. We sat for a while on a cast-iron balcony, thirty feet above ground, until we realized the danger of sudden collapse. We heard the sounds of a construction crew, evidently working on restoring one of the houses highest up, closest to the Jewish city.

Why has Lifta been left alone for so long? Perhaps not many Israelis or tourists have the same kind of troubled curiosity about such a place as does the anthropologist searching for the presence of memory in the landscape. And people elsewhere have little trouble conducting their everyday lives in and among the remains of much greater horrors.[3] We might speculate that some remains might be left precisely to indicate Palestinian guilt: as Alan Mintz suggests, "There is something in us that resists the spectacle of a destruction that is not in some sense a punishment" (1984: 18).

Such speculation is not in order, however. Answers to the mystery of Lifta are available, though I have only begun to collect them. The answers are mostly prosaic: Lifta and its lands turn out to be a scarce resource, the object of a competition that has yet to be fully resolved. Much of the village's land was sold to Jews before the State of Israel was established. Many of the houses in the village were destroyed in recent years to make room for the building of the highway to the massive Jewish suburb of Ramot. The elegant restaurant at the top of the hill — called May Neftoach after the Hebrew name for Lifta's spring — belongs to a friend of Ariel Sharon.[4] In short, it seems that Lifta as a whole remains outside Jerusalem because there is no single controlling plan as to how it should be incorporated into the victorious city.

One of the uses of this site is the rhetorical use to which I am putting it. However mundane the reasons for it, the simultaneous persistence and near-invisibility of a site like Lifta challenge us to refine the statement by Vincent Crapanzano that the ruins that Benjamin and Simmel described as merging with nature have "been replaced by... the trace, [which] becomes at once an emblem of a past evacuated of history... and a signal of the artifice of any such account, any history" (1991: 431). A bit later in the same essay, Crapanzano admits that "the post of postcolonialism is not subject to the same play, not yet at least, as the post of postmodernism.... The past of postcolonialism... cannot be reduced to a trace" (434). I would argue that at a site like Lifta, the difference between a ruin (which need not be monumental in any case) and a trace is a highly unstable one. Apparently, for the vast majority of travelers on the highway entering Jerusalem, what they see when they look at Lifta is a trace, at best; and yet this certainly does not mean that the site has "really" been evacuated of history. Depending precisely on the optic of the observer — anamnestic, naturalizing, or, perhaps inevitably, a troubled and confused combination of the two — Lifta is a subtle and picturesque relic of traditional habitation, a conundrum for the symbolic ethnography of the state, or an agonizing reminder of the violent erasure of life in this place not long ago at all.

---

3. See James Young (1992b) on Polish residents of Oswiecim picnicking on the grounds of Auschwitz-Birkenau.

4. Jeff Halper, personal communication.

The last appearance in Benjamin's work of the figure of piling up of ruins is, of course, in *The Theses on the Philosophy of History:* the Angel of History is forever blown away from paradise, toward which he stares back "while the pile of debris before him grows skyward. This storm is what we call progress" (Benjamin 1969: 258). The earlier moral and aesthetic rescue of the Baroque, the rehabilitation of the fragment, and the renunciation of the ultimate goal have here become a mortally urgent critique of the ideology of progress. In the discussion of Baroque ruins, Benjamin was already free of the very evacuation of historical pain that seems to characterize Simmel's essay. Here Benjamin would seem to say more directly that ruins are in fact nothing if not markers of past violence in the present.

Crapanzano's citation of only the first reference in Benjamin's work to ruins may help explain why he resorted to oblique, "allegorical" politics in addressing his Israeli colleagues. Thus, toward the end of that paper, he designates fundamentalism, racism, and nationalism as "retrogressive movements" (1991: 443), implying that these bad ideologies go against the grain of something good we can still unreflectively assume should be called "progress." But Lifta was not emptied of its inhabitants by fundamentalists or overt racists. Zionism is certainly a nationalist movement, but it is nationalism that in the main and for most of its history has seen itself within the same stream of progress upon which Crapanzano's denunciations of intolerance implicitly rely here.

Would it be useful to suggest that, with their predominantly Eurocentric orientation, academic (and usually Ashkenazi) Israelis belong on the side of postmodern "play" and their Palestinian Others on the side of postcolonial "pain"? The binary designation, while suggestive, is both exaggerated and misleading. The Palestinian situation, while quite diverse, is in a word more nearly colonial than postcolonial. On the other hand, postmodernism as I understand it is not only a matter of "play" but also in large part an attempt, painful indeed, to find a sense to the work of thought[5] after and within the crisis of liberal, progressive modernism epitomized in Nazism. Certainly within the relatively smooth and pragmatic bourgeois normality of Israeli secular social scientists, there is a great deal of precisely postmodern pain. This pain —

---

5. In Crapanzano's sensitive response to the earlier version of this essay (1994), he suggests that this desire to "find a sense to the work of thought" might betray a lingering desire to "master history," and he underlines the Benjaminian vision of a messianic resolution of conflicting memories that implicitly underlies the structure of this essay (even as it is questioned by my self-mocking references to a "New Jerusalem" below). I don't think so: I would rather characterize the postmodern sense *at its best* as an attempt to think responsibly while refusing the arrogance of the *cogito*. What I have tried to do throughout this book is to grow toward, rather than to master, more of the possible readings and histories tied to particular contentious ruins.

and the ruins of so many Jewish communities that, even obliterated, attest by their absence to the sources of that pain — helps to legitimate the Israeli Anthropological Association. Such legitimation may in turn have led Crapanzano to agree to address that body despite his possible misgivings about its members' privileged situation, comparable to though not identical with those of another group Crapanzano has written about — the whites of South Africa. *Vielleicht war es ganz anders* — yet such risky speculation seems justified here if only to raise the question of why an "allegorical" political message nevertheless had to be formally signaled in a footnote.

Like the rabbis perhaps, we thus heap our interpretations on top of interpretations. The expositions mount, and the ruins themselves do not cease to pile up. Not always through destruction, but sometimes indeed through a "restoration" that distorts them beyond recognition of their original, lived-in outline. The Israeli journalist Danny Rubinstein records the following incident that took place in the village of Sataf near Jerusalem, restored by the Israelis as "a model of mountain agriculture." As a result of the Israeli conquest in 1967, refugees from Sataf are sometimes able to visit the homes they were completely barred from between 1948 and 1967:[6]

> One summer day in 1988, when the site was filled with Israeli visitors, shouts were suddenly heard from an elderly woman in traditional Palestinian village dress. She was ranting against the Israelis at the top of her lungs, in the rural dialect of Arabic characteristic of the area. It turned out that the woman was a native of Sataf who now lived in a refugee camp near the West Bank city of Ramallah. One of her sons, who was living in Kuwait, had brought his family for a visit, and she took them all to her native village — a custom widespread among refugees. The woman's ire had been kindled by an error in the restoration. She discovered, to her outrage, that the wall rebuilt next to the well should not have reached as far as the mulberry tree. "It's a lie," the old woman shouted. She recalled that her little sister had once fallen there, so there couldn't have been a wall. (Rubinstein 1991: 12)

Whether through restoration or obliteration — and even where, as in the case of the martyred village of Oradour in France or the Israeli armored cars from the 1948 war, an attempt is made to preserve ruins in their pristine ruined state — the physical remains taken for the rock of memory often prove slippery. The double character of ruins — better, the double perspective with which we approach them — is captured in the prosaic title of an encyclopedia of destroyed Palestinian villages: *All That Remains* (Khalidi, ed., 1992). These stones, we hear at first, are the only things that persist; this is all that remains. And yet also the very possibility of an encyclopedia implies a plenitude: *all*

---

6. Compare the accounts of visits to their old homes by ethnic Greeks from Turkey now living in Crete and by former Cretan Muslims now living in Turkey, in Herzfeld 1991.

*that* remains... in our memory. Both memorial books and physical ruins can constitute sites of memory. The existence of Palestinian ruins within an *Israeli* landscape bears witness to a collective struggle for control of space. Can that struggle be overcome in memory? Is there a possibility of commensuration within a shared ethos of memory as constituting particular yet nonexclusive humanity — not, that is, the monumental commemoration of triumph but a ruinous commemoration "under the sign of mourning" (Koshar 1991: 57; J. Boyarin 1992, chap. 7)?

The midrash with which I started can serve as a guide here. Doubtless the Palestinian memorial literature, too, is already huge. It is not, to my knowledge, grounded in the same ancient experiences of loss to which the Western Wall attests, nor in the depth of interpretive and expositive tradition begun with the book of Lamentations. Does this mean that we can measure Palestinian loss against Jewish loss and declare one greater, one lesser? The midrash asks in astonishment: "Could it be that R. Yohanan was greater than Rabbi!" No: he who was further in time from his loss could articulate, could expound it more; he who remembered the loss directly must weep, console himself, and halt. Certainly the later master was not more "progressive" than the earlier one! Here too, the wall of the Temple courtyard is not to be measured against the lost well in Lifta. Nor should the Palestinians' more recent "exposition" — their uncertain and tortured search for the very language in which to communicate their loss — be taken as a sign that those with the more recent loss are themselves "lesser," or their loss diminished. Rather this midrashic reminder should direct us back to a greater concern with the different situations of loss and construction of self in, through, and with ruins.

•

That's the first ending, and rather sentimental at that. I mentioned toward the beginning that the temptation to reproduce in my own account the allegorical relation between geography and memory is a strong one, and until now I've indulged it: the narrow passage through the dangerous valley of theory and ethnography has led us upward toward an idealized "New Jerusalem" of empathic mutual memory.

I want to question that indulgence now, by shifting briefly to a very different and equally compelling site of competing Jewish and Palestinian ruins. Yes, I'm piling up fragments, but don't worry: I won't do so ceaselessly, and this coda will be free of theoretical detours. The place we are moving to now is a hilltop in the northern Galilee, close to the Lebanese border. Until 1948, it was inhabited by Maronite Christian Arabs. They were forcefully evacuated from their homes during the 1948 war, and, although they remained within Israel and have struggled ceaselessly to be permitted to return to their homes, they never have been allowed to move back (Chacour and Hazard 1984; Chacour 1990). During the early 1950s, their homes were destroyed by the Israeli army, so that even though there was no massacre, the place is reminiscent of some unkempt Oradour.

The village is called Bir'im in Arabic. It is an ancient settlement — so old that it is mentioned in the Talmud — and it is also an archaeological site called Biram on Israeli maps. This slight change: Bir'im, Biram, is an unusually literal example of *differance*. The place with an *i* as its second vowel is the ruin of an Arab village. The place with an *a* is, at least for the Israeli government, the site of an ancient synagogue. It must be added that many Israeli Jews — both individuals and political parties — have disagreed with that government, arguing alongside the villagers that their right to return home must be honored.[7]

Unlike at Lifta, which most Israelis or tourists would only see from a distance — from the highway or at best from the restaurant at the top of the hill — the visitor to the excavated and partially restored ancient synagogue at *Biram* is surrounded by the ruins of *Bir'im*. The site has obviously been landscaped and designed so as to encourage visitors to walk straight to the synagogue site and then to return to their cars without examining too closely the destroyed Arab houses. Thus one sign at the parking lot informs us, in Hebrew and in English, of the significance of the place:

> Site of one of the many Jewish settlements in Upper Galilee during the period of the Second Temple.
> Remains of the beautiful third century (C.E.) synagogue reflect the high standard of religious and cultural life maintained by the Jews of the region, even after the destruction of the Temple.
> The work of restoration and landscaping was carried out by the Department for Landscaping Improvement and Development of Historical Sites of the prime minister's office.

The didactic point is not lost on anyone familiar with the politics of settlement and land control in the Galilee since the establishment of the State of Israel. The "Judaization" of the north has been a fairly constant priority. The excavated synagogue (which is indeed quite beautiful) is not only a tourist attraction but a mark of the Jewish claim to this area and of the per-

---

7. "It has been more than six months since the plenary session of the Knesset authorized, by majority vote, the proposal to recognize the right of the exiles from Ikrit and Biram to return to their villages from which they were 'distanced' for two weeks by order of the IDF in 1948. Two months ago a committee of ministers was appointed to discuss their demand. However, during the meeting of the ministerial committee this week, the *Shabak* (General Security Services) said 'no!' According to the *Shabak* the implementation of the return of the Ikrit/Biram exiles to their villages would set a precedent for demands by Palestinian citizens of Israel who since the 1948 war have yet to be authorized to return to their villages. This would also weaken Israel's opposition to the Palestinians' right of return" (Anonymous 1994).

sistence of Jewish habitation in Palestine after the end of the second Jewish commonwealth.

Another sign cautions:

> National parks contain antiquities, natural sites, and hazardous terrain. Visitors are therefore advised to be careful during their stay on the grounds.

"Antiquities" presumably are things visitors should be careful not to harm by stepping on them. "Hazardous terrain" is a place visitors should avoid for their own safety. But why should anyone be cautioned about avoiding "natural sites"? The copula that joins "landscaping improvement" and "development of historical sites" in one bureaucratic slot gives us a clue here: these natural sites are freshly planted. The state is trying to grow ruins into the landscape. Please don't interfere by looking at them too closely.[8]

This visitor and his companions — one a Palestinian professor of anthropology at Bir Zeit University, the other a Palestinian-American graduate student doing fieldwork on the role of archaeology in Israeli national culture — ignored the warnings about hazardous terrain, examining closely the ruined houses, the still-intact church (used occasionally for weddings and the like), and the graveyard, where by court order the people of Bir'im are allowed to bury their dead. On the wall of perhaps the most impressive house in the village, a cross carved into the lintel had been destroyed by vandals; the date the house was built was partially legible: 19...but the last two digits had been obliterated.

The professor from Bir Zeit — himself a native of the Galilee — further broke the spell of nature cast on the ruins by the landscaping department, by engaging with the Druze gatekeeper in a detailed conversation, reminiscing about the fates and present whereabouts of various former residents of the area who were all mutual acquaintances of theirs. Doubtless there cannot be a dialogue *with* ruins: stones speak only in our metaphors. But it seems there can indeed be dialogue *around* ruins.

On the back wall of the church at Bir'im, there are graffiti in three languages: *"Biram ahuva"* — "Beloved Biram," in Hebrew; *"Hona bakun,"* "Here I will be," in Arabic; "Biram forever," in English; most poignantly ironic of all, and also in English: "Let my people return." It is interesting to note that not only do the residents — or more likely, their children — express their longing

---

8. In his account of the Palestinian exodus, the Israeli historian Benny Morris no doubt unwittingly colludes in this obfuscation of the ruins of Bir'im: "Within months, Bir'im's lands were distributed among Jewish settlements and, in the early 1950s, the village itself was levelled" (Morris 1987: 239). Unfortunately perhaps for Biram the historical site, the village itself was not — quite — leveled. For a more general account of "the politics of seeing" (see Buck-Morss 1989).

to go home in Hebrew and in English but that when they do so, they now call their home Biram.

Clearly the site of the Arab village of Bir'im/Biram is not only a ruin. It also functions as a memorial. But it remains a place of contention, so clearly it does not serve the same healing and unifying function as the usual state memorial. It is tempting to think of the destroyed village with its graffiti as a *Gegendenkmal,* an "antimonument," like the monument against fascism in Harburg, Germany, which is lowered periodically into the ground as its base is covered with graffiti. Norbert Radermacher, the designer of the antimonument, "suggests that the site alone cannot remember, that it is the projection of memory by visitors into a space that makes it a memorial" (Young 1992a). Different memories are projected by different visitors to this site in the Galilee, with and against the connivance of the state. Perhaps the destroyed modern village surrounding the restored ancient synagogue serves as a sort of antimonument for at least some Israeli visitors and as a memorial for the villagers of Bir'im who have become villagers to Biram. But in any case the ruins of the village are in no way an allegory or a prototype for all the ruined Palestinian villages. This is evidenced by the particular circumstances in which the people of the village still find themselves — refugees of a sort and Israeli citizens at the same time.

In the larger sense, unlike the double destruction of the Temple in Jerusalem that has become the prototype for all Jewish experiences of catastrophe, there is no prototypical ruined Palestinian village. They were lost, to borrow a phrase, "one by one by one." Any attempt to understand the persistence of Palestinian nationalism will have to face that loss and the ruins that testify to it; any genuine reconciliation between Israeli Jews and Palestinian Arabs will have to make room for the different modalities of the losses and commemorations that are at the heart of their respective national identities. At Biram, the attempt to impose a sense of the place as uniquely and properly Jewish is effectively undercut by the remains of an Arab village. Through their periodic returns to their homes, the villagers and their descendants ensure that this is more than a passive effect. They *make* their stones tell a story against the story told by the Department for Landscaping Improvement and Development of Historical Sites of the prime minister's office. In parody of the little booth with the lonely Druze gatekeeper inside guarding the way from the parking lot to the synagogue site, one house near the church has a single word, painted in English over its empty doorway: "Information."

# Bibliography

Alcalay, Ammiel
 1993 *After Jews and Arabs: Remaking Levantine Culture.* Minneapolis: University of Minnesota Press.

Alcalay, Reuben
 1965 *The Complete Hebrew-English Dictionary.* Tel Aviv and Jerusalem: Massadah.

Anderson, Benedict
 1991 *Imagined Communities: Reflections on the Spread of Nationalism.* 2d ed. London: Verso.

Anonymous
 1990 Judaisation of East Jerusalem: Map and Caption. *The Other Israel* 42 (July–August): 12.
 1994 Palestinians inside Israel: The Shabak vs Ikrit and Biram. *The Other Front* 258 (February 2): 4.

Arendt, Hannah
 1965 *On Revolution.* New York: Viking.

Aronoff, Myron
 1990 The Origins of Israeli Political Culture. Paper presented to conference entitled "Israeli Democracy under Stress: Cultural and Institutional Representations," Hoover Institute, Stanford University.

Atran, Scott
 1989 The Surrogate Colonization of Palestine, 1917–1939. *American Ethnologist* 16/4: 719–44.

Avruch, Kevin
 1981 *American Immigrants in Israel: Social Identities and Change.* Chicago: University of Chicago Press.

Bachelard, Gaston
 1964 *The Poetics of Space.* Boston: Beacon.

Bateson, Gregory
 1972 *Steps to an Ecology of Mind.* San Francisco: Chandler.

Benjamin, Walter
    1969    *Illuminations*. New York: Schocken.
    1977    *The Origin of German Tragic Drama*. London: New Left.

Benvenisti, Meron
    1986    *Conflicts and Contradictions*. New York: Villard.

Berger, Harry
    1989    The Lie of the Land: The Text beyond Canaan. *Representations* 25: 119–38.

Bhabha, Homi K.
    1990    Introduction to *Nation and Narration*. Ed. Homi K. Bhabha, 1–7. New York: Routledge.

Bourdieu, Pierre
    1977    *Outline of a Theory of Practice*. Cambridge: Cambridge University Press.

Boyarin, Daniel
    1990    *Intertextuality and the Reading of Midrash*. Bloomington: Indiana University Press.
    1994    *A Radical Jew: Paul and the Politics of Identity*. Berkeley: University of California Press.

Boyarin, Daniel, and Jonathan Boyarin
    1989    Toward a Dialogue with Edward Said. *Critical Inquiry* 15 (spring): 626–33.
    1993    Generation: Diaspora and the Ground of Jewish Identity. *Critical Inquiry* 19/4: 693–725.

Boyarin, Jonathan
    1988    Waiting for a Jew: Marginal Redemption at the Eighth Street Shul. In *Between Two Worlds: Ethnographic Essays on American Jews*. Ed. Jack Kugelmass, 52–77. Ithaca, N.Y.: Cornell University Press.
    1989    Voices around the Text: The Ethnography of Reading at Mesivta Tifereth Jerusalem. *Cultural Anthropology* 4: 399–421.
    1990    Letter to the editor. *Tikkun* 5/3: 6.
    1991a   *Polish Jews in Paris: The Ethnography of Memory*. Bloomington: Indiana University Press.
    1991b   That Jew's an Animal! Paper presented at conference entitled "People of the Body, People of the Book." Stanford and Berkeley, California.
    1992    *Storm from Paradise: The Politics of Jewish Memory*. Minneapolis: University of Minnesota Press.
    1994a   Hegel's Zionism? In J. Boyarin, ed., 1994, 137–60.
    1994b   Jewish Geography Goes On-line. *Journal of Jewish Folklore and Ethnography* 16/1.
    1994c   Space, Time, and the Politics of Memory. In J. Boyarin, ed., 1994, 1–37.
    1995    Before the Law There Stands a Woman: In *Re* Taylor v. Butler (with Court-Appointed Yiddish Translator). *Cardozo Law Review* 16/3–4: 1303–23.

Boyarin, Jonathan, ed.
1993    *The Ethnography of Reading.* Berkeley: University of California Press.

1994    *Space, Time, and the Politics of Memory.* Minneapolis: University of Minnesota Press.

Boyarin, Jonathan, and Daniel Boyarin
  1994    Self-exposure as Theory: The Double Mark of the Male Jew. In *The Rhetoric of Self-Making.* Ed. Debbora Battaglia, 16–42. Berkeley: University of California Press.

B'tselem
  1992    *Violations of Human Rights in the Occupied Territories 1990/1991.* Jerusalem: B'tselem.

Buck-Morss, Susan
  1989    *The Dialectics of Seeing: Walter Benjamin and the Arcades Project.* Cambridge, Mass.: MIT Press.

Budick, Emily
  1989    To Jerusalem and Back: The Place of Israel in American Writing. Paper presented at session entitled "Imagining Palestine and Israel," Modern Language Association, Washington, D.C.

Butler, Judith
  1990    *Gender Trouble: Feminism and the Subversion of Identity.* New York: Routledge.
  1993    *Bodies That Matter: On the Discursive Limits of "Sex."* New York: Routledge.

Carta
  1986    *Carta's Official Guide to Israel.* Jerusalem: The State of Israel Ministry of Defence Publishing House; Carta Ltd. Originally published in 1983.

Carter, Paul
  1989    *The Road to Botany Bay.* Chicago: University of Chicago Press.

Chacour, Elias
  1990    *We Belong to the Land.* San Francisco: HarperSanFrancisco.

Chacour, Elias, and David Hazard
  1984    *Blood Brothers.* Grand Rapids, Mich.: Chosen Books.

Clifford, James
  1990    Notes on (Field)notes. In *Fieldnotes: The Makings of Anthropology.* Ed. Roger Sanjek, 47–70. Ithaca, N.Y.: Cornell University Press.
  1993    Diasporas. Paper presented to annual meeting of the Society for Cultural Anthropology.

Clifford, James, and George Marcus, eds.
  1986    *Writing Culture: The Poetics and Politics of Ethnography.* Berkeley: University of California Press.

Cohn, Robert
  1990    Israel and Sacred Space. *Continuum* 1 (autumn): 4–14.

Comaroff, Jean
   1985   *Body of Power, Spirit of Resistance: The Culture and History of a South African People.* Chicago: University of Chicago Press.

Connolly, William E.
   1993a   *The Augustinian Imperative: A Reflection on the Politics of Morality.* Beverly Hills: Sage.
   1993b   *Political Theory and Modernity.* 2d ed. Ithaca, N.Y.: Cornell University Press.

Crapanzano, Vincent
   1991   The Postmodern Crisis: Discourse, Memory, Parody. *Cultural Anthropology* 6/4: 431–46.
   1994   Discussion of Boyarin. *Found Object* 3: 49–54.

Davies, W. D.
   1974   *The Gospel and the Land: Early Christianity and Jewish Territorial Doctrine.* Berkeley: University of California Press.
   1982   *The Territorial Dimension of Judaism.* Berkeley: University of California Press.

de Certeau, Michel
   1984   *The Practice of Everyday Life.* Berkeley: University of California Press.

Derrida, Jacques
   1992   *The Other Heading: Reflections on Today's Europe.* Bloomington: Indiana University Press.

de Santillana, Giorgio, and Hertha von Dechend
   1969   *Hamlet's Mill.* Boston: Godine.

Domínguez, Virginia
   1990   *People as Subject, People as Object: Selfhood and Peoplehood in Contemporary Israel.* Madison: University of Wisconsin Press.
   1993   Visual Nationalism: On Looking at "National Symbols." *Public Culture* 5/3: 451–55.

Eilberg-Schwartz, Howard
   1990   *The Savage in Judaism.* Bloomington: Indiana University Press.

Eisenzweig, Uri
   1981   *Territoires occupés de l'imaginaire juif.* Paris: Christian Bourgeois.

Eisinger, Chester E.
   1948   The Puritans' Justification for Taking the Land. *Essex Institution Historical Collections* 84: 131–43.

Eisner, Jack
   1980   *The Survivor.* New York: William Morrow.

Eliade, Mircea
   1959   *Cosmos and History: The Myth of the Eternal Return.* New York.

*Encyclopedia Judaica*
    1971    Vol. 15. New York: Macmillan.

Epstein, Rabbi Dr. I., ed.
    1935    *The Babylonian Talmud (Seder Nezikin)*. London: Soncino.

Fabian, Johannes
    1983    *Time and the Other*. New York: Columbia University Press.
    1990    Presence and Representation: The Other and Anthropological Writing. *Critical Inquiry* 16: 753–72.

Fischer, Michael, and Mehdi Abadi
    1990    *Debating Muslims: Cultural Dialogues in Postmodernity and Tradition*. Madison: University of Wisconsin Press.

Friedlander, Judith
    1990    *Vilna on the Seine*. New Haven: Yale University Press.

Galdon, Joseph A.
    1975    *Typology and Seventeenth-Century Literature*. The Hague: Mouton.

Genovese, Eugene
    1976    *Roll, Jordan, Roll: The World the Slaves Made*. New York: Vintage.

Gilman, Sander
    1986    *Jewish Self-Hatred: Anti-Semitism and the Hidden Language of the Jews*. Baltimore: Johns Hopkins University Press.

Goldberg, Harvey
    1977    Culture and Ethnicity in the Study of Israeli Society. *Ethnic Groups* 1: 163–86.

Goldberg, Sylvie Anne
    1989    *Les deux rives du Yabbok: La maladie et la mort dans le judaisme ashkenaze*. Paris: Le Cerf.

González Echevarría, Roberto
    1987    The Law of the Letter: Garcilaso's *Commentaries* and the Origins of the Latin American Narrative. *Yale Journal of Criticism* 1/1: 107–32.

Gostynsky, Zalman
    1973    *Shteyner dertseyln*. Paris.

Greenblatt, Stephen
    1991    *Marvelous Possessions: The Wonder of the New World*. Chicago: University of Chicago Press.

Gutman, Herbert
    1977    *The Black Family in Slavery and Freedom, 1770–1925*. New York: Pantheon.

Haberman, Clyde
    1993    For Golan Heights Winery, Will It Be Stay or Go? *New York Times*, November 7.
    1994    Israeli Rightists Now in Opposition to One Another. *New York Times*, February 9.

Hale, Charles
  1992  Enduring Fieldwork: Indian Politics and Activist Research in Los Angeles. Paper presented at annual meeting of the American Anthropological Association, San Francisco, November.

Halper, Jeff
  1991  *Between Redemption and Revival: The Jewish Yishuv of Jerusalem in the Nineteenth Century.* Boulder, Colo.: Westview.

Handelman, Don
  1991  *Models and Mirrors: Toward an Anthropology of Public Events.* New York: Cambridge University Press.

Handelman, Don, and Lea Shamgar-Handelman
  1991  The Presence of the Dead: Memorials of National Death in Israel. *Journal of the Finnish Anthropological Society* 16/4: 3–17.
  1993  National Images and the Blind Hegemony of Discourse: Rejoinder to Domínguez. *Public Culture* 5/3: 457–61.

Hanning, Robert
  1966  *The Vision of History in Early Britain: From Gildas to Geoffrey of Monmouth.* New York: Columbia University Press.

Harlan, David
  1989  Intellectual History and the Return of Literature. *American Historical Review* 94/3: 581–609.

Harlow, Barbara
  1987  *Resistance Literature.* New York: Methuen.

Hartog, François
  1988  *The Mirror of Herodotus: The Representation of the Other in the Writing of History.* Berkeley: University of California Press.

Harvey, David
  1989  *The Condition of Postmodernity.* Cambridge, Mass.: Blackwell.

Herzfeld, Michael
  1987  *Anthropology through the Looking-glass: Critical Ethnography in the Margins of Europe.* New York: Cambridge University Press.
  1991  *A Place in History: Social and Monumental Time in a Cretan Town.* Princeton, N.J.: Princeton University Press.
  1993a  Sequence of Tensions: Ancient Burdens, Modern Models. Paper presented at conference entitled "European Identity and Its Intellectual Roots," Harvard University.
  1993b  *The Social Production of Indifference.* New York: University of Chicago Press.

Herzl, Theodor
  1973  *Zionist Writings: Essays and Addresses.* Vol. 1. New York: Herzl.
  1980  A Solution of the Jewish Question. In Mendes-Flohr and Reinharz, eds., 421–27.

Hill, Christopher
   1986a    The Norman Yoke. In *Puritanism and Revolution*, 58–125. New York: Viking Penguin. Originally published 1958.
   1986b    Till the Conversion of the Jews. In *The Collected Essays*. Vol. 2, 269–300. Brighton, Sussex: Harvester.

Horowitz, L. P., R. I. Arshansky, and A. C. Elitzur
   1988    On the Two Aspects of Time: The Distinctions and Its Applications. *Foundations of Physics* 18: 1159–93.

Howe, Nicholas
   1989    *Migration and Mythmaking in Anglo-Saxon England*. New Haven: Yale University Press.

Ignatius, David
   1982    Palestinians Carve Out Lives in Distant Lands but Hunger for "Home." *The Wall Street Journal*, September 13.

Jabès, Edmond
   1989    *The Book of Shares*. Trans. Rosmarie Waldrop. Chicago: University of Chicago Press.

Jaffe, Eliezer David
   1988    *Yemin Moshe: The Story of a Jerusalem Neighborhood*. New York: Praeger.

Jehlen, Myra
   1986    *American Incarnation: The Individual, the Nation, and the Continent*. Cambridge, Mass.: Harvard University Press.
   1993    History Before the Fact: Or, Captain John Smith's Unfinished Symphony. *Critical Inquiry* 19/4: 677–92.

Kayyali, Abdul-Wahhab Said
   1978    *Palestine: A Modern History*. London: Croom Helm.

Kearney, Michael
   1991    Borders and Boundaries of State and Self at the End of Empire. *Journal of Historical Sociology* 4 (March): 52–72.

Khalidi, Walid, ed.
   1992    *All That Remains: The Palestinian Villages Occupied and Depopulated by Israel in 1948*. Washington, D.C.: Institute for Palestine Studies.

Kimmerling, Baruch
   1983    *Zionism and Territory*. Berkeley, Calif.: Institute of International Studies.

Koshar, Rudy
   1991    Altar, State and City: Historic Preservation and Urban Meaning in Nazi Germany. *History and Memory* 3/1: 30–59.

Krajewska, Monika
   1981    *Time of Stones*. Warsaw: Interpress.
   1993    *Tribe of Stones*. Warsaw: Polish Scientific Publishers.

Krupnick, Mark
    1989    Edward Said: Discourse and Palestinian Rage. *Tikkun* 4/6: 21–25.

Kugelmass, Jack
    1986    *The Miracle of Intervale Avenue.* New York: Schocken.

Kugelmass, Jack, and Jonathan Boyarin
    1983    *From a Ruined Garden: The Memorial Books of Polish Jewry.* New York: Schocken.
    1988    Yizker Bikher and the Problem of Historical Veracity: An Anthropological Approach. In *The Jews of Poland between Two World Wars.* Ed. Yisrael Gutman et al., 519–36. Hanover, N.H.: University Press of New England.

Lambropoulos, Vassilis
    1992    *The Rise of Eurocentrism: Anatomy of Interpretation.* Princeton, N.J.: Princeton University Press.

Langfur, Stephen
    1992    *Confession from a Jericho Jail.* New York: Grove Weidenfeld.

Lavie, Smadar
    1992    Blow-ups in the Borderzones: Third World Israeli Authors' Groping for Home. *New Formations* 18: 84–106.

Leckie, R. William, Jr.
    1981    *The Passage of Dominion: Geoffrey of Monmouth and the Periodization of Insular History in the Twelfth Century.* Toronto: University of Toronto Press.

Levine, Lawrence
    1977    *Black Culture and Black Consciousness.* New York: Oxford University Press.

Lloyd, David
    1989    Kant's Examples. *Representations* 28: 34–54.

Luz, Ehud
    1988    *Parallels Meet: Religion and Nationalism in the Early Zionist Movement (1882–1904).* Trans. Lenn J. Schramm. Philadelphia: Jewish Publication Society.

Lyotard, Jean-François
    1990    *Heidegger and "the Jews."* Trans. Andreas Michel and Mark Roberts. Minneapolis: University of Minnesota Press.
    1984    *The Post-modern Condition.* Minneapolis: University of Minnesota Press.

*Maasey Alfas*
    n.d.    Psakh Dovor Lemaasey Alfas. In *Makhzor Kol Bo.* New York: Hebrew Publishing.

Maier, Charles S.
    1988    *The Unmasterable Past: History, Holocaust, and German National Identity.* Cambridge, Mass.: Harvard University Press.

Margalit, Avishai
    1988    The Kitsch of Israel. *New York Review of Books,* November 24.

Marin, Louis
    1993    Frontiers of Utopia: Past and Present. *Critical Inquiry* 19/3: 397–420.

Massumi, Brian
    1987    Pleasures of Philosophy. Translator's foreword to *A Thousand Plateaus: Capitalism and Schizophrenia*, by Gilles Deleuze and Felix Guattari, ix–xix. Minneapolis: University of Minnesota Press.

Mattar, Nabil
    1989    Protestantism, Palestine, and Partisan Scholarship. *Journal of Palestine Studies* 18/4: 52–70.

Mead, Margaret
    1962    Foreword to *Life Is with People: The Culture of the Shtetl*, by Mark Zborowski and Elizabeth Herzog, 11–28. New York: Schocken.

Mendes-Flohr, Paul, and Jehuda Reinharz, eds.
    1980    *The Jew in the Modern World.* New York: Oxford University Press.

Meyer, Michael
    1988    *Response to Modernity: A History of the Reform Movement in Judaism.* New York: Oxford University Press.

Miller, Perry
    1956    *Errand into the Wilderness.* Cambridge, Mass.: Harvard University Press.

Mintz, Alan
    1984    *Hurban: Responses to Catastrophe in Hebrew Literature.* New York: Columbia University Press.

Moffatt, Michael
    1987    *Coming of Age in New Jersey.* New Brunswick, N.J.: Rutgers University Press.

Morris, Benny
    1987    *The Birth of the Palestinian Refugee Problem, 1947–1949.* New York: Cambridge University Press.

Nusseibeh, Sari
    1990    Letter to the Editor. *New Outlook,* April, 5.

Obeyesekere, Gananath
    1992    *The Apotheosis of Captain Cook.* Princeton, N.J.: Princeton University Press.

O'Gorman, Edmundo
    1961    *The Invention of America: An Inquiry into the Historical Nature of the New World and the Meaning of Its History.* Bloomington: Indiana University Press.

Oz, Amos
    1993    An Unsentimental Middle East Peace. *Harper's* 287 (October): 14–17.

Patraka, Vivian
  1992  Spectacles of Suffering: The Tropological Use of the Term "Holocaust" in Public Discourse. Modern Language Association convention, New York City.

Popkin, Richard H.
  1988  Introduction to *Millenarianism and Messianism in English Literature and Thought*. Ed. Richard H. Popkin, 1–11. Leiden: Brill.

Pratt, Mary Louise
  1986  Fieldwork in Common Places. In *Writing Culture*. Ed. James Clifford and George E. Marcus, 27–50. Berkeley: University of California Press.

Price, Richard, and Sally Price
  1992  *Equatoria*. New York: Routledge.

Rabasa, José
  1990  Dialogue as Conquest: Mapping Spaces for Counter-discourse. In *The Nature and Context of Minority Discourse*. Ed. Abdul R. JanMohamed and David Lloyd, 187–215. New York: Oxford University Press.
  1993  *Inventing America: Spanish Historiography and the Formation of Eurocentrism*. Norman: University of Oklahoma Press.

Rabinowitz, Dan
  1990  Relations between Arabs and Jews in the Mixed Town of Natzeret Illit, Northern Israel. Ph.D. diss., Cambridge University.

Rafael, Vicente
  1993  *Contracting Colonialism: Translation and Christian Conversion in Tagalog Society under Early Spanish Rule*. Durham, N.C.: Duke University Press.

Raz-Krakotzkin, Amnon
  1993  Exile within Sovereignty: Toward a Critique of the 'Negation of Exile' in Israeli Culture. (English Abstract.) *Teoriya Ubikoret* 4: 182–84.

Renan, Ernest
  1990  What Is a Nation? In *Nation and Narration*. Ed. Homi Bhabha, 8–22. New York: Routledge.

Reventlow, Henning Graf
  1985  *The Authority of the Bible and the Rise of the Modern World*. Philadelphia: Fortress.

Rosaldo, Renato
  1988  Ideology, Place, and People without Culture. *Cultural Anthropology* 3 (February): 77–87.

Rubinstein, Danny
  1991  *The People of Nowhere: The Palestinian Vision of Home*. Trans. Ina Friedman. New York: Times Books.

Rushdie, Salman
  1989  *The Satanic Verses*. New York: Viking.

Said, Edward
　1978　*Orientalism*. New York: Pantheon.
　1980　*The Question of Palestine*. New York: Vintage.
　1985　Michael Walzer's *Exodus and Revolution:* A Canaanite Reading. *Grand Street* 5: 86–106.
　1986　Reply to Michael Walzer. *Grand Street* (spring): 252–59.
　1989　Representing the Colonized: Anthropology's Interlocutors. *Critical Inquiry* 15/2: 205–25.
　1990　Narrative, Geography and Interpretation. *New Left Review* 180: 81–99.

Said, Edward, and Christopher Hitchins, eds.
　1988　*Blaming the Victims: Spurious Scholarship and the Palestine Question*. New York: Verso.

Sampson, Elissa
　1990　Exodus and Empire. Seminar paper, New School for Social Research.

Sarris, Greg
　1993　*Keeping Slug Woman Alive: A Holistic Approach to American Indian Texts*. Berkeley: University of California Press.

Scherman, Rabbi Nosson, ed.
　1985　*The Complete ArtScroll Siddur*. Brooklyn: Mesorah.

Schwab, Gabriele
　1986　Reader-Response and the Aesthetic Experience of Otherness. *Stanford Literature Review* (spring): 107–36.

Searle, Eleanor
　1988　*Predatory Kinship and the Creation of Norman Power, 850–1066*. Berkeley: University of California Press.

Segev, Tom
　1986　*1949: The First Israelis*. New York: Free Press.

Selzer, Michael, ed.
　1970　*Zionism Reconsidered: The Rejection of Jewish Normalcy*. New York: Macmillan.

Shafir, Gershon
　1989　*Land, Labor, and the Origins of the Israeli-Palestinian Conflict, 1882–1914*. New York: Cambridge University Press.

Shammas, Anton
　1989　The Two-Language Solution. Paper read at Modern Language Association convention, Washington, D.C.
　1993　Palestinians Must Now Master the Art of Forgetting. *New York Times Magazine*, December 26.

Sharif, Regina S.
　1983　*Non-Jewish Zionism: Its Roots in Jewish History*. London: Zed.

Shavit, Yaacov
  1990  Cyrus King of Persia and the Return to Zion: A Case of Neglected Memory. *History and Memory* 2/1: 51–83.

Shehadeh, Raja
  1982  *The Third Way: A Journal of Life in the West Bank.* London: Quartet.

Shell, Marc
  1991  Marranos (Pigs), or from Coexistence to Toleration. *Critical Inquiry* 17: 306–35.

Shohat, Ella
  1988  Sephardim in Israel: Zionism from the Standpoint of Its Jewish Victims. *Social Text* 19/20: 1–35.

Simmel, Georg
  1959  The Ruin. In *Georg Simmel, 1858–1919: A Collection of Essays, with Translations and a Bibliography.* Ed. Kurt H. Wolff, 259–66. Columbus: Ohio State University Press.

Slyomovics, Susan
  1994  The Memory of Place: Rebuilding the Pre-1948 Palestinian Village. *Diaspora* 3/2: 157–68.

Smalley, Beryl
  1964  *The Study of the Bible in the Middle Ages.* South Bend, Ind.: University of Notre Dame Press. Originally published 1940.

Spanos, William V.
  1990  Heidegger, Nazism, and the Repressive Hypothesis: The American Appropriation of the Question. *Boundary 2* 17/2: 199–281.

Stinson, Charles
  n.d.  "Northernmost Israel": England, the Old Testament and the Hebraic "Veritas" as Seen by Bede and Roger Bacon. Dartmouth College.

Thom, Martin
  1990  Tribes within Nations: The Ancient Germans and the History of Modern France. In *Nation and Narration.* Ed. Homi K. Bhabha, 23–43. New York: Routledge.

Tuchman, Barbara
  1956  *Bible and Sword: England and Palestine from the Bronze Age to Balfour.* New York: New York University Press.

Turner, Frederick W.
  1980  *Beyond Geography.* New Brunswick: Rutgers University Press.

Turner, Terence
  1993  Anthropology and Multiculturalism: What Is Anthropology That Multiculturalists Should Be Mindful of It? *Cultural Anthropology* 8:4, 411–29.

Viswesaran, Kamala
  1994  Feminist Ethnography as Failure. In *Fictions of Feminist Ethnography.* Minneapolis: University of Minnesota Press.

Walzer, Michael
   1965    *The Revolution of the Saints.* Cambridge, Mass.: Harvard University Press.
   1985    *Exodus and Revolution.* New York: Basic Books.
   1986    Letter to the Editor. *Grand Street* (spring): 246–52.

Wilford, John
   1990    Battle Scene on Egyptian Temple May Be Earliest View of Israelites. *New York Times,* September 4.

Williams, Robert A.
   1990    *The American Indian in Western Legal Thought: The Discourses of Conquest.* New York: Oxford University Press.

Willis, Aaron
   1992    Redefining Religious Zionism: Shas' Ethno-Politics. *Israel Studies Bulletin* 8/2: 7–12.

Winchester, Simon
   1991    After Dire Straits, an Agonizing Haul across the Pacific. *Smithsonian* 22 (April): 84–95.

Yashuvi, Na'ama
   1992    *Activity of the Undercover Units in the Occupied Territories.* Jerusalem: B'tselem/The Israeli Information Center for Human Rights in the Occupied Territories.

Young, James
   1992a   The Counter-monument: Memory against Itself in Germany Today. *Critical Inquiry* 18/2: 267–96.
   1992b   *The Texture of Memory.* New Haven: Yale University Press.

Yourcenar, Marguerite
   1954    *Memoirs of Hadrian.* Trans. Grace Frick. New York: Farrar, Straus and Giroux.

Zerubavel, Yael
   1991    The Politics of Interpretation: Tel Hai in Israel's Collective Memory. *AJS Review* 16/1–2: 133–60.
   1994    *Recovered Roots: Collective Memory and the Making of Israeli National Traditions.* Chicago: University of Chicago Press.

Zwicker, Steven N.
   1988    England, Israel, and the Triumph of Roman Virtue. In *Millenarianism and Messianism in English Literature and Thought.* Ed. Richard H. Popkin, 37–64. Leiden: Brill.

**Jonathan Boyarin** is an independent scholar trained in anthropology. He has published widely in Jewish ethnography and interdisciplinary cultural theory. Among his books are *Polish Jews in Paris: The Ethnography of Memory* (Indiana, 1992); *Storm from Paradise: The Politics of Jewish Memory* (Minnesota, 1992); and *Thinking in Jewish* (Chicago, 1996). He currently attends Yale Law School.